A SOURCE BOOK OF HINDU PHILOSOPHY

K.P. Bahadur

Ess Ess Publications
4837/24, Ansari Road, Darya Ganj,
New Delhi,110 002
Phone : 3260807

First Published 1995

ISBN 81-7000-174-9

Rs. 500/-

Published by :

Ess Ess Publications

4837/24, Ansari Road, Darya Ganj,
New Delhi,110 002
Phone : 3260807

To the memory of
My noble and loving friend
S. K. Sethi

Quem di diligunt
Adolescens moritur dum valet, sentit sapit
'Whom the gods love die young, while still
they can enjoy Health, tastes and senses'

PLAUTUS

PREFACE

Our little systems have their day;
They have their day and cease to be
They are but broken lights of thee
And thou, O Lord, art more than they.

Lord Tennyson

'What is Truth; said jesting Pilate; and would not stay for an answer'. It could have been because he wasn't sure himself what truth was. Much the same can be said about religion. Ever since man's pursuits ceased to be merely food and sex, he began to ponder over the wonder of existence. He understood waking life all right. But dreams and death baffled him. It was true what he saw when he dreamt wasn't at all logical, But it couldn't be denied. And the inexplicable thing was that with all the restless agitation the mind experienced during the dream-state, dreams turned out, as much as sleep did, to be the 'balm of hurt minds.' Death proved to him to be even more mysterious, and as science developed, and with it the science of medicine and surgery, the mystery deepened. Unbelievably sophisticated methods of treating diseases and disorders came out and are still being invented every year. Surgery has become painless and non-invasive, medicines fast-curing and life-saving. Yet death remains as inevitable and erratic as before. Then there's the never-answered questions of the 'why' and 'how'. Why should one man die under anaesthesia when others don't; why should a man survive in a major accident when the one next to him dies; why should an enemy's bullet kill one and not another; why should one man succeed and another fail in the same circumstances; why should one be born rich and another poor. Why? – the perplexing contradictions have no end. The 'what' and the 'how' are equally obscure. How did the world come about? How did creation start? How did the seasons change and the sun and the moon give light? What are the stars, planets, water, air, fire, earth and so forth. The 'hows' and the 'whats', too, are never ending. Thirdly, there was the ethics of behaviour. The old law of the jungle was 'might is right'. Soon, however, men realized that civilized society could not exist without mutual goodwill and accommodation. The earliest effort to put civilization on the rails was to devise restrictions in the form of totems and taboos. These later became the dictates of ethics in the religions and philosophies of the world.

Something was needed to calm this restlessness of the mind thus baffled by questions to which there was no answer. This disquiet and inquisitiveness were the birth-pangs of religion; for when religion came it brought both peace and pain – the peace of understanding and the pain of violent conflicts and bloodshed. Men have always been at variance with each another. When they were savages they bunched themselved into tribes. When civilization came they divided themselves into nations, sects and communities. Many religons were born. And so long as men found contentment in their own religion they were religious. When they began to feel that they must force this contentment on persons of other sects they were no longer believers but fanatics. And these were the ones who stained religion with blood.

Religion is a cauldron into which many ingredients are cast. Some of them, indeed, as for example mythology, are even odious and bizarre. It is these which are the root of religious conflicts and persecutions. These elements comprise mainly the practice of religion, not its principles. In them lie the differences, while in the philosophies and spiritual thought of religions there is oneness. If people concentrated more upon the principles of religions than upon their practices, the world would be a much happier place to live in. In religious conflicts, even as in wars, it is the less aggressive religions that are in danger of being suppressed. Of all religions Hinduism is perhaps the mildest and most accommodating. This is its strength as well as its weakness. Its strength lies in the superiority of its wisdom and its weakness in its inability to stand firmly against the fanatics of other religions who are out to suppress it either by money or the sword. Fanaticism endows people who indulge in it with zeal. All *jihāds* and crusades are as fierce as they are irrational. As George Santayana says (*Life of Reason* vol. 1) 'Fanaticism consists in redoubling your effort when you have forgotten your aim.' The irony of fanaticism is that the fanatic always pats himself on the back for the intolerance he shows. The fanatic Moslem for example, calls himself a victorious Ghazī after he has killed 'infidels' in a 'holy war'. Thus by his own lack of undertanding he looks on his 'triumphs' with a jaundiced eye, seeing virtue in evil.

The disability to stand against aggression is not Hinduism's only weakness. There are others too which are even worse, which make it the most vulnerable religion of the world. We will speak of these in detail in the introduction where we will discuss the reasons for the conflicts between religions. Here we only summarize them. There is caste which divides the Hindus into various groups at variance with one another. Exploited by scheming Hindu politicians, caste animosities have been more and more accentuated. Then there is the curious phenomenon of Hindus disparaging their own religion to appear what they proudly and erroneously call 'secular'.

In the glorious period of Indian history before the foreign conquests, there was no clash between the religion and statecraft. King were guided by *purohits* (family priests) and always followed their counsel. The *purohits* were a class of philosopher-kings, the kind Plato conceived in the *Republic*. They ensured a clean and efficient administration and a sound foreign policy. The Moslem period of Indian history tolled the bell for righteous polity. King waded through blood, often of their own sons, fathers and other relations, to ascend the throne. In the British rule the kings were across the oceans, but their representatives, the governors and the viceroys looked on India as an ideal baiting-ground for Christianity. Religion again had a hand-shake with politics but this time it was the Christian religion. When Pakistan was created to fulfil the ambitions of men on the top, India had more Moslems in it than those in the new Moslem homeland! Gradually, by the simple process of growth in numbers, the Moslems became a decisive force in the formation of gevernments in the framework of the Indian democracy. This turned Hindus, particularly ambitious politicians, into eager woers of the Moslems. The effective way to do that was to decry Hinduism. So Hindu, Hinduism and '*Hindutva*' became the whipping-boy for scheming political leaders. Hindus and Hinduism can never be put into separate compartment, for if there are no Hindus there can be no Hinduism and if Hinduism does not remain, there can't be 'Hindus'. So today we see the marvel of Hindus opposed to Hinduism, which have made them the world's laughing-stock and which seems much like a return to the middle-ages. So know-nothings have Hindus become that they are unable to distinguish between knowledge and faith. One plus one is two would be true for everyone whether he is Hindu or a Christian, a Moslem or Buddhist, or of any other religion. But religious beliefs are different. They cannot be questioned even if they are considered irrational by anyone. For example it is believed that the Holy Virgin Mary gave birth to Jesus parthenogenetically. If any one were to deny that, on the ground of its being medically impossible, he would be a fool, for the Immaculate Conception is a sacrosanct belief to be approached by all with reverence. But we find people in India wanting judicial decisions on matters of faith and belief. It's as Justice William O, Douglas of the U.S. Supreme Court, observed in a judgment delivered by him in 1944–U.S.v. Ballard, 322 U.S. 78 'Men may believe what they cannot prove. They may not be put to the proof of their religious doctrines or belief. Religious experiences which are as true to life to some may be incomprehensible to others.' And Judge Felix Frankfurter observed (310 u.s. 856), 'Government may not interfere with organized or individual expressions of belief or disbelief'.

That leads us to yet another weakness of the Hindus. For a Christian, belief in Christ is the only criterion of his being of that faith. For a Moslem it is belief in Prophet Mohammed and the Holy Quran. But Hinduism is so obscure that it has no one positive cannon. One may be an image-worshipper or believe in a God without form. Instead of one scripture it has many. There are many sects too, according to the particular god one worships, Vaishṇavas who believe in Vishṇu, Shaivites who are devotees of Shiva and so forth. True, there are some fundamental beliefs, of which we will speak in the introduction, but the differences are legion. This may be good in one way, giving the religion richness, yet it tends to act as a dividing factor. Thus we find Hinduism weakened by various forces, and whatever is strong and praisewerthy in it is slowly being taken apart by the Hindus themselves who have invented 'secularism' as their battle-cry. Secularism really means atheism and at best it would imply the co-existence of religions, *not* an attack on Hinduism or on *Hindutva*. As Leo XIII who was the Pope from 1810 to 1903 says, 'The equal toleration of all religions . . . is the same thing as atheism' (*Immortale Dei*. On the Christian Constitution of States).

There is a difference between the known, the unknown and the unknowable. The known is, of course, what one perceives by his senses—that which can be seen, heard, felt smelt and tasted. The unknown is that which has not yet come within the field of knowledge, but which man is constantly trying to explore, as for example space, the planets and scientific and medical discoveries yet in the offing which can benefit mankind. The unknowable is that which can never be known, however much one may try. This is for example, God, *brahman* (the Cosmic Absolute) death and what happens after death. Man has been trying to know the unknowable right from the time he started using the higher powers of the mind and has yet not succeeded. Nor he ever will, for the knowledge of the unknowable will mean the end of God. To fill in this gap in knowledge, different religions have given contrary accounts of the unknowable—the beginning of creation, the nature of the Almighty, accounts of afterlife like heaven, hell, the soul and its journey from its leaving one body and entering another and so forth. These accounts, however real they may seem to the followers of the religions which postulate them, cannot obviously all be true. So the unknown cannot be the meeting-point of religions. Nonetheless they are the fervent beliefs of the people. It is philosophy which is the confluence of religious currents. It is the soul of religions, their corner-stone.

What really is philosophy? It has been said to be the quest of truth. Aristotle, for example, says 'Philosophy is the science which considers truth.' and Henri Frederic Amiel, the Swiss poet and philosopher of the nineteenth centruy, believes 'It (philosophy) loves one thing only–truth'. (Journal). But then we have Bacon's observation on Pilate. Truth is hard to define. 'It is, for example, mostly opposed to a lie. However, is a lie always to be condemned? A lie which has no element of deceit might be better than truth which hurts. If one goes and tells a miser, that he's a miser, it would be truth all right, but likely to injure the man's feelings. There's a story told about this. A cow wandered into a holy man's hermitage. Immediately after a butcher with his knife hurried there and asked the sage, 'Have you seen a cow here?' The holy man thought if he told the butcher the cow was in his cottage in the adjoining garden, he would take it away and slaughter it. The protection of cows was a *brāhmin's* bounden duty. So he said 'There isn't any cow here, and I haven't seen one come this way.' The butcher then went away. So we see truth is not so easy to define. Perhaps Will Durant's comment portrays more adequately what philosophy is : 'Philosophy accepts the hard and hazardous task of dealing with problems not yet open to the methods of science–problems like good and evil, beauty and ugliness, order and freedom, life and death; so soon as a field of inquiry yields knowledge susceptible of exact formulation it is called science'. (The Story of Philosophy). One might add that these things are not likely to pass into science, for they are things of the spirit and science encompasses things of matter. So they will remain in the domain of philosophy. To induct them into science would be as vain as writing one's name on water. Cicero says about philosophy as follow:

> 'When Leon asked what philosophers were and in what they differed from the rest of the world, Pythagoras replied that the lives of men seemed to him to resemble the festival that was celebrated with most magnificent games before a concourse collected from the whole of Greece; for at this festival some men whose bodies had been trained sought to win the glorious distinction of a crown, others were attracted by the prospect of gain through buying and selling, whilst there was, on the other hand, a certain class, and that quite the best type of free-born men, who

> looked neither for applause nor gain, but came for the sake of spectacle and closely watched what was done and how it was done. So also we, as though coming from some city to find such a crowded festival, entered upon this life, and some were slaves of ambition and some of money; but there were a special few who, counting all else as vain, clearly scanned the nature of things; these men gave themselves the name of lovers of wisdom – for that is the meaning of the word "Philosophy", and just as at the games the men of truest breeding looked on without any self-seeking, so in life the contemplation and discovery of nature far surpassed all other pursuits (Cicero : *Disputations*).

There can be philosophy without religion, but there cannot be a religion without philosophy. Shorn of philosophy religion would become mere ritual and mythology. The philosophical contents of a religion gives it its value, as the more the proportion of gold in jewellery, the more precious it is. And in philosophy the most treasured constituent is the spiritual. The dictionary defines 'spiritual' as 'of the spirit or soul; of religion, not of material things; of God' (Oxford. Advanced Learner's Dictionary of Current English). Basically it is that, but something more too. It is not enough to speak of God and the soul in isolation. All religions admit the existence of a soul. It does not really need religion to tell us that. We all see and know death, and also its difference from life. What causes that difference is obviously something which irretrievably abandons the body. But what is the relationship between that and its Creator? Can the soul, while even in the body, know God? Such questions and the answers religions give, are the fount of the spiritual. Another important constituent of the philosophy of religions is ethics. Every religion tells us what is good and evil. Hinduism even points out the way in which one can sift the one from the other. The *antaḥkaraṇa* (English equivalent 'conscience') it says, is the measure of that. There are other matters too which religion deals with, like the hereafter, the cause of sorrow and the ways of its removal, the reason for inequalities in wealth, happiness, opportunity and fortune seen in the world, the nature of contentment and the ways in which it can be obtained, and so forth. These things began to vex mankind from the beginning of civilization, and religions tried to provide solutions and answers.

It is in the philosophical constituents we have briefly stated, that Hinduism excels. It is in silence only that the voice of wisdom is heard and in which the spirit of God is revealed. It was on the lonely heights of Mount Sinai that the Lord gave Moses the Ten Commandments and it was in the silence of Gethsemane that Christ prayed to his Father. The words of wisdom constituting the Sermon on the Mount were spoken from the hill-top. Hindu sages and *rishīs* went into the solitude of the forests to meditate upon the questions about the unknown and the unknowable. They discovered the immortal truths of the Upanishads there, and taught them to worthy disciples who approached them with reverence. These hermits found adequate answers to spiritual questions and discovered what Schopenhauer termed 'the products of the highest wisdom which are destined sooner or later to become the faith of the people'.

Hinduism alone, of all religions, gives an explanation of God and the soul from a point of view very much approximating to the rational. To harness reason to the mystical and the spiritual is almost an impossibility. Hindu philosophers and saints like Shankārāchārya and the guru of his guru, the illustrious sage, Gauḍapāda, proved the existence of the soul by methods which were rational, a unique achievement in the philosophies of the world. Gauḍapāda's hypothesis is contained in his *Kārikā* to the *Māṇḍūkya Upanishad.* Hinduism clearly speaks about the nature of God, both in his formless aspect and in the one with form. The former is Īshvara or Vāsudeva whose Cosmic Form (*virāṭa rūpa*) has been described in the *Bhagavadgītā* and the Purāṇas. *Brahman* is the Cosmic Absolute, the formless God frequently spoken of in the Upanishads and the Vedānta. Spiritual communion between God and man is possible even in one's own lifetime, though it can be achieved very rarely, and the union of the soul God is the state of *moksha* (emancipation). We will speak of all these aspects of Hinduism, and others too, when we narrate its fundamental concepts and beliefs. Here these are mentioned only to show that, despite the fatuous onslaughts on Hinduism and *'Hindutva'*, the Hindu religion, in so far as its philosophical content is concerned, is unequalled in its spiritual values. Afterlife, rebirth, the doctrine of karma, the nature of worldly sorrows and the ways to surmount them and other elements of the unknown are all dealt with in Hindu religion and philosophy in a clear-cut manner.

Hinduism is the mildest and most accommodating of religions. Lord Krishṇa says in the *Gītā* 'Even those who worship other gods with faith, really worship me', and 'whatever form of devotion is adopted I make it steady' (9:23 & 7:21) Nor does Hinduism divide men into believers and unbelievers. There are neither heathens in it nor kafirs. Lord Krishṇa did not force Arjuna to accept his teachings. He merely said that he had given the wisdom of the *Gītā* to his disciple. Now it was up to him to reflect upon it and do as he chose to. This is a unique feature of Hindu religion. Neither the sword nor any kind of inducement was ever used to convert people to Hinduism. Differences in the beliefs of one sect and another were decided by arguments and quoting religious texts.

Religion does not give solutions to the problems of life. Each person has to solve his problem to the best of his ability. Nor does it perform any miracles for us, even though the various scriptures show its founders and the gods performing them. In cures of diseases and ailments it is Nature which works not God. Though most religions conceive God as one who judges the acts of men and dispenses reward or punishment, such a concept can only be a guess. The Vedāntic view is more convincing—'Whatever there is in the world is enveloped by God' (*Īsha Upanishad*, 1). Everything is God—the baby miraculously formed by the fertilization of the ovum by the spermatozoa, the growth of the baby in the womb with all its different organs, each a wonder in itself, 'the lisp of children and their earliest words', adolescence, youth, romance, love, the loveliness of the sunrise and sunset, the glory of a rainbow, the countless kinds of creatures of land, water and air, the seasons, days, nights, dreams and fancies, nature in its gentle and its furious aspects, the moonlit and starry skies, the loveliness of flowers and plants: in brief the wonders we constantly see around us but do not wonder at because we take them for granted – all this is God.

While the accounts of creation, afterlife, karma, rebirth and so forth may not be convincing to all, there is no denying the fact that the philosophies of religions are comforting and consoling. At some stage or the other man has to face that which cannot be remedied, whether it is disability, deformity, death or desolation. Sorrow, frustration, dejection and depression are the consequences, and it is then that religion and philosophy come to one's rescue as Boethius says:

> 'The night was put to flight, the darkness fled
>
> And to my eyes their former strength returned. . .

'In the same way the clouds of my grief dissolved and I drank in the light. With my thoughts recollected I turned to examine the face of my physician. I turned my eyes and fixed my gaze upon her, and I saw that it was my nurse in whose house I had been cared for since my youth – Philosophy'.

(*The Consolations of Philosophy.* Book 1).

Religions insist on faith. There is much in common between faith and love. Like love, faith cannot be created by an act of will. It is something which comes spontaneously like poetry, song or the attraction to something lovely. That is why John Keats calls 'beauty truth, truth beauty.' 'Men can be attracted to, but not forced to the faith', says the eight century English scholar Alcuin. 'You may drive people to baptism, you won't move them one step further to religion'. The purity of gold is judged by heating it in the fire. So too faith is tested by suffering. Christ showed the world that one has to suffer to reach God, and took upon him the sufferings of mankind. The fire of suffering either reveals the falsity of faith as heating discloses the copper in gold, else strengthens it. It was at the most intense moment of his suffering that Jesus was united with his Father: 'Father, into thy hands I commend my spirit'. God does not forsake the sufferer in his suffering, it is the sufferer who forsakes God. But if he does not, God takes him more firmly by the hand.

In a way acceptance is faith. After struggling against what is inevitable, man accepts his destiny and resigns to God. 'Father, if thou be willing, remove this cup from me: nevertheless, not my will, but thine be done' (*St Luke*, 22 : 42). But the struggle is hard. It is in suffering that man realizes the futility of relying on human sympathy. And so through it man turns to God, as Browning says in Abt Vogler :

> 'Therefore to whom turn I but to thee, the ineffable name?
>
> Builder and maker, thou, of houses not made with hands'!

It is through suffering that man is drawn towards God. Schopenhauer says : 'Yet without doubt it is the knowledge of death and the consideration of the suffering and misery of life that conduce the most strongly to philosophical reflection and a metaphysical explanation of the world. If our life were endless and painless it would probably occur to no one to ask why the world exists and why it is as it is'. (*Man's Metaphysical Needs*).

Hindu religion has some features that make it stand apart from others. We will speak of these in the introduction where its fundamantal concepts will be discussed. It is in its philosophy that Hinduism is unparalleled.

There are innumerable writings which might be considered to be the source-books of Hindu philosophy, and many are so voluminous that a lifetime wouldn't be enough for the proper study of each of them. The Purāṇas, for example run into several volumes and so does the great epic of the *Mahābhārata*. This book gives selections from the basic philosophical writings. These strictly form the Vedānta, namely the Upanishads, the *Bhagavadgītā* and the *Brahma-sūtras*, on which most of the illustrious philosophers like Shankara, Rāmānuja, Mādhva and others have written their commentaries. To these have been added the *Mahābhārata,* the Vedas, the Purāṇas, and the *Rāmāyaṇa* of Tulsīdāsa, which are of vital significance. It is hoped that the book will prove of interest to those too who are interested in religion and philosophy in general—almost a third of the book has been devoted to this—and it may show those misguided Hindus who are vigorously campaigning against Hinduism, its greatness.

I am grateful to my publisher for venturing to bring out this book even in these hard days for book publishing, and also for the attractive format in which the book has been brought out.

POSTSCRIPT

While this book was under publication, a case of rebirth was reported in the press. As this would be of interest to readers, and it could not be included in the relevant chapter in the book where rebirth has been discussed, the news item appearing in the *Pioneer* of 23 June 1994 is being reproduced below:

Nepal's extraordinary girl
Recalls her life in last birth

PTI

Kathmandu

MISS MALA KUMARI Paswan, a seven-year-old girl of Gaur in eastern Terai Nepal, has started recalling her previous life, claiming that she was a resident of Gandhinagar in Bihar state and gave birth to a dumb son and three daughters.

Upon hearing about the extraordinary girl who is the fourth child of Mr Prem and Phuijhar Devi Paswan, a broad-sheet daily the Kathmandu Post reported, her daughter-in-law travelled a long way from Gandhinagar to Gaur to visit her and took Mata, Malka Kumari, and her present mother to her Gandhinagar home. Though she could not recall her own name of previous life, Mala easily recognized her parents-in-law and husband when she was shown an old Gandhinagar family photograph.

She also told her daughter-in-law that the photograph was taken at Badabham where she succumbed to injuries when she slipped near the hand-pump after a bath.

She has also reportedly recognized her family doctor Dr Surendra Prasad Shrivastava. She recalled that she had handed over the key of a box containing jewellery to her son—Mr Vijay Shah.

A NOTE ON THE PRONUNCIATION OF VERNACULAR WORDS

The letter 'o' (which bears no diacritical mark) is pronounced as *o* in 'm*o*re' (not as in 'lion'). The *m* nasalizes and lengthens the preceding vowel as *n* in bo*n* (French). The *ch* sound is also not to be found in English. It is pronounced with the tip of the tongue placed higher against the upper palate than in uttering the *c* sound.

The cerebrals (*t*, *th*, *d*, *dh*, *n*) are pronounced with the tongue retroflected. The dentals (*t*, *th*, *d*, *dh*, *n*) are pronounced with the tongue against the back of the upper front teeth.

Other marks are explained as follows:-

a as *u* in c*u*t

a as *a* in f*a*ther

i as *i* in f*i*t

i as *i* in mach*i*ne

u as *u* in p*u*t

u as *u* in r*u*le

e as *ay* in m*ay*

n as *n* in wi*n*g

sh as *s* in *s*ugar

g as *g* in *g*oad

t as *t* in *t*ongue

t, *d*, *n* are dentals

d as *d* in *d*ent

c as *ch* in *ch*urch

Other letters may be pronounced as they are in English. The letter 'n' on which a curved mark is put--n is to be pronounced as n in Senor (Spanish).

CONTENTS

(E) **FROM THE BHAGAVADGĪTĀ**

WHAT THE BHAGAVADGĪTĀ IS ABOUT
READING LIST
The Enlightened Sage
Krishṇa as the Lord's Incarnation
On Devotion
The Lord's Promise to his Devotees
The Divine and the Demoniacal
The Nature of Renunciation
How to Attain *Brahman*
The Supreme Path

(F) **FROM THE UPANISHADS**

WHAT THE UPANISHADS ARE ABOUT
READING LIST
About God
What Gives Liberation
Righteousness
The Oneness of *Brahman* and the Soul
The Fate of Human Beings
On the Nature of the Soul
More About the Soul
How to Know *Brahman*
Nachiketas and Yama
The Unity of Existence
One is Judged by his Deeds
The Soul in Various States of Conciousness
From Fire to Fire
The Origin of the Universe
God and the Cosmic Process

Introduction

1

THE EVOLUTION OF RELIGION

One religion is as true as another.
Robert Burton

There are those who are religious and those who aren't. Yet religion remains one of the greatest influences in the lives of human beings. Centuries back, before writing was invented, are have proof that men believed in some kind of existence beyond death. We find in the caverns in which the Palaeolithic man once lived, many paintings which depict wonder and reverence for life. Besides graves of the dead of the Stone Age have been found, in which, along with the bones of the person buried, there are articles of daily living then in use. Why should they be there, if those people did not believe in some kind of life after death ?

SLEEP AND DEATH

Natural phenomena like sunrise and sunset, day and night, stars, planets and the moon, the sudden appearance of fire when stone is struck on stone, the rain, clouds, lighting and so forth; created in ancient man a sense of wonder. That was what he found happening outside in the world in which he lived. Even more mystifying was what kept happening to himself. When he fell asleep he entered a new world. It was real as well as unreal. He saw dreams as vivid as the experiences in the waking state. Yet they weren't like what happened in the day. While awake, things were in his control. He could fling a spear and kill an animal for food. he could eat and drink and make love as he pleased. But in the bewildering world of dreams he had no control. He had to see whatever was shown to him and do whatever he was made to. The whole dream-world was fantastic. irrational and weird. Sometimes pleasing, and then again filled with awesome terror. Dreams and sleep puzzled people right from the Stone Age to the period of the Upanishads when the Hindu sages brooded over them in the solitude of forests. For example in the *Brihadāraṇyaka Upanishad* two great seers Janaka and Yājñavalkya talked about them. Yājñavalkya said :

> 'There are only two states of the soul, this worldly and the other worldly. The dream state is where these two join. Dreams, both sorrowful and joyful, are to some extent drawn from the soul's experiences in the other world. In sleep the soul takes apart its waking experiences and recreates them. No longer circumscribed by the external world it becomes a light to itself and with that light it brings forth the dreams. The soul itself creates its dream-world. There are no real chariots in it, nor animals to be yoked to them, nor roads. Yet it conjures them all in dreams. There are no pleasures there, nor delights, nor joys. Yet in dreams it makes them all felt. There are no tanks there, nor pools nor rivers. Yet it makes them all exist in the dream-world. He in deed is the dream-world's maker.[1]

The modern psychologist has succeeded in finding out more about the nature of dreams and sleep. Scientists put gadgets into various parts of the body of the sleeping man and find out how the different organs are working. They conclude that the entire machinery slows down. The rate of metabolism is at its lowest, being just sufficient to keep the various parts of the body in operation. The blood pressure drops, the pulse rate is slower, the breathing is irregular and slowed down. The body is less sensitive to stimulation by pain, light or sound. Even its temperature drops somewhat.[2] Despite these scientific observations what actually happens remains a puzzle. What is the stuff dreams are made of, no one knows. And the reality of the dream state cannot be denied. One can

1 *Brihadāraṇyaka Up.* 4, 3, 9-10.

2. *The Book of Health* ed. R.L. Clark and R.W. Cumley. Van Nostrand Co. Inc. New Jersey vol 1. p., 92.

only say that it is on a plane different from that of the waking state. The dreams the sleeping man sees, create positive emotions in him. A horrible dream causes fear. A pleasing one, delight. A wet dream, usually accompanied by some kind of sexual dream experience, causes erection and ejaculation. Different theories have been given to explain dreams. Freud, for example, says that they are repressed wishes in a symbolic form. Yet we have not really been able to understand either the phenomenon of sleep or that of dreams. The last word has perhaps been said by Shakespeare :

'Sleep that knits up the ravell'd sleave of care,
The death of each day's life, sore labour's bath,
Balm of hurt minds, great nature's second course,
Chief nourisher in life's feast'.[3]

In fact so little do we know of sleep and dreams, that we have not advanced much further in our knowledge of them than the primitive man. The difference between sleep and consciousness made him believe that there was something that transcended the body. That thing could go away and travel wondrously through space and time.

Then there was death. Those men, living more than six thousand years ago, were equally bewildered by it. They found that when someone died all his vital attributes ceased to exist – warmth, movement, speech, breath and volition. Where did they go? Since the body quickly disintegrated, it could only be the citadel of the spirit. Years later the Upanishadic seers, too., were wondering over the event of death : 'When one is weakened due to illness, those sitting around him say, "Do you recognize us? Do you recognize us?" So long as his soul has not left his body he can know them. But when he dies the soul goes upward, borne on the sunrays'.[4] The Greek thinkers were still puzzled by it, and Marcus Aurelius observed 'Both death and birth are mysteries of nature'.[5] In the nineteenth century a writer and a clergyman said on his deathbed, 'Now comes

---

3 *Macbeth* Act II scene I.

4. *Chhandogya Upanishad*, Chapter 7.

the mystery'.[6] No wonder then that primitive man considered death as something beyond comprehension and defying any rational explanation. Everyone died, and it could not be known when death would come and in what form. Thus, even as the various phenomena of nature remained a mystery to the man of the Stone Age, so too, and indeed even more, was Death and his brother Sleep. Inside the body of creatures, he reasoned, there must be some agent which governed their behaviour. As Sir James Frazer said 'The animal inside the animal, the man inside the man, is the soul'. Another thing the primitive man realized was the inevitability of death. Somewhere, sometime, he would cease to exist as the person he was. The ancient thinkers were still dwelling on the same thought. Horace said, 'Death with noiseless feet has stolen and will steal all',[7] Propertius, 'Neither beauty nor fortune will be ours forever. Near or far, death waits for every man',[8] and Homer wrote in the *Iliad*.

'Yet must I yield to death and stubborn fate,
Whenever at morn, or noon, or eve, the spear
Or arrow from the bow may reach my life'.[9]

Shakespeare, later, still found death as mysterious, and exclaimed with sad resignation :

'Ay, but to die and go we know not where;
To lie in cold obstruction and to rot;
This sensible warm motion to become
A kneaded clod'.[10]

In the *Bhagavadgītā* Shri Krishṇa also tells Arjuna that death is inevitable– *jatasya hi dhruvo mritur dhuvam janma mritasya chā* ['To whom life is given death is certain, as to the dead

5. Quod sibi ipsi scripsit, *IV*. 5.
6. Henry Ward Becher.
7. *Odes*. 2. 13. 19.
8. *Elegies*. III, 25. 11 (II, 28.57).
9. *Iliad*. *XXI*, 110.
10. *Measure for Measure*. Act 3. scene 1.
11. *Gītā*.. 2. 27.

there is also rebirth']. The inevitability of death, more than anything else, gave birth to religion. It was man alone who could realize it, for he was given the higher cerebral areas of the brain. An animal could not anticipate death. He just died when it came. But right from the time man stepped out of the ignorance of childhood, he knew that he would die some day. He did try to forget about it. 'I will not die' he thought, even though he saw others dying. Why this was, and still it, we will explain when we go on later to speak about *māyā,* the power of delusion, which is one of the fundamental concepts of Hindu philosophy.

THE BIRTH OF THE SPIRITUAL

From the higher reaches of the human brain came man's quality of reasoning and discrimination. He realized the virtue of being disciplined. He could judge between good and evil, suppress his passions and aggressive instincts and forego immediate gain for future rewards. Moreover since he could understand the significane of events happening around him, he had such feelings as disappointment, hope, regret, worry and anxiety. He had many things in common with animals and other creatures too. For example sex, hunger and thirst, the physical pain following injury, procreation, birth and death. The higher powers of the brain, however, gave him an edge over animals. This was not wholly an advantage. As a poet wrote, the animals are 'more placid and self-contained'. They are not plagued by the fear of impending death, nor by the greed of wealth. They do not need palatial houses, but are content with their humble, nests, hives, lairs holes, burrows and caves. They eat to live, not to pamper their palates. They kill only to fill their bellies, they do not murder. They do not flaunt themselves in costly and showy clothes, but make do with feathers, furs and manes—the protection against the weather which nature has provided them. As the poet Bihari says : 'See the homely pigeon whose raiments are his feathers, grit his fare, and who's happy with just his mate'.[12] Yet of all creatures man is indisputedly

12. Bihari. *The Satasai*

superior. As the Hindu sage, Shankarāchārya, says 'Among sentient creatures, birth as a human being is difficult of attainment'.[13] The reason is that man alone possesses the intellect by which he can rise above mere living, copulating, eating and drinking. He has the capacity to invent various instruments for his peasures – and sometimes alas! for his destruction – and the impetus to muse over spiritual matters.

13. *Vivekachudamani.* 2.

2

THE RUDIMENTS OF RELIGION

PRIMITIVE MEN

Having been given the higher mental faculties, primitive man was agonized by the evanescence of life, He did not live in isolation like Robinson Crusoe, but in a group or tribal society. He had his individual needs, but had also to discipline himself to fit in with the group to which he belonged. So he evolved a crude kind of ethical code. He invented myths to account for natural phenomena, prayers to placate their fury as when they took the form of eclipses, floods, famine, disease hurricanes etc., and to grant him prosperity, progency long life and health. The Vedic Hindus had gods such as Indra, the god of the firmament, Varuṇa the god of the sky, Ushas, the dawn, Agni the fire-god, Kāma the god of love, Yama of death and so forth. These later found their parallel in the Greek and Hellenic gods. The ancient men of the Stone Age were not so specific. They worshipped natural phenomena, all the same, as the sun, moon, wind etc. To enforce discipline they provided taboos, i.e., acts and things from which one had to desist.

Primitive people lived in groups and so they sought a leader to guide them. This role was assigned to some prominent person in the group who was known as the shaman. He had a hand in almost everything. He was the medicine man, doctor, priest, teacher and policeman. It was he who mediated between man and the unseen world of spirits, cured disease by incantations and spells, and instructed the members of the group in the proper carrying out of rites and ceremonies. He was the precursor of the priest, padre, mullah and pandit.

Although primitive men were sturdy, it would be wrong to conclude that they had long lives. Death and disease pursued them relentlessly. Most of them died before they reached forty, and few survived their fiftieth year. Many died in childhood. A great deal of primitive religion consisted of rituals. Symbolic ceremonies attended funerals. Most tribes chose some particular animal whose spirit, they thought, pervaded their group. They buried the heads of these animals with their dead. They also sprinkled red colour on the corpse hoping thereby to imbue it with life's glow. The Aborgines of Australia believed that if they revered the spirits, the spirits would in their turn, foster them. Strangely much the same idea is contained in the Bhagavadgītā, the most sacred scripture of the Hindus. Sacrifice as an offering to the gods is enjoined. When the gods are pleased with such offerings they also give men what is desired by them. Thus ritual sacrifice becomes a kind of bridge between gods and men.[1] The Aborgines too considered life to be such a reciprocal relation between man and the world of spirits. The earliest religion was thus ritualistic. Circumcision, knocking off the teeth, removal of body hair, making decorative patterns on the body and bloodletting, were some of the rituals practised. A few of these still remain, though they are not carried out in the crude form which then prevailed. For example circumcision is an important religious rite of the Moslems. Shaving off the hair from a child's head (called mundan) is just as important for Hindus. Tattooing is a practice in many tribes even today. Another significant belief of the ancient Aborgines was the closely knit bond between man and nature. They were convinced that the human spirit transcended space and time. Thus primitive religion developed from ignorance to wonder and from wonder to rituals and adoration.

RITUALS

All religions have five factors in common. These are rituals, mythology, ethics, philosophy and scriptural testimony. The extent of each may vary. But they are all there in different modes and forms. The beginning of religion was, as we have seen,

1. *Gītā* 3.10.

in rituals. These have persisted through hundreds of centuries. Hindus have the head-shaving ceremony in which the hair of the child's head is shaved off in some temple. The hair is placed on a thick piece of kneaded flour, rolled up into a ball and immersed in a holy river. Then there is the sacred thread ceremony (*janeyu*), singnifying that the lad has assumed his full religious duties. Women go round the *peepul* (Indian fig-tree) reciting the scriptures, to pray for a son or some other desired thing. The Hindu marriage ceremony, which takes up the greater part of a night, has many rituals like the welcome given to the bridegroom by girls singing auspicious songs (the *dwārachārya*), the mutual garlanding of the groom and the bride done with breathtaking grace (the *jayamāla*), the 'giving away' of the bride to her future husband (*kanyādāna*), the seven rounds taken by the couple around the fire with garments knotted, sanctifying the marriage and finally the *bidāi* in which the bride is tearfully sent off to her new home. Then there are the numerous death ceremonies which go on for thirteen days, ending in a community feast. India is a large country, often called a sub-continent. It is natural that there should exist in it diverse rituals some of which might appear grotesque to westerners and even to the modernized and anglicized Hindus. For example a feature writer, Anasuya Jha, describes the rituals held at Kodungallur in a temple of the Devi (one of the most revered goddess worshiped by Hindus) :

> 'The animal in us is very powerful and unless we are ever vigilant, the lower nature will upset our inner balance and equanimity, is a wise saying. Now just imagine the animal appropriates itself religious sanction for its indulgence in vices! What could be the outcome?'

Having given this salutary observation the writer goes on to describe what she thinks is a 'picture of perversion of minds'. This takes the form of obscene songs and gestures and a ceremony described thus:

> 'On Aswati, the last day of the festival, the regular service of the temple is closed at 10 in the morning. At midday three priests belonging to the non-brāhmin category enter the sanctum sanctorum and conduct a special ritual called

> *Thiruchandanapoti Chartu* (smearing the idol with sandal-powder). During this *pūjā* (worship) the outside doors of the temple are closed and the Raja and his men are the only witnesses of the ceremony'.

She goes on the say that after the doors are opened a green silken umbrella is hoisted. Devotees chant the goddess's name and beat the inside of the temple with sticks. Small packets of pepper, turmeric, whole coconuts and coins are offered to the goddess. Later cocks are given as offering which are then auctioned outside the temple and slaughtered.[2]

The account is given only to show that ritual pervades Hindu religion, just as any other. As regards the obscenity, the writer commits the same mistake in judging Hindu religion as some people do when they condemn the Shivalinga and the sculptures of Khajuraho as obscene. Hindus had a healthy attitude towards sex. One of the Upanishads [the *Brihadāraṇyaka*] even describes sex so vividly that in Max Müller's version of the Upanishads it was left untranslated from the German ! Here's an extract: 'If one wishes to make love to a woman he should insert his member, join his mouth to hers and stroking her lower parts, say "O semen, you have been produced by all my limbs and from my heart. Make this woman pliant in my hands like a deer pierced by a poisoned arrow'."[3]

The Hindu mind did not push sex into cloisters. Instead it depicted it in all its majestic frankness in holy sculptures of temples, the loves of Krishṇa, Tāntric practices and as Shakta and Shakti. As a writer says : '. . . .the Sāṁkhya doctrine does not necessarily condemn bodily pleasures as evil. The tendency of Hinduism, especially in its later development, is to assert the contrary : hence the preponderane of ritual and conduct which, as Gandhi once remarked, became "obscene" only when the Western conquerors arrived to pronounce it so. 'Possibly the Orient was wiser to permit the open parade of such tendencies within the sphere of religious ritual than in their covert parade through the dream-world, as in our Western consciousness. The worship of Shiva, with its undisguised

2. Anasuya Jha. *Sacred Obscenity. Pioneer.* 14 March 1993.

3. *Brihadāraṇyaka* Up., chapter 6.

emphasis upon the generative organs of both sexes, the *linga* and *yoni*, does not strike the Hindu, however young and innocent, as obscene : "obscenity" might rather be attributed to the tendency found almost universally in the Occident, namely to associate sexual operations with other purely automatic activities'.[4]

Other religions likewise have their rituals. The Ceylon Buddhist monks carry palm-leaf umbrellas to hide their faces. Boys of four or five years age of devout Buddhist families are made to re-enact Gautama's renunciation of the world and its pleasures, by first dressing them in princely clothes and then shaving their heads and replacing the clothes by coarse ones. Burmese officials sweep the pavement of the Shwe Dagon Pagoda in order to acquire merit, and laymen put gold leaves they have brought on its central tower. Tibetan Buddhists perform war-dances dressed in terrifying masks and costumes. The votaries of Confucius exorcise evil spirits from temples. The priest holds a sword in his right hand and in his left a small metal bowl with water in it. He takes the water in his mouth and blows it out, thereby purifying the atmosphere. The evil spirit is thus driven away. In Seattle, Washington, Chinese-American girls worship the representation of a dragon to celebrate the Chinese New Year. The dragon personifies the benign powers of nature, productive of rain, harvests and prosperity. A devout Moslem is required to make a pilgrimage to Mecca at least once in his lifetime. While there, he generally observes three main rituals. The first, performed on arrival is the circumambulation of the Kabā seven times. Then he runs seven times between two small hills across Mecca. This is to enact symbolically Hagar's frantic search for water for her son, Ishmael. The third act is going to the Mount of Mercy in the Plain of Aracat. The pilgrims 'stand here before God' from noon to sunset. They are forbidden to wear head coverings, but may carry umbrellas. There are other rituals, too which every Moslem generally observes. One is circumcision which is accompanied by feasts dances and songs. The other is the observance of fasting in the month of Ramadan. During this period the Moslem does not take any food or drink between dawn and dark.

4. Tomlin E.W.F. *Great Philosophics of the East*. London : Arrow books 1959. p., 229.

He must not even have sex. The Shites, a major sect of Islam go round the streets once a year slashing themselves with knives and sometimes pulling out their hair. Then there is walking over fire. The Maulawiyahs or 'Whirling Dervishes' dance in religious ecstasy to the accompaniment of flutes. Zar dancers exorcise evil spirits from the bodies of sick or insane people. Finally there is the sacrifice of animals on the occasion of Bakr' ldd (*kurbani*). Judaism has a number of rites. At weekday morning prayers phylacteries (*t'fillin*) are worn. These are leather straps with boxes containing scriptural verses. One is placed round the arm so as to be near the heart. The other is worn round the head. A sanctification (*Kiddush*) prayer is said at meals while holding the goblet of wine, 'Blessed Art Thou, Oh Lord, King the Universe, who createst the fruit of the vine'. Orthodox Jews observe the Sabbath so strictly that on that day they do not use the phone, or touch money or pose for photographs. At the end of the Sabbath they have the ceremony called Havadalah. Other ceremonies are observed on the Jewish New Year day, the Rosh Hashanah when special white bread (*hallah*) is dipped in honey, and the Passover when there are readings from the Holy Torah. A drop of honey is also placed on the first page of the Torah when a Jewish boy begins his studies. A small box called the *mezuzah* (meaning 'doorpost') containing 15 verses from the Scripture hangs at the door of Jewish homes. The family members kiss it whenever they pass through. Much as in the Hindu custom, a Jewish bride is completely veiled, even covering her head and face. The Jewish wedding-pavilion is called the Chupah. After being blessed by the Rabbi, the couple sip wine together to show they will share whatever fate brings. Christians have their rites mostly connected with birth, death, marriage and festivals. Pilgrims to the Grotto of nativity and the Manger, in Bethlehem, where Christ is believed to have been born, kiss the floor, hang lamps, and place small figures of Christ beneath the altar. To observe the crucifixion Catholic priests dressed in black carry a small image of Christ on a spread out white cloth. A prayer is held at the Stone of Unction where Christ's body was anointed by Nicodemus and the women. There is baptism **in early** age, marriage customs and funeral rites.

MYTHOLOGY

Dismissed by cultured minds as superstition and ignorance, nonetheless mythology has been common to many races like the Greeks, Romans, Hindus and those of the West. Ancient man, who was at a loss to account for natural phenomena, invented myths to explain them. Many myths of these kinds existed among the ancient Egyptains and Babylonians. But it was the Greeks, a nation of poets, who conceived of tales of gods and heroes, and enriched mythology. Hindu mythology generally tells the stories of gods and their deeds. Perhaps it is the most extensive of all such mythologies. Max Müller considered myths to be 'linguistic corruptions' deriving from personification of natural phenomena. Frazer (*The Golden Bough*) allied them with fertility cults and the natural cycle of birth, death and resurrection. Jung saw them as the symbolic expression of a people's collective consciousness. Myths are now considered to have a close relation to the culture and society to which they belong.

Quite a few religions and cultures believe some human figure to be the messiah of their faith. Such a person is considered to be divine. He must be so if he is the founder. Such a figure may be personified from nature, as for example Re the Sun-god. Or he may be a historical figure like Christ, Krishṇa, or Confucius, or the Egyptian Pharaoh. There are other myths like those of Arthur and the Round Table. They do have some kind of religious significance. But in them mythology and ethics are so interwoven as to be almost indistinguishable. Arthur's knights are saintly warriors who combat evil and resue people, mostly ladies, in distress. These semi-historic myths abound among the Greeks. An account of the myths is beyond the scope of this brief introductory chapter. It may be said, however, that the aim of the heroes of the Greek legends was mostly to relieve men from misery. There is, for example, the tale of the Argonauts. Phrixus and Helle were the children of the cloud-nymph, and of Athamas, the Minuan king. When a famine came upon the land, their cruel stepmother Ino wanted them out of the way so that her own children may reign. So the children were brought to the altar for sacrifice. Just then clouds appeared and out of them the Golden Ram came and bore the victims away. Athamas in his fury killed one of Ino's sons. She fled away with the other one and leaped from a cliff into the sea. She was instantly changed into a dolphin which, as is its habit, wanders over the waves sighing with its young one clasped to its breast. Athames was driven out by his people for his ill deeds. He went to the Oracle in Delphi which told him he would become a king again after wild beasts feasted him as their guest. One day he found wolves tearing apart a sheep they had killed. They fled away on seeing him. Athames ate of the sheep's flesh and, as foretold by the Oracle, founded a kingdom and became its ruler. Meanwhile the Golden Ram carried the two children over land and sea. Helle fell into the ocean, and the narrow straits where he fell came to be known as 'Hellespont'. There are two points to be noted in this Greek legend. Firstly, that the children of the cloud-nymph were being sacrificed on the altar *to save the country from famine*. So the Greeks had not advanced much from the concept of the primitive men that rituals can avoid natural calamities. The second significant point is that the legend shows how the straits of Hellespont got their name. There are a number of other Greek legends. One is about Perseus who slew the dreaded monster the Gorgon, the sight of whose head could make one turn to stone, and later dreamt that he had rescued the captive Andromeda. The legend mentions the Sea Queen, Hermes and Father Zeus, the gods and goddess of Greek mythology. It is said in this legend that the goddess Pallas Athene' appeared to Perseus in a dream and asked him to slay the Gorgon and bring her its head so that she might place it on her shield. On asking her who she was and how she came to know his name the goddess said :

> 'I am Pallas Athene. I know men's thoughts and hearts and can know whether they are noble or wicked. Those vile, fatten like sheep which feed on pastures sown by others. They grow and spread like the gourd along the ground. But like the gourd they give no shade to the

traveller, and when they are ripe death gathers them, and they go unloved into hell, and are heard of no more. But to the souls of fire I give more fire and to the manful more strength. These are the sons of the Immortals. I drive them on to fight the Titans, the monsters and the enemies of gods and men. Some are slain young, others live on to old age. But what finally happens to them only Zeus, the Father of gods and men, can know. Tell me, Perseus, which of these two kinds of men appear to you more blest ?'

'Then Perseus boldly answered "Better to die with a noble name than live at ease like the sheep, and die unloved and unrenowned".'

If we were to draw a parallel, what Krishṇa says to Arjuna in the *Bhagavadgītā* is strikingly similar. In the sixteenth chapter the lord says that there are two kinds of persons, the divine and the demoniac. Those divine, have the attributes of charity, kindness, self-control, sacrifice, wisdom. righteousness, fearlessness, purity, eagerness to know God, worship of the Lord, renunciation, compassion, truthfulness, peace, forgiveness, gentleness, fortitude; and absence of greed faultfinding, fickleness, pride and malice. The demoniac are harsh, arrogant, filled with rage and scorn. They are ignorant and godless and always coveting ill-gained wealth, taking revenge, conceited, obstinate and so forth. Such people are cast into demonic wombs and are reborn as lower animals or insects etc.[5]

Hindu mythology is perhaps the richest and the most extensive. It concerns mostly the gods and saints and their doings. We give as an example the story of Bhrigu, a sage. He rescued the sage Agastya from the tyranny of king Nahusha, who had obtained superhuman power. Bhrigu crept into Agastya's hair to avoid the potent glance of Nahusha, and when that tyrant attached Agastya to his chariot and kicked him on the head to make him move, Bhrigu cursed Nahusha, and he was turned into a serpent. On Nahusha's supplication however, Bhrigu limited the duration of his curse.

5. *Gītā.* 16. 1-20. This portion will be raproduced in detail when extracts from the *Gītā* are given later.

In the *Padma Purāṇa* we find Bhrigu as the one assigned the task of finding out who among the three gods of the Hindu Trinity held the highest place. The sage first went to went to Shiva, but did not salute him. The god was enraged and was about to curse him when he quickly apologized and assuaged Shiva's anger. Much the same thing happened when Bhrigu went to Brahmā. Thereafter the sage went to Vishṇu who was asleep. Bhrigu kicked the god on the breast. Vishṇu opened his eyes and instead of getting angry, took the sage's foot in his hands and gently pressed it, expressing himself honoured and made happy by its touch. Bhrigu was pleased with Vishṇu's humility and proclaimed him to be the highest among the three.

Another story is about how Gaṇesha, the god of wisdom and the remover of all obstacles, and the son of Shiva and Pārvatī, got an elephant's head [the god is represented as a short fat person with a protuberant belly, four hands and the head of an elephant but having only one tusk]. There are a number of legends about his elephant's head. One is that his mother, proud of her son, asked Saturn to look at him. When Saturn cast his gaze, Gaṇesha's head was burnt to ashes. Brahmā, the Hindu Creator, told Pārvatī to replace the head with that of the first creature on whom her gaze fell. This happened to be an elephant. So she fixed the elephant's head on her son. Another account is that Pārvatī went to bathe and made her son stand at the door, so that no one may enter while she was naked. Shiva happened to come just then, and the oveuenthusi-astic boy stopped him too. In his rage he cut off his son's head. To pacify Pārvatī he replaced it with an elephant's head, for he saw the beast arrive just then. One version is that Pārvatī herself wanted a son with an elephant's head. Yet another account has it that Shiva slew Āditya, the Sun, but restored him to life again. For this violence Kashyapa doomed Gaṇesha to lose his head. The head of Indra's elephant was used to replace it.

The story of Ahalyā is told in the *Rāmāyaṇa.* She was a very beautiful woman married to Gautama, the rishi. Once when her husband was away from home. Indra, who was enamoured of her, assumed the form of Gautama and ravished Ahalyā. While Gautama was returning he was amazed to see another person identical to him going out. He cursed both of them. Ahalyā was turned into stone. However the curse was made conditional. When Rāma would come that way, he would touch the stone with his feet and restore her to life. It so happened, and Ahalyā went to heaven, after singing a prayer to Lord Rāma.

Thus we find many legends about sages and gods in Hindu mythology. Nor is Hinduism the only faith with such religious stories. The various elements of religion are not isolated compartments. They often coalese. We find a great deal of the scriptures dealing with narratives of the mundane kind. The *Rāmāyaṇa* of the Hindus, the Bible of Christians and the Holy Quran as well as scriptures of other religions have such accounts. We will speak of the *Rāmāyaṇa* in detail later. Here it will suffice to say that the greater part of it tells of how Rāma lost his kingdom and was exiled, of how the demon-king Rāvaṇa carried away Sītā his wife, the battle between the rival armies of Rāma and Rāvaṇa, Rāma's return to Ayodhyā with Sītā, and his coronation. The Bible, too, has many narratives, as for example the one about David and Bath-shebha and Amnon and his sister Tamar, the building of the Ark, the Floods and so forth. In fact the Old Testament is full of such narratives.

Thus quite a bit of the scriptures of all religions contain what may be termed as legend or mythology. And a fair number of scriptural accounts deal with the world's creation. In the Holy Quran we find Joseph's interpretation of the king's dream of the 'seven green ears and (seven) others dry'.[6] Then there is the account of the origin of life:

> 'And certainly We created man of dried clay, of black mud fashioned in shape. And the jinn We created before of intensely hot fire. And when thy Lord said to the angels: I am going to create a mortal of dried clay, of black mud fashioned in shape. And when I have made him complete and breathed into him of My spirit, fall

6. *Translation of Holy Quran.* Muhammad Ali. Ahmadiyya An-juman I-Ishaat-I-Islam. Lehore 1928, p., 240 [Ch. 12 section 6].

> down making obeisance to him. So the angel made obeisance, all of them together. But Iblis (did it not); he refused to be with those who made obeisance. He said : O Iblis! what excuse hast thou that thou art not with those who make obeisance ? He said : I am not such that I should make obeisance to a mortal whom Thou hast created of dry clay, of black mud fashioned in shape. He said : Then get out of it for surely thou art driven away : And on thee is curse until the day of judgment. He said : My Lord! respite me till the time when they are raised. He said. Thou art of the respited ones. Till the period of the time made known. He said : My Lord! because Thou hast judged me as deviating. I will surely make (evil) fairseeming to them on earth, and I will cause them all to deviate, Except Thy servants from among them, the purified ones. He said : This is a right way with Me. As regards My servants, thou hast no authority over them except those who follow thee of the deviators. And surely Hell is the promised place for them all. It has seven gates; for every gate there shall be a separate party of them.[7]

We find such accounts of creation in most other scriptures also. In the Bible we have the Book of the Genesis. According to this God first created the heaven and the earth, light and darkness (day and night), the sky and the ocean, the seasons, sun and moon, trees on the earth, acquatic and winged creatures, the animals and other life on earth and last of all man whose representives were Adam, and Eve who was made from one of the ribs of Adam. Thre is a striking similarily between the account of the Holy Quran and the Holy Bible in regard to the creation of man: 'And the Lord God formed man of the dust of the ground, and breathed into his nostrils the breath of life; and man became a living soul'[8] It is said that God made the entire creation in six days. On the seventh day of the week he rested : 'And on the seventh day God ended his work which he had made. And God blessed the seventh day, and sanctified it : because that in it he had

7. ibid. p., 263. chapter 15 : 26-42, p., 263.
8. The Holy Bible. *Genesis.* 2 : 7.

rested from all his work which God created and made'.[9] Orthodox Christians observe the seventh day (Sunday) as the Sabbath, and as we have seen, they refrain from all work on it. Thus in the English calendar, which we too have adopted (along with the English language, dress, manners and social behaviour) Sunday is the weekly holiday. Even the elite markets in India are closed on this day. On the contrary as conceived by the *Gītā*, the Hindu scripture, there is no rest for God, not even for a minute. Krishṇa says to Arjuna: 'O Arjuna, though I have no duty to perform in all the three worlds, and there is nothing whatever worthy of attainment which I have not with me, still I am always working. For if I ever ceased from work O Arjuna, the people of the world will also (copying my example) stop working. So If I should remain idle all these worlds will be destroyed. Sloth will lead to the birth of illegitimate children. And it will be I myself who will be cause of the destruction of creation'.[10]

The Upanishads also give an account of creation, but it is more complex and long, lacking the clarity of other account, but much on the same lines. First we are told that there was nothing having name and form. Death enveloped all. He decided to create the mind. He felt there should be something to experience consciousness and insentient objects, so he created the soul. Then he created water. The froth of the water solidified and became the earth. He also divided himself into the various limbs of the body, head, arms trunk, belly and so forth. He brought about the congress of mind and speech. According to another account in the same continuation, in the beginning there was only the Cosmic Soul. There was none else and so he said 'I am' That's why everyone first says 'I am' and then adds his name. Man was created and the man divided himself into two and became 'a man and a woman in close embrace'. From their congress human beings were born. The Upanishad continues :

> "Why should he cohabit with me" she (the woman) reflected "after having produced me from himself ?" Thinking so, she endeavoured to hide from him by transforming himself

9. ibid. 2. 2 : 3.

10. *Bhagavadgītā* 3 : 22-24.

> into a cow. But he became a bull and was united with her, and from their union kine were born. She became a mare, he a stallion, she a she-ass, he a he-ass. And from their union animals of the one-hoofed kind were born. She became a she-goat, he a he-goat, she a eve, he a ram, and from their copulation goats and sheep were born. In this manner all life on earth was created in pair, right down to the ants'.[11]

Other faiths have some explanation for creation. The Zoroastrians, for example believe in creation emanating from the one God, Ahura-Mazda. The notable exception is Buddhism. It is concerned with they way of removing suffering rather than going into theories about God and creation. The Buddha was once staying in a forest in Kosambi (near Allahabad). He took a few leaves in his hands and asked his disciples whether these leaves were more or those in the trees of the forest. On being told that that leaves of the forest trees were obviously more, he said, 'Just so, what I have told you is only a little and what I haven't is much more'. He also gave the example of a man wounded by a poisoned arrow. If one were to insist before taking the arrow out on knowing who shot it, his caste, name, family, the kind of man he was, the sort of bow used and so forth; the victim would surely die. Therefore what is necessary is to remove suffering intead of getting involved with questions 'such as whether the universe is eternal or not', and so forth. Buddhism does not deny that gods exist. But, like men, they too are governed by the world order. They can't interfere with it, neither did they create it.

One view about mythology is that there are two kinds of myths – explanation myths and justification myths.[12] The explanation myths concern theories of creation (some of which we have given in the aforesaid accounts), how the world will end, how a city was founded and how a craft was first practised. Norse mythology is one which believes that creation as well as the

11. *Brihadāraṇyaka Upanishad.* Chapter 1. It will be seen that this Teverses the order of creation as in the Bible where man was created last of all beings.

12. This has been explained in *The Penguin Encylopedia* Penguin Books, 1965.

Creator will be destroyed by fire and thereafter a new earth and heaven will come into being. Hindu mythology also believes in *Pralaya* when the world will be destroyed. According to Hindu cosmogony there are four ages (*yugas*). Each *yuga* is preceded by a period of the *yuga's* twilight and followed by another such period of equal length. Each of these periods is one-tenth of the *yuga*. The *yugas* are periods of descending righteousness, and in each of these *dharma* declines progressively. The period of greatest righteousness is the *Kritayuga* of 4,800 years, then the *Tretā*, the *Dvāpara* and last of the *Kali-yuga*, the period of the least righteousness. These three are respectively of 3,600, 2,400 and 1,200 years i.e. 12,000 years. But these are years of the gods, one of which is equal to 360 years of ours. Thus the total period reckoned in terms of the years of men is 4,320,000 years. This forms a *Maha-yuga* or *Manavantara*. Two thousand *Maha-yugas* or 8,640,000,000 years make a *Kalpa*. A *Kalpa* is a night and a day of Brahmā, the Creator. At the end of a *Kalpa* there is the world's dissolution, which is known as *Pralaya*. The world remains unaltered (in the sense of its continuance) for one of Brahmā's days. Thereafter it is consumed by fire, the sages, gods and elements surviving. Here we pause to note the similarity to Norse mythology. Which as we have said, also believes in the world's destruction by fire. To proceed with the Hindu account, when Brahmā himself expires, and all the gods and sages too, and the whole universe is resolved into its constituent elements.

The other kinds of myths are those which explain customs, beliefs, or rituals. To this class also belong myths concerning victories of gods over one another. An example in Greek mythology is the account of the Titans, the predecessors of the Olympian gods. They were the offspring of Uranus the oldest, of the gods, and Gaea. Their leader. Cronos married his sister Rhea. Their offspring were Hera, Demeter. Plutoand Poseidon. Cronos was fore warned that one of his children would displace him and so he swallowed all of them. But Rhea gave birth to Zeus who made Cronos swallow a potion which led him to disgorge all the children he had swallowed. A war ensued in which Zeus and his brother and sisters were victorious, after which Zeus became the ruler of earth and heaven. There are myths to narrate the marriage of gods. Such stories abound in almost all religions. The Babylonians have the myths of Baal Ishtar and so forth. Lancelot, Arthur and other knights figure in British legends. The Egyptins have Horus and Isis, the Romans Janus, Jupiter etc., the Irish Conchubar and Deirde, the Welsh Merlin, and the Scandinavians Aesis and Balder.[13]

Hindu mythology also gives accounts of wars and conflicts among gods, demons (asuras) *nāgas* (the serpent race) and so forth. The myths often give accounts of seduction, sexual incontinence, abductions and so forth. Western scholars and critics often express contempt and disdain regarding these myths, forgetting that other scriptures, not excluding the Bible, have such stories also involving the chosen ones of the Lord. Such myths concern Indra. Krishṇa (whom alas! many Sanskrit and Hindi poets have used as a kind of peg to hang their dirty clothes on) and other gods and sages. Indra sent Menekā to excite the passions of sages. His rivalry with Krishṇa is mentioned in detail. Indra was worshipped by the people of Vraja. Krishṇa persuaded them to give it up. Indra sent a deluge to drown the Vraja people, but Krishṇa lifted up a mount (Goverdhana) on his finger to shelter them. Indra failed to harm the people and acknowledged his defeat. We thus see that mythology is an integral part of almost all religions. Like ritual, it too is a widening of primitive religion. The Stone Age people worshipped natural phenomena. But their adoration could not be expressed by the written word, for writing even in its crude form on leaves and barks of trees came much later. As soon as men could convey this adoration into words, they invented stories about gods, wars, defeats, victories and so forth. Many religions, if shorn of their mythology would lose much of their contents.

MIRACLES

Allied with mythology are miracles which form part of most religions. Both the Holy Bible and Hindu scriptures like the *Rāmāyaṇa* and the *Purāṇas* abound in them. So much so that even Buddha who was the founder of a religion based largely

13. An account of these would be beyond the scope of this book. However the reader may refer to *The Penguin Encyclopedia* Penguin Books. 1965.

on rationalism, performed miracles. The queer thing is that the performers of miracles were averse to them. But they performed them all the same. The Buddha forbade the display of miraculous power. One day he came across an ascetic who sat on the bank of a river. The man had practised austerities for twenty-five years. The Buddha asked him what he had got for all this labour. The ascetic proudly replied 'I can now cross the river by walking on the water'. 'This is very little gain for so much labour', the Budda said, 'seeing that the ferry will take you across for just one copper'. Yet many miracles were performed by the Buddha. He caused his body to rise up in the air, flames of fire coming from the upper part of him and streams of water from the lower. He produced a mango tree fifty hands high by merely washing his hands over a seed. He cleaned by a glance the muddy water of a stream. He fed a hundred monks on just one cake, the remnants making a huge mound [compare Christ's miracle of feeding a multitude with five loaves and two fishes]. He miraculously disappeared from one bank of a river and reappeared on the other. He divided the water when there was a flood and walked though the two walls of water [cf., the similar division of the sea in the Bible]. He restored the sight of Subha, a nun whose eyes had been torn away by a licentious man who had pursued her into a forest.

Christ too, was against the performance of miracles. 'Why doth this generation seek after a sign ?' he said to the Pharisees. 'Verily! I say unto you there shall be no sign given to this generation'.[14] However it is clear that he did not wish any publicity to be given to his miracles. When he raised from the dead the twelve year old daughter of the ruler of the synagogue, he told the parents not to tell anyone of it: 'He charged them straitly that no man should know of it'.[15] Again, after he had cured a man who was deaf and had an impediment in his speech, he asked the men present there not to tell anyone about it, though their astonishment was so great that they spread the news of the cure : 'And he charged them

---

14. *St Mark*. T. 36-37. [The Holy Bible].

15. ibid. 5. 43.

that they should tell no man : but the more he charged them, so much the more a great deal they publicised it.[16] So we see that both Buddha and Christ were against the performance of miracles, yet they performed them. When we consider the miracles of Krishṇa we do not find such reluctance. On the contrary the boy Krishṇa who subdued the Kaliā-nāg (the dreaded serpent who poisoned the waters of the Yamunā), danced gleefully on its head! The miracles performed by him in the *Mahābhārata*, too, were much different from Christ's miracles. They wern't to ease distress, but to assist the Pāṇḍvas, on whose side he was. Or as in the case of the lifting of the Goverdhana mount, to defeat and disparage some other god. Of all existing religions, Hinduism takes the lead in miracles and mythology. The Hindu gods and sages are for ever appearing and disappearing. They change forms, as the demon Kālanemi did to outwit Hanumān who was flying to the Himalayas to get the wonder drug plant which would revive unconscious Lakshmaṇa, or as the she-demon Sūrpanakhā took the form of a lovely woman to beguile Rāma. They can also become huge or diminutive as the god Hanumān who jumped the ocean in one bound, flew from the south of India to the Himalayas and back again in just one night, towered high as a mountain and becoming small as the size of a thumb entered the demon Surasā's mouth and got out through her ear! The messengers of the gods also show their prowess, as Angad who put his foot so firmly in Rāvaṇa's assembly that not even the mightiest warriors could shift it !

There are no miracles in life, despite unverified claims of our so-called sages to perform them. The Hindu mind is extremely gullible and apt to hero-worship anyone who takes a staff and bowl and dresses in ochre. So we find rings being produced suddenly from the air, coins disappearing from closed fists and so forth. In life it is nature which works and God through nature, Miracles are confined to the scriptures. But why should miracles be part of scriptural mythology at all? Surely the prophets or avatāras do not need a certificate. They would be adored even if they were not shown performing miracles.

16. ibid. 8 : 12.

It could be that they help creating faith. While Jesus was in Galilee he healed a nobleman's son who lay dying in distant Capernaum. As a result, we are told 'the nobleman himself believed, and his whole house'.[17]

In the Holy Quran we have the following passage regarding signs:

'And nothing could have hindered us that We should send signs except that the ancients rejected them; and We gave to Samood the she-camel – a manifest sign – but they did injustice by (slaying) her; and We only send signs to make (men) fear . . . .We have repeated for men in this Quran every kind of argument, but most men do not consent to aught but denying. And they say : we will by no means believe in thee until thou cause a fountain to gush forth from the earth for us : Or thou shouldst have a garden of palms and grapes in the midst of which thou shouldst cause rivers to flow forth, gushing out : or thou shouldst cause the heaven to come down upon us in pieces as thou assertest, or bring God and the angels face to face (with us) : Or thou shouldst have a house of gold, or thou shouldst ascend into heaven and we will not believe in thy ascending until thou bring down to us a book which we may read. Say : Glory be to my Lord! am I aught but a mortal apostle?'[18] The Holy Quran gives merely statements about miracles and assigns, as we see, their authorship to God. To faith, it adds the element of fear. The Bible, too, says : 'The fear of the Lord is the beginning of wisdom'.[19] The Upanishads do not speak of 'fear of the Lord' but assert that he is the one by whose command everything is in place and nature does its allotted tasks : At *brahman's* command the sun, the moon, heaven and earth stay in their places. At his command the moments (*muhūrtas*) [a period equal to forty–eight minutes or in other words 'hours'], days, nights, fortnights, months, seasons and years keep their respective periods of time. At his command some rivers flow east from the snowy mountains, while others flow westward, or in different directions according to their

17. *St John*. 4 : 53

18. The Holy Quran. Trans., Muhammad Ali. Lahore : Ahmadiyya Anjuman-I-ishaat-I-Islam. 1928. 17 : 59 & 89-93.

19. *Psalms*.

prescribed courses. By his command, Gārgi, the givers of charity gain merit, the gods are desirous of offerings made to them at sacrifices and manes are eager to receive offerings'.[20]

We see, therefore, that the ancient cult of the reverence for natural phenomena developed in religions into stories or myths and legends of gods, sages (who were considered godmen), prophets and messiahs and about some Supreme Being who was believed to control what happens in the world. The basis of mythology was to demonstrate the glory and the power of this Being, to inculcate fear of him and belief for him and to account for things unseen and beyond the purview of the five senses of human beings, yet happening mysteriously day in and day out.

ETHICS

We have spoken about taboos and totems in the beliefs of the ancient men of the Stone Age. These were more or less in the nature of prohibitions. Although there was no semblance of the kind of religion we know of, in their code of conduct, they were very strict about these. As Freud says, despite their primitive nature, these savages took measures to save the family from disintegration and prohibited sexual realtions of certain kinds. Incest was looked upon with horror and punished with death. In Melanesia, for example, if a girl came across her brother by accident, she must run away and hide herself from his gaze. In New Caledonia the girl, in case of such chance meeting would flee into a bush. Marriages in forbidden clans was prohibited, as well as temporary affairs which did not have the birth of children as their aim [curiously we seem to be less civilized than the savage in this respect, for in the West particulary, promiscuous sex is not frowned upon]. The objects of taboos were many. One was to protect important people like chiefs, priests and so forth from harm. Another was to guard the weak (as for example women and children) from spells and magical influences. A third object was to prevent contact with corpses and some prohibited foods. Fourth to protect the main acts of life (birth, initiation, marriage etc.) from interference. Fifth to escape from the wrath of

20. *Brihadaranyaka Upanishad.* 3 : 8.

the gods or spirits. Sixth to save unborn children and babies from certain forbidden acts of their parents.[21] It is interesting ot not that some of these practices have come down to us in the religions and religious practices of our times. The Hindu bathes and casts off his clothes for fresh ones, after he has come back from cremating a corpse. This is doubtless an extension of the third kind of taboo mentioned above.

Prohibitions have been incorporated in scriptures too. In the Holy Quran we are told that men should 'cast down their looks and guard their private parts', and women should 'cast down their looks and guard their private parts and not display their ornaments except what appears thereof', and 'wear theirhead-covering over their bosoms'.[22] In the Holy Bible we find a moral code of conduct given by the Lord himself:

> 'Thou shalt have no other gods before me. Thou shalt not make unto thee any graven image, or any likeness of any thing that is in heaven above, or that is in the earth beneath, or that is in the water under the earth: thou shalt not bow down thyself to them, nor serve them: for I the lord thy God am a jealous God, visiting the iniquity of the fathers upon the children unto the third and fourth generation of them that hate me; and shewing mercy unto thousands of them that love me, and keep my commandments.
>
> 'Thou shalt not take the name of the Lord thy God in vain; for the Lord will not hold him guiltless that taketh his name in vain.
>
> 'Remember the sabbath day to keep it holy. Six days shalt thou labour, and do all thy work : but the seventh day is the sabbath of the Lord thy God : in it thou shalt not do any work, thou, nor thy son, nor thy daughter, manservant nor thy maid-servant, nor thy cattle, nor thy stranger that is within thy gates : for in six days the lord made heaven and earth, the sea, and all that in

21. Encyclopedia Britannica. Quoted in Sigmund Frued.. *Totem and Taboo.* Penguin Books 1919, pp., 43. 44.
    Totem and Taboo. Penguin Books, 1919, pp., 43-44.
22. *The Holy Quran.* Trans., Muhammad Ali. Lahore, 1926, 24 : 30-31.

them is, and rested on the seventh day : wherefore the lord blessed the sabbath day, and hallowed it.

'Honour thy father and mother : that thy days may be long upon the land which the lord thy God giveth thee.

'Thou shalt not kill

'Thou shalt not steal.

'Thou shalt not bear false witness against thy neighbour.

'Thou shalt not covet thy neighbour's house, thou shalt not covet thy neighbour's wife, nor his manservant, nor his maid-servant, nor his ox, nor his ass, nor any that is thy neighbour's'.[23]

The Book of the Covenant in *Exodus* also gives a number of prohibitions and rules of conduct. These comprise many matters of social behaviour. Punishments for transgressions and evil deeds are also provided, as for example death for murder [21 : 12-15]. There are minute details about the procedure to be followed in case of theft, borrowing, lending money, sowing land, fasts and feasts, pledging goods and so forth. Similarly in the Covenants in *Deuteronomy* we find such directions some of which read almost like the ancient totemic restrictions. Certain kinds of beasts are not to be eaten : 'of them that chew the cud, or of them that divide the cloven hoof : as the camel, and the hare, and the coney [and the swine]'. Of birds too, among others, the swan, the hawk, pelican, cormorant, stork heron, lapwing and every creeping thing that flies. There are also detailed laws about marriage, divorce, adultery and so forth. For example :

'If a man be found lying with a woman married to an husband, and a man find her in the city, and lie with her; then ye shall bring them both out unto the gate of that city and ye shall stone them with stones, that they die; the damsel because she cried not, being in the city; and the man, because he hath humbled his neighbour's wife'.[24]

23. *Exodus* 1. 3-13

24. *Deuteronomy* 22 : 23-24.

However, if the betrothed woman is found in a field and then the same act is done, the man should be killed but not the woman, for she cried out, but there was no one to hear her. In case the woman is a virgin, but not betrothed, the man who forces her has to pay a fine (fifty shekels of silver) to the woman's father and marry her. In the Epistle of St Paul to the Romans, there also figure rules of ethics. But these are on the moral plane. They concern virtuous living and communion with God : 'Let love be with out dissimulation. Abhor that which is evil; cleave to that which is good. Be kindly affectioned one to another with brotherly love; in honour preferring one another; not slothful in business; fervent in spirit; serving the Lord; rejoicing in hope, patient in tribulation; continuing instant in prayer; distributing to the necessities of saints; given to hospitality. Bless them which persecute you; bless, and curse not. Rejoice with them that do rejoice, and weep with them that weep. Be of the same mind one toward another. Mind not high things, but condescend to men of low estate. Be not wise in your own conceits. Recompense to no man evil for evil. Provide things honest in the sight of all men. If it be possible, as much as lieth in you, live peaceably with all men. Dearly beloved, avenge not yourselves, but rather give place unto wrath : for it is written, Vengence is mine; I will repay, saith the Lord. Therefore if thine enemy hunger, feed him; if he thirst, give him drink : for in so doing thou shalt heap coals of fire on his head. Be not overcome of evil, but overcome evil with good'.[25] There follows a very significant observation : 'Let every soul be subject unto the higher powers. For there is no power but that of God....'. Every religion passes through three stages of development. The first is practical conduct which largely concerns acts to be done and those to be avoided. In Hindu philosophy this is the *karma-kāṇḍa* or observing the duties enjoined by the scriptures. Krishṇa makes this distinction in the *Gītā*. Duties enjoined by the scriptures must not be abandoned he says, because they purify a man. But they should be done without an eye on the fruit, i.e., with detachment. The man who is spiritually

25. *Romans.* 12. 1–21.

advanced, however does not shrink from what is disagreeable, nor does he long for what is agreeable.[26] The second stage of ethical development is on the moral plane. This is a kind of bridge or stepping-stone from the purely ritual which encourages good conduct [prayer, worship, pilgrimages, going to temple mosque or church, doing virtuous acts etc.] to the spiritual. Moral ethics is of the kind which makes people do good either out of fear of God or the working of their own conscience. The Holy Quran says : 'Then if he is one of those drawn nigh (to God). He shall have happiness and bounty and a garden of bliss. And if he is one on the right hand. Peace to thee from those on the right hand. And if he is one of the rejecters the erring ones, He shall have an entertainment of boiling water. And burning in hell. This indeed is a certain truth'.[27] To the moral stage of ethics belong prayers such as the Christian prayer attributed to St Francis of Assisi :

> 'lord, make me an instrument of your peace. Where there is hatred, let me sow love; where there is injury, pardon; where there is doubt, faith; where there is despair, hope; where there is darkness, light; where there is sadness, joy.
>
> 'o divine master, grant that I may not so much seek to be consoled as to console; to be understood as to understand; to be loved as to love; for it is in giving that we receive; it is in pardoning that we are pardoned; and it is in dying that we are born to eternal life'.

In the *Taittīrya Upanishad* we find a striking example of moral ethics. After the teacher has taught his pupils, he gives them this parting advice :

> 'Speak the truth. Practise virtue. Do not neglect your studies . . .Do not swerve from your duty or from truth. Do not be indifferent to your own welfare. Make the offerings due to the gods and the manes. Revere your parents and your teacher and be hospitable to guests.

26. *Bhagavadgītā* 18 : 5–6 and 10.

27. *The Holy Quran*. Trans., Maulvi Muhammad Ali. Karachi, 1928, 56 : 88–95 (p., 538).

> 'Whatever deeds are blameless and whatever good works have been performed by us, those only should be performed by you, not others. Honour those who are learned by offering them a seat and show obedience to them and eagerness to learn. Give with sympathy, humility and abundance. Give gladly and willingly. Never give a gift for which you are not completely willing. If you are in doubt regarding any acts or conduct of yours, you should shape them according to the acts and conduct of *brāhmins* [i.e. men of wisdom] who can judge well but not harshly, who love virtue, and who are themselves devoted to good deeds, not urged to them by others. And as to those whom people may malign, you are not to take them at their word, but behave towards them as these (aforesaid) brāhmins behave'.

The third and the highest plane of ethics is the spiritual. This is the one in which the fruits ripen and of themselves fall off the tree. The spiritually realized man needs no moral precepts, for whatever he thinks and does that itself is morality. The spiritual man has realized his identity with God. He is no more struggling with ritual or with the observance of scriptural injunctions or with the effort to discriminate between good and evil. He has known God. He has also realized that all creation, all that is called the universe, all that happens in the world, in truth everything; is nothing but God. There is nothing apart from him. The spiritual stage is not easily attained, for to know God in this way is given to some rare person. In the *Bhagavadgītā* Krishṇa tells Arjuna : 'It is after many lives that the man of wisdom realizes "All this is Vāsudeva [God]". Such an enlightened soul is very rarely found'.[29] Jesus asked his disciple one by one who they thought he was : 'And they said, Some say thou art John the Baptist; some, Elias; and others, Jeremias, or one of the prophets. He saith unto them, But whom say ye that I am?

'And Simon Peter answered and said, Thou art the Christ, the Son of the living God. And Jesus answered and said

---

28. *Taittīriya* Up., 1. 11 : 1–4.
29. *Gītā.* 7 : 19.

unto him, Blessed art thou, Simon Bar-jona; for flesh and blood hath not revealed it unto thee, but my Father which is in heaven'.[30] Krishṇa, too, says much the same thing. 'Fools seeing me in a human form are indifferent to me. They do not know that I am the Lord and Creator of these worlds', and 'Of the thousands of people some rare ones try to attain salvation and even among those there is hardly anyone who knows me as I am'.[31] The Yoga of Pātanjali begins with the primary stage of ethics (*yama and niyama*) consisting of such virtues as non-violence, the absence of covetousness and stealing, continence, telling the truth, purity, austerity, contentment. repetition of the sacred word and devotion to God. From this it moves on to the higher spiritual states of concentration, meditation and *samādhi* [the eradication of mental modifications when the thinker and object of thought is one]. The Upanishads, which, along with the *Bhagavadgītā,* are the highest expression of Hindu philosophy, frequently speak of this spiritualism. The *Kaṭha Upanishad* begins with a teaching which is purely ethical: Both the good and the pleasant approach a man. The wise man, after pondering over them, discriminates and chooses the good while the simple-minded man who is bothered only about his own good, prefers that which is pleasant'. Thereafter it culminates in the spiritual teaching : 'Only that person knows eternal bliss who sees abiding in his soul the Controller of all beings, who sees that which is eternal in this changing world'.[32] The *Taittirya Upanishad* speaks of *brahman* form which 'Words and thoughts turn back, not comprehending it. How can that man fear, who has realized its bliss ?'[34] The spiritual stage is that in which wisdom becomes identical with devotion. That is why in the *Bhagavadgītā*, Krishṇa praises both the man of knowledge and the devotee, the *akshara-brahman* [Cosmic Absolute] as well as Īshvara [the Lord Almighty]. The devotee is, however, nearer to God than the wise man, for where knowledge ends, devotion begins. Reason can only guide us in the known and the seen. When we see smoke, we reason

30. *St Matthew.* 16 : 14–18.
31. *Bhagavadgītā.* 9 : 11 and 7 : 3.
32. *Aphorisms of Yoga.*
33. *Katha Up.* 2 : 1 and 5 : 12-13.
34. *Taittirya Up.* 2. 4.

out there must be fire. When we notice the marks of shoes or footsteps on a muddy track, we surmise that someone must have gone that way. But for the unseen and the unknown there is no proof. We either accept or reject. So the devotee is like Browning's musician :

> 'Each sufferer says his say, his scheme of the weal and woe :
>
> But God has a few of us whom he whispers in the ear;
>
> The rest may reason and welcome : 'tis we musicians know'.[35]

The futility of argument has been realized by philosopher and poet alike. Arjuna was appalled by the horror of killing his own kinsmen and shedding blood on the battlefield of Kurukshetra. He was also not sure if his side [the Pāṇḍvas] would win the battle or the Kauravas. That was the basic fact. As a *kshatriya* [warrior] he was duty bound to fight, yet he didn't want to. So he advanced all kinds of arguments for not fighting. Krishṇa called these *prajñāvāda* [*prajñā* = 'intellect,] and *vāda* = 'argument']. The word *vāda* is used here to mean prevarication. Arjuna had made a decision to abstain from war and he was trying to justify that by fruitless arguments. Much the same is the case with spiritual matters such as the existence of God, the soul, afterlife, rebirth and emancipation. The believer can prove their existence by arguments and so too the agnostic their non-existence. For things beyond the cognizance of our five senses it is futile to advance arguments. As Omar Khayyam says :

> 'Myself when young did eargely frequent
>
> Doctor and Saint, and heard great argument
>
> About it and about : but evermore
>
> Came out by the same Door as in I went'.[36]

In the *Gītā* Krishṇa says that the worship of the unmanifest is more difficult than the worship of a personal God. We have different kinds of beliefs provided by various religions.

35. *Abt Vogler* XI.

36. *The Rubaiyat.* Trans.. Edward Fitzgerald. 1. xxvii.

Some are dead against image worship, as for example Islam. So much so that Moslem zealots became iconoclasts. Christianity makes Jesus Christ the intermediary between God and man. To Martha, Christ said 'I am the resurrection and the life: he that believeth in me, though he were dead, yet shall he live: and whosoever liveth and believeth in me shall never die'.[37] 'I am the way, the truth, and the life : no man cometh unto my Father, but by me'.[38] Hinduism believes in image worship. But it is the most broadminded of all religions for it admits of all kinds of beliefs. A Hindu may worship an image or believe in the formless *brahman*. He may go to a temple or say his prayers at home. Buddhism is quite different from Hinduism, yet the Buddha has been considered to be one of the *avatāras*.

DEVOTION (Bhakti)

What exactly is devotion [*bhakti* in Hindi] ? Most religions imply by it complete faith in God, unquestioned by reason, requiring no proof. The process of devotion, however, has its peculiarities. It presupposes faith of course. 'If ye have faith as a grain of mustard seed, ye shall say unto this mountain, Remove hence to yonder place, and it shall remove'.[39] The conferment of faith or its attainment, however, is somewhat mysterious. The wind bloweth as it listeth. In the Holy Bible we have the incident of Saul : 'And Saul, yet breathing out threatenings and slaughter against the disciples of the Lord, went unto the high priest, and desired of him letters to Damascus to the synogogues, that it he found of this way, whether they were men or women, he might bring them down to Jerusalem. And as he journeyed he came near Damascus : and suddenly there shined round him a light from heaven : and he fell to the earth and heard a voice saying unto him, Saul, Saul, why persecutest thou me? And he said, Who art thou, Lord? And the Lord said, I am Jesus whom thou persecutest : it is hard for thee to kick against the pricks'.[40] According

37. *St John.* 11. 25–26 [The Holy Bible]
38. ibid. xiv : 6.
39. *St Matthew* xvii : 20 [The Holy Bible].
40. *The Acts of the Apostles.* 9 : 1–6. [The Holy Bible].

to mythological belief Vālmīka, the author of the *Rāmāyana* was a robber who killed many people for their wealth. But he received Rāma's grace, and became a sage and a devotee. One of the Āḻvār saints, Tirumangai Mannan would rob wealthy men to carry out holy works of charity. It is said that the Lord appeared to him and transformed him into a devotional poet. In the *Gītā,* Krishṇa says: 'Although a man may be a villain all his life, if he loves me I do not see any evil in him. He is holy and will get peace'.[41] Thus devotion is not acquired. It is given. It is like love. You cannot create love. It is either there or not there. It is a gift from God, given to those who are worthy to receive it. We judge a man's worth by what he says and by what he appears to be to us. We do not have the capacity of peering into his heart and soul. One may smile and smile, yet be a villain, as Shakespeare says. But God is the internal observer [*antarayāmī*]. Besides, we can know only the present life. According to Hindu belief the soul passes through many existences. The belief is catching on with other thinkers too. Only God can know the totality of existence. Once we realize this many things become clear. The suffering of those who are good, the gift of devotion to those who, by worldly standards, are unworthy. Even then there remain mysteries like, death, the nature of afterlife, the purpose of creation and so forth. These we will consider later.

PHILOSOPHY

We have considered those elements of religion which were an extension of primitive beliefs – rituals, mythology and ethics. With philosophy we enter a new realm. The primitive man was puzzled by the phenomena of nature and by the things for which he had no logical explanation, as for example sleep, dreams and death. He took the easiest and the most obvious course of adoration, placation and what we would call superstition, like the driving out of evil spirits, puberty rites, blood-baths, mourning ceremonies and so forth. In order to keep intact the society in which he lived he devised prohibitions which we call taboos and totems. These were the precursors of ethics

41. Chapter 9.

as conceived by the followers of religions which later developed. The highest reaches of the human mind, however, remained unreached and unexplored. To the Stone Age man warding off evil was enough. He wasn't bothered much about the why and the wherefore of existence. These questions agitated the minds of the Vedic seers for the first time. They were not necessarily celibates or *sannyāsīs*. Quite a few were family men like the sage Yājñavalkya, and some even kings, like Janaka. Yet others were seemingly insignificant persons. Such a man was Raivaka, the man with the cart, who came to the notice of a pious and charitable king of the name of Janashruti in a unique manner. The story is told in the *Chhandogya Upanishad*. Janashruti was sleeping on his terrace. While he lay awake on his bed for a few minutes, he heard two swans speaking to each other :

> 'One of them said "Hey mind where you're flying. Be careful The light of Janashruti shines across the sky. Don't let it touch you or you'll be burnt". The other swan said "Say who's this man of whom you speak as though he is Raivaka, the man with the cart ?". "How's it with Raivaka ?" the first swan asked. "It's like a game of dice" the second swan explained. "Just as the player who throws the highest number wins and all the lower numbers thrown go to him so the merit Raivaka gained by the numerous good deeds performed by him include the good deeds of others too".'[42]

The king's curiosity was aroused and he sent men to search for Raivaka. They found him at last lying under a cart and scratching himself. He was rather annoyed at being disturbed. The king won him over with costly presents and gave him his daughter in marriage. In return Raivaka told him about the Cosmic Absolute and the soul. Whatever the standing of these men was, they had one thing in common. All of them were eager to fathom the mystery of existence, to find out, if they could, what happens after death, what the nature of God and the soul was, and what was the goal of life. They believed that solutions to such intricate questions could only

42. Chhandogya Up. 4 : 1–3.

be found by continued meditation. And for that the proper place was not the home with its worldly life and family cares, but the forest. So they dwelt in the forest solitude. They came to their own conclusions about these matters, and taught what they had learnt to disciples whom they considered worthy to receive the knowledge. Their teachings are recorded in the Upanishads.

After them there were many philosophers and thinkers in other countries. Many of them very ancient and outstanding, like the Chinese philosophers Confucius and his renowned disciple Tzu Ssu, the Zen masters of Japan, the Egyptians and the Greek (Hellenic) philosphers. In the ancient world the word 'philosophy' was used in the sense of the search after truth and the nature of the universe and man. The prominent Greek philosophers were Socrates and Plato. There were others too, like Heraclitus, Parmenides, Empedocles, Anaxagoras, the Atomists, Sophists, Stoics, Cynics, Epicureans, Sceptics, and the Greek-Christians Philo, St Justin, the Alexandrian philosophers and Plotinus.

The immediate difficulty faced by philosophers was how to express in writing the unknown, indeed often that which was beyond words. A favourite method was that followed by Plato, viz., dialogue in which the listener keeps accepting one premise after another till the whole truth is revealed. Hindu philosophy devised a similar System. But in it the listener does not just keep accepting. Imaginary objections are interposed, and these are controverted to reveal the doctrine the philosopher is establishing. Many of the aphorisms in the Six Systems of Hindu Philosophy adopt this method. Max Müller was quick to notice the felicity of expression of Hindu philosophers : 'Whatever we may think of such views of the world as are put forward by the Sāṁkhya and Vedānta, and other systems of Indian philosophy, there is one thing we cannot help admiring, and that is the straight– forwardness and the perfect freedom with which they are elaborated. However imperfect the style in which their theories have been clothed may appear from a literary point of view, it seems to me the very perfection for the treatment of philosophy. It never leaves us in any doubt as to the exact opinions held by each philosopher'.[43]

There is a great deal of difference between religion and philosophy, despite the closeness of the two. Religion is quite often dogmatic. There is in it no room for disagreement. Philosophy presents a certain point of view and leaves acceptance to those to whom, it is addressed. As Walt Whitman says :

> 'From this hour I ordain myself loos'd of limits and imaginary lines
>
> Going where I list, my own master total and absolute.
>
> Listening to others, considering well what they say,
>
> Pausing, searching, receiving, contemplating,
>
> Gently, but with undeniable will divesting myself of the holds that would hold me'.[44]

Religion is for the large part narrative, while philosophy is not. It deals only with the eternal questions about the unknown and the unseen – God, the soul, afterlife, *moksha* [emancipation] and so forth. Thus while the religion of one may be meaningless to another, philosophy is universal, for it deals with matters of common interest. One may accept what a certain philosopher says, or reject it, but the doctrine is certainly intelligible. For example in Hindu philosphy the *Gītā,* the *Brahma Sūtras* and the Upanishads [which form the Vedānta philosophy] are statements about God, the soul afterlife and so forth. These scriptures are pure philosophy. Others like the *Rāmāyaṇa, Mahābhārata* etc., are largely narratives telling a story, though interspersed with philosophical observations, Being concentrated views of things unseen, philosophy has fewer takers than religious epics. Arising, as we have said, from the higher reaches of the mind, it has to be hard of comprehension. It has 'Fit audience though few'. While religions divide people, philosophy unites them.

Philosophy has striking similarities. The Hindus believe the soul to be eternal and transmigrating from one body to another,

43. Max Müller. *Introduction to the Six Systems of Indian Philosophy.*

44. Quoted in Ralph Waldo Trine. *In Tune with the Infinite* London: George Bell & Sons. 1905 p., 114.

as a man changing clothes that are worn out for new ones. The soul cannot move by itself. So it is provided with an astral body known as the *linga sharīra* or the *sukshma sharīra* which is a kind of vehicle for journeys from one body to another. This vehicle accompanies the soul till it attains emancipation, when it is needed no longer and disintegrates. Shankarāchārya, the renowned Indian philosopher says about this, 'The *sukshma sharīra* is free from all union and unaffected by limiting factors. It performs all actions as the instrument of the ātman (soul) as chisel and other tools do for a carpenter'.[45] It is believed that the *sukshma* sharīra possesses in it the essence of the various parts of the physical body. The same conclusion was reached by an American psychologist who investigated the experiences of people declared clinically dead, but who came to life again. Their soul which emerged from the body and floated up in space had, in a subtle form, all the various parts of the physical body. Moveover it had the capacity of unimpeded motion. It could pass through doors, walls and even through living persons.[46]

The Egyptians believed, much as the Hindus, that from out the dead body a subtle body called the *sāhu* came out. It ascended to heaven and was immortal, and in it lived the soul. The physical body was known as *Khat* i.e. that which was liable to decay. Then there was the *Ka* or 'double' an abstract individuality or personality which possessed the form and attributes of the man to whom it belonged. it could wander about at will. Then there was the *ba* or heart-soul which was connected with the *Ka*. It could also assume a material or immaterial form at will. The Egyptian spriritual soul was the *Khu*. It was regarded as an ethereal being and dwelt in the *sāhu* or spiritual body.[47] Plato formulated the doctrine of Anamnesis or Recollection. According to this the soul has known the Forms in its divine existence before incarnation in a body and is 'reminded' of them by perceiving through the senses those particular things in this world which participate in them. There were differences too. The Sāmkhya for example,

45. *Vivekachudamani.* 102.

46. Dr Raymond Moody Jr. *Life after Life.*

47. Sir E.A.W. Budge. *The Book of the Dead.*

believed in there being as many souls as bodies. According to the philosophy of the Jains the soul is variable in size and capable of expansion and contraction according to the dimennsions of the physical body with which it is associated for the time being. The unalterable nature of the soul is therefore denied by the Jains.

What is significant about philosophy is that unlike religion, it does not create dissensions. There are differences, but no blood is ever shed over philosophy. There are no wars in it, only debates. Hindus called these *shāstrāthas.* When philosophers disagreed they did not break each others' heads as often happens in religious conflicts. They sat down and argued, seeking the support of scriptures (*shāstras,* hence the word *shastrārtha*). There was the remarkable religious debate between the *advaitic* Shankarāchārya and Mandana Mishra the votary of the Mīmānsā philosophy. Mandana's gifted wife, Ubhayabhārati acted as umpire by mutual consent. It was embarrassing for her to judge, when one of the contestants was her own husband. But she devised a novel way to do it. She put a garland of flowers round the necks of the two and declared that he whose garland showed signs of fading would be the defeated one. Numerous scholars and pandits came to hear the debate which went on for many days. At last Mandana began to lose ground, and the flowers in his garland started fading. Ubhayabhārati declared Shankārāchārya the winner.

Having pointed out the difference we must hasten to add that the two—philosophy and religion—have much in common too. Philosophy devoid of religion would be pedantic. Religion without philosophy would be lifeless. Even the atheist speaks of God and the soul, albeit to deny them. In truth it is the philosophical content of religion which is a measure of its greatness. Otherwise why should Aldous Huxley have called the *Bhagavadgītā* 'the most systematic scriptural statement of Perennial Philosophy', or of the Upanishads Paul Deussen said that the spiritual wisdom contained in them is unequalled in India, or perhaps anywhere else in the world'; and Schopenhauer that they [the Upanishads] 'are the products or the higest wisdom. . . . destined sooner or later to become the faith of the people' ? As Huxley says, the Perennial Philosophy which was perfected in the *Gītā*, found expression in some form or the other 'in Vedānta and Hebrew prophecy, in the Tao Teh King and the Platonic dialogues, in the Gospel according to St John and Mahayana theology, in Plotinus and the Areopagite, among the Persian Sufīs and the Christian mystics of the Middle Ages and the Renaissance'.[48] Religions, shorn of philosophy, whose only message is 'accept this, or perish' are no religions at all. The human mind rebels against compulsion in any form, whether political religious or any other. Henry D. Thoreau says :

> 'Most people with whom I talk, men and women even of some originality and genius, have their scheme of the universe all cut and dried—very *dry* I assure you, to hear, dry enough to burn dry-rotted and powder post, methinks—which they set up between you and them in the shortest intercourse, and ancient and tottering frame with all its boards blown off. They do not walk without their bed. Some, to me, seemingly very unimportant and unsubstantial things and relations are for them everlastingly settled—as Father, Son, and Holy Ghost, and the like.

---

48. Introduction to the *Bhagavad-Gītā*. Trans., Swami Prabhavananda and Christopher Isherwood. New York : Mentor Books, 1954.

The Pernnial Philosphy has four fundamental doctrines according to Huxley :

1. The phenomenal world of matter and of individualized consciousness—the world of things and animals and men and even gods—is the manifestation of a Divine Ground within which all partial realities have their being, and apart from which they would be nonexistent.

2. Human beings are capable not merely of knowing *about* the Divine Ground by inference; they can also realize its existence by a direct intuition, superior to discursive reasoning, This immediate knowledge unites the knower with that which is known.

3. Man possesses a double nature, a phenomenal ego and an eternal Self, which is the inner man, the spirit, the spark of divinity within the soul. It is possible for a man, if he so desires, to identify himself with the spirit and therefore with the Divine Ground, which is the same or like nature with the spirit.

4. Man's life on earth has only one end and purpose : to identify himself with his eternal Self and so to come to unitive knowledge of the Divine Ground.

> These are like everlasting hills to them. But in all my wanderings I never came across the least vestige of authority for these things. They have not left so distinct a trace as the delicate flower of a remote geological period on the coal in my grate. The wisest man preaches no doctrines; he has no scheme; he sees no rafter, not even a cobweb against the heavens. It is clear sky.[49]

So too John Stuart Mill says, 'in an imperfect state of the human mind, the interests of truth require a diversity of opinion. . The exclusive pretension made by a part of the truth to be the whole, must and ought to be protested against, and if a reactionary impluse should make the protestors unjust in their turn, this onesidedness, like the other, may be lamented, but must be tolerated. If Christians would teach infidels to be just to Christianity, they should themselves be just to infidelity. It can do truth no service to blink the fact, known to all who have the most ordinary acquaintance with literary history, that a large portion of the noblest and most valuable moral teaching has been the work not only of men who did not know, but of men who knew and rejected the Christian faith'.[50]

It is the same with faiths other than Christianity too. Any religion which does not stand criticism, which seeks to survive by the sword, not by reason, and which will not tolerate those who refuse to subscribe to it, will sooner or later become a shibboleth. Philosophy, therefore is the corner-stone of the religious edifice. It is what gives a religion universality, that which, even though not drawing adherents of other faiths within its folds, elicits their admiration. It must be realized that philosophy is only the expression of mystical realization. Truth is revealed neither by it nor by religion. At best both are surmises. Truth, on the contrary, is Revelation. It is gifted only to saints and mystics like St Joan of Arc, St Augustine, Plotinus the Greek mystic, Shankārācharya, Ramana Mahārshi. Rāmakrishṇa and others. These persons *knew*, and the similarities of their experiences are remarkable. Plotinus believed in the Higher Soul (the World

49. Henry D. Thoreau. *Selected Writings*. Ed. Oscar Cargill. New York : The Liberal Arts Press, Inc. 1952. p., 77.

50. J.S. Mill. *On Liberty*. Thought and Discussion. London : John W. Parker and Son. West Strand. M.DCCC. LIX.

Soul) and the Power Soul or Nature, as the Vedānta's *Parā-brahman* (lower) and the *aparā-brahman* (higher), the higher Self and the lower. Much of Plotinus, philosophy resembles that of the Vedānta. 'The mere fact of being in the human body' he says 'does not imply imprisonment in the body. It is the inward attitude that makes the difference. Man can pass from the narrowness of life to the universality of the transcendent Soul and then pass beyond Soul to take his rightful place in the world of the Divine Mind. Thence we can even pass higher though rarely. to that ecstatic union with the One in which Mind attains to the highest by leaving itself behind. The lower soul or Nature is an image of the higher Soul. Its primary activity is contemplation. This contemplation is, however, not rational, but like that of a man in a dream. Waking, intelligent contemplation, belongs to the transcendent spiritual world of the higher Soul and the Divine Mind'. This is as close as one could get to the philosophy of the *Gītā* and the Upanishads.

Philosophy, therefore, is the meeting ground of religions the unifying force in a discordant world. Through it man has demonstrated his superiority over other creatures. Religion has been only on extension of primitive beliefs. But philosophy is the gift of civilizations.

SCRIPTURES

The primitive man did not conceive God as an omnipotent Being governing the universe and Controller of birth, death and destiny. His 'religion' was a mixture of crude ethics, superstition, rites and prayers to placate the originator of sorrows and evils. As civilizations were born, with them came the great religions of the world. It became imperative to formulate creeds for these faiths, so that their followers could have something positive to guide them. These creeds found expression in the scriptures. Human pyschology requires sanctification as a prerequisite to belief. For example marriage is a union of a man and a woman for sex and companionship and for the propagation of offspring. However, to give it authority it is sanctified by a priest, pandit, mullah etc. It then becomes a sacrament. Even so the originators of the scriptures of various religions sought for them divine authority. The *Bhagavadgītā* was believed to the words of Lord Krishṇa, as

Saṁjay tells Dhritarāshṭra : I heard this greatly secret doctrine ['the *Gītā*] from the lips of the great Lord Shri Krishṇa himself'.[51] The Holy Quran was given by God to the prophet Mohammed: 'It is plainly stated to be a revelation from the Lord of the worlds, or a revelation from God, the Mighty, the Wise and so on. It was revealed to the Prophet Mohammed having been sent down upon his heart through the Holy Spirit in the month of Ramadan on the 25th or 27th night which is known as *lailat ul qadr* in the Arabic language'.[52] The Holy Bible (from Latin *biblia* too is believed to have religious authority. It has two parts, the Old Testrment, which is a record of the religious and historical thought of the people of Isreal, and the New Testament which consists of an account of the life of Jesus Christ and his teachings along with the Acts of the Apostles, the Epistles and the Revelation of St John the Divine. The Christians believe that man can be redeemed only by faith in Jesus Christ. As the Hindu Trinity is Brahmā-Vishṇu-Mahesh [Creator-Preserver–Destroyer], so too the Christian Trinity is the Father, the Son and the Holy Ghost [God, Jesus the Son of God and the Spirit of Christ]. The Holy Ghost, the Spirit is spoken of in *Isaiah*, 'and the spirit of the Lord shall rest upon him, the spirit of counsel and might, the spirit of knowledge and of the fear of the Lord';[53] Thus salvation is possible only through this Trinity. The *First Epistle of John* says : 'For there are three that bear witness, because the Spirit is truth. For there are three that bear record in heaven, the Father, the Word and the Holy Ghost : and these three are one . . . .He that believeth on the Son of God hath the witness in himself : he that believeth not God hath made him a liar; because he believeth not the record that God gave of his Son . . . .He that hath the Son hath life; and he that hath not the Son of God hath not life'.[54]

51. *Gītā* 18 : 75.
52. *Translation of the Holy Quran.* Muhammad Ali. Lahore : Ahmadiyya Anjuman-I-Ishaat-I-Islam, 1928 p., IX.
53. The Holy Bible. *Isaiah.* 11 : 2.
54. The Holy Bible. I *John* 5 : 7–12.

Similarly we have other scriptures. Judaism has the Talmud and the Torah, Sikhism has the Granth Sahib, Zoroastrianism the Zend Avesta, and Buddhism, Vinaya, Sutra and Abhidharma. Although scriptures were, as we have said, an advance on the old primitive religions, they retained, in a more refined form, some of their elements too. One was the admonition that those who did not follow the particular scripture were doomed. Allied with this was the promise that those who did so, would gain some reward like heaven or emancipation. Lord Krishṇa says in the *Bhagavadgītā* : 'Abandon all *dharmas* and take refuge in me alone. Do not grieve I will absolve you of all evil. He who teaches this [doctrine] to my devotees will doubtless come to me. Nobody is as more dear to me than he is. He who reads this [*Gītā*], worships me with the yoga of wisdom'.

Belief in Jesus Christ is fundamental to the Christian. Those men who do not have it, of whatever denomination they are, cannot be redeemed : 'Neither is there salvation in any other: [except Jesus Christ], for there is none other name under heaven given among men, whereby we must be saved'.[55] The Epistle of St Paul to the Ephesians speaks of those who have no 'inheritance in the kingdom of Christ and of God'. The idolater [among 'the whoremonger or the unclean or covetous person], is one of them.[56] Thus those who worship images or idols cannot hope to reach God. Philosophy too is out. It is even tabooed : 'Beware lest any man spoil you through philosophy and vain deceit, after the tradition of men, after the rudiments of the world, and not after Christ.[57] Akin to this is the bewildering Upanishadic observation : 'Those who are devoted to ignorance enter into blinding darkness. Into greater darkness do those enter who delight in knowledge'.[58] In the Holy Quran we find the following observation : 'Fight

55. *The Acts of the Apostles*. 4 : 12.

56. *Ephesians*. 5 : 5.

57. *Colossians*. 2 : 8.

58. *Isha Upanishad*. 9.
Commentators take 'knowledge' to imply 'knowledge of ritualistic philosophy' [Swami Shivadananda's commentary]. However the words used in the text are *avidyā*=ignorance and *vidyā*=knowledge.

those who do not believe in God, nor in the latter day, nor do they prohibit what God and His Apostle have prohibited nor follow the religion of truth. out of those who have been given the Book, until they pay the tax in acknowledgment of superiority and they are in a state of subjection'.[59] Thus we see that most of the religions emphasize that the creed they profess is the only way to salvation. *The Bhagavadgītā* is perhaps the least demanding : 'Men whose discrimination has been blunted by worldly desires, establish this or that ritual or cult and resort to various deities. according to the impulse of their inborn natures. But it does not matter what deity a devotee chooses to worship. If he has faith, I make his faith unwavering. Endowed with the faith I give him, he worships that deity and gets from it everything he prays for. In reality, I alone am the giver. But these men of small understanding only pray to what is transient and perishable. The worshippers of the *devas* will go to the *devas*. So also, my devotees will come to me'.[60] After Lord Krishṇa had narrated the entire teachings to Arjuna, his disciple, he said : *Vimrishyai tad shesheṇa yathe ichhasi tathā kuru* – 'I have given this [secret] wisdom to you. Ponder well over it and do as you it pleases you'.[61] This exclusiveness claimed by various religions viz., that their doctrine is the only way to God, and still more that those who do not subscribe to it will be consumed by fire and brimstone; is a reminder of the kind of warnings for transgressing taboos conceived by primitive men. Another element common to most religions is the principle of penances or atonement. In the *Mahābhārata* we are told that the five Pāṇḍava brothers were married to Draupadī. They had mutually agreed to visit her by turns. Once Arjuna, the great warrior among

59. Trans., Maulana Muhammad Ali. Lahore. 1928. 9 : 29.
Here too various commentators have given their views. See also f.n., in the afore said translation. However we give the translation as it is.

60. These are Krishṇa's words to Arjuna. *Gita* 7 : 20–23.
Trans., Swami Prabhavananda and Christopher Isherwood. The New American Library. 1954 p., 73. The word 'deity' has been taken to mean the Hindu deities by some commentators. Dr Radhakrishnan however, takes it in its larger sense as the Divinity as conceived by faiths other than Hinduism also.

the brothers, happened to surprise Draupadī and Yudhishṭira his brother who were disporting together. In order to atone for this fault he undertook a self-imposed exile in the forest. Christians confess their sins before the priest. The Moslems have *fathwas* against the transgressors of Islam. The Sikhs also have a system of penance.. Recently the akal takht held an author, Dr Piar Singh, guilty of hurting Sikh sentiments in his book *Gatha Sri Aad Granth.* He was sentenced to forty days 'religious punishment. As penance he was asked 'to clean the shoes of the *sangat*, sweep the floor of the *gurdwara* [the Ramsarai] and recite the prayers of *Sukhmani Sahib* and *Japji Sahib'*. After this forty days' penance he would have to present himself at the akal takht again for *ardas*, which would then get him forgiveness for his sin.[62] Scriptures are a combination of narrative, ethics and philosophy. The proportion differs, but these elements are invariably parts of them. The narrative part is the religion's private preserve. Detractors and critics who ridicule such stories in religions other than their's, forget that they are part of their religion also. And the queer and occasionally even grotesque incidents we come across in them is a common factor. For example we have demons, and gods with faces of monkeys, elephants and other animals in the *Rāmāyaṇa*. In the Holy Bible we have rods turning into snakes and so forth. Some scriptures like the *Bhagavadgītā*, Upanishads, *Brahma–sūtras* and the Buddhist Vinaya etc., are more or less pure philosophy and ethics. Let us take for illustration the two verses of the *Gītā* which speak of the cause and consequence of anger : 'When the senses dwell upon their object, attachment to those objects arises. From that comes the desire for them. And when one is addicted to them but fails to get them he feels thwarted. When he is thwarted, anger arises in him. An angry person's mind becomes confused. He loses discrimination, and that man perishes [because he is then completely lost]'.[63] Such scriptures are unladulterated philosophy. Others like the *Rāmāyaṇa, Mahābhārata*

61. *Gītā.* 18 : 63.

62. Reported in the *Poineer* 3 April 1993. 'Sikh author told toperform 40-day penance'.

63. *Gita.* 2 : 62–63.

etc., are for a large part narrative telling some story, but also delving into philosophy. Yet other scriptures have historical narratives. Nonetheless parts of them reach the zenith of spiritualism. Such are the Book of Job,. the Book of Psalms, the Proverbs, the Ecclesiastes and the Song of Solomon in the Old Testament of the Holy Bible,. and parts of the New Testament like the Sermon on the Mount, Parable on Prayer, Little Children and the Rich Young Ruler.[64] Religions can be mainly didactic or they may be philosophical and spiritual. The former kind say in effect 'It is only by believing this and doing that, that man can reach God'. The other kind do not subscribe to dogmas. They attempt to explain the unseen and the unknown – things like death, afterlife, the nature of God and the soul, the process of rebirth and so forth. In brief their object is to explain the phenomena of life, its purpose and its goal. Buddhism occupies an intermediate position. As the Buddha said, the sole purpose of life is to end sorrow, not to muse upon questions such as whether there is a God or not and his nature, the object of creation, what happens after death, and so forth. However, Buddhism decidedly comes in the category of non-didactic religions. Lord Buddha's well-known advice to his favourite disciple, Ānanda is proof of this :

> 'Therefore O Ānanda be lamps unto yourselves. Be ye a refuge to yourselves. Betake yourselves to no external refuge. Hold fast to the truth as a lamp. Hold fast as a refuge to the truth. Look not for refuge to any one besides yourselves . . . . And whosoever, Ānanda, either now or after I am dead, shall be a lamp unto themselves and a refuge unto themselves, shall betake themselves to no external refuge. but holding fast to the truth, shall look not for refuge to any one besides themselves, it is they, Ānanda, among my bhikkus, who shall reach the very topmost Height – *but they must be anxious to learn*'.[65]

Those scriptures which do not propound dogmas, but simply state their doctrines, are doubtlessly superior to those that say : this is the only way to salvation. As Lord Buddha

---

64. *St Lũke* 18. 1–27.

65. *The Sacred Books of the East.* vol. XI Oxford 1881. Buddhist Suttas.

says : 'It is not proper for a wise man who maintains truth to come to the consclusion : this alone is Truth and everything else is false'.[66]

As we have said, most religions claim to be revelation directly from God. Thus the Holy Quran is said to have been revealed by God to Prophet Mohammed, the Vedas to the *rishis*, the Holy Bible has the sanctity of Jesus whom Christians believe to be Son of God, the followers of Judaism consider that the words *Shema Yisroel Adonoi Elohenu Adonoi Echod* ['Here O Isreal, the Lord our God, the Lord is one'] were spoken to the Jewish people by God through the mouth of Moses,[67] and so forth. Allied with this is the belief that the originators of religion did not come into the world in the ordinary way. Krishṇa was born in a prison when an intense beam of light entered Devakī's womb. Rāma was born in his celestial aspect before he took the form of a baby. In Christianity we have the Immaculate Conception, the belief that Mary gave birth to Jesus parthenogenetically and the Bodily Assumption whereby at death she was physically transferred to heaven. There is also the Resurrection of Christ. The concept of divinity was found necessary to give religion authority. God was universally believed to be the Lord and Master of the universe, the Creator and the Destroyer and the Controller of destiny. Therfore religions sought him as the author of their doctrines. One could neither doubt nor dispute what came from him. Hindus claim Hinduism to be the Word of God (spoken by Lord Krishṇa to Arjuna in the *Gītā*). The Moslems believe the Holy Quran was revealed to Prophet Mohammed by God. The Christians consider Jesus Christ to be the Son of God, and Christianity is what Jesus taught. Lord Buddha got Enlightenment under the Bodhi Tree.

Yet there have been fierce conflicts and a lot of bloodshed due to religion. Not only between the followers fo different faiths but also between sects of the same religion. It still goes on. Hindus ranged against Moslems, Shias against Sunnis, and now even old friends like Sikhs and Hindus are poised

66. Walpola Rahula. *What the Buddha Taught*. Gordon Frazer.

67. This is the first prayer a Jewish boy learns, and the last ultered before a Jew dies.

in opposition. If all religions are the Word of God, why these conflicts ? Does God speak in different tongues ? In his book *Life after Life* Dr Raymond Moody Jr. says that when the Soul is before its Maker, the communication between them is in a soul-language which is thought-waves. The language of God [and the Soul] then, is neither Arabic, nor Sanskrit, nor Hebrew, Greek, nor Aramaic, nor any of the other languages of the scriptures of the world. In truth this thought-language too is the one by which the Soul speaks to God even when encased in the human body. That is why silent prayer and is more eloquent than hymns and and hallelujahs :

'More things are wrought by prayer
Than this world dreams of. Wherefore, let thy voice
Rise like a fountain for me night and day.
For what are men better than sheep or goats
That nourish a blind life within the brain,
If, knowing God, they lift not hands of prayer
Both for themselves and those who call them friend ?
For so the whole round earth is in every way
Bound by gold chains about the feet of God'.[68]

Why there should be cruel deeds done in the name of religion, when they all claim as their fount the one God ? We will analyze the reasons for this. Before that we go on to speak about the nature of religion. Thereafter we will discuss that in which they tend to oneness and that which they are at variance with one another.

68. Alfred Lord Tennyson. *The Passing of Arthur.*

3

THE NATURE OF RELIGION

No work done by any man, however great, will really prosper unless it has a distinctive religious background. But what is religion ? I for one would answer 'Not the religion you will get after reading all the scriptures of the world. Religion is not what is grasped by the brain, but a heart-grasp.'

MOHANDAS KARAMCHAND GANDHI

All religions must be tolerated ... for... every man must go to heaven in his own way.

FREDRICK (II) THE GREAT

WHAT RELIGION IS ABOUT

All worldly life moves from the universal to the particular, while all spiritual life moves from the particular to the universal. The newborn baby responds only to love, by whomever it is given. Soon he starts recognizing his parents and those who are near to them, like his grandpa and grandma. The 'shades of the prison house' begin to close. As the child grows up to be a man, he gets more and more involved in attachments. He starts with the family—his sons and daughters and wife. He picks up friendship with some people, a few, if he's an introvert and many if he's a social guy. This is the full stop for most. Right up to the moment of death one has known, befriended and cared for his close relations and companions only. He has little choice in these associations. The family is given to him by birth, the friends and acquaintances by the place in which he lives. Barring the secularists [atheists], who are so few in number as to be negligible, everyone has a religion in which, too, he has little choice. If he is born in a Hindu home he becomes a Hindu, if in a Moslem family he takes to Islam, and if in a family of Christians, a follower of Christianity [we will speak of converts later].

The intensity of religion varies with the individual. To some the visit to a church, a temple or a mosque is mere formality. To others it is an intensely emotional experience. But why should there by such intensity ? Why should one think *his* religion to be the only one worthwhile ?

Among various other things, religion is an essential consequence of egoism – the I-ness in man. He acquires his religion just as he does his mother tongue, his nationality and his patriotism. Religion, as Rāma Tīrtha said, is from *re* = 'back' and *ligare* = 'to bind'. It is therefore that which binds one back to the origin or fountainhead. This explains why people are so obsessed by their particular religion, some even so much that they become fanatics. It is like the zeal for the language one is born to. A Tamil-speaking person is so overenthusiastic about Tamil that he hates Hindi. Even if he understands it he will pretend not so. So is the case with Kannada against Tamil. A Frenchman will keep quiet if addressed in English, even if he can understand and speak that language. So is the case with one's country. Really speaking even the world is for a short time, to say nothing of ones country. Yet people die for it. Thus religion takes firm roots in the very minds and hearts of its followers. It is like food. Too little of it leaves one hungry, too much of it makes one sick.

RENUNCIATION

It is odd that the human being's God-given instinct is attachment, yet God's message as conveyed through religions is to renounce the world, that is to get rid of attachment. The *Gītā* points out the necessity of being unattached to sons, wife, family and so forth.[1] Shankārachārya says : 'When you are a boy you spend your time playing with toys. When you grow up you run after women. Old age brings grief and brooding. No one is interested in seeking God'.[2] Jesus Christ said in the Bible : It is easier for a camel to go through a neede's eye than for a rich man to enter the kingdom of God'.[3]

---

1. *Bhagavadgita.* 13 : 9 *asakttiranabhishvangah putra-dāra-grihādishu.*
2. + *Dakshinamurti Stotra.*]
3. *St Luke.* 18 : 25.

And to Peter his beloved disciple, he said 'There is no man that hath left house, or parents, or brethren, or wife, or children, for the kingdom of God's sake, who shall not receive it manifold more in this present time, and in the world to come everlasting life'.[4] In most religions there is no leeway given to worldly pleasures or the gifts, like prosprity and wealth, which human beings are given by worldly life. Hinduism, however, has a more integrated approach. The *purushārthas* [aims of living] are, according to it, *artha, kāma, dharma* and *moksha* [meaning respectively the honest pursuit of wealth, sexual enjoyment with ones spouse, following the moral world-order and seeking emancipation]. The ancient Hindus lived a full life. The first stage was that of celibacy *brahmacharya*, then married life *grihastha*, followed by a life or renunciation in two stages, *vānaprastha* (the forest-dweller) and finally *sannyāsa* (the wandering hermit). Religion, by and large, is the giving of some gift and then gradually asking us to relinquish it. It's much as though one gave someone a birthday present, with the admonition : Look, I'm giving it now, but after enjoying it for sometime you have to cast it into the dustbin. Religion takes away much of what life gives. Does it have anything to give in return ? We may answer this question by a riddle. Religion gives what life takes away.

SURRENDER TO GOD

If life was a gloriously smooth time from birth to death, maybe there would be no need for religion. But it's not like that at all. As Bacon says, 'Prosperity is not without many fears and distastes'.[5] Illness, disease, disabilities, misfortunes, sudden and untimely deaths – all these, and many more, are as much part of life as its joys and pleasures. Most of such misfortunes are beyond our control, and one – death –, is inevitable. Here, what life takes away, religion gives. For things like disability and death, there is no other way but acceptance. Acceptance is not easy. It is a long struggle, and often it is the outcome of a prolonged spell of helplessness.

4. ibid. 28-30.

5. Francis Bacon. *Of Adversity.*

So is the case with contentment. As Thackeray says at the end of *Vanity Fair* : 'Ah ! *Vanitas Vanitatum!* which of us is happy in this world? Which of us has his desire? or, having it, is satisfied ?'[6] Religion makes the process of existence less painful in many ways. When one considers himself, or others, as being responsible for one's misfortunes, he develops a kind of guilt complex. For example someone whom he loved, dies. He thinks: I didn't take him to the hospital in time. The doctor was not expert enough. He imagines all the things he could have done, but he didn't do. Or suppose someone is crossing the road. He jumps the traffic- light. A scooter hits him and he breaks his leg and has to hop along painfully all his life. Or maybe, his mobike skids and his optic nerve being damaged, he loses one eye. That man may spend all his life brooding. Why did I not rush my child to the hospital.[7] Why did I cross the road on the red light ? Why did I not bypass the puddle on the road which made my mobike skid ? Why did it to have to happen to *me* ? One can keep asking oneself a million questions of this kind. But the Moving Finger has written and moved on, and we are left with our musings. To those who keep bemoaning their adversities and keep reproaching themselves, wisdom speaks in the words of Lady Macbeth :

'How now, my lord ! Why do you keep alone,
Of sorriest fancies your companions making;
Using those thoughts which should indeed have died
With them they think on ? Things without all remedy
Should be without regards : what's done is done'.

Reason stops at logic and is therefore useless in making the acceptance of the inevitable a smooth process. That's why Krishṇa gives it as the ultimate argument for not being perturbed over 'the living or the dead' : 'Even if you think the soul is subject to birth and death you should not grieve. For to one born death is certain. And to one dead there has to be rebirth. So why do you sorrow for what is unavoidable?'[8]

6. + William Makepeace Thackeray. *Vanity Fair*
7. W. Shakespeare. Macbeth. Act 3. Scene 2.
8. *Bhagavadgitā*. 2 : 26-27.

But Krishṇa realizes that a logical explanation of anguish would not be very convincing. So he first gives the metaphisical arguments of the eternality of the soul, death being only like a man discarding old clothes for new, i.e., the soul casting off an aged and useless body for the energetic one of a newborn baby, and so forth. As Kipling says, acceptance is only a kind of compromise.

'Man propounds negotiations, Man accepts
the compromise,
Very rarely will he squarely push the logic
of a fact
To its ultimate conclusion in unmitigated act'.[8a]

To one who has resigned himself to God the thought of 'I am the doer' does not come. Krishṇa says. 'The person who is vain and foolish considers himself to be the doer of works when really works are the result of the interaction of the *guṇas* [qualities]'. And again, 'While seeing, hearing, touching, smelling, eating, walking, sleeping, breathing, speaking, grasping, relinquishing, opening the eyelids, or closing them; the enlightened yogi knows "I am not doing all these things" and they are really the result of the senses dwelling on their objects'.[9] By the surrender has of to be complete. It won't do if we hold him responsible for all our evils and give ourselves credit for the good. For such duplicity the laugh's on us, not on God. For it does not rid one wholly of the I-sense. Sri Ramakrishna Paramahaṁsa told a story to bring this out :

A *brāhmin* was laying down a garden and looked after it day and night. One day a cow straying into the garden browsed away a mango sapling which was the most carefully watched trees of the *brāhmin*. The *brāhmin*, seeing the cow destroy his favourite plant, gave it such a sound beating that is die of the injuries received. The news soon spread like wildfire that the *brāhmin* had killed the sacred animal.

8a Rudyard Kipling. *The Female of the Species.*

9. *Bhagavadgītā.* 3 : 27-28, and 5 : 9. The *guṇas* are the three qualities-*sattva* [purity], *rajasa* [activity or passion], and *tamasa* [dullness or inactivity].

'Now the *brāhmin* was a so-called Vedāntist, and when taxed with the sin denied it, saying. "No. I have not killed the cow; it was my hand that has done it and as Indra is the presiding deity of the hand, so if anyone has incurred the guilt of killing the cow, it is Indra, not I."

'Indra is his heaven heard all this, and assuming the form of a *brāhmin*, came to the owner of the garden and said, "Sir, whose garden it this ?"

Brāhmin : "Mine."

Indra : "It's a beautiful garden. You have a skilful gardener, for see how neatly and artistically he has planted the trees!"

Brāhmin : "Will sir, that is also my work. The trees are planted under my personal supervision and direction."

Indra : "Indeed ! O you are very clever. But who has laid out this road ? It is very ably planned and neatly executed!"

Brāhmin : "All this has been done by me." 'Then Indra joined hands and said, "When all these things are yours, and you take credit for all the works done in this garden, it is hard lines for poor Indra to be held responsible for the killing of the cow."[10] This complete dependence on God is not easily achieved, for in such a case man has got to believe in the unseen. But a moment's thought will show that it is the only course possible. However gregarious man may be, the individual in him keeps appearing like the heads of Hydra.[11] This individualism manifests itself as the I-sense or ege [*ahankāra*]. Of it Shankārachārya says : 'The great *ahankāra* even though apparently cut down to its roots, will, if excited only for a moment by the mind, come to life again and cause a hundred distractions, just as during the rain, clouds are scattered about by the storm.'[12] When a person seeks human sympathy, it is like looking for a needle in a haystack. Egoism and apathy make

10. Max Müller. *Ramakrishna—His Life and Sayings.*

11. A monster of the Lernean marshes. in Argolis. It has nine heads, and it was one of the twelve labours of Hercules to kill it, As soon as he struck off one of its heads, two shot up in its place. hence hydra-headed applies to a difficulty which goes on increasing the more it is combated. [*Brewer's Dictionary of Phrase & Fable*. London : Cassell 1870].

12. *Vivekachudāmani.* 312.

men indifferent to the sorrows of others. So everyone has to bear his own yoke. As the poet Rahiman says: 'Do not speak of the sorrows of your mind to others. All of them will laugh at you, but not one among them will share [and so lighten] your grief'.[13] Therefore man turns to God; for human nature has been tested and found wanting, and it would be foolish to rely upon it. All religions promise deliverance to mankind in different ways. Krishna's final exhortation to Arjuna is :

'Give me your whole heart
Love and adore me,
Worship me always,
Bow to me only,
And you shall find me
This is my promise
Who love you dearly
Lay down all duties
In me, your refuge
Fear no longer,
For I will save you
From sin and bondage'.[14]

Christianity offers mankind freedom from all sorrows through Christ. Jesus said to his disciples : 'If any man will come after me, let him deny himself, and take up his cross, and follow me. For whosover will save his life shall lose it : and whosoever will lose his life for my sake shall find it. For what is a man profited, if he shall gain the whole world, and lose his own soul'.[15] Through his agony on the Cross, Jesus took upon himself the sins and the sorrows of mankind. 'Come unto me,' he said, 'all ye that labour and are heavy laden, and I will give you rest. Take my yoke upon you,

13. *Rahiman nij man kī vyathā man hi rākao geha/suni iṭhalahiyiṁ log sab, bāṁt na paihyaiṁ koye II*

14. *Bhagavadgītā.* Trans., Swami Prabhavananda and Christopher Isherwood. The New American Library 1954 [Ch. 18 vs. 65-66].

15. St Matthew 16. 25-26 [The Holy Bible].

and learn of me; for I am meek and lowly in heart : and ye shall find rest unto your soul. For my yoke is easy and my burden is light'.[16] In the struggle for the acceptance of things which have no remedy, therefore, religion plays a primary role. But of course there must be faith before the balm of religion can be effective. The fact that a man is born into his religion is in itself an assistance to create belief in it. This confidence is made strong by the promise of reward to those who have faith and the threat of punishment for those who refute the principles of the particular religion. Krishṇa says that people who have no faith– *nireeshvara*, will be reborn in evil wombs.[17] Jesus says, 'Where fore I say unto you, All manner of sin and blas phemy shall be forgiven unto men: but the blasphemy again the Holy Ghost shall not be forgiven unto men. ..... neither in this world neither in the world to come'.[18] The Holy Quran is more emphatic : 'God will cause those who believe to do good deeds to enter gardens in which rivers flow. They shall be adorned therein with bracelets of gold and (with) pearls, and their garments therein shall be of silk. And they are guided to goodly words and they are guided into the the path of the Praised One. Those who disbelieve and hinder (men) from God's ways and from the Sacred Mosque which we have made equally for all men (for) the dweller therein and (for) the visitor, and whoever shall incline therein to wrong unjustly we will make him taste a painful chastisement'.[19]

THE DIFFERENCE BETWEEN SIN AND EVIL

All religions speak about sin. But they conceive it in different ways. One of the reasons for sin is said to be disobedience of God's commands. But what does God really command? Some religions give the answer in the form of do's and don'ts. The concept is purely ethical. Others just say, this [i.e. our

16. Ibid. 11. 28-30.
17. *Bhagavadgītā*. 16. 8 and 19.
18. The Holy Bible. *St Matthew* 12. 31-32.
19. *The Holy Quran*. Trans.. Maulana Muhammad Ali. Lāhore 1918. 22

religion] is the only good. He who does not follow it, errs and is damned. Perhaps the most universally acceptable concept has been given by the Hindu religion. Krishna says 'Following various paths, men come to me—*man vartamāna aṇuvartante manushyaḥ pārtha sarvashah.*[20] The measure of right and wrong is one's own conscience. This is called the *antaḥkaraṇa* i.e. the internal doer or guide [*antaḥ* = inside, *karaṇa* one who does or guides]. It is that which is responsible for *sankalpa-vikalpa* i.e. deciding whether to do an act or not to do it and what ought to be done. Conscience is our built-in barometer of good and evil. It has the capacity of instantly telling us whether what we are about to do is wrong or right. But like all sensitive instruments it is apt to become blunted and thus made ineffective by misuse. If one keep continually disregarding its signal, it then gives none at all. The Hindu concept of sin, or good and evil, is not that the change from sin to sinlessness is a sudden or catalytic transformation. What really happens is that men do not move from sin to sinlessness, but from good to evil. Everything that is an impediment in this progress is sin, and that which carries one forward towards good is not a 'sin'. Thus faced with a certain situation, conscience guides the person. If he follows its guidance he moves forward and comes a step nearer to God. If he does what his conscience forbids him from doing he moves backwards on the moral plane and his progress is retarded. Lecomtc du Nouy says:

> 'The Will manifests itself, therefore, through evolution, and its goal is the realization of a morally perfect being, completely liberated from human passions—egotism, greed, lust for power—hereditary chains, and physiological bondage. This does not mean the definite severing of the ties between the flesh and the spirit, which would not make sense, as we cannot conceive the latter independently of the first in the case of man, but simply the escape from the *domination* of the flesh.
>
> 'Consequently, anything which opposes this evolution in the moral and spiritual realm, anything which tends to bring

---

20. *Bhagavadgītā.* 4 : 11..

> about a regression towards the animal, to replace man under the dictature of the body, is contrary to the directing will and represents absolute Evil. On the contrary, anything which tends to deepen the chasm between man and beast, anything which tends to make man evolve spiritually, is Good'.[21]

This is near to the Hindu doctrine of the soul's search for *brahman*. The disembodied soul, the *ātman* is eternal, but conditioned by the body it has necessarily to identify itself with it, and is then known as the *jīva*. The object of life is to bring the soul to *brahman*-realization. As Hinduism believes in rebirth, unlike other religions like Islam and Christianity, this process of realizing I the Cosmic Absolute (i.e. *brahman*) goes on life after life, till the goal in realized.

MYSTICISM

Another constituent of most religions is mysticism. This means (as the dictionary says) 'the teaching and belief that knowledge of God and of real truth may be obtained through meditation or spiritual insight, independently of the mind and the senses'.[22] Prayer, meditation, chanting the Lord's name *kīrtan* telling the beads of a rosary and so forth are enjoined in all religions. However, mysticism goes much beyond its literal meaning. In the Holy Bible we have Christ's Transfiguration on the Mount: 'And there was a cloud which overshadowed them : and a voice came out of the clouds saying. This is my Beloved Son : hear him. And suddenly when they had looked round about, they saw no man any more, save Jesus only with themselves'.[23] The Agony at Gethsemane, when an angel appeared and strengthened Jesus, and the Resurrection after his crucifixion are of the nature of mysticism. The Last Supper also recalls the spiritual: 'And he took bread, and gave thanks and brake it, and gave unto them, saying. This is my body which is given for you : this do in remembrance of me. Likewise also

---

21. Lecomte du Noüy. *Human Destiny*. New American Library. 1945.
22. *The Advanced Learner's Dictionary of Current English*. Oxford University Press. 1963
23. *St Mark*. 9 : 7-8.

the cup after supper, saying. This cup is the new testament in my blood, which is shed for you'.[24] In the *Gītā* we have the Cosmic Form of the Lord (*virāṭa rūpa*) shown to Arjuna in the eleventh chapter. The Hindu concept of delusion (*māyā*), of which we will speak in greater detail later, is also a mystic concept.

24. St Luke, 22 : 19-20.

4

THE CONFLICT OF RELIGIONS

How many crimes have in religion's name been wrought !

Lucretius

The religion of one seems madness unto another.

Thomas Browne

A religion that requires persecution to sustain it is of the devil's propagation.

Hosea Ballou

THAT IN WHICH RELIGIONS ARE ONE

The primitive man who belonged to the age when civilization had not yet taken root, killed, but it was for game. It was to feed himself and his family. In this respect he was much, like the beasts who also prey on each other for food. Bloodshed for the sake of religion is the curse of civilization. And in this respect those who have killed and are killing for the sake of religion are inferior to the primitive savages.

All religions profess to lead their followers to God. Most of them claim that there is one God. This remains a riddle. Do they mean thereby that *their* God is the only God or that God is one and the same ? When we see the world's religions in their interaction with one another, it seem the former is the case.

There are several reasons for religious conflicts—egotism, lack of accomodation, divergent rituals, the element of militancy and so forth. Man is egotistic by nature. He firmly believes that only he is right and everyone else is wrong. That's why arguments and disputations are futile. Once a man takes up a particular stand, he won't budge from it, however unreasonable it may be. Extended a little further, this applies to one's religion too. As we have said, man is born to his religion just as he is to his home, family and mother tongue. As he feels himself superior to all others, so too he comes to believe that his religion is the best. And unfortunately most religions don't hinder him in this irrational belief, they rather encourage him. The Holy Quran says 'there is no altering of God's creation; that [meaning Islam] is the right religion, but most people don't know'.[1] The corollary to this belief is that the religions of others is not so good as our own. This idea leads to lack of accommodation. It pitches the followers of one religion against another, particularly, when this antagonism becomes demonstrative. An Edict of the ancient Indian ruler, Ashoka, reads.

> 'His Sacred Majesty the King does reverence to men to all sects, whether ascetics or householders, by gifts and various forms of reverence. His Sacred Majesty, however, cares not so much for gifts of external reverence as that there should be a growth in the essence of the matter of all sects. The growth of the essence of the matter assumes various forms, but the root of it is restraint of speech, to wit, a man must not do reverence to his own sect or disparage that of another without reason. Depreciation should be for specific reasons only, for the sects of other people all deserve reverence for one reason or another.... He who does deserve reverence to his own sect, while disparaging the sects of others wholly from attachment to his own, with intent to enhance the glory of his own sect, in reality by such conduct inflicts the severest injury on his own sect. Concord therefore, is meritorious, to wit, hearkening and hearkening willingly to the Law of Piety, as accepted by other people'.[2]

Ashoka's edict is worthy not only of deep thought by men of all faiths, but also of actively following and acting upon,

1. Trans., Maulana Muhammad Ali. Lahore. 1928. See also in. which says, 'Islam, according to this verse is the natural religion of man, or a religion to the truth of which human nature bears testimony'.
2. Quoted in Aldous Huxley. *The Perennial Philosophy.* London : Chatto and Windus. 1946. p., 206.

particularly at this time when religious intolerance has crossed the bounds of all decency.

Perhaps the most accomodating of all religions is that of the Hindus. We find in it both image worship as well as the worship of a formless God. It is, therefore both monotheistic as well as polytheistic. The Hindu is not required to go to any temple, though he may, if he chooses to, go to one. Normally worship is at home in a room set apart for it, called the *pūjā*-room. On the contary a Christian attends church for prayers and for a Moslem it's obligatory to go to Friday prayers in mosques. There is absolutely no indoctrination in Hindu religion, as there is in others. There is no effort to convert people of other faiths to it either by persuasion or by force. Ironically enough, that sometimes proves to be its weakness when in truth it should be its strength. This is when Hinduism comes in conflict with other religions which are not prepared to let it alone. History is eloquent witness to this.

SECULARISM AND ALL THAT

Here we must pause and consider the import of two words which have become partly distorted and partly misunderstood in India, which despite all the pretensions of its people can never be Anglicized because of its thousands of years of Hindu culture, and that [to silence carping critics] includes Dravidians as well as Aryans, wherever they belonged to, either of indigenous origin or from central Asia [we do not intend getting caught up in such academic controversies] They got absorbed in the mainstream of this country's culture. The later conquerors and invaders, didn't. We often in consequence, misuse and misinterpret English words such as 'stepney' 'dickey' and so forth. One of such words is 'secularism' which has become so popular with Indian editors, journalists, politicians and the aspiring intelligentsia, that one is sure to come across it at least once in every page, when he go through his mornig paper. The Oxford may shout itself hoarse that 'secular' means 'worldly or material not religious or spiritual' and secularism implies 'the view that morality and education should not be based on religion', but the enlightened Indian must still associate secularism with religion.[3] And that too in a country in which religious propensities are so strong that one is likely to be shot or decapitated any moment because he happens to profess a certain religion ! The other word 'fundamentalism' is as much misused as misunderstood. It is really associated with the Christian religion. Fundamentalism means 'maintenance of the traditional beliefs of the Christian religion (such as the accuracy of everything in the Bible) in opposition ot more modern teaching'.[4] Thus the Protestant creed might in a remote way be connected with fundamentalism. Largely it is tied up with ritual. As for example the Bible enjoins the strict observance of the sabbath. But the modern Christian may not observe it thus. So he deviates from fundamentalism. To clearly understand the application of this word to India we have to interpret another one, 'Hindutva', which one also finds sprawled across the pages of our newspapers and magazines, along with the other two–secularism and fundamentalism [we will presently come to yet another baffling term]. The difficulty with 'Hindutva', however, is greater than with the other two words, for it finds place neither in English, nor in Hindi to which it rightly belongs. The best one can do for it is to break it up into 'Hindu' and the suffix '*tava*' which means 'yours'. Then 'Hindutva' would mean 'your Hinduism' and it would be like telling a Hindu 'Look, this is your Hinduism' ! Whatever that may mean, in actual usage 'Hindutva' seems to have acquired a derogatory slant, and is meant to imply the furtive attempts of Hindus to demonstrate or assert that they are Hindus ! There is no Christiantva or Islamtva or any other 'tva', but, to repeat, our editor, journalist and politicians, must talk about 'Hindutva'. Now the word fundamentalist has by usage become a synonym of 'Hindutva'. So that in effect, it is only a Hindu who can be a fundamentalist. This is quite amusing, for of all religions Hinduism is perhaps the least assertive. Then we come to secularism. According to our 'Hinglish' an Indian who is not a fundamentalist, is a secularist. The two terms are antonynms, just as 'Hindutva' and 'fundamentalist' are synonyms.

---

3. *The Advanced Learner's Dictonary of Current Enlglish.* Oxford University Press. 1963.

4. ibid.

So anybody who is not a Hindu is a secularist. A Christian, a Moslem, a Buddhist and anyone, but a Hindu, is a secularist. We have in this way not only invented words but also corrupted them, imputing meanings to suit our individual fancies and conveniences – an achievement which would make Shakespeare and Chaucer turn in their graves. But wait, we had mentioned a fourth coinage. This is as hot a favourite as secularism. The word is 'pseudo-secularism'. Even a worm will turn. So when the secularists start suppressing those who are Hindutva-minded like the Queen in Alice pronouncing 'off with her head', they strike back, calling the secularists 'pseudo-secularists' meaning thereby that they profess secularism but are really not secularists. Thus the Indian political-cum-religious rigmarole goes on and on – secularism, pseudo-secularism, 'Hindutva', fundametalism – the ever-bubbling concoction in the witches' cauldron. We might here consider briefly another matter which has been agitating Indian minds for long now viz. the relation between religion and politics.

RELIGION AND POLITICS

Till the end of the Hindu period of Indian history, religion in India meant the Hindu religion, just as in Christian countries it meant, and still means, Christianity. When the Moslem conquerors came they brought Islam. Islam was quite different from Hinduism. As a British historian has said, 'It is difficult to imagine two religious ways of life more different that Islam and Hinduism'.[5] And Jinnah's view was : 'India has never been a true nation. It only looks the way on the map. The cows I want to eat, the Hindu stops me from killing. Every time a Hindu shakes hands with me he has to wash his hands. The only thing a Moslem has in common with the Hindu is his slavery to the British'.[6] In a speech he made in March 1940 Jinnah said : 'we know that the history of the last twelve hundred years has failed to achieve unity, and has witnessed, during the ages, India always divided into Hindu India and Moslem India. The present artificial unity of India dates back only

5. Stanley Wolpert. *A New History of India.* Oxford. 1977. p., 104.
6. L. Collins and D. Lapirre. *Freedom at Midnight.* Vikas. 1970. p., 104.

to the British conquest and is maintained by the British bayonet'.[7] Jinnah didn't say anything about the Moslem rule in India. But history records it, and a large part of it has been related by Moslem chroniclers themselves. For example the destruction of the famous temple of Somanath by Mahmud. Jawaharlal Nehru wrote about him : 'As a matter of fact he was hardly a religious man. He was a Mohammedan of course, but that was by the way... we must therefore not fall into the common error of considering Mahmud as anything more than a successful soldier'. But history records Mahmud as saying [when the temple priests adjured him to spare the idol] 'I come not to sell idols not to destroy them'. That surely is not the utterance of a man to whom religion meant nothing. We will not go into the painful saga of Moslem rule in India when hundreds of temples were demolished by them and the stones embedded into steps of mosques so that believers may tread on them to demonstrate the triumph of Islam; of how Hindus who refused to accept Islam were slain and their women dishonoured; and the humiliating *jizyah*, the excuse for which was that it absolved Hindus from military service and gave them 'security, personal freedom and religious toleration'.

The first honeymoon of politics and religion was the Partition of 1947. Obviously the guiding principle for that political step was religion. Thereafter Mahatma Gandhi's Khilafat movement

---

7. Pirzada S. S. (ed.) *Foundation of Pakistan*, p.,338.

8. Glimpses of World History. London : Lindsay Drummond Ltd., p., 155. Wheeler. The History of India. vol. IV. Trübner says The Hidaya mentions security, personal freedom and religious toleration promised to Hindus in return of jizyah. But in reality this was a myth. Hindus were on the contrary oppressed and religious toleration was a chimera. Regarding military service as J.C. Powell-Price says in *History of India.* Thomas Nelson & Sons 1955, p., 346, this cannot apply to India for military service there was never universal. The Dictionary of Islam in fact admits that even after paying jizyah the condition of the Hindu who pays it (zimmi) is somewhat inferior. *A Short History of Pakistan* says 'The laxity in religious beliefs . . . had undermined the morale of the Muslim people. It was necessary to invigorate them to give them a sense of responsibility. This would have been impossible without restoring the institutions of Islam. Aurangazebe had therefore to reimpose jizyah'. So the *jiziyah* was only meant to bolster up Islam.

was a political manoeuvre with religious overtones, for India had no concern with the Caliphate. It was merely to appease Moslems. Jinnah's 'direct action' in which thousands of Hindus were killed was yet another example. Thereafter almost all Indian political parties began to exploit religion. Thus the marriage of religion and politics is very old. In fact the Hindu kings like Janaka and Dashrath had sages for their advisers and no political step was taken without consulting them.

CAUSES OF REGIGIOUS CONFLICTS

To revert to out topic, as we have said, lack of accommodation is one of the main reasons for religious conflicts. Hinduism is the only major Indian religion which does not believe in conversion. Mahatma Gandhi said : 'conversion without a clean heart is in my opinion a denial of God and religion'.[9] But where is there such conversion? The Christians converted by exploiting poverty, the Moslems by the sword. Bacon says : 'Men must beware, that in procuring, or muniting, of Religious unity, they do not dissolve and deface the Laws of Charity, and humane society. There be two Swords among Christians; the spiritual and the temporal; and both have their due office and place in the maintenance of Religion. But we may not take up the third Sword, which is Mohomet's Sword or like unto it; that is to propagate Religion by wars or by sanguinary persecutions, to force consciences'.[10] Religions which demonstrate their efforts to convert people of other faiths and thus display their lack of accomodation, only expose their own weakness. If a religion is worthwhile people will follow it, or adopt it of their own volition. Still the egotism of men makes them blow the trumpets of their religion and to disparage the faiths of others.

The third factor responsible for the conflict of religions is rituals. All religions have it. It is an aberration of the human mind that it tends to believe that those unconcerned will show their interest in what they do, if the act is accompanied with pomp, show and noise. In India religion is demonstrated through

9. *To the Hindu and Muslims*. Gandhi series vol. 2. (ed., Anand T. Hingorani. Karachi, 1942, p.. 269.

10. Francis Bacon. *On Unity in Religion*. Oxford University Press.

meticulous, exacting and often raucous ritual. The recitation of the *Rāmāyana* which ought to be a quiet affair, must have a noisy mike fitted with a huge conical loudspeaker to keep the whole neighbourhood awake for a night, maybe two, for it is quite a lengthy narrative and once begun it must go on without a second's respite till the end is reached. Often that is not enough. It is followed by film-songs, holy to begin with and when these are exhausted, the not-so-holy. The reciters take turns and so each has his share of sleep and waking. But the sleeplessness of the listeners cannot be shared. And while a Hindu may lie awake in bed, and get some religious solace, to a man who is not a Hindu, it is just continuous noisy torture. Comparitively the mullah who climbs up to the minaret to give his sacred *azān* is mercifully much more brief. But he makes it up by the frequency and the odd hours. The Christian is the least demanding. His belfry-bell is rarely heard and only on special occasions like marriages and funerals. The old order changeth yielding place to the new. In days past God fulfilled himself by quiet prayer, but now with the passage of time a loudspeaker is essential for communication between him and man.

'Kabir, why, O Mullah, climbest thou up to
the minaret ?
Thinkest thou that the Lord in hard of
hearing ?
Seek in the heart for Him for whose sake
Thou so loudly callest to prayer !'[11]

Minor rituals of religions are often observed with adamant insistence and assertiveness. And when religions come into conflict, the dimensions of such assertiveness increase. This is all the more so when the opposing religions are violently antagonistic. [We will consider the element of militancy later]. Normally small things go unnoticed, were it not for zealots who blow them out of all proportion. And unfortunately it is these zealots who are the custodians of religions. As if this was not enough,

11. *Selections From the Sacred Writings of the Sikhs*. London. George Allen

there are the fanatics to aid them. Fanaticism is that strange madness, the remnant of the savage animal instinct in man which thirsts after blood and destruction. Aided by fanatics, zealots make every minor incident an excuse for the outburst of their fury. The ogre is out of the bottle and the killings go on without compunction and with typical Oriental barbarity. It seems that we are back to the state England was in the sixteenth century when religious reformers like Latimer, Cranmer, Ridley and a host of others became martyrs for religion and 300 Protestants were burnt by Queen Mary in four years![12] The followers of religions tend to ignore the spiritual and philosophical elements in them and emphasize the ritual. Thereby they concentrate on what divides religions rather than what unites them. Persecution for religion is nothing but insanity, and the effort to convert those unwilling—an admission of its insufficiency. In fact as Voltaire says, even atheism is preferable to fanaticism : 'Which is more dangerous, fanaticism or atheism? Fanaticism is certainly a thousand times more deadly, for atheism inspires no bloody passions, whereas fanaticism does; it is not opposed to crime, but fanaticism causes crimes to be committed'.[13] We have quoted Jinnah as complaining that Moslems wish to eat beef but Hindus won't let them as they are against cow-slaughter, the cow, because of association with Lord Krishna, being held sacred. Also that Hindus will wash their hands if they shake hands with a Moslem. This depicts the littleness of mind of such great men, who, despite their greatness, are avowed fanatics. It is exactly such shallowness of thought that leads to the conflicts in religion. It would be well to remember what has been said in *The Lacon* : 'Men will wrangle for religion; write for it; fight for it; die for it; anything but—live for it'.[13a]

Finally there is the fifth factor of the militancy of religions. The urge to assert one's religion finds expression in two ways. One is to effectively stop people from criticizing it and the

---

12. G. M. Trevelyan. *History of England* London : Langmans, Green and Co., 1929, p., 319.

13. *Philosophical Dictionary* Voltaire 1964.

13a. *The Lacon*. Charles Caleb Colton.

other is to insist that all religions, barring one's own, are heresy. Criticism does not mean disparagement or denunciation. All religions should be respected not only by their own followers, but by everyone. Religions are an endeavour to reach God by various ways. Nonetheless criticism of religion and revolt in it, have often resulted in widening what was a narrow perpective. In Christianity we have Martin Luther who is 1517, nailed his '95 Thoses' to the door of the Church at Wittenberg, attacking the practice of granting indulgences, and opposed celibacy among the clergy. That led to a reform movement in the Christian Church. Swami Dayananda spearheaded reform in Hinduism. Thus criticism and revolt, if used to reform and not to revile, are useful to religions. Certain faiths, however, resist reform and condemn criticism. These are authoritarian, and where they have to co-exist with other religions, they find the going rough. Besides this resistance to reform makes the chasm deeper. If the ritual part of one religion does not accomodate itself to the rituals of others, clashes are inevitable. This is not to suggest that the fundamental element of religions should be transformed, but surely the ornaments and trappings could be made to fit the universal mould. If each religion started claiming its own law and practice to be the one enforceable instead of the general one, there would be utter confusion. For example various outmoded forms of punishment are provided by different religious canons, like stoning, whipping cutting off the hands and so forth. It is obvious that these cannot be enforced in the present day civilized society. So is the case with dress. In all like matters it would be salutary for religions to outgrow their outlandishness.

Religions have two aspects. One is their spiritual content which tells its followers how to reach God. A large portion of the various scriptures is devoted to this. Then there is the part which lays down the laws, as for example the first four chapter of the Holy Quran and the Book of Deuteronomy in the Holy Bible. There are other directives also about civic and social life. Hindu religion, if we take it to mean the Vedānta and the Six Systems of philosophy, is an exception inasmuch as the only law mentioned therein is *dharma* which means righteousness. The Hindu religion is in fact unique. There are clashes on minor points between sects of the same religion, as for example between Catholics, Protestant and Quakers in Christianity and Shias and Sunnis among Moslems [the Moslem Sufis standing quite apart]. But never does a Christian revile Christianity, a Moslem Islam, a Sikh Sikhism, a Buddhist Buddism. But a Hindu can say 'Who is a Hindu ? There is no Hindu'.

So far as religions point out the way of salvation to those who are its followers, the question of their coming into conflict with other religions does not arise. But when they divide people into 'believers' and 'unbelievers' and also stongly condemn those who do not believe in the principles expounded by them, even to the limit of persecution, they open the doors of militancy. The priests, pandits and mullahs who are the self-assumed custodians of religion its – modern shamans – are quick to exploit such divisions. They are in truth the real cause of the militancy of religions which is the major cause of their conflicts. Just as the shamans were the ethical leaders of and decided how and in what way the primitive religions should be practised, so too these mullahs priests and pandits interpret the religions of today as being harshly uncompromising where accommodation is required. And when the particular religion they head, itself gives them this latitude, this intolerance turns into bigotry

The militancy of religions, while bringing no credit to the militant one, casts odium and humiliation on others towards which it is opposed. This naturally sets up a chain reaction of hatred, not to speak of the merciless cruelties and abject misery which is the offshoot. The unfortunate thing is that the modern shamans of religions will not, in their own selfish interest and to maintain their self-importance, let them co-exist in peace. And the followers of religions will not rescue them from the bigotry of this self-imposed leadership.

Although we have considered separately these four factors leading to the conflict of religions, viz., egotism, lack of accomodation, conflicting rituals and militancy; in truth they coalesce and follow one from the other. The sense of egotism leads one to believe that his religion is best. That leads him to make little account of the religions of others. In other words lack of accomodation develops. The follower of one religion frowns upon the rituals of the other. Normally he would not even take any notice of them. But the seeds of hatred have already sprouted. Intolerance has been born. To those who wish to thrive on differences, the votaries of 'divide and rule'. mostly rulers and politicians who exploit the miseries of mankind for their own narrow ends; the conflicts of religions is a godsend. From hatred to militancy is but a short step. Christ desired that men should put up the sword. But the un-Christian militants of religion take it out of the scabbard to shed innocent blood. This is not the opium of the masses, but their poison. Force or compulsion is a poor argument. It can never win over the goodwill of people but only their hatred. Besides persecution does not achieve the object with which it is done. One may behead a million followers of a certain religion becuase their beliefs are heresy to him. But that religion can never be thus wiped out. John Stuart Mill says : 'Socrates was put to death, but the Socratic philosophy rose like the sun in heaven, and spread its illumination over the whole intellectual firmament. Christians were cast to the lions, but the Christian church grew up a stately and spreading tree, overtopping the older and less vigorous growths, and stifling them by its shade. Our merely social intolerance kills no one, roots out no opinions, but induces men to disguise them, or to abstain from any active effort for their diffusion. With us, heretical opinions do not perceptible gain, or even lose, ground in each decade or generation; they never blaze out far and wide, but continue to smoulder in the narrow circles of thinking and studious persons among whom they originate, without ever lighting up the general affairs of mankind with either a true or deceptive light'.[14] So too was the case with the Moslem rulers. What has Islam gained by the eight hundred years of persecution of the so-called *zimmis*, the savage religious wars, the destruction of temples and idols, the massacre of innocent people whose only fault was that they wanted to practise their religion ?

14. John Stuart Mill. *On Liberty*. London : John W. Parker and Son, West Strand. M. DGCC. Lix, pp., 65-66.

No religion becomes great by intolerance, for as Jesus Christ said 'All they that take the sword shall perish with the sword'.[15] Persecution and bloodshed for the sake of religion leaves only hate behind.

We have now spoken about the nature of religion, its evolution and the causes of its conflicts. Religion is really a lovely tree with delicately perfumed flowers, which yields comfort to all who come under its shade. But misguided and unscruplous people rob it of its flowers, and leaves and sustenance and turn it into a dry and useless piece of timber fit only for feeding the flames of fire. Such people who profess to practice religion only to spread hatred and harm others, are traitors to their faith. For what does it profit man if he gain the world but lose his own soul?

15. The Holy Bible. New Testament *St Matthew* xxvi. 7 : 52.

5

THE RELIGION OF THE HINDUS

If I was asked under what sky the human mind has most fully developed some of its choicest gifts, has most deeply pondered on the greatest problems of life, and has found solutions, some of them deserving the attention of those who have studied Plato and Kant—I should point to India.

Max Müller

Where can we look for sages like those whose systems of philosophy were the prototypes of those of Greece : to whose works Plato, Thales and Pythagoras were disciples?

Colonel Tod [Speaking of India].

IMAGE WORSHIP

Before proceeding to extracts from the main books of Hindu religion and philosophy, it would be worthwhile to outline their main tenets. This is all the more necessary because at the present time Hindu religion in more critized than understood and 'Hindutva', which obviously means professing Hinduism, is being put in the pillory by those learned intellectuals to whom. Pope's observation can be applied, that 'a little learning is a dangerous thing, Some prominent Hindus are even questioning whether Hinduism is a religion at all or only a chimera of the mind. To them perhaps the *Gītā*, the Upanishads, the Vedas, the *Brahma-sūtras* and the *Rāmāyaṇa* a do not exist, as to the ostrich who buries his head in the sand, a desert-storm. For such as these we can only pray with Kipling 'Thy mercy on thy People, Lord!'[1] Then there are those who have taken too deep a draught of the Pierian Springs—the secularists and

---

1. Rudyard Kipling. *Recessional.*

their cousins, the pseudo-secularists, who, to prove that the Moslems were not the first invaders, create hair-splitting differences between Aryans and Dravidians, forgetting that as far as religion is concerned, both are Hindus worshipping the same gods in different temples. The monotheistic faiths frown upon idol-worship. Some indeed do not even have the broadmindedness to tolerate it. They claim superiority, dismissing the worshippers of idols as not having reached that point of civilization which *they* have. Arnold, for example, believes that even the highest form of moral idolatry are God- eclisping and therefore throw a veil on enlightenment and knowledge of reality.[2] In truth even monotheistic religions cannot claim to have completely estranged themselves from some objective representations, as for example the image of the Holy Mother Mary, or Christ on the Cross. It may be an image or just a stone, in effect it means the same. To some the images are just images. Kabir, for example says :

> 'The images are all lifeless, they cannot speak :
>
> I know, for I have cried to them aloud'.[3]

But the image of the goddess Kali spoke to Swami Ramakrishna Paramahaṁsa, and that of Krishṇa spoke to Meerā. A Sufī Moslem says :

> 'O you who sneer at the idolatry of the Hindu,
>
> Learn also from him how worship is done'.[4]

As the *Rāmāyaṇa* says : 'Each one saw in Rāma what he wished to see'. In the *Gītā* Lord Krishṇa says 'I gladly accept a flower, fruit or water offered to me by my devotee with faith in his heart'. An image is just a kind of symbol. The worshipper does not worship the stone or the metal in it, nor the form of it. When he stands before it and prays, he is praying through it to the same God which the Moslem or the Christian conceives. With all his wisdom even Swami

---

2. Aldous Huxley. *The Perennial Philosophy*. Chatto. and Windus. 1996. pp.. 260
3. *Selections From the Sacred Writings of the Sikhs*. London : George Allen and Unwin. 1960.
4. Nizami. K.A. *Some Aspects of Religion and Politics in India During the Thirteenth Century*. Asia 1961. p.. 263 op. cit.

Dayānanda the great founder of the Arya Samaj failed to understand this fundamental point. It was rather naive of him to have condemned image-worship because the mice ate up the holy offering to the image of Gaṇesha! If we are to understand religion at all we ought to clearly realize that it is a matter of faith. It is that which makes a Christian believe in the Holy Communion, the Holy Ghost and the Immaculate Conception, and a Moslem in the sanctity of the Kaaba and of the Black Stone. This being so it is quite unreasonable to denounce the Hindu for having faith in an image. The supercilious attitude of the followers of monotheistic faiths to image-worship, idolatory as it is contemptuously called, is only an expression of their lack of understanding. It is also forgotten by the detractors of Hinduism that it is both a polytheistic religion as well as a monotheistic one. Gauḍapāda, Shankarāchārya and their followers were the believers of the one Cosmic Absolute (*brahman*). Krishṇa makes it clear that the worship of God with form (Īshvara) and that of the formless God, both lead to salvation, though for human beings the worship of the unmanifest is difficult. Those who worship me with unswerving devotion, he says to Arjuna, are the better yogīs. But the worshippers of the unmanifest, changeless and eternal [*brahman*], who see the same soul in every creature, also doubtlessly come to me. However for people who try to reach me through the unmanifest, the going is rough, because to those who have been given a human body, the way of the unmanifest is fraught with grief (i.e., troublesome : *avyaktā hi gatiḥ duḥkham dehavabhidih avāpyate*[5])

THE AGE OF HINDU CIVILIZATION

The dates of the various civilizations as given in *Civilizations Past and Present* are as follows :

Egyptican	c. 5000-525 B.C.
Indian (Indus Valley)	c. 4000-2500 B.C.
Chinese	c. 200 B.C.-4th Century

5. *Bhagavadgītā.* 12 : 2–5.

Greek	c. 3200 B.C.-A.D. 195
Roman	c. 2000 B.C.-A.D. 170[6]

However more excavations [apart from the famous ones of Harappa and Mohendodoro] have been made by Professor Sharma of the Allahabad University in the Vindhyas and the Ganga valley. His findings show that civilization existed in India 8000 years ago.[7] Even these excavations might not be the last. So Hindu civilization is really ageless.

Hindu religion is much older. In Pātanjali's *Yoga-sūtras* the very first aphorism says : 'Now a revised text of yoga'. In the *smriti* of Yājñavalkya the original teacher of yoga is said to be Hiranyagarbha, the Lord of all beings and of the universe. Krishṇa says in the *Gītā* that the yoga teaching he is giving to Arjuna was given to Vivasvān, the Sun-god and he gave it to Manu, the Father of mankind, and Manu gave it to king Iksvāku. Calculating in terms of the *yugas* of Hindu cosmogony, Manu taught the *Gītā* to Iksvāku some 2,005,000 years ago. The age of the present Manu is reckoned as 305,300,000 years, of which we have crossed about 120,400,015 years. Thus the *Gītā* was taught by Krishṇa to Vivasvān more than 120,400020 years ago!

WHO IS A HINDU ? ACCUSATIONS AGAINST HINDUISM

Before we go on to speak about, some of the main tenets of the Hindu religion, we will examine three accusations frequently levied against it. The first is that Hinduism is too diffused and generalized a faith to be called a specific religion. The Moslems have one scripture, the Holy Quran, and so too the Christians, the Holy Bible, while the Hindus have a number of them like the *Gītā*, the *Rāmāyaṇa*, the Upanishads, Vedas and the *Brahma-sūtras*. Thus Hinduism has nebulous beliefs and it is difficult to say what the exact creed of a Hindu is. The second charge is that Hinduism is morbid and pessimistic, emphasising sorrow and the dark side of life. For example, it calls the world *mrityu-loka* i.e. 'the abode of death'. The

6. Scott Foreman and Co. USA. *Civizations Past and Present*, 1959.

7. P.T.I. 22 Dec. 1978. Paper read in the Post-plenary Symposium of the 10th International Congress of Anthropological and Ethnological Sciences on Recent Advances in Indopacific Prehistory, 1978.

third charge is that the entire goal of human life as conceived by Hinduism— *moksha*, or emancipation—is a negative concept. It speaks of the eradication of man's personality and the merging of the soul in God. Personality is all that a man has, and if it reduced to nothingness, what is there left to him ?

THE CASTE SYSTEM

Of these the first charge is the gravest inasmuch as it is often supported by Hindus themselves, mostly political leaders who wish to decry Hinduism ['Hindutva', as they call it] for their political gain and for vindicating their 'secularism'. However before we proceed to answer it, it might be well to acknowledge two glaring evils in Hindu society.[8] One is the caste system and the other is dowry. The caste system is the canker of Hindu society. It has been castigated by many social reformers like Gandhi and Rāma Tīrtha. They tried to end it, but never to exploit it to their own advantage. The same cannot be said of our power-hungry shallow-minded leaders of today, who in their attitude have not departed from the British one of *divid-et-impera.* We find them dividing the country still more, pitching the scheduled castes, the 'backward' and the 'other-backward' [their contribution to Manu], against the upper castes. The gradual corruption from *varṇa* to caste is too well-known to call for any repetition. In the old concept of varṇa which we find in the *Gītā*, it was nature *(svabhāva)* and occupation which determined it, not birth. In the *Mahābhārata* [see subsequent part of the book giving extracts from it—'Questions for the Wise'] Dharma (the god of Righteousness) asked Yudhishṭhira, one of the Pāṇḍva brothers what made a brāhmin, learning or good conduct ? Yudhishṭhira said 'It is good conduct which distinguished him. Neither was it birth nor learning. Caste must surely be eradicated. But the remedy being applied by our political leaders is worse than the disease. By lowering standards to benefit the lower castes, they are condemning them to a state of permanent mediocrity and providing crutches to them instead of making them stand on their feet. The only way to end this social slur which has made Hinduism

8. It must be emphasised that caste and dowry are the bane of Hindu *society.* Religion has no concern with them.

the laughing-stock of the world, is to abolish caste itself once for all. It would sound a bold step, and is certainly fraught with difficulties, but a festering sore can be cured only by a painful incision. But no, our men is power wish to turn the sore into a tumour just to remain glued to their chairs. And our secularists and intellectuals keep writing words words words about it, without the slightest effort to end it.

DOWRY

Then there is dowry. Open the pages of any newspaper and you find someone somewhere in India has burnt a newlywed out of greed. Punishments are given by courts to culprits. Social organizations of sorts keep agitating against it. Yet brides keep on being burnt. And the amazing thing about it is that most of the culprits are of the moneyed classes. The remedy lies in creating social awareness. Perhaps the ancient practice of ostracism might work. Having said this much about the two evils of Hindu society, we proceed to the charges levied against Hinduism.

Hindustan is what was earlier called Bhāratavarsha, the land of the Bhāratas. Later it came to be known as Hindustan. Babur, the first of the Moghuls called it Hind. When his men began to feel homesick, an amir of his army wrote on the wall.

> If safe and sound I cross the Sind
> Blacken my face ere I wish for Hind.

The diversity of Hindu religion is its strength not its weakness. For the first time a religion went into the unknown. It tried to analyze the mystery of life and death, to understand the soul and afterlife. He went beyond the ethical into the spiritual. It was Hindu religion alone which did not insist on one dogmatic creed. Even atheism is not despised by the Hindu faith. There is a school of thought, the Chāravākas recognized by it, the creed of which is hedonism. Western thought, particularly the Christian and in that the New Testament, has much that is noble and spiritual. The Books of the Old Testament, too, such as the Psalms, Proverbs and Ecclesiastes are highly philosophical and the poetry of the Song of Solomon is unequalled.

The western attitude of branding everything eastern as inferior, however, is regrettable. And still more so the castigation of the Hindu faith by Hindus themselves who contemptuously call it 'Hindutva'. Rejected by the west and disowned by the east, Hindu thought has been admired by those whom religious bigotry or political ambition has not corrupted. Schelling. Schopenhauer, Goethe, Max Miiller, Tod, Tolstoy and Paul Deussen are among those who have extolled Hindu philosophy. Tomlin says.

> 'Where as so many western philosophers, especially of the modern era, dwell upon minute technical problems and appear to avoid generalizations about the universe as a whole, the great philosophers of the Orient never lose sight of the fundamental problem namely that which concerns life's meaning and purpose. From the oldest of coherent philosophical speculations in the Hindu Vedas and Upanishads to the sages of modern India, the quest not so much for certainty as for truth has continued without relaxation. Nor has this preoccupation been confined to a few men of distinction, learning, or piety in each generation : it has exercised the minds of those anonymous, patient toiling millions with which to the western eye the Orient is peopled'.[9]

Another western writer says : 'Truth is for Hinduism an indivisible treasure; spiritual immediacy is widely distributed, the mystic path is open to everyone. In its purest forms, this religion becomes a type of wisdom, that wisdom which impressed the ancient Greeks when they visited India and which could be of some fruitfulness again for our blasè cultures'.[10] But the writer draws a distinction between wisdom and spirituality and feels wisdom is the right word to be applied to Hinduism. This isn't quite true. The quest for soul-knowledge and for the mystery of afterlife is nothing if not spiritual. The doctrine of *māyā* [delusion] and Shankara's belief of the world's unreality till *brahman* is understood are spiritual insights of the highest order. Then Renou's observation that maturity in Hinduism

9. E.W.F. Tomlin. *Great Philosophies of the East.* London : Skeffington & Son Ltd., 1952. p., 19.
10. Louis Renou. *Hinduism* London : Prentice–Hall International. 1961. Conclusion, pp., 56–7.

will come about only when 'certain crude Indian institutions' like caste, will disappear, too, depicts a confusion between 'society' and 'religion'. Society in the advanced Christian countries like America, Europe and so forth is in a decadent state. Sex seems to have dominated it with wife-swappings stag-parties and licentiousness. A Pentagon inquiry report says : 'naval aviators and their guests also engaged in consensual oral sex and sexual intercourse in full view of other participants, contributing to a general atmosphere of debauchery'. Marine pilots grabbed the buttocks and breasts of a women officer Lt Paula Coughlin'.[11] It would be as illogical to say that Christianity will come only when these crude and un-Christian acts cease, as that Hinduism will mature only when institutions like the caste-system go. Hinduism is really the most broadminded and accomodating religion. It has no shibboleths, no pre-conditions of faith. To the Christian redemption is possible only through Christ. A Moslem believes that God is only for those who follow Islam. But Krishṇa says in the *Gītā* : 'It does not matter what deity a devotee chooses to worship. If he has faith, I make his faith unwavering.... Even those who worship other deities and sacrifice to them with faith in their hearts are really worshipping me...[12] Thus Hinduism is the most accomodating and tolerant of religions. That is why it has survived the persecution of Moslems and the missionaries of British rule.

WHAT ALL HINDUS BELIEVE

Despite its broad ambit, Hinduism is not vague as some of its critics make it out to be. Nor is it mere wisdom devoid of spirituality. There are some fundamental beliefs to which all Hindus subscribe. One is the eternal cycle of Nature without beginning or end. The cosmic unit of time is believed to be a Kalpa which is a day of Brahmā, the Creator. This is equivalent to 43,200 lakh years. Brahmā creates the universe in the morning of his day and at night earth, heaven and hell and return to chaos. Next morning these are re-created.

11. UNI Washington. US navy officers face trial for sexual assault. Reported in the *Pioneer* 27 April 1993.

12. *Gita* chapters 7 and 9. Trans., Swami Prabhavananda and Christopher Isherwood. New American Library. 1954.

So it goes on till Brahmā reaches the hundredth year of his life. At the end of this period all gods sages, demons and men, the three worlds and even Brahmā- himself cease to be. This is called *Mahāpralaya* or the 'Great Dissolution'. Then follows a hundred celestial years of chaos, after which another Brahmā is born. Thus the process keeps on repeating itself. Brahmā's day is divided into a thousand *Mahāyugas* of equal length. Each consists of four *yugas*—Krita, Tretā. Dvāpara and Kali. These are respectively of 1,728000; 1,296,000; 864,000; and 432,000 years [we are living in the last of these, the Kaliyuga]. Righteousness progressively declines from one *yuga* to another.

All Hindus accept *dharma* [morality or righteousness] as the law of the universe. *Dharma* implies various things. It is that which upholds the world order, protects society and makes it stable. It brings about harmony and peace among people. It promotes good works, conduct and thoughts. It causes human beings to discriminate between what is proper and that which is improper. It implics virtues such as honesty, fairdealing restraint, dispassiong and desisting from vices like greed, avarice, iasciviousness and so forth. It means performing one's prescribed duty in the face of all dangers and odds. It also means one's nature (*svabhāva*). *Svadharma* in the *Gītā* means following one's natural *dharma [sreyan svadharmo vigunah* : one's own *dharma* is the best' 18:47]. A fish can live only in water, a bird in air, so too man can exist, only in his particular *dharma*. When someone asked the great sage Vyāsa, the author of the *Māhābhārata* what *dharma* was, he said : 'I tell you in brief what *dharma* is. Hear and practise it. Do not do to others that which causes hurt and harm to you'.[13] In other words do as you would be done by. Hindus believe in a full life. Despite its spiritualism, Hinduism accepts that worldly existence involves other things as well. Thus it considers the aims of living as four—*artha, kāma, dharma* and *moksha. Artha* (wealth or money) is that which is earned by honest toil (not as it is being earned in the world today by bribery, corruption, greed and cuts). Krishṇa considers those persons

13. *Shrutām dharma sarvasyam, shrutva chaivāv dhāryatām ātmanah prati kūlāni, parēshān na samācharēt* ||

of demoniac nature who try to appropriate the wealth of others by unfair means [*anyāyena artha sanchayan ihante* : *Gītā*, 16:12] *Kāma*, which means passion or sex, is recognized as one of the necessities of balanced living. But sex means the union of man and woman for the sake of offspring, the kind of union of which Milton sang :

'Hail wedded love, mysterious law, true source
Of human offspring, sole propriety'.[14]

It does not mean promiscuous sex, or sex for the purpose of mere enjoyment which Krishṇa decries : *kāma haitukam – Gītā*. 16:8. We have already said what *dharma* is. The fourth and ultimate object of human existence is *moksha* (called nirvāna by Buddhists). We will speak of this in detail later. Here it will suffice to say that *moksha* means the merging of the soul with God and freedom from the cycle of births and deaths: in one word, emancipation.

Connected with the *purushārthas* are the four *āsharamas*, or stages of life. These provide a complete and integrated life. The first stage is that of the pupil (*antevāsin*). The student must be obedient and submissive to his teacher and have complete faith in him. He must be eager to acquire knowledge. He must observe celibacy (*brahmacarya*). The teacher was more or less like a guru. The schools were called *gurukuls*. Education was affectionately given and obediently acquired. It was not as now, a commercial commodity aucationed to the highest bidder. The sceond stage was that of the family man, the *grihastha*, It was as a *grihastha* that the man realized the three aforesaid aims of life – *artha, kāma* and *dharma*. After the *grihastha* was the stage of the *vānaprastha*, the forest-dweller (*vana* means 'forest'). The pursuit of weath and pleasure was now given up for the higher quest of knowledge of the soul. Vedic sages, like Yājñavalkya, were such family men, usually wealthy, but eager to learn about life's mystery, who left for the woods to meditate. The last stage was that of a homeless wanderer (*sannyāsī*) in which allties with the world were severed. The, *sannyāsī* had no home. He would move from place to

14. *Paradise Lost.* bk., iv 748–50.

place, generally on the outskirts of villages and beg for alms, for of course he needed food to keep living. He would call out once and generally the housewife would come and place whatever food she could spare, in his bowl. If no one came, the hermit moved on to another house. He was prohibited from calling out twice. Thus the Hindu conceive a balanced life, a life of enjoyment as well of abnegation.

The third universal belief of all Hindus is in afterlife and rebirth. Tied up with this is the doctrine of *karma* (words). The *Kaṭha Upanishad* says : 'Like corn man decays and like corn he is born again'.[15] Krishṇa says to Arjuna 'You and I have passed through many births. I know them all, but you do not know them'.[16] The theory of *karma* is that man reaps good for the good deeds he does, and evil for evil works. The *Brihadāraṇyaka Upanishad* says : 'A man becomes good by good deeds and bad by bad deeds'.[17] Most religions also subscribe to the principle of divine judgment, but it is only Hinduism which ties it up with rebirth. The consequence of works (*karma-phala*) cannot be worked out in a single lifetime and so the soul has to have several lives [we will discuss *karma* in detail later].

A fourth belief common to all school of Hindu philosophy is *moksha*. This is the goal of all endeavour. It has been wrongly understood to be a state of nothingness. It is not. It is the state of unending bliss (*akhaṇḍa sukh*). As the Upanishad says : 'Losing name and form, the wise man goes to *brahman* as the river flows into the sea' [we will speak of *moksha* too in more detail later].[18]

Another concept common to Hindu schools of philosophy is the universality of suffering. There are three kinds of suffering: *ādhyātmika* (disease and mental grief), *ādhibhautika* (suffering arising from the world of living creatures) and *ādhidaivika* (arising from the supernatural. (like the influence of stars and planets). It is acknowledged that life involves suffering and

15. *Kaṭha Upanishad.* 1. 6.
16. *Bhagavadgītā.* 4 ; 5.
17. *Brh. Up.* 3. 2 : 13.
18. *Muṇḍaka Upanishad.* 3 : 2 : 8.

one of the aims of Hindu philosophy is to find ways and means of removing it. The way is to seek salvation which is the realization of *ḅrahman*. Then the chain of worldly existence is broken. The soul is freed from the world of sorrows. Buddhism goes deeper into this question. In fact for it the removal of suffering is a primary objective. We will consider this is detail later.

What contributes to the unity of Hinduism is common scriptures, deites, ideals, beliefs and practices. The Vedas, Upanishads the *Bhāgavata Purāṇa* and the epics, the *Rāmāyaṇa and Mahābhārata,* are recognized by all schools, Deites such as Brahmā, Vishṇu and Shiva (the Hindū trinity) and Saṛasvati, Lakshmī and Shakti, their consorts, as also Rāma and Krishṇa the *avataras* of Vishṇu—all these are accepted by all Hindus. Individuals may worship a particular deity, but no Hindu will deny the others. Common ideals are purity, self-control, truth, detachment and non-violence. Hinduism prescribes rituals in the lower stages of life. But when these give place to *sannyāsa,* the emphasis shifts from scriptural practices to meditation and renunciation. There are no rituals for *sannyāsīs*. Yoga, worship (like prayer, chanting God's name and so forth), and going on pilgrimages, are other common practices. Having answered the question, Who is a Hindu ? we proceed to the two other misconceptions about it, viz. that it is pessimistic and its concept of emancipation is a negative one. If pessimism means recognizing a fact, then certainly Hinduism is pessimistic. Its critics consider it so, just because it believes that life involves suffering. Dr Albert Schweitzer for examples refers to the 'life-negating] ascetics imposing their gloom on their followers,. One can't deny that there is suffering in the world, just as there are pleasures. As for as religion is concerned it is meant to provide comfort. As Jesus says, 'Come unto me, all ye that labour and are heavy laden and I will give you rest'.[19] We need consolation only when we suffer. In our pleasures we are by ourselves. It is when we are beset with pain and sorrow that we turn to religion. It is for this reason that religions try to provide the means of relief from suffering.

19. *St Matthew*. xi. : 27.

Hinduism does not extol suffering, but neither does it ignore it. It analyzes it and gives solutions to end it. We have already mentioned the three kinds of suffering. The *Gītā* gives another categorization. That which brings nectar-like joy in the beginning, but is in the end like poison, cannot be classified as real happiness.[20] Bacon says, 'Prosperity is not without many fears and distastes; and adversity is not without comforts and hopes'.[21] These comforts are provided by religion which counsels us to accept when there is no way out. It provides divine help, when human agencies fail. The *Isha Upanishad* says : 'One should live a hundred years, always engaged in works'.[22] This surely is not a pessimistic view of life. The Vedas are full of observations about a long and happy life. Friends bless newlyweds in these words :

Here now remain, nor ever part
Enjoy the whole expanse of life,
With sons and grandsons joyous sport
Be glad in heart within your house
Give her many sons, O Indra,
And joys and pleasures in her life
May she have ten children, and as eleventh
Her dear and loving faithful spouse.[23]

The charge of moroseness, gloom and pessimism again the Hindu religion is without foundation. In fact those who think so have completely failed to understand the spirit of the *Bhagavadgītā*, its most renowned scripture. Doubtless Krishṇa advocates renunciation for the sages, but for the men of the world he counsels ceaseless and desireless works.

The third point concerns *mokshà*, which as we mention, before, implies merging of the soul with God. In some way or the other all religions believe the soul 'our life's star' to be of the nature of God. They do not speak of any merger of

20. *Gītā.* 18. 38.
21. Francis Bacon. Essays. On *Adversity.*
22. *Isha Up.* 2.
23. *Rig Veda.* 10 : 85 : 42 & 45.

it with God, but they all believe it goes to the celestial regions. The argument against the Hindu belief mainly revolves round the loss of a man's '*personality*', the literal meaning of which is 'the state of being a person' or 'existence as an individuality'.[24] The loss of personality means, therefore ceasing to be the individual person. But for a deeper insight we go to the Buddhist idea of khaṇḍas. The Buddhists do not subscribe to the Hindu concept of an unchanging soul (the *ātman*). Personality consists of five *khaṇḍas*, namely 1. The material body or factor, 2. Feeling [pleasure, pain or the neutral feeling i.e. neither pleasure nor pain]. 3. perceptions [recognizing and naming]. 4. *Shankhāras*, or the 50 other mental accompaniments, especially the will, that are apt to arise when consciousness is stimulated, and lastly consciousness itself. Delusion consists in thinking that any of these five khaṇ ḍas either (1) is the soul, or (2) is an attribute of the soul, or (3) is in the soul, or (4) contains the soul; just for instance (a) as flame and its colour may be considered one, or (b) as its shadow is an attribute of the tree, or (c) as the perfume is in the flower, or (d) as a casket contains a jewel.[25] It is clear from the above analysis that no element of a man's personality is allied with the soul. It must, therefore, be connected with the body. And since the body is consumed on the funeral-pyre or decays in graves, 'personality' is in any case irretrievable lost when the body perishes. *Moksha*, which concerns the soul, not the body, has thus nothing to do with it. The fear that *moksha* implies loss of personality and so in a negative concept, is without foundation. Having considered the common misconceptions about Hinduism, we will go on to consider its various concepts.

---

24. *Advanced Learner's Dictionary of Current English.* Oxford University Press.

25. *Sutta-Pitaka- Patisambhidamagga* 1 : 143-45 Mrs Rhys Davids. *Buddhism.* op. cit.

6

THE FUNDAMENTAL CONCEPTS OF HINDUISM

Most religions start where reason ends. Hinduism is somewhat different. As for other religions most of its beliefs are metaphysical. But with Shankarāchārya and the monists one re-enters the realm of reason. Like other religions, too, Hinduism asks us to accept certain beliefs as if they were axioms, as for example the soul, the Cosmic Absolute, *karma*, rebirth and *moksha*. A distinctive feature of Hinduism, however, is that it provides several paths to salvation. Krishṇa tells Arjuna : 'Surrender your mind and wisdom to me and think of me alone. If you can't do that try to reach me through the yoga of devotion. If that too in not possible for you, find your salvation by doing works desirelessly. And if you can't even do that surrender to me completely all works and all the fruits of works'.[1] Devotion, desireless works and the way of wisdom are equally praised by Krishṇa in the *Gītā*. Thus Hindu religion points out various ways of redemption. It does not say, belief in this only can save you. Nor does it speak a word about non-believers. It's the difference between the eucalyptus and the banian tree. The former provides shade for only one but the other for everyone who may care to rest beneath it. In fact some of the Hindu systems of philosophy like Nyāya, Vaisheshika and Mīmānsā do not even speak of a God. There are, however, some concept which stand out, and it is these we now proceed to tell.

BRAHMAN AND ĀTMAN

These can be equated to the Cosmic Absolute and the soul. *Brahman* is conceived of as *'neti neti* or *na-iti, na-iti'*, meaning

---

1. *Bhagavadgītā.* 12 : 8–11.

'not this, not this'. In other words that which is beyond all thought and expression. In the Holy Bible (Book of Exodus) when Moses asked the Lord what he should tell the Israelities, was his name, the Lord said tell them 'I am that I am' This conveys the same idea, namely that the Absolute Being is not capable of expression in human language. The soul (*ātman or ātmā*) is of the nature of *brahman*, that is to say, it is divine. It is clear therefore that the quest for *brahman* is also the quest for the soul. All persons, however, do not bother about the soul, and many have doubtless never even heard of *brahman.* Krishṇa says in the *Gītā* 'Of thousands there is perhaps only one who strives for perfection and of these too it is only some rare person who can know me as I really am'.[2] Who then is that lucky one ? Ramana Maharshi, an enlightened sage, says that the person who does not identify himself with the body, seeks the soul. It is not at all easy to dissociate with the body, for it asserts itself in many ways. One associates all the pleasures in the world with it. It is the body which enjoys food, sex, drinks, coolness in summer as in air-conditioned rooms and warmth in bitter cold. It is only when the body suffers that one turns to God or the soul. According to Shankarāchārya the seeker of *brahman* is the person who has a strong intellect, who is learned and has the power of comprehension, who is without attachment, or avarice, and who is even-minded and desirous of obtaining emancipation. For obtaining such a grounding four kinds of preparatory training are essential : 1. Discrimination between the eternal and the transitory, 2. Renunciation of the desire to enjoy the fruits of action here and hereafter, 3. The attainment of the six qualities, viz., tranquillity, restraint, renunciation, resignation, concentration and belief, and 4. The longing for liberation.[3] In answer to Arjuṇa's question, How does the man established in *brahman* conduct himself ? Krishṇa says : 'He is free from all desire and craving. He is always happy and is not shaken by adversity. He neither grieves when unpleasant things happen to him, nor hankers after pleasures. Fortune

2. *Bhagavadgītā* 7 : 3.
3. *Vivekachudāmani.* 302 and 311.

does not make him rejorce, nor does he sorrow when misfortunes overtake him'.[4] To possess so many virtues and exercise such restraint is obviously not easy. Hindu religion recognizes this. The *Kaṭha Upanishad* says : 'This path, sharp as the edge of a razor and hard to cross, is difficult to tread'. Christ also spoke of the way to the divine as 'the narrow path'. But then when is a worthwhile thing easy of accomplishment?

There are various views about *brahman.* It is not possible to give a detailed account of these in this brief introduction. We will give just an outline 1. *Brahman* is the Creator, Ruler and Destroyer of the universe (*adi asya yata iti* – Bādarāyana-sūtras). Shankara gives it the name Tajjalām i.e. the Creator, Preserver and Destroyer of the universe. In the Upanishads the sage Yājñavalkya says 'At the bidding of *brahman*, O Gārgī the sun and the and heaven and earth stay at their places. At his bidding the moments, minutes, days and nights, fortnights, months, seasons and years keep their respective periods in time. At his command the rivers flow in their prescribed course. It is by his command people give charity and gods and manes are desirous of offerings made to them'.[6] The world also dissolves in him, and thus he is the Destroyer also : 'At the end of creation, O Arjuna, all beings return to my nature. And at the beginning I create them again'.[7]

2. *Brahaman* is the sole Reality. There is nothing apart from him. He is *satasya satyam* – 'the Reality of reality'. All life springs from him as the web from the spider's string and from fire the tiny sparks.

3. *Brahman* is not known throught knowledge in the sense of learning etc. It is beyond knowledge and it reveals itself to whom it chooses.

4. *Brahman* is the state of *turīya* i.e. beyond the waking, the dream and the deep sleep stages of consciousness. It is also the innermost sheath of the body. These concepts need to be explained. When one wakes up from sleep, he is not a new man. It's only that while dreaming and in deep sleep,

4. *Bhagavadgītā* 2 : 56–59.
5. *Ka. Upa.* 1 : 3 : 15.
6. *Brihadāraṇyaka Upanishad.* 3. 8. 9.
7. *Bhagavadgītā* 9.7 and 9. 17–19.

he has entered different planes of consciousness. On waking he remembers all that has passed before, the things he has resolved to do, the places he had to go to, and all his engagements. Thus there is a continuity between these three states of waking, dream and sleep. Moreover when one is in deep slumber he is unaware of the external world, yet when he wakes up, he *knows* that he had been asleep. In order to know this there must have remained something awake in him to be able to convey to him that he had slept. We can't know of anything unless we are aware of it through one of our five senses. For example we be can be sure we have met a friend and have seen him and greeted him. The blind know things through touch. We know we are hearing a song when it is heard by means of our ears. When we are in deep slumber, however, all our senses are ineffective. Someone might put a book on the table, but it can't be seen. People talk, but the sleeping man cannot hear them. If all our senses were dormant, who or what was there to tell us that we had slept ? Hindu philosophy call this thing, the Witness, or the *turīya* state (meaning 'the fourth). It is that which ever keeps awake while a is alive, whether he is waking, man dreaming or in deep slumber. It is the 'Eternal Witness', and this is the soul, the Self or *brahman* [as we have said, Hinduism equates the soul with *brahman*]. Ramana Maharshi says about it : 'There are three states only, the waking dream and sleep. *Turīya* is not a fourth one; it is what underlies these three. But people do not readily understand it. Therefore it is said that this is the fourth state and the only reality. In fact it is not apart from anything, for it forms the substratum of all happenings; it is the only truth; it is your very being. The three states appear as fleeting phenomena in it and sink into it alone. Therefore they are unreal...*Turīya* is only a second name for the Self. Aware of the waking, dream and sleep states, we remain unaware of our own Self. Nevertheless the Self is here and now. It is the only Reality There is nothing else. So long as identification with the body lasts, the world seems to lie outside us. Only realize the Self and they are not'.[8] Another example may be given to

8. *Talks with Sri Ramana Maharshi*. vol. 2 Sri Ramanasarama, 1955. pp., 440–41.

explain the *turīya* state. if a coin contains three pence, each penny in it represents the three states of waking, dream and deep sleep, but the entire coin, which includes each penny in it represents the *turīya*. *Brahman* is also the inmost sheath (*kosha*). It is believed the embodied soul (*jīva*) has five sheaths. These are called so merely in a figurative sense, for they do not really lie one over the other as peels of a fruit or the layers of the human skin. The sheaths are a sort of coverings over the soul which obscure it in varying degrees. For example if we cover a lamp with thin muslin it will seem brighter than if we cover it with a coarser cloth. Even so these sheaths progressively cover the soul and obscure it in varying degrees. The sheaths are *annamaya* [of food from *anna,* meaning food], *prāṇamaya* [of the vital airs from *prāṇa*, 'the vital breath'], *manomaya*, the sheath of mind [from *mana*, meaning mind], *vijñānamaya*, the sheath of intelligence [from *vijñāna*, the intellect] and *ānandamaya*, the sheath of bliss [from *ānanda,* meaning bliss]. The *ānandamaya* (inmost sheath) being closest to the soul is identical to it.[9]

5. *Brahman* is the personal God, Īshvara. As such he can be worshipped in various forms but, in reality through these gods [like Gaṇesha Hanumān and so forth] one worships Īshvara alone. He (Īshvara] alone is the inner guide (*antarayāmī*) and is superior to all the lesser gods. The *Kena Upanishad* illustrates this by an allegory. There was once a fight between the gods and the demons. *Brahman* caused the gods to win. But they began to believe that the victory had been won by them. *Brahman*, being the inner dweller of all, knew this. To cure the gods of their vanity he appeared before them in a finite form. The gods did not recognize him. They sent Agni, the

9. Tait. Up., 3. 10.

This is the sheath known as *sūksma sharīra* of which we will speak later. It accompanies the soul in its journey after death. The *Taittirīya Upanishad* says : 'The soul in man, and *brahman* are one. When a person who knows this dies, he transcends the outermost sheath of food, then that of breath and then of the mind. Having done so, his soul enters the sheath of the intellect, from that to the sheath of bliss. Thereafter his soul can traverse all the worlds at will, and it keeps chanting the praise of the ones of *brahman* "wonderful ! O wonderful ! O wonderful".'

god of Fire to find out who the Spirit was. The Spirit [*brahman*] asked Agni, 'who are you ?' Agni said 'Well I am the Fire-god and I have the power of burning everything'. 'Indeed'. *brahman* said. 'All right, here's a straw. Burn it'. Agni rushed towards it, but try as he might, he could not burn it. Then the gods sent Vāyu, the Wind-god. *Brahman* put a straw before him. He huffed and he puffed but it wouldn't even move. Then the gods sent Indra, their king. When he came the Spirit disappeared and in its place Umā the daughter of the Himalayas came before them. The gods were amazed and asked her who the Spirit was. Umā said 'It is indeed *brahman* through whom you obtained victory over the demons'.[10] The *Kaṭha Upanishad* says that even Indra and Prajāpati, the doorkeepers of the heavenly world, cannot prevent the entrance of the soul of a knower of *brahman*.[12]

6. *Brahman* is the Light of lights, complete bliss and *sachidānanda* (i.e. Being-Consiousness-Bliss).

In the conversation between Janaka, the emperor of Videha and Yājñavalkya, the sage, we have the following :

Janaka : By the light of what do men do their tasks in the world?

Yājñavalkya : The sun's light.

Janaka : And when the sun has set?

Yājñavalkya : By the light of the moon.

Janaka : And when there's no moon?

Yājñavalkya : By the light of fire.

Janaka : And when the fire too has gone out?

Yājñavalkya : By the help of speech or sound.

For by their help on can locate the spot from where they are coming.

10. *Kena Upa*. 3 & 4.

11. *Kaṭha Upa*. 6. 3.

12. *Kaushitaki Upa*. 1. 5.

Janaka : And when speech too has stopped, what then is the man's guide?

Yājñavalkya : Then his guide is his own soul, for the soul is a light to itself. It is by the soul's light that a person sits, moves about and does his work'.[13]

In the *Kaṭha Upanishad* we are told that the light of the sun, the moon, stars, fire and all lights are derived from *brahman*. When he shines then only can they possess their light.[14]

Yājñavalkya describes the soul's bliss by giving the example of a husband and wife clasping each other : 'As a man who clasps his wife limb to limb, is immersed completely in bliss and is unaware of everything else, the individual soul enfolded by the Supreme Soul knows neither inside nor outside. It has fulfilled all desires and no longer craves for anything. It has transcended both desires and sorrows....the state of *brahman* is the highest bliss.[15] But the *ātman* and *brahman* are identical in their natures only. They can't be the same. The wave is of the nature of the ocean, the spark is of the nature of fire and the sunrays of that of the sun. Yet the wave is not the ocean, nor the spark the fire, nor the sunbeam the sun, It's only that the wave the spark and the sunray arise from the ocean, fire and the sun and go back to it.

'Our birth is but a sleep and a forgetting :
The Soul that rises with us, our life's star.
Hath had elsewhere its setting,
And cometh from afar :
Not in entire forgetfulness.
And not in utter nakedness
But trailing clouds of glory do we come
From God who is our home :'[16]

13. *Brihadāraṇyaka Upanishad.* 4. 3. 4.
14. *Kaṭha Upanishad.* 5 : 15.
15. *Brihadārnyaka Upanishad.* 4. 3. 19–33.
16. Wordsworth. *Ode. Intimations of Immortality.*

THE SOUL WHEN EMBODIED AND THE SOUL BY ITSELF

Hinduism makes a rather subtle distinction between the *ātman* and the *jīva* (the embodied soul). This we go on to explain. Different religions conceive the soul differently. The Buddhists, as we have said, do not believe in an eternal soul beyond change and ever-existing without any alteration. The Hindu concept of the *ātman* is refuted. Nothing, including the soul, can, according to them, be exempted from the universal law of change. So for Buddhism everything is constantly changing, whether it is the soul by itself, or when it is contained in the body (the *jīva*). Jainism believes the *jīva* to be variable in size and capable of expansion and contraction according to the physical body with which it is associated for the time being. Still, there is some similarity between Hinduism and Jainism inasmuch as both believe in the distinction between the soul by itself and the soul-in-the-body (*ātman* and *jīva* of Hinduism). In its pure state, the Jains believe the soul to possess perception, knowledge, bliss and power. When in bodies the souls are covered with a thin veil of *karma*. These obscurations are of many kinds, some obscuring knowledge, other, bliss, right conduct, faith, the doing of good acts etc. Some obscurations even determine one's length of life, nationality, caste, family and social standing. These *karmas* stick on to the soul and are got rid of by a process of purging called *nirjarā*. Jains believe that even elements like, earth, water, fire and air have souls, In fact minute souls or nucleus-forming clusters pack the whole space of the world like powder in a box. These replace those souls which on getting emancipation are merged in God. Even a small portion of these soul-clusters can replace an infinite number of *moksha*-attained souls. The *jīvas* are divided by the Jains according to the number of sense-organs they possess. Thus souls of plants have only touch, of worms touch and taste, of ants touch taste and smell, of bees in addition vision, of vertebrates all the five senses, while souls of human beings have all five senses and in addition *manas* or mind-power. Other religions speak of the soul, or spirit as they call it, but do not enter into such detailed analysis of it.

The Hindu viewpoint finds place in the Sāṁkhya and Vedānta. Sāṁkhya calls the soul *purusha*. It has however to some extent the Jain principle of obscuration of the soul. Different bodies obscure the soul in varying degrees. So the souls of individuals are not all alike. Thus it believes in the plurality of the soul. The *purusha* combines with *prakriti* (Nature) to form creatures. How this combination is brought about is not quite clear. But it is said to be an automatic process like iron filings being attracted to a magnet by close proximity. The concept of the soul in Vedānta is somewhat different. The soul is eternal and constant. Krishṇa tells Arjuna that it cannot be limited or destroyed. It can't slay or be slain. It is unborn, everlasting, unchanging, deathless, birthless and eternal. Water can't wet it, fire cannot burn it and the wind cannot dry it. It can't be wounded by any means. It dwells in all beings, changeless and for ever. Neither the senses, nor the mind, nor thought can grasp it.[17] The Upanishads speak of the soul in many of their passages. The soul is small as a thumb and lies within the heart. It is tiny as the point of a goad and bright as the sun. Though minute, it is infinite. Neither male nor female nor even neuter, it identifies itself with whatever body it is contained in.[18] In answer to Janaka's question 'What is the soul ?' the sage Yājñavalkya says : 'The soul is often mistaken for the mind, but it is not the mind. Though remaining with the sense organs, it is yet different from them, for it is the light which lights up the mind'.[19]

THE SŪKSHMA SHARĪRA

The soul (*ātman*) is thus eternal and changeless. It is the same in all creatures, and dwells in them from their birth to the moment of death. Then the soul departs to be reborn in another body, the kind of rebirth depending on its deeds. The mechanism of rebirth and of the soul's journey from the body after the body's death will be considered under the section on rebirth and afterlife. Here we will only state how the soul, which according to the Hindu belief is quiescent

17. *Bhagavadgītā.* 2. 17–24.
18. *Svetāshvatrara Upanishad.* 5. 8–10.
19. *Brihadaraṇyaka Upanishad.* 4. 3.

and incapable of moving, makes this journey which involves locomotion. Hinduism, like Jainism, draws a distinction between *ātman* and *jīva.* When the soul occupies a body it is called *jīva.* While the *ātman* is free from joys, suffering, pleasures and pains, and unaffected by them, its union with the body makes it conditioned by these feelings and emotions. For example if we place a red cloth beneath a sheet of glass, the glass though transparent, *appears* to be red. But it isn't really so. It seems red only so long as the red cloth is beneath it. At the same time it shares the cloth's redness, even though temporarily. So too the embodied soul, the *jīva*, becomes a sharer in the ups and downs of the body in which it is encased. When we say 'I am wearied, I am distressed, I am happy, I am sad' and so on, we mean both the soul and the body. It is really the body which suffers, but the captive soul cannot evade the suffering. A very interesting question arises from this. Why do some men faced with the same amount of sorrow, feel it less than others ? True both the body and the soul are co-sharers in troubles, but their proportion can vary. This variation follows the extent to which one identifies himself with the body. To those who thus identify themselves completely, the suffering is most, to those who do not do so at all it is least. In between there are varied intensities of it.

So much for the embodicd soul. When it leaves the body, it moves with the help of the subtle body, the *sūkshma sharīra* (also known as the *linga sharīra*). It is conceived as the replica of the gross body but in a subtle form, a kind of thin wisp-like film encasing the soul and having the essence of all the parts of the gross body like hands, feet limbs and so forth. This is the soul's vehicle and accompanies it in all its wanderings, till emancipation (*moksha*) is reached. It is also the receptacle of all merit and demerit and of the tendencies which the soul acquires during its contact with various bodies. As Shankarāchārya says : 'The *sūkshma sharīra* is free from all union and unaffected by limiting factors. It performs all actions as the instrument of the *ātman*, as chisel and other tools do for a carpenter. For this reason the *ātman* is free from all union'.[20] The tendencies stored in the *sūkshma sharīra* are known as *sanskāras*. These *sanskāras* are a sort of record of the various inclinations of the soul., which in turn are governed by *svabhāva* or the nature of the human being. *Svabhāva* is in its turn dependent on the actions man performs. Man has the choice of doing good or evil, of helping others or bothered only for himself. Every action creates an impulse and these impulses combine to form that man's tendencies (*svabhāva*). The *Gītā* says that man has the choice of action: *Karmaṇi adhikārāḥ te* (2:47) But once the choice is exercised it becomes final. There can be no going back upon it. The accumulated acts become tendencies. Krishṇa tells Arjuna that man, even one who is wise, is bound by his tendencies. 'Even a wise man has to act according to the tendencies of his own nature. All beings follow their tendencies. What is the use of fighting against them (repressing them)?'[21] The acts and tendencies of each lifetime keep accumulating. These become *sanskāras,* and are contained in the *sūkshma sharīra.* When these *sanskāras* are good they lead to birth as a human being in good families. Krishṇa tells Arjuna : 'No one who does good can ever come to grief—*Kalyaṇakrita durgatim na gacchati.*[22] Since the choice in action is ours and it is from action that the entire chain leading to *sanskāras* is set into motion, are we to suppose that we are the controllers of our destinies? In order to answer this question we have to consider what action is. All our action, whether good or evil, whether by our hands and feet, speech or following from the mind's resolve, says the *Gītā*, have five constituents: the body which is the stage where all that happens to us takes place, the doer, the sense organs though which all works are done, the various kinds of endeavours, and fifthly the divine will.[23] Of these the first four are in our hands for the endeavours or the motives with which we work, are of our making. But the fifth is beyond our control. That is why human beings can never have complete mastery in works. All that they can do

---

20. *Vivekachuḍamani,* 102.
21. *Bhagavadgītā.* 3 : 33.
22. *Bhagavadgītā.* 6. 40.
23. ibid. 18. 14–15

is to act with due wisdom and discrimination and with a good motive. We have quoted the first part of Krishṇa's observation in the *Gītā* on works, i.e., you have the right to work. The second part is even more significant 'but never to the fruits thereof' : *mā phaleshu kadachana* (2:47). Thus what the outcome of our endeavours will be, we do not know. Neither can we have any control over that. And since destiny encompasses both the act as well as its outcome, we have no control over it. That is why the Moving Finger moves on after having writ, and Destiny guides our ends rough-hew them how we will.

MĀYĀ, OR DELUSION

One of the fundamental concepts of Hindu philosophy, and one peculiar to it, is that of *māyā*. The word, not having any exact equivalent in English, can be translated as 'illusion' or better still 'delusion', which is the closest we can get to it. In fact its meaning has been changing in its usage in the various Hindu Sciptures. It meant 'spiritual power', 'mysterious will-power' or 'wondrous skill, in the *Rig Veda*. In the *Atharva Veda* the mystery aspect was emphasised, and the meaning ascribed to it was 'magic' or 'illusion'. The sense of illusion adhered to it. But, as we have remarked, 'delusion' would be a nearer equivalent.

Māyā has be conceived to be the principle of creation. Often the entire creation has been said to be *māyā*, and Shankarāchārya used it to denote the illusoriness of the world. We will speak of this more fully in the section concerning the world as illusion. *Māyā* is said to be the power of the Lord, to whom it is subordinate as to the master his slave. In the *Gītā*, Krishṇa says that when evil prevails on the earth, the Lord incarnates himself through his *yogamāyā* (*ātmamāyayā*).[24] Thus it is power of his *māyā* which makes the Supreme Being take on a human form for the redemption of mankind. The idea is almost analogous to the concept of Christ in the Christian religion, except that Jesus came as the Son of God while Krishṇa was the incarnation of God (Vishṇu) himself. Christ too took human form as Jesus to redeem mankind from sin.

24. *Bhagavadgītā.* 4. 6.

He suffered on the Cross while Rāma (who too, like Krishṇa, was Vishṇu's incarnation) had to undergo his tribulations in the fourteen year's exile in the forest.

While for the Lord *māyā* is the instrument by which he executes his purpose, in its relation to man it is like the ever-delusory mirage. The reason is that factors like time, the taking place of events like birth, death, the states of existence like the past, present and future, and of the various lives on earth through which the soul passes; have quite different meanings and significance for God and man. For example, we know only the present life which we are living. Krishṇa tells Arjuna: You have passed through many lives. You do not know them, but I 'know them all'. So too is the case with time. Even we find an hour flit past as though it was a moment, when we are enjoying ourselves. But that same hour when in pain or sorrow, never seems to end. Much more so is the difference between God's experience of time and ours. What is a lifetime to us might mean just a moment to him. Then there is the delusion of attachment. We think 'this is *my* son, *my* wife *my* daughter, *my* husband' and so forth, knowing fully well all the time that these are only temporary relationship due to the accident of birth and are to end with the advent of death.

'Remember this O Mind ! Nobody is your own :
Vain is your wandering in this world
Trapped in the subtle snare of *māyā* as you are
Do not forget the Mother's name.
Only a day or two men honour you on earth
As lord and master, all too soon
That form, so honoured now, must needs be cast away,
When Death, the Master, seizes you'.[26]

When we view creation as a whole we find it beyond our understanding. *Māyā* is said to have three characteristics. It has the capacity to veil the truth by its quality of *āvaraṇa* (lit a 'cover' or 'screen' and misrepresent it by its quality

25. *Bhagavadgītā.* 4. 5.
26. *The Gospel of Srī Ramakrishna*

of *vikshepa* (meaning 'confusion'). For example the truth is that all men, being mortal, will die some day. Even though one is aware of it, he says 'Oh, so and so is dead', but never realizes that his innings will also end some day. Thus under the influence of *māyā* the truth of his death is veiled from him. Then again it is quite evident that it is soul which is the body's living principle, for when it leaves, life can't exist a moment. Yet misguided people, deceived by *māyā* take the body itself to be the source of life. Thus *māyā* misrepresents the fact of existence. The third quality of *māyā* is its inscrutability. It is impossible to understand it. there is a story narrated in the *Matsya Purāṇa* which illustrates this.

'No one can comprehend my *māyā*', said lord Vishṇu to the sage Sutapas who wished to know about it, 'and none has ever comprehended it. There will never be anyone who can penetrate its secret. Long ago there lived a holy sage. Nārada, who was the son of the god, Brahmā himself, full of fervent devotion to me. Like you, he merited my grace and I appeared before him, just as I am appearing now to you. I granted him a boon, and he too wanted to know the sercet of my *māyā*. Though I warned him not to inquire about it, he insisted just like you. And I said to him "Plunge into yonder water and you shall experience the secret of my *māyā*. Nārada dived into the pool. He emerged again–in the shape of a girl.

'Nārada stepped out of the water as Sushīlā, the virtuous daughter, of the king of Benares. And presently, when she was in the prime of her youth, her father married her to the son of the king of Vidarbhā whose realm adjoined that of the king of Benares. Sushīlā experienced the delights of love. When the aged king of Vidarbhā died, her husband became the king. The couple were extremely happy and lovely Sushīlā had many sons.

'However after some time a feud broke out between Sushīlā's husband and her father, and this ended in a furious war. In a single battle many of her sons and grandsons, her father and her husband, all were slain. Sushīlā was sunk in sorrow on seeing their bodies on the battlefield she got a huge funeral pyre lit and the dead bodies of her sons, grandsons, father, brothers, nephews and other relations placed on them. When the flames mounted she cried aloud "My son, my son !" and herself jumped into the blaze. The flames immediately disappeared and the pyre bacame a pool. Amid the waters Sushīlā found herself–but again as the holy Nārada. Vishṇu, holding the sage by the hand, was leading him out of the crystal pool.

'When the god and saint had come to the pool's edge, Vishṇu asked with an equivocal smile : "Who is this son whose death you are bewailing ?" Nārada stood confunded and ashamed. Vishṇu continued "This is the the semblance of my *māyā*, woeful, sombre, accursed. Not the lotus-born Brahmā, not any other of the gods, Indra [their king], nor even Shiva, can fathom its immeasurable depth. Why or how should you know this inscrutable".'

In the *Bhāgavata Purāṇa*, we are told that the sage Mārkaṇḍeya also wished to know what the Lord's *māyā* was. Vishṇu promised to disclose it. While the sage was meditating, lo ! a storm suddenly arose. There was deafening thunder. Lightning flashed all round and rain poured continously from the skies. The tremendous deluge rose and submerged the entire world and the sage saw only the huge waves of the ocean all round. The entire universe including heaven, earth, sky, the stars and planets were covered by the surging waters. Only the sage survived, awed, mystified and maddened by the deluge. He drifted helplessly all about, tossed by the stormy wind not knowing the directions or the earth and the sky. Conflicting emotions overtook him. At times he was overcome with grief, troubles and diseases and felt he was about to die. The very next moment he experienced pleasures and bliss. Sea-creatures kept biting him and causing him agony. Thus millons and billions of years passed by. Then he saw a young banian tree with fruit and foliage sticking out on a small piece of earth. One one of its branches he saw a lovely child of dark complexion and incomparable beauty. The baby was sucking his own toe. The very sight of that infant removed all the sage's grief. On going near him he was drawn inside the baby's body as though he was an insect. There inside the body of that child the sage saw the entire universe arranged again as systematically as it was before the deluge. He saw in the baby the gods and the demons, forests, countries, rivers, seas; time with its varied divisions – in brief the whole orderly universe. In excess of joy the sage proceeded to embrace the child, but instantly the infant, who was in fact the Lord Vishṇu himself, vanished, and along with him the tree, the waters and the storm. The sage found himself in his own hermitage, as though nothing had happened.[27]

On another occasion Brahmā stole the calves and cowherd boys of Vrindāvana. Krishṇa from whom nothing can remain hid, knew of this. He produced exactly the same boys and calves from his own body. When Brahmā came back after hiding the calves and the cowherd boys, he was amazed to see them all there as before. He acknowledged the power of *māyā* of the Lord who casts the whole world into delusion, but whom no one can delude.

The *rāsa krīḍā* of Krishṇa with the cowherd maids of Vrindāvana is yet another example of Krishṇa's delusive power. In this circular dance he assumed as many forms as the girls, so that each one of them found herself dancing with him.[28]

In the *Rāmāyaṇa* we have the episode of the sage, Nārada. He sat in meditation for such a long time that Indra, the king of the gods, began to suspect he was all out to oust him and become heaven's ruler. So Indra sent Kāmadēva, the god of love, to interrupt Nārada's meditation and defeat his attempt. Kāmā tried all his tricks, but failed to disturb Nārada. He begged the sage's forgiveness and returned. Nārada felt proud of his victory over Kāma. He went to Shiva and told

27. *Bhāgavata Purāṇa.* 12. 9. 1–34.

28. ibid. x. 13. 1–44.

him about it. Shiva knew he was bragging. So he said 'All right, you have told me, but don't ever speak a word about it to Lord Hari (Vishṇu). Even if he asks you, just keep mum'. But God's (Hari's) will is supreme [*hari icchā balavān*]. Nārada was so greatly filled with vanity that, he paid no heed to Shiva's advice and went to Lord Hari. The Lord heard from him all about it and said 'You are an observer of the vow of celibacy and steeped in wisdom. How can Kāma ever have any effect on you ?' But the Lord, who knows the hearts of all, knew that Nārada was prey to vanity, and as he is kind to all his devotees, he decided to remove Nārada's conceit. So the Lord evoked his power of *māyā [shripati nij māyā tab prerī]*. He created a city which was more glorious and lovely than heaven itself and extended to eight hundred miles. It was peopled by charming girls who exceeded in beauty even Rati, Kāma's wife. This kingdom was ruled by a king of the name of Shilanidhi whose court exceeded in grandeur even that of Indra. His daughter Vishvamohini was so beautiful that even the goddess Lakshmi wondered at her form. Nārada went to the king, who saluted him and bringing his daughter, asked the sage to tell him what the girl's future would be. As soon as he saw her, Nārada fell madly in love with her and forgot his vow of celibacy. He also divined that he 'who would marry her would have eternal life and the entire world would be at his feet. He prayed to Lord Hari to be his helper. Hari appeared before him and the sage told him everything. 'Please give me your form, Lord' he prayed, so that I may be chosen by Vishvamohinī as her husband. Do what you feel is to my advantage'. Seeing the result of his *māyā*, the Lord smiled to himself *[nij māya bal dekhi bisālā hiyaṁ haṁsi bolē dīnadayālā]*. He said 'Listen Nārada, a vaid (physician) does not give his patient anything which is likely to harm him. So too, I will do that in which lies your good'. The Lord made Nārada's face extremely ugly and repulsive. At the *Swayamvara* (husband choosing ceremony), Vishvamohinī was appalled to see the frightening form of Nārada. The Lord had also appeared there in human form. Vishvamohinī did not even look towards Nārada and put the garland (signifying her choice) round the Lord's neck. Then one in that assembly said to Nārada 'Just go and see your face in a mirror'. The sage went to a pool and looked into the water. He was enraged to find that the Lord had turned his face into that of a monkey. In his anger he cursed the Lord saying 'Monkeys will be your helpers. And as you have prevented me from union with Vishvamohinī, the girl I desired, you will also suffer the pangs of separation from your wife'. The merciful Lord honoured the sage's curse by undergoing separation from Sītā, when he incarnated himself as Rāma. Lord Hari withdrew the influence of his *māyā [nij māyā kai prabapatā karashi kripānidhi līnhi]*. The entire illusory city along with the king and his daughter vanished.

This is the Lord's inscrutable *māyā*, which must be distinguished from *māyāvī. Māyāvī* means trickery or artfulness. Demons possess such power. They can take various shapes and create different kinds of illustions, as for example Mārīcha become a deer to lure Rāma away from his hermitage in the forest, so that Rāvaṇa could carry away Sītā. However, while *māyā* is the power of the Lord, those exercising *māyāvī* power are gods, demons of false sages. The power of *māyā* is always for the good of mankind while the other is for selfish or evil ends.

The creation of illusion is *māyā* in its lowest reaches. In its broader sense *māyā* is the creation itself, and everything in it. As Prospero says to Ferdinand :

Our revels now are ended : these our actors,
As I foretold you, were all spirits, and
Are melted into air, into thin air :
And, like the baseless fabric of this vision
The cloud-capp'd towers, the glorious palaces,
The solemn temples, the great globe itself
Yea, all which it inherit, shall dissolve,
And, like this insubstantial pageant faded,
Leave not a rack behind : We are such stuff
As dreams are made of, and our little life
Is rounded with a sleep'.[29]

Thus in a sense the entire world and existence on it is a delusion. We have spoken about dreams. They vanish with

29. Shakespeare. *The Tempest.* 4. 1.

waking. So too the 'dream' of life vanishes when we leave the world, To the soul which leaves the body what are all the worldly relations with which the man was associated? Suddenly they do not mean a thing. When Arjuna was sorely distressed on the death of Abhimanyū, his son, and Krishṇa found no way to comfort him, he said 'All right, come with me. I will show you your son who is now in heaven'. Arjuna went with Krishṇa. He saw Abhimanyū sitting there and began to speak words of endearments. Cutting him short, Abhimanyū said 'But who are you? I do not recollect having seen you'. 'I'm your father' Arjuna said. 'Have you forgotten me?' 'I have had so many fathers and been father to many sons, in various lives. How can I know who you are?' Thus existence it self is a delusion just as dreams are. In the *Rāmāyaṇa* Lakshmaṇa asked Rāma to explain what *māyā* was. The Lord said, 'I and mine, you and yours—this is *māyā* which has taken hold of all living beings. The objects of the senses, and in truth whatever the mind can conceive,—that is *māyā*'.[29a] Does this mean that there is nothing in the world which is not *māyā* ? That would be denying the world altogether. It would be like admitting that a play is being held but denying the stage on which it is being held. The truth is that there is both the play and the stage, the world and the saga of existence. The difference is this. When the audience witnesses the play, or the movie on a screen, it is swayed by the emotions being displayed. Someone dies in the movie. We feel sad. There is a reunion amid celebration and song. We in the audience, feel elated. And all this, knowing fully well that it's only pictures projected on a screen. As soon as the movie ends everything is forgotten. Existence too is like that. Events keep happening. Births, celebrations, marriages, accidents fortunes, misfortunes, disease and death. Why they keep happening and why to some, not to others, are questions with we will deal later when we speak of sorrow and destiny. Here we are concerned only with the fact that they happen. When we are adults we forget what we were like when we were children. When we are old we do not remember the

---

29a. *Rāmacharitamānasa Araṇya-kaṇḍa.* 14. 1-2

days of youth. The events are the same, our reaction to them different. Things which were very important to us at the moment they happened are of no significance later. For example one had trouble with his boss. He wasn't getting along well with him. It kept him worried to death. He lost his sleep because of it. But the whole thing straightened out. The man changed his job, had a new employer and he was happy. The old episode which then vexed him so much was forgotten. Thus we move along in life from sorrow to happiness, from pain to pleasure, from regret to elation, helplessly carried along like a boat in a storm, till finally death puts a full stop, final or only for this life? We do not know and can only surmise :

'Tomorrow, and tomorrow, and tomorrow.
Creeps on this petty pace from day to day,
And all our yesterdays have lighted fools
The way to dusty death. Out, out, brief candle !
Life's but a walking shadow; a poor player
That struts and frets his hour upon the stage,
And then is heard no more : it is a tale
Told by an idiot, full of sound and fury
Signifying nothing'.[30]

Māyā dominates life. It deludes us into the fallacy that we are the shapers of events : 'I am the master of my life, I am the captain of my soul'. But really it is like the pieces of glass in a kaleidoscope falling into varied patterns as it keeps turning round. Call it chance or destiny or the Divine Will; it is something which keeps eluding our grasp. Though the comparison of waking life with the dream-world has been made so often as to have become worn out, it is nonetheless very apt. In the *Rāmacharitamānasa* Lakshmaṇa says to Nishāda: 'Meeting and parting, good and bad experiences, foes friends and those who are indifferent to us – all these are but snares of delusion. Birth and death, fortune and misfortune, works and time – all that which comes within the entanglement of worldly existence; the earth, home, wealth, country, family, heaven

30. Shakespeare. *Macbeth.* Act V Scene V.

and hell and so forth, whatever is within reach, what is seen, heard or thought of– all this is founded on ignorance, not reality. A king may dream that he has become a beggar and a beggar that he has become a king, but on waking neither the king has lost anything nor has the beggar gained anyting (i.e. on waking the beggar remains a beggar and the king, a king). So too is this delusive world. Thinking thus one should neither show anger nor blame anyone [for what happens]. All beings are plunged in the sleep of delusion and keep seeing various kinds of dreams. Only those sages who are unaffected by this delusive world are awake here. The soul is awake only when it has shaken off all the sense-pleasures of the world. When it is so enlightened by the removal of delusive pleasures, then only does it become godlike'.[31]

Of existence itself there is very little that we really understand. From day to day we irresistibly move, every morning waking with hope in our hearts. But he sun does not shine always. Dark clouds of troubles gather we know not how or why. Sometimes driven to desperation by some maddening grief the sufferer mournfully asks 'God, why me ?' To such questions there is no answer. It is the unknown factor working in our lives. That, we might know as *māyā*. It is 'the third' which Eliot speaks of, whom we do not really know :

'Who is the third who walks always beside you?
When I count, there are only you and I together
But when I look ahead up the white road
There is always another one walking beside you
Gliding wrapt in a brown mantle, hooded
I do not know whether a man or a woman
–But who is that on the other side of you.[32]

Rāma Tīrtha, who spoke sometimes in parables, related one about how 'The Pājī became a qāzī' (a high-ranking excutive officer under the Moslem rule). A Moslem emperor called his qāzī and asked him three questions. If he could answer

31. *Ayodhya-kāṇḍa.* 91 : 1–4, 92 : 1–3.

32. T.S. Eliot. *The Waste Land.* London : Faber and Faber.

them correctly, he promised to give him the governorship, a post the qāzī aspired for. One of these questions was 'What does God do ?' The qāzī's mind was rather dull, but he had a very clever servant called Pājī. The servant offered to help him out. He went to the king and said. "I will answer your question, but one who answers is a teacher and he who listens is a pupil. So I must sit on your chair and you on mine". The emperor agreed, and they exchanged chairs. But he said that if the question was not correctly answered, the qāzī would be beheaded. The servant then called for the qāzī. He made him sit in the place he himself was to occupy, asked the king to take the qāzī's place, and himself sat on the throne. "This is the way God works", he told the king. He turns a servant into a king, the king into a qāzī and the qāzī into a servant". This is just a story. But such a thing actually happened, and history has recorded it. When Humayun, the Moghul emperor, was once fleeing, having been defeated in battle by the treachery of his own men, his horse sank while carrying him across a stream. Seeing him in danger of being drowned, Nizām, a *bhishtī* (water-carrier) distended his leather bag (*mashaq*) and offered it to the emperor, who holding on to the bag, was able to safely get across. In return he promised the water-carrier to make him sit on his throne. The lowly man was made emperor for a day.

Thus we find *māyā* working; the strings that keep pulling the human puppets. Only we do not see the strings. This unknown factor works out our pre-ordained destinies. It is the Divine Agent which decrees destiny. We only live it out. How is it done ? We revert to what Krishṇa says in the *Gītā*, 'O Arjuṇa, the all-knowing Lord seated in the hearts of all beings, keeps making them go round and round by the power of his *māyā*'.[33] Every act performed by human beings may be considered as consisting of four stages. First is thought. An idea comes into the mind that one should do a certain thing. The second stage which follow the birth of the idea, is volition. Whenever we are set upon doing something, various alternatives suggest themselves. These are,

33. *Bhagavadgītā.* 18 : 61.

to use a cliche, the pros and cons, the arguments for and against. Then follows what we may call discrimination. In other words we think it over and decide what course of action should be adopted. It is from here the Divine Will, the Moving Finger takes over. We delude ourselves that it is we who decide. The decision is really made for us and from it follows the fourth and the final stage of action, the result. Since the Divine Will enters at the stage of decision, it can introduce certain new factors which will influence it and turn the scale in favour of one course in preference to another. Let us take a concrete example, an incident which actually happened and was reported in the papers. A certain pilot was scheduled to fly a plane on a solo flight. However, he felt a little unwell and another fellow-pilot readily agreed to take it. Just as he was about to start off, the other pilot suddenly arrived and said he was feeling all right. He would take the flight as originally scheduled. 'But it is just a few miles' his colleage said. 'I'll go and be back in a jiffy'. He started the engine and was off. After a few minutes the plane developed some mechanical defect and crashed, killing the pilot. Now why did the other pilot feel unwell and then well and insisted on taking the plane, yet his willingness came to naught and he escaped, while, the other pilot died ? It would be impossible to give any logical answer, except it happened because the moment of death of the first pilot had not come, while that of the other, had. Another incident, also reported in the papers was as follows. Some passengers were travelling in a bus. At one stop it so happened that a black cobra entered the bus from outside and coiled itself round one man's foot. Not only the poor man, all the occupants too, were scared to death. The cobra showed no sign of moving away. The passengers decided that the best course was to get the man out so that the others would be safe. So they made the man sit outside on a culvert. The place is full of trees and foliage, they reasoned. Quite posibly the natural surroundings would make the reptile slink away. The bus continued its journey. leaving the man, with the snake still coiled round his leg, to come by the next bus. The bus had gone just a kilometre when it fell into a *khud* (a pit) killing all those who were in it. As soon as this happened, tha cobra left the leg of the man sitting on the culvert, and disappeared into the thick roadside bushes. Thus the Lord, as the *Gītā* says, makes people go round and round (i.e., to do as he wills) by the power of his *māyā (bhrāmayan māyayā)*. But God does not do so arbitrarily. Largely it is according to the man's *karmas* (works), though God has final say. We will speak about of works and rebirth later.

In the *Gītā māyā* is often equated with *prakriti* (Nature). This is really a Sāṁkhian term. *Prakriti* is believed to be constituted of three *guṇas* (qualities). These are purity or goodness (sattva), activity or passion (*rājasa*) and dullness or inactivity (*tāmasa*). All creatures have these in varying proportions, and the preponderance of one of these over the other, determines the proclivity of a human being. The *Gītā*, however, conceives of *prakriti* in a sense quite different from what it implies in Sāṁkhya. In Sāṁkhya *prakriti* is an entity parallel to the *purusha* [the Sāṁkya equivalent to the *ātman* of Vedānta]. *Prakriti* in the *Gītā* is completely subordinate to Īshvara. While the *Gītā* subscribes to the Sāṁkhian view of *prakriti* comprising the three *guṇas*, it conceives of it as *aparā* (lower) and *parā* (higher). The lower *prakriti* consists of earth, water, fire, air, ether, mind, the intellect and the ego or the I-sense. The higher or *parā prakriti* is that which is the cause of the creation, sustenance and destruction of the universe.[34] Existence is nothing other than the interplay of the *guṇas*. Whatever actions are performed are because of this interplay. Good works are the result of the *sattva guṇa*, those involving activity rise from *rājasa*, and the man whose achievement is nothing, whose ideal in life is just ease, comfort and luxury, is impelled by *tāmasa*. The way to escape from the snare of the *guṇas*, or in other words from the clutches of *māyā* is pointed out by Krishṇa to Arjuna in the following words : 'That person is said to have transcended the *guṇas* who keeps calm and is not affected by their inter-action because he knows that all that's happening is due to them. He is neither attached

34. *Bhagavadgītā.* 7 : 4–6.

to the *guṇas* when they are active, nor longs for them when their activity has ceased. He is the same in happiness and grief (i.e. unaffected by either. He is calm and indifferent to praise or blame, Gold is as valueless to him as stones and mud (i.e. he desires no wealth). He considers alike foe and friend, honour and dishonour. He never initiates any works (as he has no desires). He has unswerving devotion to God and attains God, who indeed is the upholder of righteousness and the bestower of that happiness which knows no end'.[35] Thus according to the *Gītā* the way to get out of the clutches of *māyā* is detachment (*tyāga*) and complete devotion to God. Although wisdom and desireless works, too, can lead to this goal, Krishṇa advocates devotion (*bhakti*) as supreme [*Gītā*. 18 : 65-6].

The concept of *māyā* in the Vedānta revolves round the world's unreality. We have already made a mention of it. The idea has often been likened to Kant's doctrine of the thing-in-itself. According to him we can know objects only as they appear to our senses, not as they are in themselves. Only the appearance of things can be known. Thus everything appears only in our thoughts.

The representation of things as we see depends on our understanding and that decides their truth or falsehood. Schopenhauer also believed in the world as Idea. As such it has two fundamental halves—the object consisting of forms, space and time, and the subject which is not in space or time for it is present entire and undivided in every percipient being. Each of these halves appears with the other and vanishes with it. These concepts approach Shankārāchārya's idea of the world as illusion. Kant, however, does not believe in a soul eternal and everlasting. Death is, in his view. the end of all experience which concerns the soul as an object of experience. Bodies, of course, cannot exist as bodies apart from one's thoughts, but neither can the soul without the living body in time. Thus the concept of the *ātman*, which is a fundamental one in the Vedānta and on which the idea of the world

35. *Bhagavadgita*. 14 : 22–27. Not initiating works does not mean ceasing from works. but foregoing their fruits.

as māya exists, is opposed to Kant's doctrine. Francis Thompson's lines, too, have the import of the world being there, yet not there :

'O world invisible we view thee,
O world intangible we touch thee,
O world unknowable we know thee,
Inapprehensible, we clutch thee'.[36]

Shankara's guru was the sage Gauḍapāda, who wrote a teatise (*Kārikā*) on the *Māṇḍukya Upanishad*. This is in four parts, namely the *Āgama*, *Vaitathya*, *Advaita and Alātashānti*. We have already spoken of the *turīya*, the Eternal Witness, which is present through all the different stages of consciousness, namely, wakefulness, dream and deep sleep. It can't be denied that these three are not the same. Yet it is the same soul which passes through all the three states. To say that there is no difference at all between the waking state and the sleeping, is not borne out by experience. Shankara's views about this underwent a change between the time he wrote his commentary on Gauḍapāda's *Kārikās* and on the *Brahma-sūtras*. In the former he held that world experiences were like dreams, but in the *Brahma-sūtras* commentary he was of the view that the world of objects and senses had some sort of existence outside thought. For example if a boy wears a fearful mask, as boys often do in play and stares with it at a baby who has no understanding, the baby will be frightened. But a man who knows that the mask is make-believe will be indifferent to it. So too for the man who has spiritual understanding, the world still remains. But it has no effect on him. He is not deluded by it. But those who have not realized the Spirit come under the influence of the world's delusive power, its inducement of greed, honour and power and that which separates people into compartments of mine and not-mine. The difference between the waking experience and dreams may be summed up as follows. 1. The world and its objects remains for all in an identical manner, while that of sleep differs. For example, a chair, or a table, or a jug remains so for everyone. But all persons

36. Francis Thompson. *The Kingdom of God.*

do not dream the same dreams. 2. We have some kind of control over waking experiences. One may shift the table, or the chair, or the jug whenever he likes. He may turn on the TV if he wishes to watch it, or turn it off if he doesn't. But of dreams he is the helpless experiencer. 3. There is a positive sequence and orderliness in the waking state while the dream-world is topsy turvy. 4. There is continued remembrance in the waking state while most dreams are forgotten. So much for the differences. Now the similarities. The objects of the waking world evoke different reactions and feelings in various persons. One person may admire a flower, another be indifferent to it. One sees a bird like a stately duck, or a glinting fish as a thing of beauty. Another will think 'How delicious will its flesh be'. In the variation of thought the universal reality of the waking-world is questionable. Again, the waking-world is not a continuous experience. It is interrupted by dreams and deep sleep just as much as dreams cease in the other two states. The waking experience is also interrupted permanently by death. The waking experience, despite its comparitive reality is open to error. For example a rope is liable to be mistaken for a snake. And while the error lasts the reaction too follows the imagined object. Till the error of the snake in the rope is not removed, fear remains. The Hindu belief that the world does not exist for him who has realized his Self betrays some confusion of thought. The world ever exists. It constantly changes, as the Buddhists believe. But it keeps on existing. What really happens is that one's concept of it changes. And this is even for the same person. Things which attract one in youth, no longer do so in old age :

> 'Crabbed age and youth cannot live together
> Youth is full of pleasance, age is full of care'.[37]

What changes is really the thoughts about things rather than things themselves. It is true that we cognize the objects of the waking world in a consistently uniform manner. That is to say that a book is seen as a book and a cup as a cup by every person. But this is only under normal conditions. The person all of whose senses are working can cognize the

37. Shakespeare. *The Passionate Pilgrim.*

object in its entirety. It is very doubtful that the thing-in-itself exists apart from congnition, as Kant and the *advaitists* believe. Such a concept savours of mere hair-splitting. All that can be positively said is that the object is cognized so long as the senses are working. The waking world does not exist in the mind or in thought, but in the senses. Let us take an example. The blind poet Milton says :

'Thus with the year
Seasons return, but not to me returns
Day, or the sweet approach of ev'n or morn,
Or sight of vernal bloom, or summer's rose,
Or flocks, or herds, or human face divine;
But cloud instead, and ever-during dark
Surrounds me, from the cheerful ways of men
Cut off, and for the book of knowledge fair
Presented with a universal blank
Of Nature's works to me expung'd and raz'd,
And wisdom at one entrance quite shut out.[38]

For the blind person, much of the waking world of objects is non-existent. So it is for those who might have the misfortune of having been deprived of other senses—hearing, touch, taste and smell. Let us imagine the case of the person who has been deprived of *all* his senses. Does the waking world exist for him?

In a way it does, for it is still there. In a way it doesn't for it has no meaning for him. To him there is only this difference between sleep and waking—he dreams while he is asleep, he doesn't when he is awake. The knower of *brahman* is in a somewhat separate category. He cognizes the waking world just as much as anyone else. But his mind is not in it. He is like a man whose hook has just been swallowed by a fish. He is busy tugging the line, all his attention taken up by the task of getting the fish he has caught, out of the water. Someone who is visiting a friend stops at this

38. John Milton. *Paradise Lost* bk. iii.

moment and asks him 'Do you know, sir, where so and so lives ?' The fisherman does not even hear him. The man and his voice do not exist for him. So is the case with the knower of *brahman*. The world of joys and pleasure is there, but he is no longer interested in it.

Māyā makes us centred in ourselves, our family, our relations and friends. It makes us hanker after wealth with the greed of Midas. It encourages us to regale our ears with the song of the Sirens and to seek Elysian pleasures. It makes people fight and murder for property when it is evident that everything is God's—whatever there is in this changeful ephemeral world is enveloped by the Lord. Support yourself by renouncing it. Do not covet what belongs to others.[39] *Māyā* makes us blind with the darkness of ignorance, keeps us away from the quest of the Unknown and turns us away from God :

'All our ignorance brings us nearer to death

But nearness to death no nearer to God,

Where is the Life we have lost in living?

Where is the wisdom we have lost in knowledge?

Where is the knowledge we have lost in information?

The cycles of Heaven in twenty centuries

Brings us father from GOD and nearer to the Dust.[40]

As Yama, the lord of Death says to Nachiketas the *Kaṭha Upanishad* : 'To the foolish person whom wealth deludes, there seems to be no other world than this one. Thinking thus he does not escape from the cycle of births and deaths'.[41] Thus works that inscrutable power of God which Hindu philosophy calls *māyā*. As we have said, it also meant in the beginning 'wondrous power'. Though it would be preposterous to apply the terms to any but Hindu philosophy, we find instances of the Lord's power manifested in the Holy Bible also. The Lord appeared to Moses in fire that was not of the earth: 'and he [Moses] looked, and behold the bush burned with

39- *Īsha Upanishad.* 1.

40. T.S. Eliot. *Two Choruses from 'The Rock'.* Faber and Faber, MCMXI.

41. *Kaṭa Upanishad.* 2 : 6.

fire, and the bush was not consumed . . . .God called unto him out of the bush and said, Moses, Moses. And he said, Here am I. And he said, Draw not nigh hither : put off thy shoes from off thy feet, for the place whereon thou standest is holy ground. Moreover he said, I am the God of thy father, the God of Abraham, the God of Abraham the God of Jacob'.[42] The seven plaguers were brought upon the people of Egypt when Pharaoh did not let the Israelites leave. By the Lord's power the waters of the Red Sea were divided and the Israelites were able to go through the sea thus with their cattle and goods. But when the Egyptians pursued them the waters again closed in drowning Pharaoh's army. When there was no food for them in the wilderness, the Lord rained manna (coriander seed) from heaven for the people of Israel.[43]

Māyā in the sense of the wondrous power of God, is found acting in other scriptures also. But in Hindu philosophy it takes the form of delusion. We see it working day in and day out, making millionaires paupers and paupers millionaires, causing people is forget the purpose for which they have come into the world, namely to realize God, and instead running after 'woman' and 'gold', eating, drinking and feasting, till Death suddenly knocks at the door to says 'Your time is over'.

KARMA AND REBIRTH

The question Nachiketas asked Yama in the *Kaṭha Upanishad* was, When a person dies doubt exists whether that is the end, or is there some existence even thereafter. What is the truth about this?[44] This question has agitated mankind right from the beginning of civilization. The primitive man seemed to believe that there was some kind of life after death. As we have said they buried with the dead body implements and things used in living. The Egyptians believed that if the prescribed prayers were said and the appropriate ceremonies properly performed over the dead body by duly appointed priests it acquired the power of developing from out of itself

42. *Exodus.* 3 : 2–6.

43. Holy Bible. *Exodus* 7 : 14 et seq.

44. *Kaṭha Upanishad* 1. 20.

an immaterial body called the sāhu which was able to ascend to heaven and dwell with the gods there. The sāhu took the form of the body from which it sprang and was immortal, and in it lived the soul.[45]

Plato believed the soul to be divine. It has, he said, existed always, before its indwelling in any body and will continue to exist after it has won final release from its chain of incarnations. He was very emphatic about the soul being punished or rewarded in the next world according to its deeds performed in conjuction with the body. Plato expounded the doctrine anamnesis or recollection. According to this the soul has known the Forms (the Reality knowable only by the pure intellect) in its divine existence before incarnation in a body, and is 'reminded' of them by perceiving through the senses those particular things in this world which participate in them. Thus Plato believed in life after death and reward or punishment according to karma (works).

Religions, other than Hinduism, do not believe exactly in rebirth, but they do accept some kind of revival after death, the Resurrection of the Christians and Qiyāmah of Moslems. They also believe in Divine Judgment and punishment for evil deeds. According to the Holy Quran death does not bring man's life to an end. It opens the door to a higher form of life. The Resurrection is known as the *as-sā'–ah* literally 'a portion of time' or 'the hour'. According to Raghib, the lexicologist of the Holy Quran there are three such hours – 1. *kubrā,* 'the greater, which is the rising up of the people for reckoning, 2. *wustā*, 'the middle'. which is the passing away of one generation, and 3. *sughrā* 'the minor', which is the death of the induvidual. The *yaumul giyāmah*, is thus the hour of reckoning. Life after death is one of the fundamentals of Islam :

> And whoever desires the hereafter and strives for it as he ought to strive *and he is a believer*, their striving shall be recompensed . . . .See how We have made some

45. Sir E. A. W. Budge. *The Book of the Dead.*

of them to excel others, and certainly the hereafter is much superior in respect of excellence'.[46]

Islam also believes that good shall be rewarded and evil punished :

'He who has done an atom's weight of good shall see it'. 'And We will set up a just balance on the day of resurrection, so no soul shall be dealt with unjustly in the least; and though there be the weight of grain of mustard seed, We will bring it, and sufficient are We to take account'. 'And the measuring out on that day will be just; then as for those whose measure of good deeds is heavy, they shall be successful. And as for those whose measure of good deeds is light, these it is that have made their souls suffer loss'.[47]

It seems that the Holy Quran also believes in the grace of God. For one thing while the good are rewarded hundredfold, the evil are treated with indulgence, though they do not escape punishment. The Holy Quran says :

'The parable of those who spend their property in the way of God is as the parable of a grain growing seven ears with a hundred grain in every ear, *and God makes it manyfold for whom He pleases :* and God is Ample–giving, Knowing'. 'Whoever brings good, he shall have better than it, and whoever brings evil, those who do evil shall not be rewarded for aught except what they did'. 'And whatever affliction befalls you, it is on account of what your hands have wrought, and He pardons most of your faults'.[48]

The similarities between the Hindu and the Islamic views are obvious. Both believe in life after death, the consequences of good and evil deeds and the grace of God. However, the mechanism of afterlife is different. Hinduism does not believe in a particular day of judgment. The evalution of karma takes place immediately after the soul goes before God. Besides there is no resurrection, Day of Judgment, or as the Christian

46. The Holy Quran. Tran., Muhamad Ali, Lahore : Ahmadiyya Anjuman -I-Ishaat-1- Islam 1928.

47. ibid. 99 : 7,8; 21 : 47; 7 : 8, 9.

48. ibid. 2 : 216; 28 : 84; 42 : 30.

belief is, the Last Day. Neither Islam nor Christianity believe in rebirth in the sense that Hinduism does. The doctrine of grace, however is common to most religions. Christ said 'I am the Resurrection and the life'. Father O'Brien relates about a woman. fate had condemned :

> 'Some time ago we had occasion to prepare for death a mother who had been bed-ridden for several yaers because of a serious spinal injury. Widowed after the birth of her fifth child, she had worn herself to the bone to keep her little brood together, a roof over their heads, and clothes on their backs. After some seventeen years of incessant labour, which included taking in washings, ironing, sewing, and all manner of other work, she suffered an injury that made her a hopeless invalid with half of her body paralyzed. In the last year cancer set in. Always cheerful, never complaining, she bore her burden like the Christian heroine that she was, in spite of the intense pain caused by the inroads of the cancer. The joys which every mother craves, of nestling in the home she has made, of leaning proudly in the arms of her stalwart sons, of listening to the tender confidences of her lovely daughter aglow with the meaning and mystery of life at the threshold of romance, were denied to her. The sequel to her seventeen years of unremitting toil and four years of invalidism, she knew full well, would be death.
>
> 'One day when we visited her, the dread carinoma was eating like a glutton into her emaciated body and her failing strength told her that the end could not be far off. Out through the hospital window she could see people passing, happy, gay and free from care. Fighting to hold back her tears she said to us. "Father, these last four years have not been easy. At times the pain has been almost unbearable. I've worked so hard for my children. I love them and I hate to leave them now. But God knows best. And I bow to his will. But if I did not believe there is a God *and a future life*, I think I would go mad".'[49]

49. John A. O' Brien Ph. D., L.L.D. *Shall We Live Again ?* Paulist Press, 1946. pp. 18-19.

Dhammapada. 127. Trans. Paul Dahlke.

According to Buddism there is both karma (called in Buddhist language '*kamma*') and rebirth. In fact *kamma* is responsible for the chain of births and deaths, which according to Buddhism comes to an end with nirvāna or *nibbāna*. Escape from the consequence of *kamma* is not at all possible.

> Not in the heights of heaven, not in the depth of the sea
>
> Not in the caves ot the mountains, taking a refuge there,
>
> Nowhere at all may be found a single corner of earth
>
> Where, taking footing, a man may be loosed from his evil deeds.

Hinduism believes the last thoughts of the dying man determine the nature of his next birth. Krishṇa tells Arjuna : 'Whatever a man remembers when he is dying, he will become that in the next life, because he will think at the hour of death according to his ideas throughout his life. If he departs with my name on his lips, he will realize me'.[50] The Buddhist view is similar to this but not quite. At death the body is completely disintegrated and the mind ceases to work. But the last impluse of the mind before it stops (which Buddhists called *viññāna*) has in it the desire to enjoy or possess ,a clinging or grasping after life, which is conveyed to some embryo about to get life. This embryo can be anywhere. It can be in the nextdoor neighbour's house, or in some world other than ours. The result of an act performed is twofold according to the Buddhists. The one is immediate, the other timeless. For example a man collides against someone, which causes that man to fall in the path of an oncoming car and he is killed. Though the act was accidental, the immediate result would be that the man who collided with the victim may be beaten up by bystanders, or hauled up by the police at least for the time being. The ultimate result, which is not in the purview of human judgment might be in some later life. Here we see the similarity between Buddhism and Hinduism, for Hinduism also believes that the fruit of works are reaped in some future existence. An interesting point is whether there

50. *Bhagavadgītā*. 8 : 5–6.

is punishment for acts which, while causing harm and suffering to others, are unintentional and purely accidental. Hinduism does not clearly answer the question, but lays down *prayashichat* (atonement) which presumably clears the wrongdoer. In Islam repentance, if shown forthwith, gets rid of the evil consequence: 'Repentance with God is only for those who do evil in ignorance and then turn back (soon) . . . And repentence is not for those who go on doing evil deeds, until when death comes to one of them, he says, Now I repent; not for those who die while they are unbelievers'.[51] However repentance's reward is only for believers : 'And whoever desires a religion other than Islam, it shall not be accepted from him (fn. "as nothing but submission to Divine laws is acceptable to God"). . . Except those who repent after that [i.e. they first disbelieved and then believed] and amend, for truly God is Forgiving, Merciful. Those who disbelieve after their believing then increase in disbelief, their repentence shall not be accepted, and these are those who go astray.[52] The Buddhist belief is that the person whose accidental acts lead to evil consequences was unmindful. He did not have awareness. He was not bad but unskilful.

Reverting to Hinduism, it believes positively in karma and rebirth. Karma forms an essential constituent of the doctrine of the *Gītā.* Krishṇa says that no human being can escape from works. Indeed he could not even stay alive if he did not work. From the time we arise from bed till we go back to it to sleep, we are constantly engaged in works. Some works are done to keep alive. One has to earn his living. Others are those enjoined by the scriptures like *yajñas* (oblations) worship, pilgrimages, prayer and so forth. These bring a person peace and lift him up morally. Yet others are done for the benefit of others, like charity, looking after the afflicted, poor and heedy. Such works are termed as 'good' by the Upanishads. The *Kaṭha Upanishad* says : 'The good and the pleasant are quite deifferent. Good comes to the doer of good and he who chooses the pleasant is lost. Both the good and the

51. The Holy Quran. Trans. Maulana Muhammad Ali. 4 : 17.

52. ibid. p.. 65. 3 : 84 & 88–89.

pleasant approach a man. The wise man carefully discriminates between the two and sticks on to the good while the fool chooses the pleasant through avarice and attachment'.[53] The works we have mentioned before like austerity, charity, worship, purity non-violence and so forth are the good ones. The pursuit of wealth beyond one's requirements, of sex beyond marriage, of enmity, jealousy, crime, violence self-aggrandizement, the lust for power, envy, hatred and indulging in evil and vice, are works which debase a person. Krishṇa condemns the doers of these as of demoniac nature. Their punishment is descent into a lower form of life. The main teaching of the *Gītā* is that works should be performed desirelessly. When we make the fruits of works the incentive, works become impure and tainted. Besides the outcome is either elation or depression and disappointment. Both disturb the mind's calmness. Elation is like wine. The inebriation spurs the mind suddenly to galloping joy, and precipitately pulls it down to uneasy agitation Buddhism classifies pleasures too under the head of 'sorrows', calling them *viparināma-dukkha*. A happy feeling or condition, not being permanent, changes sooner or later. When it changes, it produces pain, suffering and unhappiness. Therefore even elation is not permanent bliss. As the poet says : Pleasures are like poppies spread/You pluck the flower, the bloom is fled. The *Gītā* says that true happiness is like poison at first but in the end sweet as nectar while the reverse is the case with deceptive joys. For example drinking. As they say, first the man takes a drink then the drink takes a drink, and then the drink takes the man. Telling ones beads or counting on the rosary is nerve-wracking to begin with. But it gives peace and calm in the end.

As we have said, the *Gītā* accepts the doctrine of rebirth. Before the soul acquires a human body it passes from birth to birth for countless ages in the realms of plant and animal life.

It is said the soul acquires a human body after 84 lakh previous lives. Men die at the time which has been preordained in accordance with their deeds. The nature of their deeds

53. *Kaṭha Upa.* 2 : 1–2.

also determines the path the departing soul takes. It goes either by the way of the *devas* (*devayāna*) to the the worlds of *brahman*, or by the way of the Fathers (*pitrayāna*) to the moon. The stages of these two ways are as follows :

1. *Devayāna*—The soul first passes through the world of the *devas* (gods) to the sun. From there it goes to the moon. There it is tested for its worthiness. If it passes the test it goes through lightning. A Person who is not human, but made of mind, then guides it to the world of *brahman*. In the coure of this journey to the *brahman*-world it sheds its good and evil deeds. The good deeds fall on the relations he loves and the evil ones on those he hates.

2. *Pitriyāna*—When the soul takes this path, it goes to the atmospheric world (*bhuvar-loka*) and exists as a disembodied ghost (*preta*) till the *shrāddha* ceremonies (prescribed by the Hindu custom, in which *brāhmins* are offered food to honour the manes) are completed. After that the spirit gets an adequate body and takes his place in *pitra-loka* (the realm of the Fathers). After dwelling there for some time, he goes through space to the moon. He remains there till his merit is exhausted. Thereafter he again enters space and passing through wind, smoke, mist and clouds, the soul is carried by the rain on the earth again. Thus brought to the earth it enters some vegetable plant and stays in that vegetable till that plant or vegetable is eaten by someone. The creature eating the vegetable determines the form the soul is destined to take by virtue of its previous karmas (deeds), devotion, enlightenment and so forth. For example if it is to take a human form, that vegetable will be eaten by a human being. If it has to be reborn as an animal it will go through that vegetable to an animal. Those good are born in high and noble families. Those evil acquire lower forms of life such as worms, moths, pigs, dogs, and so forth.[54]

---

54. The account has been given by Douglas P. Hi.ll : *The Bhagavad Gita* However the *Gītā* nowhere gives such an account in regard to the soul getting into the vegetable kingdom and then through that into the creature who eats it. The *Brahma-sūtras* do have this account. However they make it clear that it should not be taken literally. The plants serve only as a waiting place for the soul. The soul is a kind of guest there. The factor deciding rebirth is karma. See extracts from the *Brahma-sūtras* Section D. chapter 3. section 1. given in this book

There are others, who are the very wicked ones. They go neither the way of the *devas* nor that of the Fathers. They dwell in hell (*naraka*) and suffer agelong torments. If their evil deeds are not exhausted even after that they are hurled down to the nether regions (*pātāla*). Those whose children fail to perform the prescribed ceremonies following death, become ghosts. Krishṇa tells Arjuna that on rebirth, a human being takes the form which was the mode of his worship. Those who worship other deities are really worshipping me, he says, though with a mistaken approach. Such men must return to the earth (by 'other deities' Krishṇa means the lower forms of Hindu worship). Those who sacrifice to such deities go to them. Those who worship the ancestors go to the ancestors, while the worshippers of elemental powers and spirits go to them. My worshippers, says Krishṇa, come to me.[55]

The aforesaid Hindu concept of the soul's journey after birth and the manner of rebirth are doubtless fantastic. Most of this must therefore be classified as mythology, in which imagination can body forth according to the narrator's will. Nonetheless it is almost universally recognized by all religions that there is afterlife in some form. The Orphic religion which came with Orpheus in the 6th Century B.C., believed the soul to be an immortal god imprisoned in the body and doomed to successive rebirths, unless released by following the Orphic way of life. The next world was more real and important than this one. It was, as the Orphics believed, a place of joy and feasting for the blessed and of torment for the not-blessed. The Pythagoreans also believed in the soul's rebirth life after life till it purified itself by knowing the truth of its divinity and immortality.

While one cannot really prove rebirth logically, because the Unknown is beyond understanding, certain characteristics make it a strong probability. All persons are born with tendencies and predilections which cannot be accounted for by the present life. Let us take the example of Saul, who 'made havock of the church, entering into every house and haling men and

55. *Bhagavadgītā.* 9 : 23. 25. The two paths taken by the soul find place in *Gītā* 8 : 24–26.

women committed them to prison' (Holy Bible. *Acts*, 8:3); and breathed threatenings and slaughter against the disciples of the Lord' (*Acts*, 9:1); yet he became a staunch follower of Christ. This was because, in the words of the Bible, he could not 'kick against the pricks'. These 'pricks' are the innate tendencies of man which he is born with and which come from some previous existence. Peter denied Jesus thrice. Yet it was he whom Christ gave the keys of the kingdom of heaven. It is God who knows the hearts and all the lives of being; God alone. As Krishṇa said in the *Gītā*, 'Arjuna, I and you have passed through many lives. You do not know them, but I do'.[56] It is sometimes said that in such case it there is rebirth, man should rember the incidents of his past life, which he does not. We do not remember our dream experiences on waking. The effects of lessons learnt in boyhood do not last through old age. So too we cannot deny an earlier existence just because we do not remember the details of past lives. As we have said before, it is possible for the soul to move from one body to another because of the subtle body (*sūkshma sharīra*) which is its vehicle. We also find that often some children show intellectual advancement much ahead of what is normal at that age. That could be possible only because of extraordinary development in the past life. The famous Indian woman who is a wizard with figures is able to instantly work out sums which would take hours. The correct answer just flashes through her brain. Macaulay's memory, Kalidasa's and Shakespeare's unmatched genius, can only be explained by accelerated powers of the mind in previous lives. Sometime back there was the account in the *Reader's Digest* of Arigo, the 'doctor' with a rusty knife, who could operate successfully with just that, and affect miraculous cures. He was a surgeon in his previous life who had left his work unfinished and longed to continue it. God gave him the opportunity to do so in his next life. This man, Arigo, was born in Brazil on 18 October 1918. His formal name was Jose Pedro de Freitas. Early in age he would see a bright light 'so brilliant it nearly blinded me', and hear a voice

56. *Bhagavadgītā.* 4 : 5.

'that spoke in a strange language'. At about the age of 25 he began to have persistent dreams of himself being in an operating theatre. There was a stout bald man speaking to the nurses. in the voice which Arigo had heard when a child. This man said (in the dream) that he was Dr Adoplho. Fritz who had died during the First World War. His task was not completed and so his soul had entered Arigo and commanded him to complete his work. Dr Fritz's voice would speak to Arigo and he could hear it in his left ear. Arigo did countless operations with his knife without anaesthesia, antiseptics or sutures. They were painless and almost bloodless cases considered incurable were cured. Highly qualified surgeons testified to this by personal observation. While he was administering the cures his Portugese would acquire a thick German accent and his words were interspersed with German phrases. It wasn't Arigo, he would tell his patients, but Jesus who brought about his cures. He would say 'I do not want to know what your religious convictions are. All religions are good. Is this not true ?'[57]

The above account, compiled from authentic sources, clearly shows that there is rebirth. Man's innate fear of death is due to sufferings undergone in previous life. If one swings a baby from near the edge of a highrise roof stark fear shows in his eyes. Infants also take instant dislike to some people without apparent cause and are attracted to others. Their suckling of the mother's milk involves a rudimentary kind of exercise of the will (*saṁkalpa*). Sometimes the sight of a beautiful thing makes one wistful. This can be caused by the recollection of some love or friendship in a previous life. The birth of some human beings in prosperous and good families, and of others in poor and low famies could only be due to karma (works) done in previous lives. The Hindu doctrine of karma makes rebirth a necessity. One lifetime is too short to exhaust the consequences of accumulated karma and for the ultimate realization of *moksha* (emancipation).

The are hundreds of cases of rebirth reported in a Hindi magazine published by the *Gita Press* Gorakhpur, India. Two,

57. *Readers Digest.* May 1975. *Arigo : Surgeon of the Rusty Knife.* John Fuller. pp. 144–176.

however, are in the author's personal knowledge. These are given below (the names have been omitted to save embarrassement to the families concerned).

1. Son of an advocate of a prosperous Thakur family. When the child was about four year's old he was staring on the street from the balcony of his roof. All at once there was an accident and the screech of a car's brakes. The sound revived the child's experience when in the past life he was driving a car which crashed against another vehicle, killing him on the spot. He insisted on being taken to the city of– – – – –where he lived in his previous life. He was then in a Sardar family. He guided his parents to the road where he used to live and from there to the lane. In his previous life he was the son of a wealthy Sikh gentleman owing cinema houses. He rushed up the stairs to the room which used to be his, and recognized several articles of his which were in obscure places in the room and were taken out one by one on his directions.

The boy reborn thus in the advocate's family refused to have the customary hair-shaving ceremony (*mundan*) performed and remains unshaven like a Sikh and wears a turban.

2. The fourth son of a lawyer was being made to observe the ceremony which marks the child starting reading and writing. In his caste, the child is dressed up then in a bridegroom's clothes. When he was made to put on the dress, he suddenly got up and said 'No, I will not wear this because I am already married'. The boy recognized the woman who was his wife in his previous life. He himself directed his parents to the house in which she lived.

Works are of three kinds. One is those performed in the previous life which finds fruition in the present life. This is known in the Vedānta as *prārabdha* karma. Ordinarily the consequences of this are unavoidable. The second kind is *sañchita* karma i.e. accumulated works. These are works which have been performed in previous lives i.e. the ones prior even to the one immediately before, the consequences of which have not yet started bearing fruit. Then there is *āgami* karma which is works being performed in the present life. Whether we have any control on these is a matter not very free from doubt. If we believe that it is God who makes man do everything and man has no free will of his own, the question of our excercizing any control over works, even the ones being done in the present life, does not arise. We will take up this rather complicated aspect of Hindu philosophy presently. Meanwhile we give Swami Nikhilananda's analogy about karma:

> 'A hunter carries in his hands a bow and an arrow, and on his back a quiver full of arrows. He dischages the arrow at what he thinks to be a deer, and not wanting to leave anything to chance, is about to shoot a second one, when he discovers to his dismay that his target was man. In his revulsion he might now throw away the second arrow and also the quiver, but he cannot take back the arrow which has left the bow. The arrow which has left the bow represents the action which has been determined the man's present body; the second arrow, about to be shot, the action performed after the attainment of knowledge, and the arrows' in the quiver, the past actions which have not yet begun to bear fruit'.[58]

Two things are noteworthy in the view expressed above. The meaning of the word 'knowledge' and the significance of throwing away the quiver, which, of course, means doing away with the result of actions done in lives other than the previous one. The sense seems to be that the *āgamin* karma, the one we are about to perform is in our hands, in as much as we may avoid the evil consequence of deeds by staying our hands in time. For example if we are going to slay innocent creatures, but refrain from doing so on mature thought, we have averted an evil act which if done would have led to suffering by becoming *prārabdha* of the next life. Or taking another example, one is about to utter words that might hurt someone. But he makes a split-second comeback and stops them midway, so that they die on his tongue. It is not merely physical injury which pains but also hurtful words uttered in anger or hate. The understanding which makes a human being

58. Swami Nikhilananda, *World Perspectives.* London : Allen and Unwin, 1959.

desists from evil is not knowledge in its ordinary sense. It is the discrimination which comes from years, nay lifetimes, of discipline and the practise of virtue. The reward or punishment for karma also similarly covers years of lifetimes. The saints, the real ones, not imposters who hide selfish ambitions beneath the ochre robe, can never hurt. As the *Rāmāyaṇa* says they are pure as sandalwood, which imbues even the axe which cuts it, with perfume. They have triumphed over anger, hate, jealousy and sense-pleasures, What Swami Nikhilananda means by knowledge is not learning. nor wisdom, but the touch of divinity. Then there is the observation about throwing away the quiver. i.e. getting rid of *sañchita* (accumulated) karma. These works have not begun to bear fruit. Can one really escape their consequences, and if so, how? Once we believe that we can nullify works, we will have to admit that *all* works can be thus neutralized. Then why not *prārabdha*? The arrow has left the bow. But between that and its striking the target there is still a second. Much can happen in even less than a second. A boy fallen on the track can be pulled away before the wheels of an oncoming speedy train crushes him into pulp. A soul may come into a body, or go out of it in just an instant. A moment can make the difference between life and death :

> 'One Moment in Annhilation's Waste,
> One Moment, of the Well of Life to taste—
> The Stars are setting and the Caravan
> Starts for the Dawn of Nothing—Oh, make haste !'[59]

The question next arising is how can the effect of karma be changed? The doer of works is apparently man, though the view that man is only the plaything of God also finds place in Hindu philosophy (*Gītā* 18:61 and *Kushītaki Upanishad,* 3 : 8; *Muṇḍaka Upanishad,* 3:2:3). This in truth, is the vexing aspect of Hindu philosophy. We are told emphatically that karma determines not only reward or punishment for good or evil works, but also the form of future life. Yet it is

59. Edward Fitzagerald. *Omar Khayyam.* xxxviii ed. 1.

urged that God is the doer, not man. Nay, he even makes a man do works good or evil as he chooses. If man is not the doer of karma, why should he be made responsible for its consequences? It would seem that while God is the arbiter of destiny, he still leaves man free in some works. This is the vies of Sri Ramakrishna, the guru of Vivekananda:

> 'Is there anyone who has free will or anything like that? It is by God's will alone that everything has always happened and shall happen. Man understands it in the long run. But then something has to be added. Just as when a cow is tied to a post with a long tether, it can stand at a distance of one cubit from it or the whole length of the rope; so it is with the free will of a man. A man ties a cow with the idea "Let her lie down, stand or move about whenever she wills within that area". Similarly God has given man some power. And he has given him freedom to use as much of it as he likes and in any way. This is why man feels he is free. But the rope is fastened to the post. And mark this : If anyone prays to him in all humility, he may remove him to another place and tie him there; or he may lengthen the tether or even remove it completely from his neck. . . . There is, however, one thing. He does not give one power, if the little given is not properly used. That is why individual effort and perseverence are necessary. Don't you see everyone has to make some effort, however small, before he gets God's grace? When one does so, the experiences of ten lives are crowded into one and then all comes to an end'.[60]

That clinches the argument, but what is the 'effort' required to get Gods grace. Sri Ramakrishna mentions one – praying to God in all humility. The *Gītā* says that God's devotees are of four kinds : 1. The man who is grieved (he prays God to remove the grief), 2. The man of wisdom (i.e., the seeker of spirituality), 3. The man who wishes to get something he desires (he prays to get that desire – 'Seek and ye shall find') and 4. The man who wishes to know the true nature

---

60. Jagadananda Swami. *Sri Ramakrishna. the Great Master.* Madras : Sri Ramakrishna Math. p. 81.

of God. Of these the man with unswerving devotion, who wishes to know about God is the one who is the most favoured. 'Such a man loves me', says Krishna, 'and he is my beloved devotee'.[61] The significance of this is that God's grace is obtained by the person who strives for knowledge of God. What then is really in our hands for which men are judged ? Divine judgment is acknowledged by all religions though the name by which it is known and the modes of its working varies. Islam believes in *qiyaāmah, yaumul hisāb* (the day of reckoning) and so forth, Christianity in the Last Day and the Resurrection and Hinduism in karma. In his book *Life After Life* an American psychologist who investigated cases of people having after-death experiences (i.e. what they experienced after being declared dead clinically but thereafter revived), concluded that their souls quickly passed on to a Light, the kind never seen on earth and having a Voice too. The Light talked to the soul, but not in any earthly language. It was a kind of thought-communication, thought-waves going too and fro. The soul was shown a three-dimensional playback of the entire life it has lived on earth in the previous body. The Voice kept asking in a gentle loving tone if it had not been better if he had done something else instead of what had actually bee done. In other words gently and lovingly ticking off the soul for deeds which were not good. [For example it the person had neglected his ailing sister the Voice could ask 'wouldn't it have been better had you looked after her ?']. The Voice laid particular stress on 1. What the person had done for others, and 2. What effort he had made to gain *spiritual* knowledge, which the Vioce said a was continuing process through several lives.[62] The account testifies to judgment immediately after death, not at some distant period. Secondly, individual judgment on the basis of deeds for each soul, not a consolidated judgment of souls at any one time. Thirdly, that God is merciful. He is indulgent to faults, but nonetheless takes them into account and finally that reward and punishment must be according to karma (else why the playback and the questioning?). This investigation and the

61. *Bhagavadgītā* 7 : 16–17.

62. Dr Raymond A. Moody. *Life After Life.*

conclusions drawn from it, accord with Hindu philosophy. Dr Moody found that most persons after death found themselves, i.e., their souls floating encased in a gossamerlike film which contained all the limbs of the physical body in the minutest form. This sounds very much like the subtle body (*sūkshma sharīra*) the soul's vehicle which we have spoken about. The emphasis on doing good to others and the spiritual quest emphasised by the Voice are also to be found in Krishṇa's teaching to Arjuna. 'One who does good works never suffers' Krishṇa says.[63] 'The ignorant people work with a selfish motive, but wise men work for the welfare of the world'.[64] 'Pious men eat of the remains of the offering made to the gods but those who are full of sin cook food only to eat of it themselves (i.e. they care only for themselves and have no urge to help others)'.[65] So too the *Rāmāyaṇa* says : 'Nothing is difficult of attainment for those who have ever at heart the good of others'.[66] The spiritual quest has been constantly emphasised in the Vedānta. Just to give one example, Krishṇa says: 'The man who has mastered his mind, (i.e., controlled it), is indifferent to heat and cold, joy and grief, honour and dishonour'.[67] Once Swami Rāma Tīrtha took part in a competition to climb a hill in America. He was honoured with the winner's prize because he beat all others at it, but he declined to accept the award.

---

63. *Bhagavadgītā*. 6 : 40.
64. ibid. 3 : 25.
65. ibid. 3 : 13.
66. *Ramacharitamanasa*. Araṇya–kāṇḍa 30 : 5.
67. *Bhagavadgita*. 6 : 7.

A view which can betaken [it is the author's and not confirmed by any scripture] is that there is no such 'judgment' after death as Hinduism and most other religions conceive. All that happens could be a kind of computerized result. Every act, every thought of man is etched, like a song on a disc, in the sanshāra or tendency which accompanies the soul. All that is necessary is to computerize the conclusion. The sanskāras is the 'computer'. The whole 'judgment' is automatic. The sanskāras like the cassette which records the heartbeats in a holter test, are automatically interpreted. The soul is tehn consigned to the kind of life it deserves. According to this interpretation there is no Judge, no judgment, no cross–examination. The whole process is automatic and goes on thus for ever till the world lasts.

According to Hindu philosophy, therefore, karma is the deciding factor in man's destiny and in the joys and sufferings he goes through. The consequences of karma may not necessarily be worked out in one lifetime. Some karmas yield fruit early, others late. For example a lemon tree will yield lemons in 3 or 4 years. A wood-apple, mango or tamarind tree will take much longer. Therefore more than one lifetime is necessary to exhaust the fruits of action of a single life. But then even while man is reaping the consequences of works performed in previous lives, he is doing works in the present one. And these will again bear fruit in some future existence. Thus the whole process goes on in a never-ending chain. The chain can, however, be broken and ended for ever. Both grace and good works aid in ending it. God helps the spiritual man by carrying his burden, and by nullifying the consequences of his karma. Krishṇa tells Arjuna that he looks alike on all men, but he is in those who are his devotees and they are in him. And of such men, he says :

'Quickly I come
To those who offer me
Every action,
Worship me only
Their dearest delight,
With devotion undaunted.
'Because they love me
These are my bondsmen
And I shall save them
From mortal sorrow
And all the waves
Of Life's deathly ocean'.[68]

Those who call the world and worldly existence a vale of tears, the abode of death (*mrityu-loka*) or the house of sorrows, are likely to be dubbed as pessimists. Maybe there is some

68. *Bhagavadgita*. 12 : 6–7 Translation Swami Prabhavananda and Christopher Isherwood. New York : New American Library. 1944.

truth in it also. Nonetheless there is also much substance in the view. Life is not an unmixed blessing. Nor did there ever exist an Utopia on earth. That is the reason why all religions conceive a heaven which is free from suffering. Hindu philosophy considers *moksha* or emancipation as the goal of one who has realized God. We have already clarified that this is not a negative concept and does not imply the eradication of the essential in man. *Moksha* is complete bliss, unadulterated and endless. There is not even the shadow of suffering in it, nor uncertain happiness that ever remains poised on the edage of grief's precipice. The Vedānta believes that this state can be reached even in one's lifetime, though it is not easily got. For as Krishṇa says in the *Gītā,* only perhaps one among thousands strives for knowledge of *brahman*, and even among these there is some rare person who achieves it. The *Brihadāraṇyaka Upanishad* says :

> 'As one acts and conducts himself so does he become. He who is virtuous achieves goodness and he who is evil reaps evil. Others, howver say that it is desire alone which impels a man to action. As is one's desire so is his resolution. As his resolve, so his act. And as his act so the fruit thereof .. . . .So much for the man who is shackled with desire [He is reborn for futher works]. But death is no change for him who has no desires, who being satiated with desires, has become desireless; who longs for soul-knowledge only. Such a man attain *brahman* in this very life. His soul merges with *brahman*.

> 'When every passion vanishes
> That finds a home in the human heart
> He who is mortal becomes immortal
> Here already he has attained to *brahman*.'[69]

SORROW AND HOW TO END IT

To Sorrow
I bade good-morrow,

69. Brh. Upa. 4 : 4: 6–7 (verse from Paul Deussen. *The Philosophy of the Upanishads,*.

And thought to leave her far away behind;
But cheerly cheerly,
She loves me dearly
She is so constant to me, and so kind

John Keats. Endymion

What do you think, O ! monks ! which may be more, the flow of tears you have shed on this long way, running again and again to new birth and new death, united to the disliked, separated from the liked, complaining and weeping or the waters of the four great oceans? . . . But how is this possible? Without beginning or end, O monks is this round of rebirths. There cannot be discerned the first beginning of beings, who sunk in ignorance and bound by thirst, are incessantly transmigrating and again and again run to a new birth. And thus, O monks, through a long time you have experienced suffering, pain and misery, and enlarged the burying ground, truly long enough to be disgusted with every kind of existence, long enough to deliver yourself from it.

Samyutta Nikāya : Trans., T.r.v. Murti

To the Buddhists suffering is involved in existence itself. Buddha's effort was concentrated in the removal of suffering rather than theorizing about God, the soul and afterlife. He does not deny that there is happiness in existence, such as material and mental happiness, sense-pleasures, the joys of family life and so forth. But all these are included in sorrow, because they are shortlived. A beautiful person or a longed for possession makes only happy. But when one is deprived of that person or thing, happiness turns into sorrow. Suffering has, the Buddha said, three aspects. One is ordinary suffering like old age, sickness, death, separation from beloved ones, association with the unpleasant and deprivation of the pleasant, grief, lamentation and distress. In other words universally accepted pain and suffering. Secondly, suffering produced by change. That is change from a state which is pleasant to one which is unpleasant.

The third is the five elements of attachment emanating from the I-sense. These are matter (the senses and their functions, mental thoughts and the elements); sensations of various kinds, experienced through one senses (these may be pleasant or unpleasant); mental formations (all volitions, karma or *kamma* etc.); perceptions which are of six kinds; and consciousness, including mental consciousness and material, i.e., for external objects. These five constitute the ego or 'I'. They are all constantly changing and so impermanent. And what is impermanent is suffering. There are three distinct stages of suffering according to Buddhist psychology. Bodily suffering is of the lowest stage. Man shares this with animals. The next higher stage is mental suffering. This covers unsatisfied desires, the gap between illusion and reality and the disappointments that beset us in life. The third stage is when we regard the sorrows of others as our own. As the poet says :

'To each his suffinng : all are men
Condemned alike to moan;
The tender for another's pain
Th' unfeeling for his own'.[70]

According to the Holy Bible human beings were condemned to sorrow for not following the Lord's command. In the Book of Genesis God says : 'Unto the woman he said, I will greatly multiply thy sorrow and thy conception : In sorrow thou shalt bring forth children; and thy desire shall be to thy husband, and he shall rule over thee. And unto Adam he said, Because thou hast hearkened unto the voice of thy wife and hast eaten of the tree, of which I commanded thee, saying, Thou shalt not eat of it : cursed is the ground for thy sake; in sorrow shalt thou eat of it all the days of thy life; thorns and thistles shall it bring forth to thee; and thou shalt eat the herb of the field; in the sweat of thy face shall thou eat bread, till thou return unto the ground; for out of it wast thou taken : for dust thou art and unto dust shalt thou return'.[71] Thus sorrow comes to human beings because

70. Thomas Gray. *Ode on a Distant Prospect of Eton College.*
71. *Genesis.* 3 : 16–20.

they do not follow in the ways of God. But Jesus Christ, by his crucifixion took away man's suffering by his Agony on the Cross.

The Islamic view does not appear to be much different. Suffering is meant to turn men towards God, so that they may humble themselves before him :

> 'And We did not send a prophet in a town but We overtook its people with distress and affliction in order that they might humble themselves . . . And certainly We sent apostles to nations before thee, then We seized them with distress and affiction in order that they might humble themselves'.[72]

Hinduism, as we have said, believes suffering to be of three kinds (*trividha duhkha–trividha* = threefold; *duḥkha* = suffering). These are 1. Those that emanate from the sufferer himself. This is known as *ādhyātmika* (arising from the *ātmā* i.e. one's own self). 2. The suffering caused to human beings by other creatures. This is known as *ādhibhautika duḥka* (from *bhūtas* 'created beings'). This is the pain caused to men from birds, beasts and so forth. 3. Suffering caused by supernatural forces. This arises from the ill effects of stars and planets, evil spirits and *devas* (gods). This form of suffering is known as *ādhidaivika* (*daivya* 'divine'). According to the Sāṁkhya ordinary things, like money and sensual enjoyment, cannot remove suffering for it comes again when that enjoyment is removed. Thus the means of removal of suffering must be through spiritual realization. Besides material things can remove grief only temporarily and what is required it to remove suffering permanently.

Christianity believes that sin or sorrow can be removed through belief in Christ. Islam too emphasises that only believers can be freed of sorrow. Both stress obedience to God and Buddhism, which as we have related, makes a most thorough analysis of suffering, considers that it can be got rid of by the Eightfold Path. The four Aryan Truths of Buddhism are 1. Sorrow,

---

72. The Holy Quran. 7 : 94 and 6 : 42 Trans., Maulvi Muhammad Ali. Introduction p., lxvi. Lahore : Ahmadiyya Anjuman–I–Ishaat–I–Islam. 1928.

2. The cause of sorrow, 3. The ending of sorrow, and 4. The Way to end sorrow.

In the *Majhima Nikāya* the Buddha says : 'Just this have I taught and do teach—sorrow and the ending of sorrow'. The Way of ending sorrow is through the eightfold path (*aṭṭhangikama'gga*). This is in essence, a kind of code of ethics, which boils down to the practice of morality, mental culture and insight into truth. The path is 1. Right views, which means to see life as it really is, that is seeing it as ever-changing, insubstantial and fraught with suffering. The idea is that when a man realizes that life is like this, he is not disturbed or disappointed when he experiences it as such. As Housman says :

I to my perils
Of cheat and charmer
Came clad in armour
By stars benign.
Hope lies to mortals
And most believe her
But man's deceiver
Was never mine.
The thoughts of others
Were light and fleeting
Of lovers' meetings,
Or wealth, or fame :
Mine were of troubles
And mine were steady;
So I was ready
When troubles came.[73]

2. Right Mindedness. This means having friendly thoughts, with goodwill to all creatures.

73. A. E. Housman. Poems.

3. Right speech. This means speech which is truthful but not unkind, what may be termed in Hindi as *priya satya* (*priya* = loving; *satya* = truth).

4. Right action. This means acting with due foresight, with sympathy to all beings. At the same time avoiding violent effort (volition). This is what the *Gītā* (14 : 25) terms as *sarva ārambha parityāga*, i.e., not initiating any action [because the contented man does not feel that there is anything he lacks].

5. Right Livelihood. This means living in such a way that neither the person nor those whom he comes into touch with, infringe the law of morality. As Hindu philosophy would say, following *dharma*.

6. Right Endeavour. The practice of perfecting oneself and the pursuit of that which is noble.

7. Right Mindfulness. Having self-awareness, self-reliance, equanimity and compassion for all.

8. Right concentration. That contemplation which brings wisdom and intellectual intuition.

The chain that shackles people to the world of sorrow is as follows : From ignorance there is craving; from creaving, attachment; from attachment activity; and from activity, rebirth. This is the Buddhist concept of the Wheel of Becoming. Thus ignorance is the main cause of man's bewilderment and the suffering arising from it The *Samutta Nikāya* says : 'Existence is without cognizable beginning. Beings caught in the web of ignorance rush here and there, not knowing what to do'. Thus the culprit is ignorance. And this can be overcome by knowledge of the four noble truths of suffering.

Among the Hellenic philosophers, Plotinus has something to say about suffering. The suffering individual, he says has no more right to complain than the tortoise who is crushed under the feet of the choral dancers at the climax of that dance. Thus existence itself involves suffering, at least that of the physical kind. The wise man, Plotinus believes, may suffer bodily pain, but he does not feel it because he is detached in spirit. The higher self of man abides above in the spiritual world and does not take part in the conflicts and tribulations of physical existence for the ordinary man who is not able to rise to that level, who is not a philosopher, there is no hope. The weak foolish and wicked suffer because of their own fault. They cannot expect the gods to help them when they are themselves in the wrong. It is because of sinning that the soul enters a lower body, (i.e., of animal and the like. Thus soul-purification is, according to Plotinus, of the utmost importance. While we have the opportunity of having been endowed with a human body we ought to strive for the spiritual. This account of spiritualism recalls Shankarāchārya's observation: 'He who, hraving with difficulty obtained a human body does not even then strive for emancipation and instead runs after elusive objects, destroys himself'. However, it is doubtful if philosophy can mitigate physical pain. As Shakespeare says:

> 'For there was never yet philosopher
> That could endure the toothache patiently.[74]

What could be possible is that the subjective reaction to pain could be different. At the same time the extent of the Divine Hand in the alleviation of pain is certainly mysterious and often without any logical explanation. Let us take, for example, the case of Arigo, we have already related and which is based on substantial evidence. One of his many cures is narrated in the account. In this case the patient was a woman who was on her death-bed because of cancer of the uterus. The priest had given her the extreme unction and gone. Arigo bowed his head to pray. suddenly there was a strange kind of tingling in his head and his eys clouded. He took a large knife from the kitchen and plunged it straight into the woman's vagina, probing violently. Jabbing the blade several times he removed it and thrust in his hand. In a few seconds he pulled out a huge tumour. The dying woman made a complete recovery. She had been fully concious throughout and had felt no pain.[75] Similarly Arigo removed an almost blind woman's

74. *Vivekachuḍāmani.* 4
William Shakespeare. *Much Ado About Nothing.* iv. ii 34–5.

75. Reported in the *Reader's Digest* May 1975 John Fuller. *Arigo : Surgeon of the Rusty Knife.* p., 156.

cataracts from both eys with just a pair on nail scissors. There was no pain or bleeding. This was witnessed by Immesi, a judge. How did Arigo get these powers? He told the judge. Eleito Soares, who examined him, that he began with the Lord's prayer. He saw or knew nothing else. People said he wrote out prescriptions, but he did not remember having done so. It was the same with the operations he performed. 'I do not do it' he said. 'I am just an intermediary between the people and the spirit of Dr Fritz'.[76] Two points emerge from this. When a human being, endowed with God's gift can take away the pain and suffering of others, obviously hundreds of times greater must be the healing touch of the Divine. Secondly, physical pain is not immutable. Even a simple human device such as administering an anaesthesia can cause suspension of pain. We will consider the effect of one's mental and spiritual attitude to pain later. Meanwhile let us see what Hinduism is to offer as a panacea for suffering.

As we have said, the Sāṁkhya view is that suffering is due to natural and extrinsic causes like disease, infirmity etc., by other creatures and by divine and supernatural agencies. The Veda, the most ancient of Hindu scriptures, does not have any way out. Some of the Vedic sacrifices involve sacrifice of animals. Surely religions which believe that destruction of life and causing pain by offering animals as sacrifice, will find favour with God, are advocating a misconceived belief. Besides, ornate religious ceremonies require a great deal of money, and can be performed only by the rich. Sānkha offers only one remedy and that is knowledge of the Sāṁkhya-kārikā. This however, is dogmatic and hardly a solution. The Vedānta conceives of *moksha* or liberation. That could be a way out. But it is more or less begging the question. *Moksha* is the merging of the soul with God (*brahman*) and thus getting rid of rebirth. In other words since there is no more worldly existence there is no sorrow. That is like saying, because there is no pipe there is no tune. Since one in millions may achieve *moksha* it is not a remedy for suffering at all. We are concerned equally, or even more, with those countless human beings who

---

76. ibid. p., 165. and p., 161.

are still struggling with life. The conclusion one can come to is that while religions recognize sorrow, the general way advocated by them to avoid it is to follow their individual doctrines. This cannot be taken to be a universal remedy, though the followers of different religions might derive comfort from their respective faiths. The approach to suffering will therfore have to be an objective one.

The first thing about suffering is that it is universal. Like all generalities this has exceptions too. There are people who never have to suffer the agony of the deaths of those near to them, or diseare or the want of the wherewithal to subsist. But such fortunate persons are rare indeed. The only universal sorrow, which none can escape, is the fear of death. The next point is that the distribution of sorrow, like that of weath, is unequal. Indeed in some people it might be so concentrated as to lead on to believe that they were marked out for it. Thirdly, contrary to the belief of most religions, that goodness and the practice of morality (*dharma*) wins God's favour, we find in reality it is not those good and virtuous who escape suffering. In fact suffering appears to have no relation to the practise of virtue. Fourthly, pain or suffering can be (a) of temporary nature, like an illness or a successful operation or an accident like fracture and so forth, which comes and goes, (b) grief which is permanent, as for example the death of one's children (which is classed by Hindu philosophy as sorrow next in intensity only to starvation), deformity, disability to perform one's normal functions, like blindness or the loss of any of the senses, speech, hearing etc., loss of limbs paralysis and so forth. Pain which is of passing nature is an ordinary condition of existence. But that of the latter kind is as Wordsworth says 'permenent, obscure and dark. And shares the nature of infinity'. Fifthly, there are two aspects of suffering. One is the suffering itself, the other the sufferer's mental reaction to it. Sixth is the relation of the I-sense with suffering, which in this respect is like attachment. Just as attachment is less and less as ones circle widens, so does suffering. Putting it plainly one's own sorrows are sorrows, another's just nothing. One hears that someone's wife, husband or child has died. Maybe for an instant he feels sorry for the sufferer. That's all. But the same grief falling on him leaves him inconsolable. Our condolences are mere lip-service. As the Holy Bible says: 'Is it nothing to you, all ye that pass by? behold, and see if there be any sorrow like unto my sorrow'.[77] The natural instinct of human beings is to feel only their own suffering. But as we have said in another context, when one is able to get out of his shell of himself and his family he feels the sufferings of others too, at least to some extent. And particularly so if he has himself suffered. As Philemon says:

'From suffering learn too to sympathize
Who's suffered thus shall sympathize with thee'.[78]

Finally there arises the questions, Why should there be suffering at all? The view that everything is suffering, even joy and happiness, seems to be an extreme view. However quite a bit of life, is.

These being the fundamentals of suffering, let us see what Hinduism has to say about it, for we are considering here chiefly its doctrines. The universality of suffering has almost the same significance in it as in Buddhism and as in the philosophy of Plotinus, which we have narrated. Existence itself involves suffering. The world is called in the *Gītā* the abode of sorrows Once there is birth there is also disease, old age and death. Existence brings with it attachments. When one becomes attached to a person or a thing (the Sanskrit *bhūta* includes both – from *bhava* = 'becoming') the deprivation of that thing or person, causes sorrow. That is why the *Gītā* says that *sanga* (attachment) sets a chain-reaction which finally results in the man's destruction.

The chain is gloating over sense–objects – attachment to them – desire for them – anger when one is thwarted in this desire – bewilderment – loss of memory i.e. confusion – destruction of the power to discriminate–complete cessation of the wherewithal to act i.e. unfitness to do any thing (as Arjuna's state was when he cast down his bow and arrows – *visrijya sasharam chāpam* : *Gītā* 1–47). Ordinary human beings cannot escape

77. *Lamentations.* i. 12.

78. Philemon. *Fabulae Incertae. Fragment* 51 B.

this chain-reaction. And the inability to do so causes frustration and sorrow. It is only the saints who can rise above attachment. But the world consists largely of ordinary men. Existence also causes inevitable suffering in the deaths of those who are near, old age disease and death (*jarā-maraṇa*). Such suffering is inescapable. Hindu philosophy does not, however rule out pleasures and happiness. But the wise man remains the same in both. Pleasures do not make him lose his balance nor do sorrows grieve him. Krishṇa tells Arjuna repeatedly that the man of settled intelligence is the same in heat and cold, sorrow and pleasures—*samaduhkha sukhaḥ* (*Gītā,* 14 : 24 etc).

Suffering is unequally distributed. The reason for this, as explained by Hindu philosophy, is a man's karma, the deeds performed by him in various lives. These account for suffering. The *Rāmacharitamānasa* says : 'Birth, death, pleasure and pain, enjoyment, loss and gain, meeting and parting are dependent on time and works (karma). They keep ever occurring as night and day. Foolish people find joy in pleasure and lament when in sorrow. But wise people are the same in both'.[80] We have already accounted for the contradiction in the view that on the one hand it is God who makes us do works as he wills and on the other we suffer for our deeds. It's like a murder case in which the judge announces the death sentence. The president may, however grant a reprieve and reduce it to life imprisonment. But he will also take the circumstances of the case into consideration. If its a wilful brutal murder he will perhaps refuse to interfere. If there are extenuating factors he may reduce the sentence. So is the case with the grace of God. He has the final say. But he does not act arbitrarily. To receive his grace one must prove worthy of it. There can be various views about how much is in our hands and in how much we are driven helplessly on according to destiny or God's will. Tusidāsa says : 'Loss and gain, birth and death, honour and dishonour are in the hands of God'.[81] According to the *Gītā,* our right is to do works only. The result of works is in the hands of God. Yet another view, also endorsed by the *Gītā,* is that man

80. *Ayodhyā-Kāṇ ḍa,* 14. 9 : 3.

81. *Rāmacharitamānasa. Ayodhyā-kāṇḍa,* 171.

wrongly believes himself to be the doer of action. It is really God who works through him. An interesting, though not very convincing story, is related to account for the suffering of those good. Once Lakshmī and Nārāyaṇa came down to the earth. The Lord went to the house of a staunch devotee. The man instantly recognized him and most reverentially prostrated himself. He brought water and washed the Lord's feet. Making the divine couple sit on a high seat he served them fruits and the choicest of sweets. After the Lord had eaten, he made ready to depart. While going he said 'May your son die'. The man had only one son whom he loved very much. As soon as Nārāyaṇa had spoken, the boy feel down dead. Thereafter Lakshmī and Nārāyaṇa went to the house of a very wealthy man. He was counting out his money, and was annoyed to be interrupted. 'What a time to come' he shouted, 'Can't you see I'm busy. Scram !' The Lord turned back and on departing bessed him saying 'May your wealth increase fourfold'. Lakshmī could contain herself no longer. 'Strange my Lord', she exclaimed. 'Is this the way to treat your devotees? That man to whom we first went and who was so devoted to you, you gave the sorrow of the death of his only son. And this other, who seems to be averse to you, you gave untold weath !' 'Ah ! Lakshmī', the Lord said, 'you have not understood. That man who welcomed us is almost mine. The only thing which prevents him from attaining me is his attachment to that son of his. I have removed that obstacle. Now he will speedily come to me. And that other man is miles away from me. He can never reach me. So I thought, why not throw him a little further away'. Ovid says :[82]

> Those who are suffering e'en the gods will spare
>
> And grant them at the last surcease from pain.

And Hypsaeus : He whom the gods love dies young'.[83] Thus God seems to consider existence to be full of sorrow, or else he would not call his loved ones back so soon! This

82. Trede mihi miseris coelestia numina parcunt,
Nec semper leasos et sine fine premunt.
Ovid. *Epistolae ex Ponto,* III. 6, 21.

83. Hypsaeus. Stobaeus. Florilegium, CXX, 13.
(Also Menander. DisExaparaton. Fragment 4).

is in agreement with the *Gītā* calling the world an abode of sorrows. Also, it seems God imposes suffering on those he loves. As heating gold red-hot in fire removes the dross and purfies it, and also tests its purity, so too it seems suffering is the testing ground of devotion. The man whose faith remains unshaken when sorrows lay him low is the true devotee. All lamps will burn in a windless place. But only the one whose flame is strong will survive stormy winds. Meister Eckhart says:

> 'Five things there be which in whomever has them are sure signs that he will never lapse from God. First, though most grievous things befall this man from God or creature, never a murmur does he make; no word but praise or thanks is ever heard. Again, at the most trying times he never says one word in his excuse. Thirdly, this man desires of God what God will freely give and nothing else; he leaves it all to him. Fourthly, nothing in heaven or earth can ruffle him; so settled is his calm that heaven and earth in topsy-turveydom would leave him quite content in God. Fifth, nothing in heaven or earth can cheer him; for having reached the point where naught in heaven or earth can sadden him so neither can it gladden him, except as trifles can'.[84]

In regard to the suffering which is of a permanent nature the only way out is acceptance As we have said in the earlier part of this introduction, acceptance does not come easily, It involves a struggle, the end of which is resignation to suffering, willingly or unwillingly. Some people accept it as destiny, which in effect is the same as God's will, for it is he who it the dispenser of fate. Tulsidāsa says : 'Whatever happens is ordained by the Lord. Why should men question it and give rein to doubt?'[85] Then, 'Whatever is destined by God cannot be averted by the gods, demons, human beings, nāgas, nor the sages'.[86] There remains the question of one's own sorrows as against those of others. Krishṇa praises that man as being near to him, who hates no living creature and

84. Franz Pfeiffer. Meister Eckhart.

85. *Rāmachritamānasa. Bāla–kāṇḍa.* 51 : 4. *hoihi soī jo Rāma rachi rākhā/ko kari tarka baṛhāvai sākhā.*

86. ibid. 68. *jo bidhi likhā lilāra/ deva danuja nara nāga muni, kōu na meṭanihara.*

87. *Gītā.* 12 : 13.

whose heart goes out to all beings and who sees the same soul in every creature.[87] That man has realized God who knows that the same *ātman* which is in him is in all other beings, and all creation is in that *ātman.* He is so much concerned about the sorrows of others that he actually feels them as his own : *ātmaupamyēna sarvatra samam pasyati vā sukham yadi vā duḥkham.*[88] As Euripides says :

'A friend in troubles faithful, is a sight
More welcome than a calm sea is to sailors'.[89]

Thus there are people of different grades of sympathy. One kind are indifferent to sorrows of others than their own. Another realize the sorrows others. Finally there are those to whom the sorrows of the world are as their own. They are the ones who truly realize the soul's universality. they are like the bow which when it plays a mournful tune on the violin strikes every string on it to draw out the tragic not A saint can take on the sorrow of others even to the extent of transferring another's disease on to himself. Nag Mahasay, a disciple of Sri Ramakrishna had such power. When Ramakrishna was himself suffering from fatal cancer of the throat, his disciples insisted that he should go to Mother Kalī and pray to her to cure him. He came back and told Naren (Vivekananda), 'I said to her I couldn't eat anything because of the pain in my throat. "Please make it possible for me to eat just a little". The Divine Mother showed all of you [his disciples] to me and said "Why, you are eating through so many mouths!"' Krishṇa appeased the hunger of all people in the world, particularly of the sages who had come to Kuntī's cottage when the Pāṇḍavas were in exile, by himself eating half a grain of boiled rice. The reaction to suffering depends undoubtedly to a great extent on one's mental attitude. For example once Karṇa of the *Mahābhārata,* who was really one of the Pāṇḍavas, was attacked by a creature of the forest. It went on hurting him almost beyond endurance. Karṇa bled profusely. But he silently bore the pain because his guru was asleep, his head pillowed on his thighs.

88. ibid. 6. 29–32.

89. Euripides. Orestes, 727.

Thus there are various attitudes to suffering. The noblest is the one conceived by *Gītā* in which one feels the world's sorrows as intensely as his own.

THE WORLD AS IDEA

We have spoken of the *turīya* state of the soul's consciousness. This is the Eternal Witness through all the three states of waking, dreams and sleep. There are three stages in the philosophy of *advaita*, of which Shankara is the main exponent, about the unreality of the world. The first is that the world is absolutely unreal. This is something which is impossible to conceive. For example a hare with horns. We all know that there can't be such a hare. The next stage is what we may call the seemingly real. This 'reality' has a temporary and apparent existence. The classical example is the snake in the rope. or silver in a lump of nacre (mother of pearl). One who sees a rope lying ahead and mistakes it for a snake, is possessed of the same fear as a snake causes. This fear can go away only when the misconception is removed. So is the case with the man who mistakes nacre for silver. Thus the 'snake-in-the-rope' and the 'nacre-in-silver' has a temporary 'existence', till the doubt is cleared. But till then the illusory serpent and silver exist. Shankara believed the same thing about the world of existence. He says : 'Though the universe is the subject of daily experience and constant intercourse, it is unreal like a dream in as much as its *existence* even in the moment next to its birth is not provable. For instance dreams are unreal on waking; nor is the waking state possible in dreams. Both are not to be found in dreamless sleep. And the condition of dreamless sleep is not found in waking and dream. Thus these three states (waking, dream and dreamless sleep) are merely the creations of *māyā* (delusion). The Real stands apart as the Witness of all these conditions . . . The jar exists in earth, the ring in gold and silver in nacre—*but in mere name.* So too is the existence of *jīva* in *brahman*'.

We have, therefore, so to say, three states—the absolutely unreal, the apparently real, and the Real amid the unreal. However Shankara went all out to contradict the Bauddhas in their own denial of an external world of objects. They maintained that there was no difference at all between the world of dreams and the world of external objects. The notions of external things like a pot, cloth and so forth, can be accounted for by *saṁskāras* or mental impressions left by previous experience even as impressions of the waking state give rise to a number of experiences of the dream state. In trying to contradict the Bauddhas, Shankara had to somewhat modify his own original view of the world as illusion. The *Brahma-sūtras* said 'External things are experienced. Hence it cannot be said that they are non-existent. The waking state is not like that of dreams, because the state of consciousness between the two differs'.[91] Thus Shankara's idea of the illusoriness of the world underwent change between the time he wrote his commentary on Gaukapāda's *Kāriḍās* and that on the *Brahma-sūtras.* Previously he considered world-experiences exactly like those of dreams. Later he affirmed that the world of objects and senses has some kind of existence outside thought also. The Vedānta too accepts the latter view. Indeed one must allow that the two have some differences too. For exmaple. dreams are seen and sooner or later forgotten. Thus they have a momentary existence. The world is something continuous in form *as well as in thought.* One remembers on waking whatever one had resolved to do the previous day. All the objects, as for example a book, a file, a vase, his wrist-watch, are all where he placed them. The dreamer has absolutely no control over what he dreams. And neither is there any logical connection in the sequence of what he sees

---

90. Shankarāchārya. *Aprokshanubhūti* 56–60.

91. 2.2 29–29 [*nābhāvaḥ upalabdheḥ* (sūtra 28) *vaidhamaryā cha na svapnādivat* (sūtra 29).

92. For the purpose of illustration, the author gives below a brief account of one of the dreams seen by him and remembered next morning: 'I am in a small inspection house. A young man who gives his name as Mathur and says he is a lecturer, is there also. Lask someone to get me some information. He retorts "You are very lazy. Why can't you find it out yourself". A boy and a girl come in and say someone is very ill. Can I perform his funeral rite. I say I can't do it as I do not know the Moslem way—the the man is a Moslem. An old man totters while coming through the door. His leg gets entangled in an electric wire. Mathur scolds him for it. I say "Was there any current in the wire ?" Food arrives. There is some liquid in small bottles. I pour some into a wine-glass. But it is flat at the top and the liquid spills out. My wife, who is there, says, "Drink it straight from the bottle". There is a tall building, built on a very small space with English inscriptions on it'. One cannot equate all this with orderly, consistent waking experience.

in dreams. Also while the objects of the external world are vividly experienced by *everyone*, dreams are the individual creation of the dreamer's mind. The vividness, too, is absent.[92]

There are, however, two similarities between the dream experience and that of waking. Firstly, both cause reactions in the mind which have a kind of uniformity. If one sees a burglar, a tiger about to pounce, someone near pointing a knife or dagger at the sleeper, in dreams; the emotion of fear is created just as it would be in life. So with other feellings like joy, sorrow, rage and the like. Secondly both states—the dream as well as the waking—are non-continous inasmuch as they are terminated by each other.

The real meaning of the world being illusory seems to be 1. Mostly it is out of our control. We are helplessly drawn to works as volition directs. Assuredly thought, or deliberation precedes action. So while what we *see* is not illusory, what we *do* is. And here we have not much more control than over dreams. A thought comes into the mind. 'I must do this'. Say, it is to go and buy something. On the way however the scooter hits a road-divider. It falls. The rider gets a fracture, and instead of buying what he set out to, he lands in a hospital where his broken hand is plastered. Who sends the thoughts? Of course it is the mind that thinks. But why should the mind think one thought in preference to another? And here, as we have quoted Krishṇa before, comes the truth that we are made to determine a particular course of action. 'Arjuna, the Lord seated in the hearts of all beings as firmly as the driver of some machine, keeps making them go round by the power of his *māyā* ?[93] It is clear therefore, that little of what happens to us is in our control. What *is*, we have already discussed earlier when speaking of fate and free will.

The external world obviously comes to a dead end when death comes. Hinduism, however, believes it can be ended also, in a sense, by realization of *brahman*. The world remains. Only to one who has realized *brahman* its turbulence ceases to exist. It's like the sea. While previously the waves had tossed and the water foamed, it is now a calm sheet of water.

93. *Bhagavadgītā.* 18 : 61

It's not that the man has no more setbacks and sorrows. But they have ceased to disturb him. In the words of Morris he is above the tumult of the living world :

> 'Thou shalt do the deed and abide it, and sit on
> thy thone on high.
> And look on today and tomorrow as those
> that never die'.[94]

Such a knower of *brahman* is the man who has conquered his lower self by the higher. Having realized that he is not the doer of works he surrenders all works to God. But this *brahman*-knower is not to be found in air-conditioned houses of the modern styled *maharshis* and *āchāryas*. He does not have untold wealth like they have. He does not possess and move about in stately foreign cars, Planes and coptors. He does not surround himself with lovely young girls calling them 'secretaries' or 'disciples' as camouflage for his sensual delights. Nor is the *brahman*-knower to be found among the ocre-robed sadhus with matted locks. Shankarāchārya says: 'With' matted hair, shaven head, plucked hair, and dressed in coloured cloth and various other kinds of garments, the fool appears in many forms for the sake of filling his belly. Even seeing this, he does not actually see'. But the true yogi is one who lives in temples under trees, sleeps on the ground, wears only a loin-cloth and renounces all enjoyments . . . .Wearing only the tattered garment found on the road, and following the path devoid of both merit and demerit, the yogi, engrossed in deep meditation, rejoices like a child or a madman'.[96] Thus the knower of *brahman* never advertises himself. In fact he shuns people. Most think him a crank a madcap or a crazy person. He does not go out to people, and loves to live far away in solitary places, caves, forests and hills. But he has attained liberation even in this life. What is that which he has attained and which people strive for; which is, according to Hindu philosophy the goal of existence? That thing, called *moksha*, we will go on to relate.

---

94. William Morris. *The Wisdom of Brynhild.*
95. Shankarāchārya. *Bhaja Govindam.* 14. Divine Life Society Rishikesh.
96. ibid. 18 & 22.

REACHING THE GOAL–*MOKSHA*

For the majority of people it is very difficult to conceive of anything other than the world. Everyone knows about the inevitability of death. No one, of what follows it. Buddha was reluctant to go into things which were speculative, things like afterlife and so forth. He was silent about such things. Though Buddhism does speak of nirvāṇa, the Hindu equivalent of *moksha*, it is not so forcefully expressed as moksha is. Nirvāṇa is the reality beyond all change, unfading, calm, undecaying pure and full of bliss. It is the realization of truth. Literally the Buddhist nirvāṇa, or *nibbāna*, means the blowing or going out of a flame. The *Anguttara Nikāya* gives a more positive definiton. It says that nibbāna means the destruction of craving and passion. It is the cessation of all works and of all that causes rebirth. Sometimes it is conceived by Buddhism to be like a dying flame which no one knows where it went. The *Dhammapada* says : 'Now are you seen. O builder of the house, you will not build the house again. All your rafters are broken, your ridgepole is destroyed, your mind set on the attainment of nirvāṇa has attained the extinction of desires'.[97]

The Buddhist idea has been set forth to show that it does bear some similarity to the Hindu concept. In bothliberation implies bliss. It is the cessation of rebirth (as the Anguthara Nikāya says). Nonetheless, even if nibbāna is not wholly nihilistic, it wavers between the positive and the negative. As one writer says according to the Buddhist concept 'the Annihilationists who taught the destruction death of the soul, were in error as much as the Eternalists who taught its continued existence'.[98] The fundamental concept of Hinduism about *moksha* is firstly, that it is a state of *unending* bliss (*akhaṇḍa sukh*); and secondly that it can be achieved either after death of the body or even in one's own lifetime. The world is not annihilated. Only the person who has achieved *moksha* in his lifetime is no longer attached to it. According to Shankara, *moksha* is absolute reality. It is changeless, immutable, eternal and like ether all-penetrating. It is undivided and completely satisfying. Its nature is its own light. Neither good nor cause nor evil nor

97. *Dhammapada*. Trans. Dr. S. Radhakrishnan. Mrs Rhys Davids. *Buddhism.*

98. Dr. S. Radhakrishanan. *The Vedānta According to Shankara and Rāmānuja.*

effect past, present, nor future has any place in it. When the soul gets emancipated it does not become *brahman*, but only of the nature of *brahman*. Such a state can be achieved, says Krishṇa in the *Gītā* by wisdom of the divine (as distinguished from learning or mere academic knowledge), desireless works (*nishkāma* karma), or devotion either to the personal Īshvara or the impersonal *brahman* (the easier one being devotion to a personal God—Īshvara or Vāsudēva). But such devotion must be unswerving and single-minded. Half-hearted devotion is no good. The true devotee surrenders everything to God—his works, his thoughts and aspirations and even his strivings. The *Rāmacharitamānasa* says, 'How much reliance can I (Rāma) place on one says he is my devotee, yet places his trust in men ?'[99] Sri Ramakrishna Paramhaṁsa used to actually consult Mother Kali in every little thing he thought of doing. When the Vedānta swami. Totapuri, expressed the desire to initiate him into the *advaita*, Ramakrishna said 'I must ask the Holy Mother first'. The goddess approved and told him to go ahead for it was she who had sent Totapuri to him. It is common practice for staunch devotees to dress the divine image in neat clothes and ornaments and offer *prasāda* (holy food offering).

Devotion has been given prime importance in Hindu philosophy. The *Gītā* places it above all else. The Rāmāyaṇa eulogizes it. Even Shankarāchārya, the great monist, considered it in *Bhaja Govindam* to be the only way to God. Whenever he visited any place on his journeys his first act was to pay obeisance to the god of the local temple. If he found a temple without an idol he would himself install one.

99. Mōra dāsa kahāī nara āsā/kari tau kahahu kahā bisvāsā// Shri Rāma's words to Hanumā *Uttara-kāṇḍ* 45 (1). The author knows a woman who spends the day in serving the idols she worships as though they were human. She covers them with a small quilt in winter. Puts cooling devices in summer. She feeds them. fans them, dresses them up every day and puts them to by singing holy songs. So much so that she will write down the vegatables and foodstuffs on bits of paper and putting them before the images, pick up three or four of the folded paper slips, and cook for the day's meals whatever the Lord may thus direct. Ordinary people would call her a crank. But that woman does. shows her entire surrender to God. And as for the eccentricity, one might recollect what Shankara says of the knower of *brahman*.

The positive aspect of has already been explained. It is not the disintegration of personality. For some thinkers and intellectuals it seems difficult to accept such a state. The reason is that they are obsessed with the 'I'. Assailed by *māyā* which, as we have said, has the the power of misrepresenting truth (*vikshepa*), they consider this 'I' or personality, or the body as the reality. In brief they mistake the body for the soul. For example Joad says, 'For a condition in which I shall cease to exist to feel as an individual or indeed to be an individual, is a condition in which I shall cease to be at all. Why should I hope to seek to realize such a condition unless my individual personality is of no account'.[100] One senses the fear of death in such an observation, coupled with the dread of what is unknown. As Shakespeare said, 'Aye, but to die and go we know not where'. Krishṇa had to explain Arjuna about this 'I' which one takes to be his individuality, so precious to him. Arjuna did not wish to kill his kinsmen on the Kaurava side and that meant abandoing the battlefield. As though a soldier might refuse to pull the trigger on an enemy he has on the hindsight of his gun. Krishṇa explained to him that one could never kill the soul which was immortal and which no weapons could slay. It would only be the bodies of his kinsmen that could be slain. He added, 'And, Arjuna, even if you fail to understand this and think at death everything dies – both soul and body – even then it is pointless for you to grieve for the inevitable. For him to whom birth has been given, death is certain. Just as who dies must be born again. So why sorrow for that over which you have no control?[101] Sri Ramana Maharshi says : 'The real I or Self is not the body nor any of the five senses, nor the sense-object, nor the organs of action, nor the breath, nor the mind, nor even the deep sleep state where there is no congnizance of these. The "I" is really being-consciousness-bliss, in which there is not that slightest trace of the I-thought. This is also called silence (*mauna*) or the Self (*ātman* or soul)'. But as they say, if one is to use a elicle', the proof of the pudding is in the eating. So instead of spinning thoeories, we will

100. C.E.M. Joad, *Hibbert Journal*. October 1952.

101. *Bhagavadgītā*. 2 : 17–27.

go on to give actual experiences faithfully recorded or based on actual investigation. These will show that the Reality is something quite apart from what it is ordinarily conceived to be, and that it is what Hindus call *ānanda* or bliss. Swami Vivekanand, who was known as Naren then, was a complete agnostic who did not even believe in God. But just at a *touch* of his guru, Sri Ramakrishna, something strange happened. We will narrate it in his own words :

> 'Everything in the room began to whirl around rapidly and vanished into nothingness the walls, the floor, the roof and all the objects in the room—and there was a great void. The whole universe, as also my I-ness seemed to vanish. There was nothing, nothing at all—no experience, nothing to be experienced. I thought I was dying and cried out "What is this you are doing to me. I have parents at home!" At that he [Ramakrishna] stroked my breast and laughing aloud said "All right, let it be. It is enough for now. Everything will come in due tim". Instantly was as it was, leaving me amazed'.

We proceed to give accounts based on investigation of after-death experiences of persons who had been declared dead by doctors but later came to life. We have already mentioned the findings of Dr Raymond Moody in *Life After Life*. He found the the dead man's soul floated above, enclosed in a filmy diaphanous body. It was surprised to see the lamentations on his dying, for he himself was perfectly happy. Other cases have been studied by various writers. We give briefly some accounts. This is that of a person who had died and then come back to life. He experienced two consciousnesses, one belonging to the body and the other to which the ego attached itself. The body consciousness became weaker, while the other one gained strength. *The I–consciousness seemed to be quite separate and outside the body.* Through it everything could be seen. 'Not only my body and the bed on which it was lying but the entire home, garden etc. I was not only seeing things at home but in London and Scotland, in fact to wherever my attention was directed'. The I–consciousness had awareness even beyond the three-dimensional. It was four dimensional and even more.

There was also a kind of psychic stream emanating from it, which was extremly iridescent.

A mountaineer who had such an experience says : 'I know now that death is not to be feared. It is a supreme experience, the climax and not the anti-climax of life . . . Time no longer existed as time . . . Then suddenly this feeling was superseded by a feeling of complete indifference and detachment as to what was happening or likely to happen to that body. I seemed to stand apart from my body and not the least concerned at what was befalling it'.

A soldier knocked down by a bomb blast could 'see' his body from twenty feet above the ground. He said 'This experience has convinced me that there is a part of the person that survives after death . . . .*I am certain that when I do eventually die or rather when my body dies,* part of me will carry on to where or to do what I do not know'.

Another experience was that of a physician whose soul, for a time came out of his body. He said it was the removal of the fear of death, because of the extraordinarily pleasant experience of what one felt and became aware of when one was apparently detached from one's body. 'I felt no further interest in my body, and had an intense feeling. Why are these people bothering about my body ? I am entirely content where I am'.[102]

Yet another account is that of an American soldier who fainted at the onset of pneumonia. Later when he came to, his doctor told him that he had apparently died, but a shot of adrenalin had brought him back to life. 'He said he found he had leapt out of bed to dress [he was about to catch a train when he got the pneumonia attack]. Then he saw what seemed to be himself lying on the bed and wearing his fraternity ring. Terrified, he fled from the room. No one took any notice of him and eventually he felt he should get back to his body. When with some difficulty he found it, a sheet had been drawn over the face, but he recognized the ring on his hand. "This is what we human beings call death"

102. Accounts from Arnold Toynbee and others. *Man's Concern With Death.* Hodder & Stoughton. 1986. p.. 195 et seq.

he thought, "This splitting of the self". He experienced the room "flooded with the most total compassion I have ever felt. It was a presence so comforting, so joyous and all-satisfying, that I wanted to lose myself for ever in the wonder of it". Then he went to a far journey packed with experiences – and then he woke up in bed'.[103]

The above accounts make it clear that 1. The nature of the soul is bliss, 2. That the soul is different from the body, 3. That there is only the destruction of the body at death and the 'I' is *not* destroyed because this 'I' which is, in ignorance associated with the body is *not* the body, but the soul, 4. That, as Hindu philosophy conceives, the soul on leaving the body is encased by a subtle body (*sukshma sharīra*), and 5. That death does not in any way put a stop to the experiences of the soul. There assuredly existence after death.

Moksha can be achieved in life itself. Then it is called *jivan-mukti.* Shankara believed this to be possible. But according to Bādarayāṇa's view, as contained in the *Brahma-sūtras* the consequences of works done in the previous life (*prārabdha* karma) have to be exhausted in any case. There is no escape from them. In such case *moksha* can be attained only at death after exhausting *prārabdha.* It is then called *videha-mukti.* The latter view seems to be more realistic. We find even saints and men who have achieved enlightenment, suffering. This can be explained by the fact that they must suffer *prārabdha.*

Hindu philosophy is perhaps the most penetrating and deep among philosophies. And in it the teaching of the *Bhagavadgītā* is of the greatest significance. Unfortunately, its perceptiveness has not been adequately recognized. Religion and philosophy concerns the unknown. And the unknown can only be surmised. No one ever comes back to narrate about it. Nonetheless Hindu philosophy essays to explain mystical experiences rationally too. For example the concept of *turīya*, the Eternal Witness, rebirth, karma, suffering and so forth. Right from the beginning

103. S. Smith *The Enigma of Out-of- the Body Travel.* Helix Press. New York, 1965. p., 185. Quoted in Arnold Tonybee and others. *Man's Concern With Death.* Hodder & Stoughton 196 8. p.. 168.

of civilization up to the present time, existence and non-existence and the world phenomenon, has agitated the minds of human beings – those who are not single-mindedly engrossed in the pursuit of weath and the pleasures of the senses. To such as never think of anything other than the worldly, all philosophy is meaningless. But to those who look beyond, philosophy is the essence of existence. We repeat the words of the great Shankarācharyā, perhaps the greatest of the world philosophers:

> 'One who having with great difficulty acquired a human existence, is deluded into not striving for emancipation, and instead runs after illusive objects, destroys himself. Who is there on this earth with soul so dead that having been born as a human being still seeks the attainment of selfish pleasures . . . The only way to attain salvation is by the knowledge of union with spirit'.[104]

We have tried to explain the main tenets of Hindu philosophy. We go on to record the most significant passages from the main Hindu scriptures and philosophical treatise.

104. Vivekachudāmani 4–6.

SELECTED PASSAGES

Shall we say that the great *Upanishads* are the deep, still mountain tarns fed from the pure water of the everlasting snows, lit by clear sunshine, or by night, mirroring the high serenity of the stars?

The *Bhagavad Gītā* is perhaps the lake among the foothills wherein are gathered the same waters of wisdom, after flowing through the forest of Indian history, with the fierce confliet of the Children of Bharata.

Then in the *Brahma Sūtras*, we have the reservoir, four-square, where the sacred waters are assembled in ordered quiet and graded depth, to be distributed by careful measure for the sustenance of the sons of men.

CHARLES JOHNSTON

(A) FROM THE MAHABHĀRATA

THE MAHĀBHĀRATA – WHAT IT IS

The *Mahābhārata* is the world's longest epic. It is said that what is not in it will be found nowhere. It has a hundred thousand verses and is about eight times the length of the Illiad and the Odessey put together. Originally it had eighteen books, (*parvas*) to which another was added later. It is believed to have been written by Maharshi Vyāsa, the great sage. Devout Hindus however believe it to be of divine origin. There are many subsidiary stories interwoven with the central plot. Parts of it are highly philosophical, though it is mainly a literary work. It has been telecast on the Indian TV and appreciated the world over. The literature to which the *Mahābhārata* belongs is called Itihāsa and Akhyāna. The epic abounds in picturesque description and expressive comparisons. Like the Aeneid and the Georgics of Virgil it has a large mythological content and high moral ideals. But its canvas is much wider and bears comparison with the great Greek dramatists. The characters of the *Mahābhārata* have been described so vividly that they stand out as living persons. Droṇācharya is 'robed in white with the sacred thread, sandals and garlands, also white and with snowy hair'. Colour has been harnessed to give living reality to Vyāsa's picturesque descriptions. The bright lustre and glow of fire seems to light up the entire epic in a brilliance: ascetics wearing garments like glowing embers, women's limbs like the fire's glow, the battle raging like a holocaust which will burn up the entire world, warriors standing on the battlefield like pillars of fire and warriors surrounding some valiant fighter of the other side as a circle of fire formed by a burning torch rotating. The turbulence of battle, the onrush of soldiers as 'dust scattering and settling down mixed with blood' and the 'mounted warriors with cuts and bruises all over them exhausted by fighting lying on the temples of their elephants like tired lovers on the bosoms of their girls' – are all narrated in the most vibrant language. All the various emotions are to be found in the epic – the heroic, love, laughter, compassion, wrath, wonder, dread, the silent and the awesome. These are the *rasas* (emotions) which according to Bhoja make poetry charming. The erotic element is expressed in the story of Rishyashringa in which a young ascetic discovers for himself the charms of women from whom he had been completely isolated. Gāndhārī moaning over the slain warrior, Bhurisravas, whose hand Arjuna had foully cut off, says to Krishṇa 'Look, this is the hand which used to open the girdle, explore the waist and fondle the breasts of the lovely woman, his wife'. There are fights with horrible demons. Blood flows as plentifully as tears. Treachery, as the Kaurava plan to burn the Pāṇḍava brothers and Draupadī in the wax palace, the irony of Yudhishṭhira, the upholder of *dharma* (virtue) speaking a lie in proclaiming the living Asvatthāmā as having been slain and bartering away even Draupadī in his addiction to dice; the perfidy of Draupadī's disrobing by Duḥshāsana in the assembly of wise men; the terrible deed of Bhīma tearing open the dying Duḥshāsana's breast drinking his blood [for which reason he is called '*bhīmakarmā*' i.e. one awesome deeds in the *Gītā*]; the fierce nature of the war in which every rule and norm made was finally thrown to the winds; lamentation, woe, sorrow, and agony such as that of Karṇa, who even while having known he was the eldest of the Pāṇḍava brothers, fought with them and was slain by Arjuna, and of Bhīshma, who, aware of the black deeds of the Kauravas still found himself obliged to fight on their side – such is the marvellous diversity of narration in this great epic. And set in this scintillating garland of wondrous stories is the unmatchable gem of the *Bhagavadgītā*, the Lord's voice speaking of the soul's immortality.

THE STORY

It is said the *Mahābhārata* was recited by the sage, Vaishampāyana at the Snake-sacrifice held by Janamejaya, son of Parikshit. Vyāsa had it all in his mind and was anxious to teach it. Brahmā appeared to him and asked him to call upon Gaṇesha. The god came and promised to write down the poem provided it would be so correctly spoken that his pen would not have to stop even for a moment. So Vyāsa began to dictate and Gaṇesha wrote on. This is the story :

King Uparichara (also called Vasu) ruled over Chedi. He was married to Grikā. One day he was filled with desire but Grikā was not to be found. so his semen came out of itself. A hawk carried it away. But it fell into the waters of the Yamunā river. An Apsarā who had taken the form of a fish swallowed it. Due to it she had two children, a girl and a boy. The boy became a powerful monarch called Matsy. The girl became a lovely woman named Satyavatī. Satyavatī was left by the king with some fishermen. There, by the blessings of the sage Parāshara she got a son who was Vyāsa, the *Mahābhārata's* author He promised to appear to Satyavatī, his mother, whenever she called upon him.

In the race of Ikshvāku there was born Mahābhīsha, a great king, lord of all the country. One day he was in the presence of Lord Brahmā where the celestials were worshipping the god. Gangā the queen of the sacred river of that name was also there. It so happened that a gust of wind blew her garment aside exposing her nakedness. Mahābhīsha stared at her exposed body. For this he was cursed by Brahmā to be born on earth. He was born as the son of Pratīpa. Gangā went away and on the way she met the eight Vasus who, due to a curse, had to be born as humans. They implored her to make them her sons, but asked her to cast them into the water as soon as they took birth. Gangā agreed, but on condition that one of them should live on. They assented to this. However, the one who would live was to remain childless for ever and not beget any children.

One day Pratīpa was sitting at the place from where the Gangā took its source. The lovely Gangā, queen of the river rose from the water and sitting on Pratīpa's right thigh offered herself to him. But she had sat where daughters and daughters-in-law customarily sat. So the king said 'I can't marry you but I'll accept you as my daughter-in-law. Thus Mahābhīsha, Pratīpa's son, also known as Shāntanu was pledged to Gangā. One day he was going on a hunt along the river when the charming Gangā appeared from the waters. The two instantly fell in love. Shāntanu asked for her hand in marriage. She agreed, but made him promise that he would never question what she did. If ever he did that, or spoke harshly to him she would leave. They had seven sons. Gangā threw them all into the waters of the river one by one, as soon as they were born. Then came an eighth. Shāntanu could contain himself no longer and stopped her. 'You are the murderess of your own sons and a sinner' he said, and held back her hand. Gangā told him about the Vasus. 'These were all really those', she said. 'This eighth one is really Dyaus. By the rishī's curse he is destined to suffer worldly existence and will be denied the pleasure of women'. After telling him this, Gangā disappeared into the river. She took the babe also, promising to restore him to Shāntanu after he had become learned in the Vedas and adept in the use of weapons. This eighth son of Gangā was Devadutta, better known as Bhīshma.

Shāntanu was heart-broken. One day he happened to see Satyavatī, of whom we have spoken before. He became enamoured of her and wanted to wed her. But her fisherman father refused unless Shāntanu promised that *her* progeny would succeed to the throne. That meant, of course, bypassing Bhīshma, whom Gangā had returned and who was an adept warrior with the boon that he would die only when he himself willed so. Shāntanu could never think of doing that. So he went about torn between his desire and his duty. Bhīshma, however, curious to know why his father remained so sad, did some investigation on his own and found it all out. He made a solemn vow never to marry. The gods rained flowers on him in appreciation of his great sacrifice. Shāntanu and Satyavatī were married. Shāntanu had two sons by Satyavatī – Chitrāngad and Vichitravīrya. The first died early. Vichitravīrya became king. Bhīshma learnt that the king of Kāshī was holding a *swayamvara* for the marriage of his three daughters, Ambā, Ambālikā and Ambikā. He went there and defying all the suitors, carried away the three girls for wedding Vichitravīrya. Ambā pleaded that she was secretly engaged to Sālva, so she may be allowed to go. Bhīshma at once let her off. But Sālva backed out. Then Ambā returned to Bhīshma and asked him to marry her. But he had taken the vow of celibacy and refused. The frustrated maiden persuaded Parashurāma to assist her. Bhīsma, however, defeated him in a duel. Then she performed severe austerities to Shiva. The god was pleased. After burning herself she emerged a Drupada's daughter and later changing sex, became Sikhandī, who was destined to assist in slaying Bhīshma later. Vichitravīrya died without having any children. Now Satyavatī feared she would have no heir. So she summoned Vyāsa to assist her. The sage first went to Ambikā. She was so frightened at his uncouth appearance that she closed her eyes. So the son Vyāsa gave her was blind. His name was Dhritarāshṭra. Ambālikā turned pale with fright on seeing Vyāsa, so to her was born Pāṇḍu (meaning, 'the pale'). Satyavatī pressed Ambikā again to receive the sage. But she wished to avoid him and so secretly substituted her maidservant in her place. The maid cordially agreed to Vyāsa's visit, and pleased him. So Vidura, a wise and virtuous son was born to her.

As Dhritarāshṭra was blind he was passed over. Pāṇḍu became king. He married Kuntī daughter of Surasena king of the Yādavas and sister of Krishṇa's father, Vasudeva. Surasena had given her to Kuntībhoja, his friend, who had no child. While yet a child she had attended to the sage Durvāsā who had given her a boon that she could repeat a *mantra* (sacred formula) and call upon any god she wished. The god would at once appear and give her a son. While she was still a virgin, curiosity made her test the sage's boon. She called on Sūrya, the Sun-god. Lo ! he appeared. She pleaded that she was a virgin and had only called him to test the *mantra* But the Sun-god told her he was bound by it. He gave her a child. He was Karṇa who was born wearing an armour. Fearing censure, she put him in a basket and set him afloat. Karṇa was picked up by Rādhā, wife of a charioteer named Adhiratha. Pāṇḍu also married Mādrī sister of Shalya, king of Madra. After some time he decided to go to the forest for a short outing, and left with his wives Kuntī and Mādrī While hunting in the forest he accidentally shot an arrow, fatally wounding a *rishī* and his wife who were making love. The dying sage cursed him saying, 'Just as you have killed us, so will you die, the moment desire for intercourse with your wife enters your mind'. Threatened with the extinction of his dynasty, Kuntī used the power of Durvāsā's *mantra*. She got Yudhishṭhira from the god of Dharma, Bhīma from

Vāyu, the wind-god, and Arjuna from Indra the god of the firmament. Mādrī got twins, Nakula and Sahadeva from the two Ashvins. Thus all the five Pāṇḍava brothers were born with a divine origin. But one day Pāṇḍu saw Mādrī lying in dishabille in the forest and could not restrain his desire. Immediately the sage's curse came into play and he died.

Dhritarāshṭra married Gāndhārī, the daughter of Subala. As her husband was blind, she too bandaged her eyes out of love for him. Vyāsa had given her a boon that she should have a hundred sons. But instead, she gave birth to a hard mass of flesh. Vyāsa came and divided it into a hundred and one pieces. He sprinkled them with cold water and put them into jars filled with clarified butter. In time these became a hundred sons, the eldest of whom was Duryodhana, and a daughter named Duḥsalā. As Pāṇḍu had died and Mādrī had immolated herself on his funeral pyre, Kuntī and her sons began to live with Gāndhārī, and Dhṛitarāshṭra, presiding over the household at Hastināpura. As children, the sons of Dhritarāshṭra (the Kauravas) and those of Pāṇḍu (the Pāṇḍavas) did not get along well. Duryodhana particularly hated the Pāṇḍavas. Meanwhile Satyavatī and Ambālikā retired to the forest and after performing many austerities, died.

Kripa who was to become the instructor of the Yādava youth had a strange birth. Saradvat, son of the great sage Gautama, who was an ascetic, saw one day a celestial Apsarā of unmatched beauty, scantily clad. He was filled with lust and his semen came out and fell on shrubs growing on wasteland, and divided into two parts. From these sprang up two children, a boy and a girl, who were twins. One of Shāntanu's solidiers saw them and brought them to the king who took pity on them and kept them in the court. They were given the names Kripa and Kripī. Kripī later married Droṇa. Droṇa too had an unusual birth. One day the sage Bharadvāja was bathing in the Gangā river when he saw the Apsarā Ghritachī rising up from it. As she came up her garment got loose and the *rishi* saw her nakedness. His semen gushed out, but he held it in a water-pot (*droṇa*). From this was born a child who was given the name Droṇa (i.e. one born in a water-pot).

Droṇa was very poor. He became friendly with Drupada, the Pānchāli prince, who promised to help him when he became king. But when Drupada ascended the thone, he spurned Droṇa saying that friendship could exist only among equals! While staying with Kripa, Bhīshma was impressed by Droṇa's mastery in the arts of war. He therefore gave him the job of instructor to the princes. Arjuna became Droṇa favourite pupil. But one day Karṇa arrived and challenged Arjuna to a duel. Since he was only a charioteer's son (his real parentage being unknown to any but Kuntī). Arjuna refused to compete with a man of low birth. Duryodhana (who was dead set against Arjuna) crowned Karṇa as the king of then and there. Karṇa was ever obliged to Duryodhana for helping him out and saving him embarrassment. He pledged lifelong support to Duryodhana for it.

Droṇa, who remembered the shabby way in which Drupada had treated him, asked Arjuna to attack him. The Pāṇḍava brothers defeated Drupada, but Droṇa humiliated him in a very subtle kind of way. He said, 'You considered friendship possible only among equals, so I will divide the conquered kingdom between us and give you half'. Drupada took this to heart. He performed rituals to get a son who would be Droṇa's slayer. He got Dhrishṭadyumna, and also Draupadī, who, a celestial voice prophesied, would be the cause of the destruction of the *kshatriyās*. Ambā had also been born as Drupada's progeny in fulfilment of her vow to be the cause of Bhisma's end.

As Yudhishṭhira was the most suitable successor to the kingdom of Hastināpura and also the seniormost, Dhritarāshṭra crowned him as heir-apparent. But Duryodhana could never tolerate this. So he conspired to burn all the five Pāṇḍavas and Kuntī in a palace made of wax. He persuaded his father to send the Pāṇḍavas to Vāraṇāvata where the festival of Shiva was to be celebrated. Meanwhile he got a stately palace made for their stay, but all of it was of wax. The idea was to set fire to it and roast Kuntī and the Pāṇḍavas in it. But Vidura, who discovered the plot, pre-warned them and they escaped secretly from an underground tunnel which he got made for them. By chance a tribal woman and her five sons had also been there and when their charred bodies were seen after the fire, it was believed that the Pāṇḍavas and Kuntī had been burnt in the palace.

The Pāṇḍavas and their mother wandered about in the forest, fearing Duryodhana's evil designs. Here Draupadī married all the five brothers. Arjuna won her hand in a *swayamvara*. Kuntī had advised her sons to share whatever alms they got. When Arjuna came with Draupadī, he said to his mother 'Today I bring you the most precious of alms'. Without looking up Kuntī said 'Share it between yourselves'. She was aghast to find Draupadī standing before her. Nonetheless she had spoken, and her words were beyond recall. So Draupadī wed all the five Pāṇḍava brothers.

Thus the Pāṇḍavas now became strong, having powerful allies like the Pānchālas. So accompanied by Draupadī, Kuntī and Krishṇa they returned to Hastināpura. Dhritarāshṭra thought it best to divide the kingdom between Duryodhana and Yudhishṭhira. He gave Khāṇḍavaprastha, also known as Indraprastha, to the Pāṇḍavas and the rest to his sons. Though the portion given to the Pāṇḍavas was the worst part of the land, yet by hard work they developed it into a majestic country. Krishṇa and his brother Balarāma returned to Dwārakā, which was their realm. Arjuna was persuaded by Krishṇa to carry away by force his (Krishṇa's) sister, Subhadrā, with whom he (Arjuna) had fallen in love. Bhīma married Hiḍimbā sister of a demon. They had a son called Ghaṭotkacha whose head was like a water-pot (*ghaṭa* = pot). He was a tall and awesome giant.

The Pāṇḍavas were now very powerful and prosperous. They successfully held the *rājasūya* sacrifice which established their undisputed suzerainty. Duryodhana was raving with envy. On the advice of Shakunī (brother of Gāndhārī), a ruthless and scheming man, he invited Yudhishṭhira for a game of dice. In this the Pāṇḍava prince staked everything—his brothers and even Draupadī. Shakunī was adept at cheating at dice. The upshot was that Yudhishṭhira lost. Draupadī was insulted by Duḥshasana at Duryodhana's bidding. He dragged her by her hair and brought her before all the elders. Duryodhana bared his thigh, insultingly inviting her to sit on it. Not content with so much, Duḥshāsana pulled her sari to bare her body. But Krishṇa, on whom she called for aid, held one end of it. The more Duḥshāsana pulled, the longer it became, till he fell down exhausted. The enraged Bhīma made a solemn vow to smash Duryodhana's thigh. He declared that Draupadī's tresses (which she had in remorse decided to leave unbraided) would be braided. And for this he would wet them with Duḥshāsana's blood. He also vowed to slay all all the hundred Kaurava brothers.

Bad omens occurred portending some great calamity. Dhristarāshṭra rescinded the whole gambling match and restored the Pāṇḍavas their realm. But Duryodhana prevailed on his vacillating father to summon the Pāṇḍavas again for playing dice. The same thing which happened before was repeated and this time too, the Pāṇḍavas lost the wager which prescribed twelve years' exile in the forest and staying one year thereafter incognito in a city without being found out. If they were found out it would result in further twelve years of exile.

Kuntī stayed on in Hastināpura, while the Pāṇḍavas went into exile. A number of incidents occurred during the period of exile. Vidura and Krishṇa paid them a visit. Krishṇa was grieved at the turn of events and comforted Draupadī. He took Subhadrā and Abhimanyū (Arjuna's son) with him to Dwārakā. Vyāsa asked Arjuna to seek celestial weapons from Indra. Indra said that first he would have to meet Shiva. This encounter took place in a strange way. Both Mahādeva and Arjuna shot their arrows at a boar who was really a demon out to kill Arjuna. Each of the two 'hunters' claimed the kill. So they began to fight over it. Finally overcome by the god in disguise, Arjuna recognized him and, falling at his feet, begged his pardon. Shiva gave him the unequalled Pashupata weapon, which no one, god or man, could stand against. He also gave him the Gāṇḍīva bow. Arjuna then went to Indra's kingdom. He live there five years and learnt dancing, and vocal and instrumental music from Chitrasena. Urvashī went to him at Indra's behest to teach him how to mix with women. But he worshipped her as mother of the Puru race. Thus spurned, she cursed him to live among women as a eunuch. Bhīma met Hanumān, the monkey-god, who was his brother. He promised to be present on Arjuna's flagstaff when the battle was fought. At one time Jayadratha, king of Sindu happened to see Draupadī and was infatuated with her. He forcibly carried her away in his car. Arjuna and Bhīma rescued her. They spared him, but disgraced him by shaving his head. Vowing revenge, Jayadratha prayed to Shiva, who appeared. But he said he could grant him victory over Yudhishṭhira's army only for one day. Indra approached Karṇa and asked him for his armour and ear-rings, and (with which, as related, he had been born). Indra was disguised as a *brāhmin* and Karṇa had vowed never to refuse anything to a *brāhmin*. But he had been instructed by his father, Sūrya, to ask Indra for his indestructible dart in return. Indra had to give him that. In yet another incident the Pāṇḍavas were tested by Dharma. He asked each of them several questions before they drank the water of a stream. Each of them refused to answer and died, except Yudhishṭhira who replied to them and thereby also obtained the revival of his brothers.

In the thirteenth year the Pāṇḍavas disguised themselves and took service in the court of Virāṭa, king of Matsya. Kīchaka, the queen's brother and a great warrior, got enamoured of the disguised Draupadī who had entered service as maid. Bhīma, who was disguised as cook of the royal household, killed him. Meanwhile Duryodhana wished to find out the Pāṇḍava's whereabouts. So he sent spies. Kīchaka's death made him suspicious, for only a person as powerful as Bhīma could kill him. He got his whole army, including all warriors and veterans like Bhīshma and Kripa to attack the Matsya kingdom. Arjuna, who was disguised as a eunuch, however, obtained his weapons, which he had hidden on a tree, and single-handed routed the entire Kaurava army. Uttarā, whom Arjuna used to teach dancing, married Abhimanyū, Arjuna's son. The Pāṇḍavas had completed the thirteen years' exile, and the stage was set for war. Krishṇa, acting as a peace-messenger, made a final effort to avoid it, but Duryodhana was adamant. The Pāṇḍavas even agreed to desist from war if they were given just five villages. Duryodhana said he would not give them land even to the extent of the point of a needle!

The eighteen day's war waged fiercely. There was great destruction on each side. Krishṇa was Arjuna's charioteer and gave him the famous discourse known as the the *Gītā*. Bhīshma was killed by Arjuna by placing Sikhanḍī before him. Bhīshma stayed his hand as he would not send his arrows at a woman. Droṇa was killed treacherously by Yudhishṭhira's lying that his son Ashvatthāmā had been killed. He abandoned his weapons in despair and Dhrishṭadyumna chopped off his head. The brave Abhimanyū, Arjuna's son, was surrounded by a number of veteran Kaurava warriors, and slain, though after a valorous stand. Arjuna took an oath to slay Jayadratha, who was mainly instrumental in Abhimanyū's death, by sunset the next day. But it was only with Krishṇa assistance that he could do so. Krishṇa threw a dark veil over the sun and created darkness. Jayadratha thought he had been saved. But Krishṇa lifted the veil of darkness and Arjuna was able to fulfil his vow. Karṇa's chariot-wheel got stuck the mud. Once long back, Karṇa had posed as a *brāhmin* and being admitted by the sage Parashurāma as his disciple had learnt from him the *mantra* needed to use the Brahmāstra, the divine weapon of Brahmā. When later the sage found that Karṇa had spoken a lie by saying he was a *brāhmin*, he said 'As you have practised deceit on me, you will forget the *mantra* when you have need of it'. So now Karṇa, with the wheel of his chariot stuck, failed to recall the *mantra* which would have enabled him to discharge his celestial weapon at Arjuna. Though Arjuna was reluctant to kill Karṇa as he was engaged in pulling out the chariot-wheel, Krishṇa urged him on, and Arjuna's arrow put an end to that most valiant of warriors, and ironically his own real elder brother! Duryodhana was cooling himself under water to get rid of his wrath, when Bhīma challenged him to fight with maces. Gāndhārī had caused her son's body to be solid as iron, but due to Krishṇa's stratagem, she had to leave the waist and upper part of his thighs as they were. Bhīma blows had no effect on him. Seeing this, Krishṇa motioned him to strike him on the thigh, though this was against the rules of combat. Bhīma hit him there and broke them, thus also fulfilling his vow taken when Draupadī was disgraced. Bhīma also redeemed his pledge to kill Duḥshāsana and bring his blood to wet Draupadī's tresses.

Kripāchārya, Kritavarmā and Ashvatthāmā cruelly killed the sons of the Pāṇḍavas in the night while they were asleep thinking that they were the Pāṇḍavas. After this foul deed Ashvathāmā went to Vyāsa to do penance for it. The sage told him that he had really killed the sons of Draupadī, not the Pāṇḍavas, as he thought. Meanwhile the wailing Draupadī urged her husband to go and kill Ashvatthāmā and bring her the gem he wore on his forehead. In frustration Ashvatthāmā discharged the Brahmāstra to kill the foetus in Uttarā's womb and thus end the Pāṇḍava race. But Krishṇa revived her son by his divine power. He also asked Ashvatthāmā to pluck out the gem from his brow and hand it over. Draupadī gave the gem to Yudhishṭhira to wear.

Thus ended the horrible battle. All the hundred sons of Dhritarāshṭra lay dead. Grief-stricken Gāndharī cursed Krishṇa that his kinsmen would also be destroyed. The curse was effective and they killed each other. Yudhishṭhira became king and performed the great horse- sacrifice. Dhritarāshṭra, Gāndharī and Kuntī went away to the forest. Krishṇa passed away, thus ending the Krishṇa-avatāra of Lord Vishṇu. Balarāma ended his life sitting in yoga, a great stream of light emitting from him. The Pāṇḍavas crowned Parikshit, son of Abhimanyū as emperor and left for the Himalayas. They died one by one and only Yudhishṭhira reached heaven in person. Before he entered he was tested by Indra. A dog got into the heavenly chariot. Indra drove it away saying there was no place for a dog in *swarga* (heaven). 'Then there is no place for me either', Yudhishṭhira said. At this, the dog vanished. He was really Dharma come to test his son. Thus Yudhishṭhira entered heaven, where all the Pāṇḍavas and Kauravas too were. Here, in heaven, there was no enmity, no hatred. The spirits of all rejoiced and the melody of the divine sage Nārada playing on the *vīṇa*, a filled all space, echoing in the three worlds.

READING LIST

Translations

Dutt, M.N. *The Mahābhārata* Calcutta 1895-1905.

Dutt. R. *The Mahābhārata*. London, 1929

Hopkins, E.W. *The Great Epic of India* New York, 1920

Lal, P. The *Mahābhāratha.* Writer's Workshop.

Rajagopalachari, C. *Mahābharata.* Bombay : Bhavan Book University, 1951.

Roy, Pratap Chundra. *The Mahābhārata of Krishna Dwaipayana Vyasa* 13 rols. Calcutta : Bharata Press, 1883-1890.

Subramaniam, Kamala. *Mahābhārata.* Bombay : Vidya Bhawan, 1980.

There is a *Sanskrit* text with comentary by Sukthankar, Vishnu S., 7 vols. Bhandarkar Oriental Institute 1933-54.

Critical Studies

Held, G.J. *The Mahabharata, An Ethnological Study* London, 1935.

Patil, N.B. *Folklore in the Mahābharata.* Delhi : Motilal Banarsidass, 1983.

Siddhanta, N.K. *The Heroic Age of India.* London, 1929 Tatatirtha, R.C. *Mahabharata Laksha-shlokarahasyam* (A study regarding the exact number of verses in the Mahabharata. Calcutta : Firma K.L. Mukhopadhyay, 1974.

Vaidya, C.V. *The Mahabharata. A Criticism*. New Delhi : Cosmo Publications, 1983.

The Bharat Publishing House Karachi has brought out material on the *Mahābhārata* in several volumes by N.V. Thadani.

EXTRACTS

THE SAGE AND THE SCRIBE

[Vyāsa was the son of the great sage, Parāshara. He conceived the story of the Mahābhārata, but he did not know how such a long narrative could be written. So he prayed to Brahmā to tell him the way. Brahmā advised him to request Lord Gaṇapatī (Gaṇesha) to write it. Gaṇesha agreed but on condition that his pen must not stop even a moment while he wrote. 'You must speak out continuously without pause' he said. 'All right', Vyāsa said, 'but you must first get the meaning of what I say, before I go on'. Gaṇesha guessed what Vyāsa was at. Smilingly, he agreed. Thus Vyāsa would occasionally compose some verse which was not instantly understood, and while Gaṇesha paused to get its meaning, the sage would compose the next few verses.]

Beyond these fleeting shadows lies the One
Whose million forms we see around us spread
Where knowledge stops and from where words return
Failing to capture what is beyond thought.
These worlds are his kingdom, and his chaste abode
Is in the hearts fo men. Even then we seek
Him outside us, as a traveller leaves
To vainly search for peace in distant lands.
He is always shining from the sky
On souls heavily burdened; our joys and griefs
We ourselves make. And who can understand
The working of his laws, reaching beyond
One lifetime? In a moment are contained
The seeds of times to come, the blossomings
Of times past. Still on the earth, he descends
To uphold virtue and to punish vice.
So was he there himself on Kurukshetra
Amid the blaring conches to teach

Arjuna, his beloved disciple, noble ways
Of truth. Of that great incident and all
That led to it, the sage Vyāsa wished to sing
Blessed by Lord Brahmā. Gaṇapatī set down
The holy words; thus were the two engrossed
In their sweet task; the scribe pausing awhile
To delve into the trammels of some verse,
At which the sage turned to his lofty thoughts
And carefully carved out each loaded rhyme.[106]

EMPEROR YAYĀTI - THE EMPTINESS OF SENSE-PLEASURES

One of the ancestors of the Pāṇḍavas, the great and invincible emperor Yayāti, was a virtuous king who was loved by his subjects, as their welfare was his sole concern. He had been cursed by the sage Shukrāchārya with premature age. This was because Yayāti had been unfaithful to his daughter Devayāni whom he had married, by having wedlock in secret with Sarmishta, her attendant. Though the curse made him an old man he was still filled with sensual longings. He had five sons. One day he called them and said. 'The sage's curse has brought about this condition which has deprived me of youth and beauty and has brought misery on me. You are all young. He among you who will agree to give me his youth and take on himself my old age, shall succeed to my kingdom'. He asked his eldest son first if he was ready to do this. The boy said. 'If I take on myself your old age I shall be the laughing-stock of servants and pretty women. Ask my brothers, whom you love more than me'. The next son also refused. 'Father' he said, 'old age destroys not only strength and beauty, but wisdom too. I regret I can't do this'. The third son said 'An old man's speech falters. He can't even ride a horse or get on an elephant. He becomes helpless. Sorry, I can't take all this on myself'. The fourth son also

106. Note : Only the concluding 5 lines are from the *Mahābhārata.* The rest is the author's own creation, as a kind of prologue.

didn't agree. The youngest, Puru, however, loved his father very much and assented. So Puru took on Yayāti's old age, and the emperor became young again. Having regained his youth he went to Kubera's garden and for a long time enjoyed the favours of a lovely Apsarā. He found, however, that desire was unquenchable. It was like a flame which rose up more, the more it was fed with ghee. So returning to Puru, he said 'Dear son, I had heard that sense-gratification can never make a man happy. It is insatiable. Having indulged in such pleasures, now, I realize the truth of it. Neither good food, nor wealth, nor possessions, nor congress with women, can satisfy man's desires. Only control of the mind, getting rid of attraction and aversion, and the calm and bliss that follows the realization of *brahman*, can bring contentment. So take back your youth and be a good and wise ruler'. Speaking thus, Yayāti surrendered his youth and went away to meditate in the forest. After practising many austerities he went to heaven.

THE ASCETIC WHO HAD NEVER SEEN A WOMAN

[We have narrated in the Mahābhārata story, how the Pāṇḍavas lost the wager in dice and had to go to the forest in exile for twelve years. During their wanderings there, they went to pay their homage to Lomāsa, the sage, who took them visit Rishyashringa's āshrama (hermitage) in the forest, where that ascetic used to live. This in the story about the young ascetic which Lomāsa told the Pāṇḍavas]

A controversial issue which keep arising in society is whether there should boys and girls be kept away from each other. In all such controversies following the middle-path (one of the principles advocated by Lord Buddha) is perhaps the best. Extremes are fraught with danger and will not work. The Mahābhārata relates the story of Rishyshringa, to illustrate this.

The *rishi* Vibhandaka, a sage of great virtue, lived in the forest along with his son, Rishyashringa, who led a life of perfect chastity, so much so that he had never seen a woman. Once there was a great famine in Anga. Crops dried up because of the failure of the rains. People began to die of starvation. Romapāda [or as sometimes called, Lomapāda], the king of that country was greatly worried. So he called, his priests and asked them how the famine could be ended. They said, 'There lives a young sage in the forest who is a chaste ascetic. He has the power of causing rain to fall wherever he is present. If you can have him brought here, the rains will come and the famine will be over'. The king talked the matter over with his ministers and devised a way in which the task could be done. He called the most captivating courtezans in his kingdom and told them to bring Rishyashringa somehow.

The courtezans got hold of a large boat on which they made a hermitage surrounded by a 'garden' containing many artificial trees and creepers. The boat was rowed and moored in the river, close to Vibhandaka's hermitage. As it happened, luck was with them and they found the ascetic lad alone, as his father had gone away somewhere. The courtezans were all dressed in hermit clothes, which not only added to their charm, but also left parts of their bodies barc. One of them went up to the lad and, as was customary with ascetics, inquired about the welfare of the *āshrama*. 'Are there enough roots and fruits to eat? Is it peaceful and calm, and is your father, the illustrious sage all right? Are your studies of the holy scriptures going on well?' Rishyashringa was touched by her solicitude. But even more he was fascinated by that lovely ascetic. The natural human instincts took possession of him. He found a strange kind of seductive attraction for her surging in himself. After making her the usual offerings of fruits etc., he said 'You seem to be a very divine sannyasin. Where's your hermitage? What kind of austerities are you engaged in?' The courtezan said, 'My hermitage is close by. Perhaps some day you may do me the kindness to visit it'. Offering him some fruits she had brought, she said, 'You are a great and enlightened sage, so I am not fit to receive your blessings by prostrating myself. I will greet you according to the custom we observe. Saying this, she clasped him tight, breast to breast, and put sweets into his mouth to eat, with her own hands. She put perfumed garlands round him, gave him drinks and embraced him again and again. After thus awakening in him that sexual lovging which had lain suppressed in him all these years, she hurriedly left saying it was time for her to perform the *agnihotra* offering, for she feared Vibhandaka's return.

When the sage came back he was surprised to see that the hermitage had not been swept as usual. Everything was in a mess. His son's face had lost its calm and showed agitation. It was glowing with passionate desire. On questioning Rishyashringa he found out that some woman had surely visited the place. The artless boy told him that a most lovely and alluring ascetic had done him the honour of coming. 'He was very cordial, sweet and bright. He embraced me with great love.[107] I experienced such joy as I have never yet known. My whole being craves for that ascetic's company. My heart pants to see him again. O I would give the whole world to find him out'. Vibhandaka guessed the truth and said, 'Son, it was no ascetic who met

107. The young ascetic had never seen a woman. So he used the word 'he' instead of 'she'.

you. He was a demon. These wicked demons can take any form they like. If he comes again don't have anything to do with him. Just drive him off'. The sage searched the forest areas nearby to discover the person who had played this trick on his son, but he could never imagine that there could be a boat nearby.

After some time the courtezan took another chance. By lurking about the *āshrama* she was assured that only the lad was there. She went up to him. The moment. Rishyashringa saw her he got up quickly and ran to embrace her. He said, 'My father will be out for sometime. Meanwhile I'd like to come and see your hermitage, and be back before his return'. The courtezan was overjoyed. This was just what she wanted. The boy came to the floating-hermitage. As soon as he entered it, the boat was freed of its moorings and floated down the river, the hidden rowers taking the oars. The courtezans, all dressed up in lovely half-revealing ochre dresses entertained the hermit lad, who was so engrossed with their fond welcome that he forgot all about the forest, the boat and the river. The courtezans brought all their enticing allurements into play. On that journey in which the hours seemed moments, Rishyashringa learnt many things of which he was completely ignorant and particularly that in which these charming 'ascetics' were different from him. The calm of abstinence was destroyed by passion's longing as fire burns away a haystack of dry hay.

Romapāda was delighted to find that the courtezans had succeeded in luring away Rishyashringa. He gave his daughter, Shāntā in marriage to him and got a luxurious chamber prepared for them. As foretold the rain fell in torrents as soon as the young ascetic set foot in Anga. The rivers and lakes filled up. The drying crops revived and the famine was over. The king was afraid of Vibhandaka's wrath. He knew the sage would soon find out where his son was. So he lined up the entire route with liveried servants and cattle, and asked the villagers to welcome him at each halt. The sage, who by his powers got to know all about his son's seduction, came to Anga, burning with anger. He resolved to curse the king for his act. But when he saw the many cattle [which were in those days a sign of wealth and status], the servants and the welcome he got, his anger became less and less. When he entered the city his reception was even grander. He was taken to the palace where he saw his son sitting on an ornate throne with the princess Shāntā of charming beauty, by his side. Vibhandaka gave his blessings to Romapāda. To his son he said 'Obey the king in all he says. When a son is born to you by Shāntā, come with him to my *āshrama* in the forest to get my blessings'. With that he left Anga.

Lomāsa concluded his story and said to Yudhishṭhira. 'See, this is the hermitage by the riverside where Rishyashringa lived. This spot has been sanctified by many sages and virtuous men and women, yes, even by the gods. It was here that Nala and Damayanti came. Sītā and Rāma, Aruṇdhati and Vasishṭha, Lopamudra and Agastya all came here. And Now you and Draupadī have come to this holy spot. Bathe in these sacred waters, which will purify you'. Hearing Lomāsa so speak, the Pāṇḍavas bathed in the river, meditated and performed devotions.

PERFORMANCE OF DUTY IS THE GREATEST VIRTUE

[This again is an incident relating to the period when the Pāṇḍavas were in the forest during the period of their exile. The sage, Mārkaṇḍeya came to see them. The sage praised the virtue of women, their large-heartedness and sense of duty to their husbands, parents and in-laws. 'A woman gives birth to her child in such pain and labour and is devoted to its care. She is of a forgiving nature and gives love to her husband even though he may be harsh and neglectful. How wonderful is a woman's nature!' The sage went on to tell the Pāṇḍavas the story of Kaushika].

There once lived a holy *brāhmin* called Kaushika who was learned in the scriptures and had taken the vow of celibacy. One while he was sitting under a tree reciting the Vedas, a crane which was perched on the tree-top dirtied his head with its droppings. The *brāhmin* gave it a fiery glance, and such was the power of it, that the bird fell down dead. When he saw the dead crane, he felt very sorry and repented that he had been responsible for killing it.

Sometime later he went to beg alms. It was customary for mendicants to beg for food, as being hermits, they had no arrangements for cooking their meals. They would go to neighbouring villages bordering their hut for this. The lady of the house where such a mendicant went would gladly come out and give him food. It was, in fact considered to be a sacred duty, never to let such a person go without giving him alms.

Kaushika stood before the door of a house and called out. The housewife was cleaning her utensils and thought she would go out to give the alms after finishing her work which was almost near its end. But at this moment her husband came, tired and hungry, so she attended to him, giving him water to wash his hands and feet, and serving him food. Thereafter she went with alms for the mendicant. 'I'm sorry I'm late' she said. Kaushika, who was angry at having been kept waiting so long said 'Lady, you should not have delayed. It isn't right for you to keep a *brāhmin* waiting'. The housewife was apologetic and explained him that she was attending on her husband. She was duty-bound to do so as a virtuous and faithful wife. But the *brāhmin* did not cool down. Then she said 'Look, I was only doing my duty towards my husband. I think that should not cause you annoyance. Everyone is bound to do his allotted and assigned duty. No harm can come to a woman who is thus devoted to her husband. And I'm no crane that I'll fall down dead merely by your angry glance'. Kaushika was amazed. How could she know about the crane'? The woman spoke on, 'O great sage, you should know that anger is man's greatest foe. Pardon me for this delay. Go to Mithilā where there lives a man called Dharmavyadha. He will disclose to you what living a good life implies'. Kaushika thanked the woman for pointing out his fault and went to Mithilā.

When he arrived, Kaushika was on the look out of the man to whom he had been directed. He thought it would be some saint or scholarly person living in a lonely cottage somewhere on the outskirts of the town. But there was no trace of the man there. Then he entered the grand city with its lovely gardens and mansions and inquired about Dharmavyadha. 'Oh! that butcher' a passerby said, 'he must be at his meat-shop. Look there he's sitting'. The *brāhmin* was astounded. Shocked at the chunks of meat in the shop, he went and stood well away from it. The butcher got up quickly when he saw him. 'Welcome, sir' he said. 'I hope you are well and happy. Did that virtuous *brāhmin* lady send you to me?' Kaushika was dumbfounded. He was now sure that some divine hand was guiding him. The butcher closed shop and took him to his house. Kaushika saw everyone happy in his family – his wife, his parents and his children. The butcher served them all with a deep sense of duty. He honoured his wife and loved her and his children. He looked after his parents with great care and showed them the utmost respect. Kaushika was impressed by the peace and goodwill prevailing in the family. He went back chastened and a wiser man, and began to attend on his aged parents, whom he had neglected till now.

Hindu philosophy considers the performance of duty to be the greatest virtue. In the Gītā when Krishṇa found Arjuna backing out of a righteous war (dharma-yuddha) he upbraided the warrior. A kshatriya's duty was to fight and never turn his back in war. Arjuna was recoiling from it. The Īsha Upanishad says: 'The man of renunciation who considers the universe as enveloped by God should desire to live in the world for hundred years always engaged in the duties imposed on him by dharma'.[108] *What renunciation really means is renouncing evil desires, anger, jealously greed, the thirst for sense pleasures and so forth. Merely getting away to a forest is no good if such evils are still with the person there. Of the debts one owes, called riṇa in Hindu philosophy, one is to one's forefathers and one to the gods. The pitririṇa is discharged by producing a son. Looking after one's parents in their old age is considered one of the most important duties of a son. In the Rāmāyaṇa we are told about Shravaṇakumāra who carried his blind parents on his shoulders, and kept looking after their needs. This was the lesson the butcher taught Kaushika.*

108. *Isha Upa.* 2.

DRAUPADĪ' S ANGUISH

[The most tragic and shameful episode of the Mahābhārata is the account of the game of dice between the Kauravas and the Pāṇḍavas in which the players were Yudhishṭhira and Shakunī, and the consequent attempt by Duḥshāsana to disrobe Draupadī. Vyāsa paints the scene very vividly in words which express the wounded anguish of Drapupadī, the enigmatic and cowardly silence of the elders present there—Bhīshma, Kripa, Droṇa and Dhritarāshṭra himself; the guile of Shakunī the pent up rage of Bhīma, the unchivalrous callousness of Duryodhana, Karṇa and Duḥshāsana, the outspoken and courageous condemnation of Vikarṇa and the divine deliverance of Draupadī by Krishṇa. The incident has been described and sung by many Hindi poets and writers].

When Shakunī, the brother of Gāndharī had mooted his wicked plan to Duryodhana, both of them went to Dhritarāshṭra to get his permission for inviting Yudhishṭhira and the Pāṇḍavas for a friendly game of dice. Shakunī asked the king why he was paying no attention to Duryodhana his own son who was in great sorrow. Dhritarāshṭra asked Duryodhana what made him sad when he had all the pleasures he could long for and the opportunity to study the sacred scriptures. Duryodhana said that the splendour of the Pāṇḍavas in their capital at Indraprastha was much greater than his. 'A *kshatriya* must never be content with his lot. He should try to add to his prosperity. Fear and pity do not behove kings'. He told him that the spendour of the Pāṇḍavas was gnawing into his contentment and that was what saddened him. Dhritarāshṭra told him to remove hatred of the Pāṇḍavas from his mind. They were his own kinsmen. Yudhishṭhira was a virtuous man and harboured no ill-will towards them. Why then should he be jealous? Duryodhana said 'One who is learned but devoid of commonsense is like a wooden ladle immersed in tasty food, which it can neither taste not be benefitted with. You may be wise but do not know statecraft. A king should not be forbearing and content. He should try to be victorious and all-powerful'. Shakunī then disclosed his plan. Dhritarāshṭra wanted to consult

Vidura, his advisor, and called him, notwithstanding Duryodhana's opposition. The virtuous minister said that the act would sow hatred and bring ruin. But Dhritarāshṭra was too weak-willed and indecisive to oppose his son whom he loved to distraction. So Vidura was ordered to go and invite the Pāṇḍavas.

Vidura's heart was not in conveying this invitation, yet he had no choice because he had to obey his king. Yudhishṭhira said, 'Gambling is no good. It creates bad blood and is the source of great evil. All wise men should avoid it. Eh, what do you think?' Vidura said 'Everyone knows wagering is bad. I myself didn't like the idea, particularly as there would be cheats there also. But I have been ordered to invite you. So do as you please'. Drawn by fate, Yudhishṭhira consented. When he was in the assembly-hall set apart for the game, he said, 'Gambling is a game of chance. All the wise sages like Asita and Devala have advised that it should not be played because it gives scope for deceit. Battle is all right for *kshatriyas*, but not gambling'. It was a last-ditch stand. But Shakunī was a cunning man. He played on Yudhishṭhira's weakness for the game. 'What is the difference between a game of dice and a battle, or even a religious debate? They have but one end, defeat or victory. Are you afraid of playing because you feel you'll lose?' Thus incited, Yudhishṭhira gave way and even agreed to the condition that while Duryodhana would draw the stakes, Shakunī would cast the dice. Shakunī knew well how to cheat at dice. So he kept on winning. Yudhishṭhira staked all his wealth and kingdom and lost. Then the wise king who was the embodiment of virtue and honour, acted most foolishly in staking his valorous brothers one by one, and finally even the faithful and guileless Draupadī. Shouts of condemnation arose from all sides, but the deed was done. Tears rolled down the cheeks of those witnessing it. The lovely lady fair as Shrī herself and blossoming like a lotus was staked and lost. The *Rāmacharitamānasa* says : 'No one is either wise or foolish by himself. As Shrī Rāma (i.e. God) turns his mind, so does he instantly becomes'.[109] Thus it was with Yudhishṭhira. He was just another pawn in the game of Destiny, and just as helpless as any other person.

---

109. *Bāla-kāṇḍa,* 124 (A).

Duryodhana asked Vidura to fetch Draupadī. 'She has become ours now' he said. 'She shall work as a maid and clean and sweep the floor'. 'Are you mad'? Vidura said, 'Your foul victory has deranged your mind. Don't you see that you are summoning your own ruin by such rashness. It seems you and your brothers do not wish to listen to salutary advice and are bent on their self-destruction'. Then Duryodhana called his charioteer, Prāthikāmī, to fetch her. He went and told Draupadī all that had happened. The enraged queen said 'Go back and ask Yudhishṭhira whether he first lost himself in the game or me [meaning thereby if he had lost himself to the Pāṇḍavas, his right to her was ended, so how could he stake what no longer belonged to him?]. Yudhishṭhira had no answer. Then Duryodhana asked his charioteer to tell Draupadī to come and ask her question herself. When she insisted on the answer being conveyed to her, Duryodhana flared up and turning to his brother, Duḥshāsana and said, 'This man is afraid. You go and fetch her. Bring her here even if you have to drag her'. The vile Duḥshāsana joyfully proceeded to Draupadī's apartment with bloodshot eyes. He shouted 'Come lady, why do you keep us waiting. You have been won by us and are ours now. Come'. The grieved queen, trembling with fear and rage, tried to flee to the chamber of Gāndhārī but Duḥshāsana caught hold of her long blue hair and began to drag her to the assembly-hall. She was moaning and weeping and saying 'Wretch, I am in my unclean period and wearing only a one-piece garment. I can't appear before my elders thus. Leave me. Let me go'. But the wicked man whom reason and righteousness had long ago deserted, kept dragging her mercilessly on the floor and pushed the weeping and dishevelled lady into the assembly-hall. Amid her sobs Draupadī cried out 'I cannot stand before these people in the state in which I am. I am in my periods. Fie on the Kurus who are looking on without saying a word. Why do the elders, Bhīshma, Droṇa, Vidura, Kripa and Dhritarashṭra not condemn this evil deed? Ah ! woe is me. The Kurus have daughters and daughters-in-law, yet they are not speaking out at a married and virtuous woman being thus dishonoured. How could my husband stake me when he had himself been lost to the Kauravas?' No one could answer her question. Duḥshāsana gave loud laugh and called her slave! slave ! again and again. Karṇa too, rejoiced and joined in the laughter. So did Shakunī and Duryodhana. The elders held their heads in shame, but spoke not a word.[110] But Bhīma could not contain himself. With a roar of anger he got up and shouted 'Even professional dice-players would not have the heart to stake the harlots who live with them, while you, brother have staked the virtuous and fawn-eyed Draupadī and left her helpless before these scroundrels. Sahadeva, go and bring fire, so that I may burn the hands which rolled the dice'. Arjuna, however, calmed him. Vikarṇa, one of Dhritarāshṭra's sons, could not, however bear the sight of the weeping queen. He stood up and said 'Why are the *kshatriya* warriors silent? Their silence forces me to speak, though I am just a lad. The whole proceedings of the dice-game were unfair. It was a deliberate plot to entrap the Pāṇḍavas. Yudhishṭhira had no right to stake Draupadī for she was not his wife alone [she had wed all the Pāṇḍavas]. So the wager was not proper. Besides Yudhishṭhira had already become a serf of the Kaurava king when he staked himself and lost the wager. How could a man who is another's lay claim to the woman who was his wife? Can a slave stake anyone of his who is his no longer? Then again it was Shakunī who suggested to him to stake her. According to the rules of the game, neither party can suggest a wager. The staking has to be purely voluntary. So I feel that Draupadī has been won by deceit'. The whole assembly was hushed into silence. Wisdom dawned on them and there were shouts of approval. However Karṇa supported Duryodhana and rebuked Vikarṇa. 'You are a mere lad' he said, 'and yet pretend to know what is right and what is wrong. Who are you to speak thus before the

---

110. Of all the elders present there Bhīshma was the senior-most. Why didn't he speak up and ask the Kauravas not to disgrace Draupadī? One reason could be that, as we have said in narrating the *Mahābhārata* story, Bhīshma, son of Gangā was one of the eight Vasus who, due to a curse, had to be born in the world in human form. While all of the them were cast into the waters by Gangā immediately after birth, one was destined to suffer by prolonged life on earth. And this was Bhīshma. So here he was suffering the injustice of it all and the sorrow of the Pāṇḍavas and Draupadī too, but suffering in silence.

elders here. You are harming the family in which you were born, as a stick which rotates to produce fire, produces it and then burns up the very source of the fire (that is, the stick). You are like an evil bird that fouls its own nest. It is quite clear that after he lost the stake, Yudhishṭhira ceased to be a free man. He, and all that is his are now Shakunī's. Duḥshāsana, tear off the clothes of the Pāṇḍavas from their bodies. They are no longer theirs. Nor is Draupadī's garment hers'. Hearing this, the Pāṇḍavas flung away their upper kingly garments. Then Duḥshāsana caught hold of Draupadī's sari and began to pull it off her by force, and make her naked. The elders looked on this shameful scene in stunned silence, yet spoke not a word. Then the helpless Draupadī called on Krishṇa 'O Janārdana, you are the Lord of the universe Do not forsake me at this hour. Save my honour. Save me! Save me!' Krishṇa, from whom nothing can be hid, came to her aid, unseen by all. And lo! as the wicked Duḥshāsana pulled away the garment it seemed to have no end. He pulled and pulled, and the hall was covered by the stack of cloth. But the sari went on growing in length of itself. Duḥshāsana was bathed in sweat as the piled up cloth of Draupadī's sari grew more and more. His hands got tired of pulling and refused to move. He staggered with exhaustion and fell. Yet Draupadī remained clad in her garment as though nothing had happened. The whole assembly was astounded. The people in it were wonder-struck and wept and prayed. Then Bhīma took a terrible vow. Raising his voice in anger he said, 'May I never see the abode of my ancestors if I do not tear apart Duḥshāsana's breast and drink his heart's blood'.

Draupadī appealed to Bhīshma. 'Tell me', she said 'whether I have been fairly won or not. I have been wronged in this august assembly. I have never been of subjected to public gaze, except in the *swayamvara* in which I was won by Arjuna. I am the wife of a king, and as honourable as the other princess. Tell me, do you consider me to be a servant?' Bhīshma did not say a word. Nor did any of the Pāṇḍavas. Karṇa said 'Go inside and work as a servant. Choose another husband'. As if to give weight to Karṇa's wicked words, Duryodhana bared his thigh motioned to Draupadī to sit on it. Seeing this the enlarged Bhima Bhīma's shouted. 'Let me be destroyed, 'if I do not break that thigh of this vile rogue'. At this moment there were ill omens. Jackals cried and asses brayed. The eerie shrieks of fearful birds resounded in the hall, portending calamities.

In this way the great Lord, Krishṇa, saved the honour of Draupadī. No harm can ever come to one who worships God with single-minded devotion. This is what Krishṇa said to Arjuna: Make me your refuge. I will save you from all sins and free you from all bondage'.

THE DISCOURSE OF BHĪMA AND THE SAGES

[The extract given below is from the Shānti Parva, the twelfth book of the Mahābhārata. When the great bloodshed at Kurukshetra was over, and the Kaurava warriors lay slain on the field of battle, Gāndhārī, wife of king Dhritrāshṭra, was filled with sorrow as she herself went there to witness the slaughter. In great sorrow, her anger flared up, and she said to Krishṇa, 'You could have prevented this slaughter, O Mādhava, but you failed to do so'. This was not at all fair, for before the war it was Krishṇa who had gone to Hastināpura on a peace mission. He wanted to make a last-ditch effort to avoid the battle. When in Dhritrāshṭra's assembly-hall, he had said : 'I have come desiring peace between the Kauravas and the Pāṇḍavas. O Dhritrāshṭra, if you can control your sons, I shall ensure that the Pāṇḍavas do not fight. Allow the Pāṇḍavas to live and serve you and fight your battles. Let there be peace between your sons and those of Pritha'. But Dhritarāshṭra had shied away from his responsibility and said that it all depended on Duryodhana, his son. Duryodhana was not willing for peace. So it was really Duryodhana who was responsible for the slaughter caused in the battle, not Krishṇa. Anyway the wrathful Gāndhārī cursed Krishṇa saying that thirty-six years hence his kinsmen, the Yādavas of the Vrishṇi clan, would kill each other and be exterminated. Krishṇa smiled and told her that nothing could be done against his will. But he himself had been trying to do what she wished and now her curse had assisted him to accomplish it. Then Krishṇa said: 'A brāhmin woman gives birth to sons for them to practise austerities; a vaishya woman so that her sons may increase the number of cattle, (i.e., wealth, for in those days wealth was reckoned by the number of cattle); a shūdra woman to add to the number of servants; but a queen like you [of the kshatriya race] bears sons to fight valorously, and be slain if needs be, on the field of battle'. Thereafter the funeral ceremonies of the dead warriors were performed. Yudhishṭhira was filled with grief to see the slaughter, and particularly because, in ignorance, Arjuna had slain Karṇa who in truth was the eldest of the

Pāṇḍavas. The rishīs came to comfort him. The Pāṇḍava brothers asked him to assume kingship. And to them Yudhishṭhira expressed his doubts. The talk he had and the doctrine of peace is set down in the extract we give now].

Yudhishṭhira as Emperor

The Pāṇḍavas wanted Yudhishṭhira to be Samrāt, that is the king of the earth. Yudhishṭhira said to Arjuna, their spokesman: 'I have read the scriptures. They say that one can realize the Soul by controlling desires which arise in the mind. If one ceases from working to achieve desires, he is contented. Then why, O Arjuna, do you thrust the enjoyment of wealth and domain on me?' The rishīs Devasthāna and Vyāsa then said : 'Even ascetics, O king, are engaged in works. The scriptures enjoin one to follow the duties of a *grihastha* (householder). Besides a *kshatriya* king must have the strength to punish [erring subjects]. A battle is a *kshatriya* king's *yajña.* By reigning with wise polity, mercy and impartiality, a great king achieves heaven. Success can stem only from action. So to do works is necessary. Thereafter Krishṇa said, 'Those who have been slain cannot now become alive. As dreams vanish when one wakes, so too is this life'. However, finally Yudhishṭhira was made to give his consent..

Bhīshma's Hymn in Praise of Krishṇa

Bhīshma was lying on the battlefield on his bed of arrows. [These were the arrows that had pierced him from all sides so that they had become his bed. He could die only when he wished to]. Krishṇa said 'Bhīshma is still alive. Let us come to him'. So he and the Pāṇḍavas went to him. Bhīshma knew, of course, that Krishṇa was the incarnation of Lord Vishṇu. So he greeted him with a hymn of praise :

'O Lord of beings, O Universal Soul,
You have no end or beginning.
The whole universe of mind and matter
Is as a garland of threaded-flowers round you.
The senses cannot know you, nor mind comprehend,

O One of many forms, O Golden-hued :
Salutations to you, Lord of the universe,
You are *māyā's* Master, from you is all knowledge
You are the All, I seek your refuge, Lord'.

Bhīshma's Discourse on Sāṁkhya and Yoga

The devotees of Yoga believe that only he who is convinced of the existence of God can achieve liberation. According to Sāṁkhya one who has true knowledge of all objects is liberated. Yoga implies direct perception while Sāṁkhya says that this is possible only by study of the scriptures. Then only can the truth be perceived. However, both systems commend purity and mercy.

Vasishṭha's Teaching

King Janaka asked the sage, Vasishṭha : 'It is said that the relation between Nature and soul, that is to say between that which is liable to destruction and that which is indestructible, is like that of a man and a woman. Each cannot create a child without the other. If then Nature and the Soul oppose each other, how can liberation be possible?' Vasishṭha answered: 'There is no difference between Sāṁkhya and Yoga. Wise men see them as one. Objects are derived from objects and the senses from the senses. Thus qualities arise from Nature and disappear into it. The Supreme Being is quite apart. He is without matter, senses, seed, body, or qualities. The individual soul is different from the Supreme Soul. When the soul inhabits the body it is invested with qualities. But when it rises above these qualities (the *guṇas—sattva*, *rajasa* and *tamasa*) it becomes the Supreme [We have already in the introduction explained the difference between the soul as *ātman* and as *jīva*]. The wise man knows that the nature of the individual soul and the Supreme [*brahman*] is the same. But the ignorant person considers them to be different. The soul is beyond the twenty-five categories [of Sāṁkhya]. When the knower, the known and knowledge are viewed as one, then the yogi gets realization of the Supreme.

The above is the teaching so Yoga, Vasishṭha said, now I will proceed to tell you about Sāṁkhya. The Sāṁkhya system is built on Nature (*prakriti*). From it comes *mahat* or principle of greatness, *ahaṁkāra*, and the five suble elements of sound, touch, form, taste and odour. From these eight categories arise sexteen others. These are the five gross elements of ether, fire, water, air and earth, the ten senses of knowledge and action and the sixteenth, mind. Thus these twenty-four constitute the Sāṁkhya categories.

That which is produced keeps being merged with that which has produced it. Thus creation keeps moving forever forward. When destruction takes place the order is reversed. So creation and destruction keep continually occurring. When there is universal destruction (*pralaya*), only the Supreme Being remains. Everything else is destroyed. From him again the various forms arise when the universe is recreated. Nature (*prakriti*) is the Field (*Kshetra*) and the Soul [called *Purusha* in Sāṁkhya] is the Knower of the Field. When the Soul knows the Supreme Soul after dissociating itself from Nature, it is liberated and becomes one with the Supreme.

Both Nature and the Soul [*Purusha*] are beginningless and endless. Both have their own separate supremacies. The Sāṁkhya admits of no other entity beyond the twenty-five enunciated by it. But the Yoga speaks of the One without the second, which is *brahman*. When the Soul or *Purusha* knows the Supreme Soul by dissociating itself from *prakriti*, it achieves union with the Supreme Soul. Knowledge of *prakriti* by the Soul restores it to its real nature. Then that knowledge which is the twenty-sixth principle is attained. The qualities (*guṇas*) fall off from the Soul. That is how he achieves that which is Supreme.

Bhīshma said to Yudhishṭhira : Nārada, the great sage adored Nārāyaṇa, the Lord in a hymn as follows :

What Nārada Said

Salutations to you. O Lord,

You are the Infinite, the Supreme *Purusha*

Manifest and unmanifest. You are the Sun.

As the breath within, you sustain life, you rule over the waters,

You are desire and sacrifice, you live in every heart..
Reclining on the lotus, you are the world's origin,
The sun, the moon, the mind and *māyā* :
You are *Om*, you are the Cause and the Creator,
You deal death with one hand, *moksha* with the other.

Then Nārada came there and decribed the greatness of Krishṇa. 'He is power supreme', Nārada said, 'and he is the Soul of all creatures. The body consists of five elements–earth, water, fire, air and ether. Vāsudeva (Krishṇa) enters these and then only can life arise in them. It is this Spirit which is the life within. Without it the body cannot exist even for a moment. The entire universe emerges from Nārāyaṇa who is above the *guṇas*. He does not act, yet it is he who is the doer, the effect and the cause. It is he who pervades all creatures.

The Destruction of the Vrishṇīs and the End of the Krishṇa-avatāra

[Dhritarāshṭra had retired to the forest along with Gāndhārī, Vidura Saṁjaya and Kuntī. Vidura died by assuming the yoga posture and entering the body of Yudhishṭhira, who, along with the other Pāṇḍavas, had gone to pay Dhritarāshṭra and others a visit. By the power of the sage, Vyāsa, while they were bathing in the Gangā river, Dhritarāshṭra had a vision of all the warriors who had been slain on the battlefield. He and Gāndhārī saw them and were happy for a moment. Therafter, a sacrificial fire that had been lit at the bidding of Dhritarāshṭra accidentally burnt all those who had retired to the forest. Only Saṁjaya was saved.

The thirty-sixth years after the battle now came. This, it might be recollected, was the time when the Vrishṇīs were destined to be destroyed].

Remenbering Gāndhārī's curse, Krishṇa asked the Vrishṇīs to go on a pilgrimage and bathe in the holy waters. They went along with their families and dwelt on the sea coast. The Vrishṇī warriors mixed wine in food and distributed it to all. They got drunk. Yuyudhāna insulted Kritavarman. Then Sātyakī rushed and chopped off Kritivarman's head. The Bhojas and Andhakas killed Sātyaki and Krishṇa's son in the melee. The enraged Krishṇa took some blades of *eraka* grass. These turned into deadly thunderbolts. He killed all who were near him with them. This was a signal for a general conflict. Whoever plucked a blade of the grass found it converted into a thunderbolt, providing a formidable weapon of destruction. Thus they fought on killing each other, till all the Vrishṇīs lay dead.

Balarāma sat in meditation in the yoga posture. A strong white snake with a thousand heads came out from his mouth and was cast into the ocean. Thus Balarāma surrendered his soul.

Krishṇa knew that the time had come for him to go, as his purpose for descending on the earth had been fulfilled. He knew the truth of all things. But to uphold the three worlds, he who was the Lord of the universe, sat down in meditation, awaiting that which would rid him of the human form. A hunter of the name of Jarā, mistook him to be a deer and pierced his heel with an arrow. Thus ended the Krishṇa-avatāra.

Dāruka came to Hastināpura and told the Pāṇḍavas of all that had taken place. Arjuna at once went to Dwārakā. The city looked like a widowed woman. When the sixteen thousand women who had been wedded to Krishṇa saw him there came from them a heart-rending wail.

Krishṇa had left Arjuna a message before he died. Vasudeva, Krishṇa had said, 'I am Arjuna and Arjuna is myself. His directions should be followed. After he leaves, the sea will submerge Dwārakā'. Soon after Vasudeva, Krishṇa's father died. Then Arjuna got the funeral rites of the dead perfomed, and taking with him the widows of the Vrishṇīs and the Andhakas departed for Hastināpura. After he had set out, the ocean flooded Dwārakā and the entire city was submerged in it.

[But Arjuna could not give protection to the women he had taken to rehabilitate them at Hastināpura. On the way they were attacked by robbers. The great Gāṇḍīva bow of Arjuna failed, and the arrows in his quiver which never knew exhaustion, were finished. He could not remember the celestial mantras for wielding his weapons. The robbers carried away many of the Vrishṇī and Andhaka women. Arjuna proceeded with those who were left and provided homes for them at Hastināpura. With tears in his eyes he went to Vyāsa and told him all that had happened. The sage consoled him and said it was destined and was bound to come to pass. The time has also come for you and your brother to go, he said].

QUESTIONS FOR THE WISE

[The Pāṇḍavas had lost the wager again in the second game of dice and had, as a consequence brought upon themselves twelve year's exile in the forest. Many incidents occurred during their forest-sojourn, some of which we have related. It was here that Bhīma met his brother Hanumān (Māruti) the Wind-god, Arjuna obtained the pashupata, Shiva's divine weapon and Krishṇa satiated the hunger of the fiery sage Durvāshā and his disciples by himself eating just a grain of boiled rice. The incident which now follows also relates to the time when the Pāṇḍavas were wandering in the forest. The story is related by Vaishampāyana to Janamejaya].

In those days ther were no safety-matches for lighting as we have now. The way to kindle fire was by rubbing a wooden stick against a hollow wood block, It so happened that a deer rubbed itself against the fire-kindling block of a *brāhmin* and got so entangled in it that when he fled out of fear, it carried away the poor man's fire-device too! The *brāhmin* ran after it to retrieve his wooden mortar, but how could he keep up with the swift deer! Seeing the Pāṇḍavas, he cried out to them for help. They pursued the deer, but it eluded them. Tired by all the running about they sat down to rest under a bunyan tree. Yudhishṭhira was feeling thirsty, so he asked Nakula to climb up the tree and see if he could spot a place where there was likely to be water. He went up and saw water-plants and cranes, some distance away. There is bound to be a pond there, he thought to himself and coming down, went of fetch water. True enough there was a pool there with nice clear water. He was thirsty himself, and thought he'd have a drink first and then carry some water for his brothers in the pot he had brought, He bent down to drink, but instantly a voice startled him. 'This is my pool. You can't drink water from it before answering some questions I'll ask'. Nakula was very thirsty. Besides, he dismissed the voice as some kind of hoax, and started drinking. As soon as he had done so, a drowsiness overpowered him and he fainted and fell down as though dead. When Nakuka did not come, Yudhishṭhira sent Sahadeva, who met with the same fate. Then Arjuna went, and seeing his brothers lying lifeless, he was filled with rage. He challenged the person whom he thought had killed them, saying 'Show yourself. I will riddle you with arrows'. But he heard only mocking laughter. 'Answer my questions and you may then drink of this water, for the pool is mine'. Arjuna decided to deal with the man after he had refreshed himself by the water of the pool. As soon as he drank, he too fell into a faint and dropped down beside his brothers. When Arjuna, too, failed to return, Bhīma went to see what held them. On seeing his brothers lying by the bank of the pool, he was filled will grief and anger. This could be the foul work of the *yakshas*, he thought. He vowed to kill them all, but first he would slake his thirst. As he sat down to drink, the voice cried. 'You must first answer my questions, Bhīma. If you drink water from this pool which mine you will share your brothers, fate'. Bhīma did not pay any attention and started drinking the water. Instantly all his strength ebbed away and he dropped down and lay still. When Bhīma too did not come back, Yudhishṭhira was greatly worried for their safety, and feared they had come to harm. He hurried onwards and came upon the fearful sight of all his brothers lying lifeless beside the pool. He wept and was heartboken. The exile was about to end and with it the period of their trial and woes. And now this tragic end had overtaken them He was puzzled too. All his brothers were among the most valiant warriors on earth. How could they have died like this and that too apparently without a struggle. Their bodies bore no wounds. Could it be that Duryodhana had played some trick? Or was the water poisoned. Anyway he was awfully thirsty, so decided to first take just a sip of water. The voice again cautioned him. 'Your brothers died because they did not listen to what I said. You must answer my questions first and then drink of my pool'. Yudhishṭhira realized that rashness would not pay. The sight of his brothers lying there convinced him of that. It was most probably the doing of a *yaksha*, for they possessed magical powers. 'Proceed with your question' he said 'I'll answer them'. The questions asked and Yudhishṭhira's answers to them were as follows:

Q. What causes the sun to shine every day?

A. *Brahman's* light. Without him the sun can have neither light nor heat.

Q. What is *that* by which a man avoids all dangers and comes out unharmed from them?

A. Courage.

Q. By studying what can a man achieve wisdom?

A. Wisdom cannot be got from books. It is attained by the company of wise men.

Q. The earth gives sustenance. Is there anything more sustaining than that? If so what?

A. The earth sustains, but even more so does a mother. She gives birth to her children and does everything possible for their good.

Q. What is higher than the sky?

A. One's father. He is the highest being for his son.

Q. What is swifter than the wind?

A. The mind.

Q. What is more blighted than a dried straw?

A. A man's heart which is afflicted by grief.

Q. What helps a traveller?

A. Learning.

Q. Who is a man's closest companion at his home?

A. His wife.

Q. Who is that who befriends and accompanies a man even after death?

A. It is *dharma* (righteousness) which is the man's advocate and pleads for him. If he has walked in the way of righteousness, he will find favour with God.

Q. Which is the most commodious vessel?

A. The earth, for it contains all.

Q. How is happiness achieved?

A. By displaying good conduct.

Q. By abandoning what does a man become agreeable to all?

A. Pride. A humble man is universally loved.

Q. What is that, the loss of which brings joy?

A. Anger. When one frees himself from anger he is rid of sorrow.

Q. What make a man a *brāhmin*? Is it birth, or good conduct, or learning?

A. Neither birth nor learning. A *brāhmin* is distinguished by good conduct.

Q. What is the greatest wonder in the world?

A. Every day one sees or knows of people dying. Yet he never thinks that one day he too will die.

Thus Yudhishṭhira gave adequate answers to all the questions asked. The voice then said 'I will revive one of your brothers. Whom do you want me to bring back to life?' Yudhishṭhira chose Nakula. 'Why Nakula?' The voice said. 'Why not Bhīma and Arjuna who are supreme in might and also very dear to you?' Yudhishṭhira said 'My father had two wives, Mādrī and Kuntī I, Kuntī's son, am still alive. So to be fair, one of Mādrī's sons should come back to me'. 'I am pleased with your sense of fairness and justice' the voice said. 'All your brothers will be revived'. Instantly all the Pāṇḍavas rose, as though from a swoon. 'Know son, that I am Dharma, your father. It was I who took the form of the deer to draw you away to this pool. It was I who asked you these questions to test you. You will pass through the thirteen years [twelve of exile and one living incognito]. No harm will befall you'. So saying the god of appeared before them and Dharma blessed Yudhishṭhira

YUDHISHṬHIRA'S ASCENT–THERE IS NO RANCOUR IN HEAVEN

[The Krishṇa-avatara had ended and Balarāma had surrendered his earthly body. Now with the passing away of the Pāṇḍavas and the ascent of Yudhishṭhira to heaven we reach the end of the Mahābhārata story. A doubt could arise why of the Pāṇḍavas brothers, only Yudhishṭhira was chosen to ascend to heaven. It was he who had staked his brothers and Draupadī at the gambling match. Indeed, not learning from his mistake he had played again and brought misery upon the Pāṇḍavas by the twelve year's exile. He had lied about the 'death, of Droṇa's son, causing the ignoble slaying of Droṇa. Then why was he considered the worthiest of the five ? On the credit side, however, as we have related in the previous episode, he had, by his wisdom, saved his brothers. He alone had been calm when his brothers showed anger. He was never in favour of war. Nothing could ruffle him. And as we shall relate in the account which follows, he got through creditably in the final test to which he was subjected].

Kuntī's last blessing to Yudhishṭhira before she retired to the forest was 'May you always follow the path of righteousness'. When the Pāṇḍavas learnt about the end of Krishṇa and the destruction of the Vrishṇīs, they had no longer any interest in existence. So, after crowning Parikshit, Abhimanyū's son, as king of Hastināpura all of along with Draupadī left the capital. They visited many holy places and finally directed their steps to the Himalayas. As they trudged along, they fell down exhausted on the way, one by one. A dog, which had joined their company somewhere, and Yudhishṭhira, the eldest of the brothers, alone went along. After a long journey when they were somewhere high up. Indra, the king of heaven, met the two the man and the animal. 'I have come to conduct you to heaven' Indra said to Yudhishṭhira. When the Pāṇḍava prince got on to the heavenly chariot, the dog followed him. 'What nonsense' Indra said, pushing out the dog. 'There is no place in heaven for a dog.' 'Then there is no place there for me too,' Yudhishṭhira said. 'Either the dog goes with me, or I don't go. I can't desert this faithful creature who has befriended me till the last.' As he said this the dog vanished. Dharma's voice spoke out 'I had taken the form of this dog to test you, son' it said. 'I am well pleased in you.'

When Yudhishṭhira reached heaven, he saw there, of all persons, Duryodhana. He was sitting on a stately throne in all his glory, with angels attending on him, and resplendent as some god. The Pāṇḍavas were nowhere to be seen. 'Where are my brothers?' Yudhishṭhira asked the guide who was taking him. 'I can't stand the sight of this vicious man, who devised so many foul and wicked schemes to torture us even when we had never harmed him. He tried to burn us all in the wax-palace, he cunnignly made us play dice and got Shakunī to cheat and win the game. He got Draupadī, that virtuous and innocent woman, dragged before the assembly, and publicly disgraced her. I can't bear his sight. Where are my brothers? I would like to be with them'. And thus cursing Duryodhana, Yudhisṭhira turned his back to him. Then Nārada, the heavenly sage appeared and said : 'Tut tut, king Yudhishṭhira, this isn't right. No ill-will is harboured by anyone in heaven. Duryodhana fought valorously as a warrior should. He did his duty. This is not the place to remember hatreds but to forget them. You have come here with your human body, hence aversion and ill-will are sticking on to you. This is not proper. Eschew such thoughts'. Yudhisṭhira however, was, not convinced. How could this man who was full of sin, who caused so many persons to die and suffer, who never tried to distinguish between right and wrong, and who made avarice and cunning the sole incentives of his actions, be a candidate for heaven. Surely his noble brothers, Draupadī who had suffered so much, and Karṇa who, despite his animosity, had a noble streak and was his own brother, must be in some more blessed part of heaven. He asked to be taken there. When the angels heard this, they asked an attendant to take him to where his brothers were.

As they went, it became darker and more gloomy. Wierd and revolting sights were seen. Yudhishṭhira found his path slimy with blood. Offal bones, carrion, skeletons and horrible things came to view. An awful strench, almost unbearable assailed his nostrils. 'How far are have we to go?' he asked the messenger, halting in disgust. 'If you so wish, we may turn back' the attendant said. The sickening foul smell made Yudhishṭhira hesitate. But just then he heard voices 'O Yudhishṭhira, stay, don't go. Your presence has brought us some respite and relief. O son of Dharma, stay, even though it be for a little. It brings us much comfort in our tortures.' Heaing the voices lamenting and pleading with him and moved by their anguish, Yudhishṭhira asked who these wretched souls were. 'I am Karna'. one of them said. 'I am Bhīma, I am Arjuna, I am Draupadī, I Nakula, I Sahadeva.' Hearing the piteous voices of his brothers, Yudhishṭhira was maddened with gried. He was also filled with rage and said to the messenger. 'Go back. Tell your masters that I shall stay where my brothers have been unjustly confined for no fault of theirs'. The messenger went and told Indra all about it.

Thus a thirthieth part of the day passed. Then Indra, and Dharma [or Yama, the god of death who is identified with him]. appeared where the pained Yudhishṭhira stood. Dharma said 'O wise one, this is the third time I have tested you. You have chosen to stand by your brothers and to share their tortures. This is commendable. *Kings and rulers have inevitably to pass through hell, even though it may be for a short while.*[111] So for the thirteeth part of the day you had to endure the tortures of hell. Nobody is in hell This was only an illusion. This is not hell, but heaven. Don't you hear the sweet notes of the sage Nārada's *vīṇā*? Stop sorrowing. Then Yudhishṭhira shed his human body and shone with splendour. All anger hatred and grief left him. He saw all his brothers including Karṇa, and also all the sons of Dhritarāshṭra. They were all serene and free of animosity and anger. And Yudhishṭhira experienced unbroken peace and boundless bliss.

111. Cf. Christ's saying 'It is easier for a camel to pass through the needle's eye than for a rich man to enter the kingdom of heaven'.

THE LOVELY WOMEN OF THE MAHĀBHĀRATA

[We see that even saints and ascetics were attracted to lovely women and Apsarās. There were, of course lovely damsels like Draupadī, Satyavatī and so forth, but some were of divine origin, like Gangā, the goddess of the river of that name, and others were Apsarās. These Apsarās were the famous nymphs of Indra's heaven, parallel to Aphrodite, like Urvashī who approached Arjuna when he went to Indra's kingdom. These women were models of beauty. But it was by no means the concept of beauty which the modern world knows, and by which 'beauty queens' of today are judged ! The reader will find out the difference for himself by the descriptions which now follow]

DRAUPADĪ

[As we have related, Yudhisṭhira staked Draupadī in the game of dice between the Pāṇḍavas and the Kauravas. Here by gives a description of her. The account is in the Shabhā Parva of the Mahābhārata]

Yudhishṭhira said, now I will play with you [O Duryodhānā] with Draupadī as stake. She is of medium height, neither too thin nor too fat. The locks of her hair are blue and curly. Her eyes are like lotus-petals and her body has the fragrance of lotuses. Her lovelines is no less than Lakshmī's or Shrī's, whom she resembles in grace and symmetry. When she prespires her face has the softness of the lotus and the jasmine. This slender-waisted princess of Pānchāla has a hairless body, flowing locks and red lips. With this lady of waist slender as a wasp, I will play, staking her, O son of Suvala.

[After her beings dragged before the assembly the poor princess was in a sorry state. This is described now, in the Vana Parva]

Saying thus [in protest], that lady of gentle speech hid her face in her hands, soft as lotus-buds. Her tears coursed down her big deeply-divided and shapely breasts bearing auspicious marks.

[The description of Draupadī, also in the Vana Parva, which follows is when she becomes exhausted wandering in the forest with the Pāṇḍavas, during the period of their exile]

That lady with plump arms and lovely dark eyes, of graceful form stood on her thighs resembling the trunk of an elephant and closely touching each other. But she could not even stand becuase of exteme exhaustion and fell down, her limbs trembling as leaves of a plantain tree. Nakula saw her dropping as a bent creeper and hurried to support her.

[We have related in the Mahābhārata story how Jayadratha, the Sindhū king, seeing Draupadī in the forest, known as Kāmyaka, was so enchanted with her that, casting aside all morality and lusting after her, he carried her away. Subsequently she was rescued by Arjuna and Bhīma. Here we have a brief description of her beauty by Jayadratha. in the Vana Parva].

She was exquisitely charming and of stately form. As she moved her body shone in the woods as lightning in a dark cloud. She appeared in the forest darkness as a flame of fire fanned by the breeze.

[Another description of Draupadā is found early in the epic in the Ādi Parva, sections 1 - XI]

She was slender-waisted like the wasp, neither too tall nor too short, and her body had the fragrance of the blue lotus flower. Her large eyes were like the leaves of the lotus. Her full thighs were round and fair, and her body gleaming like an emerald, had auspicious marks. Her dense curly back hair cascaded down her back.

URVASHĪ

[*Arjuna was asked to go to Indra's heaven in search of celestial weapons to be able to successfully stand in battle against the Kauravas. There Urvashī met him and wanted to make love to the handsome warrior. But Arjuna repulsed her, for which she cursed him to remain a eunuch for some time. This later stood him in good stead when the one year of living in disguise had to be undergone. Arjuna could, as a eunuch take the name of Brihannalā, and teach Virāṭa's daughter Uttarā*]

When the twilight was about to fade into night and the moon was up, that Apsarā, Urvashī, went to Arjunā's apartment. Her high hips swayed as she moved and she seemed enchanting with bunches of flowers adorning her long and smooth braided hair. She vied with the moon itself in beauty, her graceful body undulating, her eyebrows sending vivacious glances, her soft voice murmuring love and her face glowing like the moon. As she moved, her finely full pointed breasts on which a gold chain dangled, anointed with heavenly and fragrant sandalwood paste and unguents, began to tremble. The heaviness of her breasts caused her to walk slowly along with bent head and to shake her slender waist as though it found the big breasts a burden. The three folds of her belly were bared. Her perfect loins, the charming dwelling place of the god of love, were topped by fair raised full and round hips sloping down as a hillside. Those hips, on which rested a gold chain seen through her diaphanous garment, were enough to agitate the hearts of saints and ascetics. Her shapely ankles and feet with flat soles and her toes straight, without blemish were golden-hued like burnished copper. The dorsa was high and curved as the back of a tortoise, with jingling anklebells which charmed all who heard their sweet sound. The upper part of her body dressed in thin gossamerlike cloth was like a wisp of cloud with the moon moving across it in the sky.

TAPATĪ, SEEN BY KING SAMVARAṆA

She was of large eyes. Her body shone as a flame of fire and her loveliness vied with the moon. That maiden of black eyes shone with the glitter of gold. So bright she looked that the plants and the creepers around her seemed to assume a golden hue. The king had never seen a woman as charming as she was. He cried out 'O lovely damsel with tapering thighs your sweet smile enchants me. O faultless one, the beauty of your form surpasses that of the ornaments with which it is decked. Your moon-like face and your eyes like lotus-petals enslave me and it seems I am being grounded by the god of love. O maiden of enchanting smiles, round swelling hips, dark eyes and voice melodious as the singing of *kinnaras* [musicians dwelling in heaven]'.

[Note - This account in from the Ādi Parva of the *Mahābhārata*].

THE COURTEZAN WHO WENT TO RISHYASHRINGA

[*We have already related the story of the ascetic Rishyashringa whom Romapāda the king of Anga enticed through a bevy of lovely courtezans so that rain would fall and famine may be ended in his kingdom.– see 'The Ascetic who had Never Seen a Woman'. Here the ascetic describes to his father the courtezan he saw. He calls her 'he' and uses 'his' for 'hers' all through the narrative, for he thought he was seeing a man, but we have used the correct pronoun in order to avoid confusion*]

That lovely damsel was playing with a ball [done usually by women out too charm, to display their limbs to advantage]. Every time she picked up the ball she resembled a lovely creeper bent in two. She was of medium height, (i.e., not disproportionate) with large lotus-like eyes and golden hued. Her bright, graceful figure was like that of some god [ought to be 'goddess', but since the ascetic takes her to be a man, he says 'a god']. She was very fair, blazing like the sun, dark-eyed and graceful-bodied. Her blue-black fragrant hair was braided and tied with gold threads. Her jutting round breasts were charming, each being balls of flesh without a single hair on them [this distinguishing feature of the courtezan must have bewitehed the youth most!]. Her waist was slender with a shapely navel and the flesh about her ribs was soft and smooth. Her face was wonderful to see, her voice pierced my heart and her words were like a blackbird's song. She smelt sweet like the fragrance of the vernal forest swept by the breeze. O father, [addressing the sage Vibhandaka, his father] her perfumed body stole my senses. Her lustrous hair parted from the middle lay massed behind. Her lovely eyes were like the *chakrava* birds extremely alluring.

HOW KRISHNA BECAME ARJUNA'S CHARIOTEER

[*When it was evident that war between the Pāṇḍavas and the Kauravas was imminent, both sides became eager to get assistance from Krishṇa, who ruled over Dwārakā, and whose army was believed to be the largest and most powerful. The Nārāyaṇas, Krishṇa's tribesmen were strong and almost invincible. Both Duryodhana and Arjuna were equally close in relationship to Krishṇa, so each hoped to get his assistance*].

Arjuna set out for Dvārakā on this quest. Meanwhile Duryodhana learnt about his departure through his spies. So he too, got his chariot made ready and went posthaste to meet Krishṇa, who had returned to his capital shortly before. Both of them by chance arrived at the same time. Being closely related to Krishṇa, the doorman allowed them to enter his bedroom. They saw him fast asleep. Duryodhana, went in and sat on an ornate chair which was at the head of the bed, while Arjuna stood standing at its foot. Both of them awaited Krishṇa's waking up. When Krishṇa woke he saw Arjuna standing humbly by his bedside. He greeted him warmly. Then he saw Duryodhana sitting on the chair and greeted him also. 'Well, what brings you two to Dwārakā?' Krishṇa asked.

Duryodhana was the first to speak. 'It is apparent that soon the Kauravas, my brothers, will be engaged in war with the Pāṇḍavas. So I have come to ask for your assistance'. He stressed the fact that his claim for Krishṇa was just and honourable. So he hoped, as indeed he was entitled, he would be given first choice. Krishṇa listened patiently and then said that it was true that he had come first, but on waking, he had seen Arjuna before he saw him. Besides, Arjuna was the younger of the two. So from that angle, too, he should be listened to first. 'Both of you are equally close to me, and so have an equal claim on me' Krishṇa said. 'I am bound, therefore to assist you both. Hence I make a proposition. On one side shall be my invincible army, and on the other me alone and that too unarmed, for I will wield no weapons and take no part in the actual fighting.' Saying this, Krishṇa turned to Arjuna and said 'Think over this well. You are younger than Duryodhana. So you are entitled to the first choice. Would you like to have the assistance of my whole grand army, or me alone unarmed and a non-combatant?' Arjuna did not hesitate a moment. In a tone of reverence he said 'I would prefer to have you on my side, even though you will not fight.'

Duryodhana was overjoyed. In fact he had come specifically to ask for Krishṇa's army, which was unequalled in might. The fool, Arjuna, had given it to him on a platter. What would he, Duryodhana, gain by one unarmed man who wouldn't wield weapons or fight. He was elated and went off to seek the blessing of Balarāma, Krishṇa's elder brother, and an invincible and feared warrior. He told him all that had taken place. Balarāma said that he told Krishṇa that for them the Pāṇḍavas and the Kauravas were the same. In any case he regretted he couldn't side with Duryodhana against Krishṇa. So he had to remain neutral. He asked Duryodhana to acquit himself as a brave *kshatriya* should. Duryodhana was happy. He had feared that Balarāma might line up with his brother. At least that situation had been avoided. He returned to Hastināpura full of high spirits, and said, 'That fool of a Arjuna has declined to have Krishṇa's huge army, and now it will fight on our side. Balarāma has also spoken kindly to me. Vāsudeva's army will not be with the Pāṇḍavas.'

After Duryodhana had left, Krishṇa said. 'Arjuna why did you make such an unwise choice ? Why did you choose me, unarmed in preference to my splendid army?' Arjuna said, 'You can face all the princes and warriors single-handed. I will also derive glory by your presence. I had long desired that you should guide my chariot. I hope you will agree to this as you have resolved not to wield weapons or fight'. Vāsudeva was pleased with Arjuna, and blessed him. Thus he became his charioteer.

Duryodhana was brave but rather foolish. Anger and vanity often obscured his wisdom. Draupadī had called on Krishṇa in the assembly when Duḥshāsana was bent on disrobing her. He ought to have realized the Krishṇa was not just a human being. Of course neither Arjuna nor he knew that Krishṇa was Vishṇu's avatāra. But Arjuna realized his divinity, while Duryodhana didn't.

HOW A SERVANT SHOULD BEHAVE

[*As we have related, when Yudhishṭhira played the second game of dice, the condition was that the side which lost would go to the forest and live there for twelve years, and thereafter would follow a year's residence without being discovered. The Pāṇḍavas spent the thirteenth year disguised as servants in the household of king Virāṭa. It was of course very humiliating for them to work as servants, but there was no way out. When they had decided to take this course, Dhaumya gave them some advice on how servants ought to behave. This was necessary also because the Matsya king had to consider them genuinely to be servants. Any suspicion to the contrary might have wrecked their disguise. The advice given to them is set forth below*].

The king's servants, said Dhaumya, must always be alert. They should do their work silently and avoid talking too much. They should not volunteer any advice and give it only when it is asked for. They should always praise the king as occasion demands and never speak ill of him or of any members of the royal household. Everything, however insignificant, should be done only with the king's prior permission. 'You should neither avoid the king', Dhaumya said, 'lest he should feel himself ignored, 'nor should you linger too much near him. Even though you may have his explict confidence and trust, you should always remember that the relationship between master and servant is one of convenience only. You always stand the risk of dismissal. It would be foolish to think that you will enjoy his confidence for ever. Never sit in the king's chariot or any vehicle he is using, for kings frown upon such liberties being taken. A king's servant should be very active. He ought to exercise self-restraint too. If he receives praise or honour he shouldn't rejoice, and on being pulled up or slighted he ought not to be dejected.

'He should not reveal to anyone the king's secrets, nor should he accept any tips or presents from his visitors. It is the king's prerogative to put any servant in charge of any work he likes. One should not think thus : I am wiser than that man. Why wasn't I given this work instead of that fool ! A servant should be circumspect in his conduct towards the ladies of the king's household. There should be not the slightest suggestion of indelicacy'.

Thus did Dhaumya bless the Pāṇḍavas and instruct them. Cheering them up he said, 'Be patient. The year will soon end and then you will have successfully passed through the period of living in disguise and will regain your kingdom'.

Dhaumya's advice was very salutary. The Pāṇḍavas followed it strictly, and so adequately did they discharge their duties, that never once in the one year's period did Virāṭa, the Matya king, or any member of his household suspect them to be playing a role.

THE OUTCOME OF VANITY AND LUST.

[*Once Indra, king of the gods became so drunk with vanity that he was discourteous to the sage Brihaspati, preceptor of the gods. The sage got annoyed and left heaven, Indra's kingdom. Ever since heaven lost its glamour, Evil beings and demons got the upper hand. Clearly Indra's day was over. His place was contested by Vrita who sprang from the sacrificial fire kindled by Vishvarūpa, a young anchorite. Indra managed to defeat Vrita, but by unfair means. Hence out of sheer shame he hid himself. Thus there was no one to rule in heaven. Nahusha got that place, and this is his story*].

When Nahusha became king of heaven he became vain and lustful. One day he saw Sachī, Indra's wife, and was enamoured of her. He desired that she should come to him. 'I am king of the gods and she should be mine' he said. In desperation Sachī went to Brihaspatī and sought the sage's protection. He assured her that Indra would soon regain his kingdom and she would come to no harm. When Nahusha came to know this he was extremely wrathful. The gods prayed to him to keep to the path of righteousness and not to lust after another's wife. But Nahusha refused to pay heed. He said : 'Indra lusted for Ahalyā. Why didn't you all prevent him then ?[110]

'What did you do when he shamelessly killed Vishvarūpa and Vrita, both, by deceit? Sachī must come to me. I will have her, for am I not your king now? You must bring her to me.' The gods were greatly frightened and went to Brihaspatī. They urged him to send Sachī to Nahusha to submit to his desire. Poor Sachī went weeping to the sage. 'I can't do such a deed' she said. 'How can I be unfaithful to my husband?' The sage said 'Do not be afraid. He who, after having promised one protection, does not protect one who has appealed to him, will surely meet with destruction. If he casts seeds upon

110. Analyā was wife of the sage Gautama. Indra was captivated by her. One day when Gautama was out, he took his form and approached Ahalyā. She thought him to be her husband returned, and yielded to his embraces. Meanwhile Gautama came back. He saw another person exactly like him going out of his hermitage. Recognizing Indra by his divine power. he guessed the trick Indra had played and had thus violated Ahalyā.

the earth, they will not sprout. Nahusha's end is near. Don't worry. Go to him and tell him that you are willing, but after some time'. Sachī went to Nahusha. As soon as he saw her he was delighted and cast many a lustful gaze on her. 'I am the lord of all the regions. Why do you hesitate, O fair one, in granting me your favours'. His passionate demeanour made her tremble with fear, but controlling herself, she said 'O king of the gods, I will yield to you and be yours. But let me first find out if Indra is alive or not. I will search for him, and after I have failed to find him, I will come to you. I can then wed you with a clear conscience.' 'Very well' Nahusha said, 'but don't fail to come when, after having looked for him, you are not able to find him'.

Sachī returned to Brihaspatī. The gods went is a body to Nārāyaṇa, the great Lord. 'It was your power, Lord, that destroyed Vrita. Now Indra, feeling responsible for it, his taken the sin on himself and has concealed himself in a fibre of a lotus stalk, awaiting better days. We pray to you to find out a way of deliverance for him'. Vishṇu said, 'Let him worship me. He will be absolved of all sin, and Nahusha will be destroyed'. Sachī went to the Mānsarōvara lake where grew the lotus in whose stalk, Indra, having become small as an atom, was hinding. She wept and told him of her plight. Indra said, 'Your sorrows will cease soon, and Nahusha will be destroyed. You should go to him and tell him that you are willing to become his wife, but he should come to fetch you in a palanquin carred by ascetics'.

Sachī went to Nahusha and asked him to come and fetch her on a palanquin carried by *rishīs*. Nahusha was overjoyed. Sachī had come to him as he had asked her to. That made him confident that she would readily yield to his desires. His passion clouded his wisdom. He said 'I am your slave and ready to do your bidding. I am lord of the three worlds. I will come to fetch you with all due honour just as you desire, in a style which Vishṇu or the Rudras or Asuras will envy. I will myself come on a palanquin carried by seven *rishīs*. It is very suitable that the bride of one so great as heaven's king should be fetched thus majestically'. With these words, Nahusha, whom desire had overpowered, called the *rishīs* and ordered him to themselves carry his palanquin. The three worlds were aghast at this sacrilege and trembled. As the *rishīs* went along, Nahusha's mind was inflamed with thought of the pleasures awaiting him. He wanted the palanquin to be taken more speedily. He started goading the *rishīs* to go faster. The thought of Sachī waiting for him, whom he would enjoy, made him eager to be with her as soon as possible. To make things worse he was mad enough to kick the sage Agastya [one of the most revered among sages] and to ask him to speed up. '*Sarpa* ! *sarpa* !' he cried out. ['*Sarpa*' means 'to move'. But it also means 'a snake']. Nahusha had insulted the *rishīs* by making them carry his palanquin. Even more so by goading them on. And now kicking Agastya was the limit. The sage cursed him saying 'O you vilest of the vile, may you become a serpent and fall on the earth.' Nahusha at once fell from heaven and became a python in a forest on the earth. Indra regained his kingdom and Sachī's grief was at an end.

[The story of Nahusha was told by Sālya, Yudhishṭhira's uncle. 'Those who are patient, he told Draupadī and Yudhishṭhira 'are rewarded. They attain victory. Arrogance and haste are self-destructive. It is true that you, your brothers and Draupadī have suffered much. But your sufferings will soon be over as Indra's were. Your kinsmen and the vile Karṇa will be destroyed as Nahusha was. Evil may raise its head for some time, but it can never triumph So have patience and stand up courageously. You will regain your kingdom'].

YUDHISHṬHIRA SEEKS THE ELDERS' BLESSINGS

When the armies of the Pāṇḍavas and the Kauravas were ranged for battle, facing each other. Yudhisṭhira did something which baffled all who were there for a while. All, except Krishṇa the dweller in the hearts of all beings, from whom no thought or act can remain hid. Unarmed, Yudhishṭhira got down from his chariot and proceeded on foot towards the Kaurava army. In the beginning of the battle, the rules of war were strictly followed [though towards the end they were violated]. So no one thought of harming him. The Pāṇḍavas were mystified. But Krishṇa smiled and said 'He goes to seek the benediction of the elders before starting the battle. That's why he is unarmed'. When Yudhishṭhira approached the Kauravas thus, Duryodhana exalaimed 'He is frightened to fight. The warriors ranged on our side have sobered him and he fears defeat. So he comes to beg for peace.'

Yudhishṭhira, however, went past everyone, warriors as well as soldiers and going to Bhisma bent low and prostrated himself 'Allow us to begin the battle, grandrise,' he said. 'We have to perforce fight against you who are unconquerable and without compare. We seek your blessing', 'You have acted worthily, Bhīsma sâid. 'I am happy to see you. I am obliged to fight on the Kaurava side. But you will not be defeated'. Yudhishṭhira similarly went by turns to Droṇa, Kripāchārya, and Sātya his uncle, and sought their blessings. Then the battle began.

[Yudhishṭhira's conduct was doubtless upright and honourable. But not always so. It was he who staked Draupadī and spoke the lie about Ashvatthāmā's being slain. But we find he was not the only to do foul deeds. Towards the end of the battle the rule was 'all's fair in love and war' Droṇa was slain when he was unarmed and meditating. Abimanyū by all the veteran warriors combined. Duryodhana by hitting below the belt. Even Krishṇa sometimes dealt with the Kauravas unfairly to make the Pāṇḍvas win! It was a war full of cruel and foul acts. just as numerous as those of valour].

(B) FROM THE PURĀṆAS

WHAT THE PURĀṆAS ARE ABOUT

Literally 'Purāṇas' means 'old' or 'ancient'. Eighteen in number, they embody in them the ancient tradition of the Āryans. They contain the ancient religious customs of the Hindus, such as burning incense to worship the Mother goddess, (the goddess Lakshmī), the adoration of the sun as one of the gods, cremation of the dead on the ghats (banks) of a river and so forth.[113] The study of the Purāṇas is also useful in throwing light on many historical controversies, as for instance whether the Āryans were of indigenous origin and whether they were against idolatory as certain scholars believe, or were they a race coming from Western Asia between the years 2000 and 1500 before Christ.[114]

There are eighteen main Purāṇas and a like number of upa-Purāṇa (minor Purāṇas). The main Purāṇas are classified under three heads according to the *guṇa* (quality) uppermost in them. The ones in which the quality of purity *sattva* is predominant are Vishṇu, Nāradiya, Bhāgavata, Garuḍa, Padma and Varāha. In these six the Lord Vishṇu gets preeminence. The next six, which are said to be mainly of the element of *rājasa* (activity or passion) are Brahma, Brahmaṇda, Brahma-vaivarta, Mārkaṇḍeya, Bhavishya and Vāmana. The remaining six, in which the element of gloom or inactivity (*tāmas*) is marked, are Matsya, Kūrma, Linga, Shiva, Skanda and Agni.

The upa-Purāṇas are—Sanat-kumāra, Nara-siṁha (or Nrī-siṁha), Nāradīya or Vrihan, Shiva, Dur-vāsasa, Kāpila, Mānava, Aushanasa, Vāruṇa, Kālikā, Shāmba, Nandi, Saura, Pārāshar,. Āditya, Māheshwara, Bhāgavata and Vāsishṭha.

The classifications are not strictly adhered to, but Vishṇu predominates in most of them. Agni and Shiva are the other prominent gods.

---

113. Mackey, Earnest. *Early Indus Civilization. London.* 1948. op. cit. pp. 104-107: p.S3;p., 29.

114. The indigenous belief is of seholars such as. Budhda Prakasha. *Rig Veda and the Indus Valley Civilization.* Calcutta. and as. *India and Jambu Island.* 1931 and A.C. Dass. Rigveda Culture Culcutta. 1925.

The Purāṇas succeed Itihāsa, wich is the class of. Hindu scriptures under which the epics fall. According to Amar Sinha, an ancient Sanskrit lexicographer there are five subjects which each of the Purāṇas deals with These are :

1. The creation of the universe.
2. The destruction of the universe and its re-creation.
3. The geneaology of the gods and the patriarchs.
4. The Manawantaras or periods in time of the various Manus.
5. The history of the kings of the Solar and Lunar races.

This can however, be a very rough classification. The Vishṇu Puraṇa perhaps comes closest to it. In any case the Purāṇas contain a great deal of historical information and accounts of society and social customs then existing among the Hindus. They are not a closed literature like the Vedas and the Upanishads. They give evidence of accretions and extensive revisions. Thus scholars kept the text updated as we have encyclopaedias having different editions to keep pace with the growth of knowledge. This elasticity and modern approach is unique to them. This has balked some western scholars who debunk the Purāṇas because they appear to foretell the future. But we find scriptures of other religions, as for example, the Old Testament, following this practice too. So there is nothing unusual about the Purāṇas if they do the same. The original compilers of the Purāṇas had studied various branches of knowledge like history, geography, medicine, astronomy, law and of course, religion. They formed the Pur*āṇ*a Saṁhita under the illustrious scholar Bādāryaṇa. Its founder was Vedavyāsa. Amendments to the Paurāṇic literature could be made only by this body. Therefore Vedavyāsa became known as the author of the Purāṇas. The Purāṇas were very popular among people eager to learn about [Hindu] religion. Many talks and discussions about them used to be held.

The Purāṇas served the great end of bringing some kind of unity among the various Hindu sects. As the *Atharva Veda* says, India was a land of many different sects, languages and cultures [*bahudhā vivāchasam nānā dharmāṇam*], and so also the *Rig Veda,* that which men consider as many, the wise know to be one' [*ekaṁ sad vipra bahudhā vadanti*] Hindu society was in danger of being being split up by internal dissensions as well as foreign invasion. The authors of the Purāṇas played an important role in consolidating it. For example when Buddhism became influential, Lord Buddhā and Pārshva began to be regarded as avataras of Vishṇu. The Gupta monarchs made a prominent contribution towards this unity. The Purāṇas were systematized in their times.

The editing of the Purāṇas had started even in the ancient Vedic age. The *Vrātya-sukta* of the Atharva Veda refers to the *Itihāsa-Purāṇa.* Other Sanskrit texts, like the *Chhāndogya Upanishad*, too, mention them. The *Vāyu Purāṇa* says : 'A *brāhmin's* knowledge of the scriptures connot be complete until he has thoroughly studied the Purāṇas. He should supplement his knowledge of the Vedas by that of history (Itihāsa) and the Purāṇas.'[115] The Purāṇas give us the genealogies of various rulers and their efforts to expand their kingdoms, and the names of the various states then existing and their relations with one another. They also give a lot of geographical information—something not found in the ancient Vedic texts. Another new element contained in the Purāṇas is a detailed account of the cults and of how they evolved. The customs, laws and rules prevailing are detailed in them and the various ways in which their development came about.

It is difficult to say who the original writers of the Purāṇas were. As we have said they were a growing and expanding literature. There are four lakh (400,000) verses in the Purāṇas. They mention the names of many kings of the medieval period of India history. Some of them mention Moslem rulers, others even the coming of the British (called Goraṇda). However, this should not be taken to mean that they are not of ancient origin. F.E. Pargiter says 'The Purāṇas must have existed at least as early as the beginning of the fifth century B.C. and this lower limit would be shifted 150 to 200 years earlier.'[116] Western writers are loath to consider any scriptures of the Hindu religion as existing before the Christian era. So they

115. *Vāyu Purāṇa.* 200-201.

116. *Ancient Indian Historical Traditions* 1962, p. 51

assign dates from which these scriptures were put into writing. So is the case with the Purāṇas. A writer says 'The Purāṇas originate from the beginning of our era to the tenth century and even later.'[117] It is forgotten that most scriptures were put into writing much later than the time of their origination. The Holy Bible was written in the late first or early second century A.D. But the Vulgate (in Latin) version came in 400 A.D. and the Authorized edition as late as 1546.[118] The Purāṇas originated, as F.E. Pargiter says, round about the 5th to 7th century *before* the Christian era. As we have said there have been many compilations since then on various dates. But their ancient origin is indisputable.

READING LIST

M. Monior-Williams *Indian Wisdom*, Allen, 1876.

Muir, J. Original Sanskrit Text. 5 vols. London, 1858.

Sources of Indian Tradition. New York, 1958.

The Sacored Books of the East. Oxfond, 1879. *The Sacred Books of the Hindus*, Allahabad.

Pargiter, F.E. The *Mārkaṇḍaya-Purāṇa*. Calcutta : Asiatic Society, 1904.

Wilson, H.H. The *Vishṇu Purāṇa* London : Trubner 1864.

Note : Translations of the various Purāṇas have been published by Motilal Banarsidass, Bunglow Road, Delhi.

FROM THE MATSYA PURĀṆA

The Matsya Purāṇa is considered to be one of the three oldest Purāṇas. the others being the Vāyu and the Brahmānanda. It describes the various kingdoms of ancient India. their kings and often their dynasties too. Tura Kavasheya. who is said to have performed the horse sacrifice belonged to the Tora tribe as mentioned in this Purāṇa. This tribe did not originate from Afghanistan. according to J. Forbes Watson. a British explorer. Thus it would show that the so-called Dasyus. the people of the Indus Valley Civilization were really part of the Āryan society. The Matsya Purāṇa gives us a great

117. *Hinduism* ed. Louis Renou. Prentic-Hall International London. 1961. p. 162

118. *The Penguin Encyclopedia.* Penguin Books 1965.

deal of information about the geography of the medieval period of Indian history. The story of creation after the Great Floods is descibed in this Purāṇa. This confirms the belief that life originated from the waters. The Holy Bible and the Holy Quran also speak of the Flood in their own manner. According to the Matsya Purāṇa the fish that saved mankind from the floods was the first incarnation of Lord Vishṇu—Vishṇu is the eternal Sun.

THE BENEFITS OF PRAYĀGA

[Prayāga (now called Allahabad) is situated at the confluence of the sacred river Gangā and Yamunā and the mythical subterranean Saraswati (which is believed to be one boundary of Brahmāvartta the home of the early Āryans). The Gangā is believed to have been brought down to the earth by the prayers of Bhagīratha to purity the ashes of the sixty thousand sons of king Sāgara who had been burnt by the angry glance of the sage Kapila. To save the earth from the shock of the fall of Gangā, Shiva caught the river in his matted locks. Prayāga is considered to be one of holiest of Indian cities. The greatest religious gathering, perhaps in the world, is held once in twelve years here. Hindus consign the ashes of their dead at Prayāga at the Sangam, the confluence of the Gangā and the Yamunā rivers. Prayāga is also known as Tirtharāja i.e. 'the king of holy places'. According to legend all the holy shrines were placed on one pan of the balance and Prayāga on the other. The pan with Prayāga remained lower. [This account is from chapters 104-111 of the Matsya Purāṇa].

Mārkaṇdeya said I will tell you about the benefits of a pilgrimage to Prayāga, 'From the town to Pratishṭhāna up to the deep of Vāsuki and the Kambala, Ashvatara and Bahu Mūlaka consecrated to the Nāgas, is the Prajāpati-kshetra which is well-know in the three worlds. Those who bathe here go to heaven. For those who die here there is no more rebirth [i.e., they achieve *moksha*]. Those who live here are protected by the gods. Sinners cannot go there. Even the memory of that sacred place washes away small sins and the graver ones are removed by rubbing the body with the mud there. There are five deep channels in Prayāga. The Gangā flows in the middle of these. The moment one enters Prayāga all sins disappear. A man is absolved of all sins the moment he remembers the Gangā river even from a distance of a thousand *yojanās* (a *yojanā* or *yojana* is distance of four, eight or sixteen miles depending on various methods of calculation). Even evildoers attain emancipation by merely taking the sacred name of the Gangā. By bathing in and drinking of the waters of the river one purifies not only his own soul but those of his ancestors of seven generations also. Those who abstain from sex for a month at Prayāga and offer the waters of this river as libation to the manes attain all their desires. The Lord Shiva remains present at the confluence of the Gangā and the Yamunā rivers.

'The person who thinks of Prayāga at the hour of his death, wherever he may be—even in a foreign country—goes to the world of Brahmā. Such a man goes to a land full of gold where live holy men and sages. There, on the bank of the Gangā, he gets the company of thousands of lovely women, sages and holy people who have come on pilgrimage. He gets all he desires and is reborn as king of Jambudvipa.[119] The sages say that those who are sick and old and those of gentle nature, go to a place where all their desires are fulfilled, if they die at Prayāga at the confluence of the two sacred rivers. They go in a flying-chariot (*vimāna*) shining bright as gold. Till being born again, the departed spirit is honoured in heaven. He wears ornaments of precious stones and celestial nymphs (Apsarās) surround him and sing melodious songs. Thereafter he is reborn in some prosperous family, and remembering the greatness of Prayāga, goes there.'

Then Yudhishṭhira asked the sage Mārkaṇḍeya 'Please tell me in what fashion one should go to this holy place?' 'One should not go there', the sage said, 'in a vehicle driven by bullocks. If she does so he will surely go to hell. His offerings will not be accepted by the manes. A man should not drink the water of the river where his children have bathed. He

---

119. Jambudvīpa is one of the seven continents forming the world. Mount Meru lies in its centre and Bhāratvarsha (India) is its best part. It consists of nine *varshas* or divisions Meru is the fabulous mountain on which *swarga* or heaven lies—the Olympus of the Hindus. The meaning is that one is reborn in heaven or Bhārat which is nearest to heaven. One of the Moslem invaders is reported to have said of India 'If there is a paradise on earth it is here' *agar firdaus bar-rūhe zamīnast/ Hamīnaste, hamīnaste hamīnast.*

will derive no good then. *Brāhmins* should not yield to temptation and accept gifts at holy places. besides one who gives them such gifts with conceit in his mind does not derive any merit. Thus a sacred place ought to be visited on foot and not on any conveyance.'

[*The sage continued telling Yudhishṭhira about the sacredness of Prayāga. Much of what he said was repetition. However we give some interesting parts of his discourse*].

Mārkaṇḍeya said, 'Visiting Prayaga is like going to sixty crore and ten thousand holy places (a crore is ten million). He who dies there gains the merit of one who is devoted to yoga. There is a place famous in the three worlds on the eastern bank of the Gangā. This is a well known as Samudra-*kūpa* and near to this *kūpā*=well is the place called Pratishṭhāna. [This is identified as the township of Jhūsī in the modern city of Allahabad, by which name Prayāga is known]. It one resides in Pratishṭhāna (Jhūsī) for three nights observing continence and giving up all bad thoughts, he is absolved of all evil and attains the merit which is got by performing the horse sacrifice (ashvamedha). The same kind of merit is obtained at the pilgrimage to a place which lies north of Pratishṭhāna, known as Haṁsaprapatana (ie. 'where swans dwell'; from *haṁsa* = 'a swan'). This place is on the east bank of the Gangā'.

Mārkaṇḍeya went on the relate the merits of another tīrtha (place of pilgrimage) called Urvashiramaṇa where too there are swans in plentiful (Urvashī was a famous and captivating Apsarā of Indra's heaven–see the Women of the *Mahābhārata* ante, in selection 'from the *Mahābhārata; ramaṇa* means 'to enjoy'). 'One who dies in this place,' the sage said, 'goes to heaven and lives with the manes for sixty thousand and six centuries. He is revered by the *rishīs* the Gandharvas and the Kinnaras and others.[120] He is ever in the company of

120. The Gandharvas dwell in the sky or atmosphere. They are said to be partial to women and have a mystic power over them. They are the gods' singers and musicians and prepare the soma-juice. The Apsārases are their wives or mistresses. Their chief is Chitraratha.

Urvashī. After exhasting his store of virtue, he becomes lord of a thousand towns. He enjoys hundreds of women as charming as Urvashī herself. The melodious jingling of the anklebells and waist-ornaments (*kardhanī*) worn by these nymphs wakens him in the morning.[121] After enjoying these pleasures he goes back to Urvashīramaṇa.

'The man who eats once a day, wears a white dress and desists from sex becomes a king and enjoys hundreds of charming wives, adorned with beautiful ornaments. He rules over a vast kingdom whose boundary extends to the sea'. 'The Gangā', Mārkaṇḍeya said, 'can be approached easily at all points, except at Gangā-dvār, Gangā-sāgara and Prayāga. Those who bathe at these three places go to heaven and are freed from the cycle of births and deaths. There is no other source of bliss to the sinner as meritorious as the Gangā.'

The sage told Yudhishṭhira, 'He who balances himself on his head (the yogic *shirshāsana* posture), swings over the flames of fire, lives in heaven for a hundred thousand years. He who cuts off his flesh and offers it to the birds resides on the moon and then taking birth becomes a very pious king. There is to the south of Prayāga, on the northern bank of the Yamunā a most sacred place of pilgrimage known as Riṇamochana (*riṇ*a='debt'). One who spends a night there and bathes in the river, is able to pay back all his debts. He never incurs any debts again, and goes to heaven'.

Yudhisṭhira asked Mārkaṇḍeya, 'What happens to those who cannot suppress desire either for worldly things or in the form of attachment to people (like one's family, kinsmen etc.); and pray how fares the man who does dishonest trade following unfair practices? Can bathing in the Gangā at Prayāga condone such evil?' The sage said, 'Such a man, who bathes in the holy river at Prayāga for a month after getting rid of all passions, can be absolved of his sin. Even a man who treacherously kills another, can get rid of his sin by living on alms and bathing three times a day, for a period of one month. A

121. A *kardhanī* is worn by women round the waist like a wide belt. It is of gold with many tiny bells attached to it.

person who without any previous intention to go to a holy place, yet visits it, goes to heaven, and after reaping the fruit of his virtue, is reborn in a prosperous family. One who having resolved so, goes to such a holy place as he had intended to, obtains eternal happiness and redeems all his ancestors who may have been dwelling in hell'.

'Why is it that Brahmā, Vishṇu and Shiva are ever present in Prayāga?' Yudhishṭhira wanted to know. The sage said, 'The town of Prayāga is spread over an area having a circumference of five *yojanas.* Due to the absence of sin Brahmā is present in the north, Vishṇu is in Veṇimādhava, and Shiva has taken the form of the sacred bunyan tree. Apart from them the gods, *gandharvas* and sages are at the boundaries to keep sin away from Prayāga. Brahmā, Vishṇu, Mahesh, the seven *dvīpas*, the oceans and the mountains, and all the gods dwell there for ever. Brahmā and the other gods have created the universe after placing themselves in Prayāga. Therefore, O Yudhishṭhira, now that you have regained your kingdom, [after the Mahābhārata war], bathe here in the holy waters along with your brothers and wash away your sins'.

THE STORY OF SĀVITRĪ AND SATYAVĀNA

This is the well-known story of Satyavāna and Sāvitrī. Sāvitrī was daughter of king Ashvapatī. She loved Satyavāna and insisted on marrying him although the sage, Nārada, had foretold that he had only one year left to live. On the fatal day he was cutting wood and lay dying. Sāvitrī supported his head on her lap. While he was thus lying, was she a figure approaching and found out that it was Yama, the god of Death (and also of Dharma) who had come to take away the soul of Satyavāna. As Yama gathered his soul and departed, she followed him. Her devotion pleased Yama. He told her that she may ask for any boon, except for the soul of her husband. She asked for three boons and then prayed to Yama, who was so taken in by her devotion that he restored *Satyavāna* to life. The story is told in chapters 208-214 of the Matsya Purāṇa.

King Vaivasvata Manu wished to know about women who are *pativratā* (i.e., perfectly chaste and devoted to their husbands). 'Who among them', he asked the Lord, 'is a model of chastity?' Matsya said, 'Even the god of Dharma is powerless to harm women of unquestioned chastity. I will now relate about one such woman'.

In the Madra country lived a king called Shakala Ashvapatī. He wanted progeny, so he devotedly worshipped Sāvitrī. Pleased by his devotion the goddess appeared and promised that he would in time have a charming daughter. The queen Mālavī gave birth to a beautiful baby girl whom the king named Sāvitrī as she had been born by the blessing of the goddess. When she grew up, the king promised to wed her to Satyāvāna. After he had done so, the sage Nārada came and said that Satyavāna would die within a year, so he should not give his daughter to him. But the king said he would not break his promise, whatever the circumstances. It wouldn't be the right thing to do. Sāvitrī was married to Satyavāna. Her father-in-law was blind. So he was deprived of his kingdom and was living with his son, Satyavāna, in the forest. However, despite all these adversities, Sāvitrī devotedly looked after both her husband and her in-laws with great affection and care. When there remained just four days for Satyavāna to die, as foretold by Nārada, Sāvitrī fasted for three nights. Thereafter, with her father-in-laws permission, she and Satvāvana went to the forest to gather flowers and fruits. But her mind was greatly distressed, thinking of the approaching calamity. Seeing her sad Satyavāna pointed out to her the lovely flowers and sights of the forest.

He named the various flower [these are omitted so as not to make the account tedious reading]. 'The beauty of the forest flowers in this spring season, is overpowering', he said, 'and fills one with amorous longing. How soothing and fragrant they are.! It seems the god of love is present here. The peacocks, filled with desire for copulation, are following their mates. The cuckoos are making love on the mango trees. The other birds are also enjoying themselves thus – the *chātaka,* the parrot, the crane and crow. So too the beasts. The lioness lies in the lion's embrace, the male and the female rhinoceros are licking each other, the wolf is making love to his female in the cave, the pair of hares are lying clasped each to each, the passion-filled ox is making love to the cow, and even so all other animals, big and small – the monkeys, cats, elephants, bears, deer and so forth – are passionately enjoying their mates'. Satyavāna said, 'Darling, you have plucked the flowers, but the firewood remains to be gathered. You wait here. I will go and get it.' 'Don't go far, dear', Sāvitrī said. 'I am frightened. Remain in my sight'. Satavāna went and she saw he was lying down on the ground. So she hastened to his side. Satyavāna said, 'Sweetheart, I am feeling faint and have a terrible headache. My eyes are also clouding and I can't see clearly. It seems I am exhausted. I feel like resting.' Sāvitrī cradled his head on her lap, and he slept. While they were thus, the god of Death came and taking out Satyavāna's soul from him fastened it by a noose and was departing with it. Sāvitrī got up and followed him. With her agitated heart beating fast she folded her hands. reverentially and said : 'One who is devoted to his mother is full of happiness in this world. He who is devoted to his father goes to the mid-regions and he who is devoted to his guru goes to Brahmaloka. These three should be served daily. He who does so follows *dharma* (righteousness).' Dharmarāja (Yama) said, 'What you say is doubtless true. But don't come after me. I am being delayed and you are full of grief. Go and serve your guru. Thereby you'll get peace of mind.' Sāvitrī said 'A woman's husband is like a god for her, he is her support. He is everything for her. So a virtuous woman should never forsake him. It's true that a father, a brother and a son are of great significance. But a husband is above them all. So I'm not doing anything improper in following my husband. The moment I'm not able to do so, I will give up my life. Who would want to live like a widow, unadorned, and an eyesore to society?' Yama said 'Your words please me. You may ask for a boon, short of your husband's life. Him I must take with me'. Sāvitrī asked that her father-in-law may get back his vision and regain his lost kingdom. Yama gave her the boon and asked her to go. But the determined woman did not turn back. 'Who can feel troubled in the company of one such as you?' she said. 'Saints are the refuge of all persons. The man who is ill-disposed to the world without reason, who causes pain and grief to others is a vile person. He is more harmful than the snake's venom, fire, or poison. Such people are destroyed and go to evil wombs after death. But good men serve the world and are ready even to die in another's service. A virtuous king should reward good people and punish evildoers. Such a king goes to heaven. And you are the controller of those who somehow escape the king's justice. You are the chastiser of the wicked and the support of virtue. So you are greater even than the gods. I don't find any sorrow at all in your company.' Yama said, 'I am pleased with your words of wisdom. Ask for a boon, but not for your husband's life.' Sāvitrī said, 'I wish to have a hundred brothers. My father has no son. Grant sons to my father.' Dharmarāja said. 'It shall be so. Now return and perform your husband's funeral rites. His soul has to go to another world. You can't follow him there. Your husband has shown great reverence to his guru. He has been very virtuous. That's why I've myself come to fetch him. Normally this job is done by my messengers. As you say, a wise man should be devoted to his teacher and his guru. One should give a teacher, parents, an elder brother, and particularly a *brāhmin*, the utmost respect. The sufferings parents have to undergo in order to bring up their children are very great. The debt due to them for this cannot be repaid even in a thousand years. Serving a teacher, one's parents and elder brother is the highest form of austerity. Nothing should be done without their permission. It's they who are in truth the three Vedas, the three realms and the three sacrificial fires [which according to the scriptures are ever to be kept burning]. Now go back. You will get all you have asked for. Don't tire yourself.'

Sāvitrī said, 'There is no suffering in pursuing *dharma*. You are its personification, so I adore your feet. *Dharma*, *artha* (honest wealth) and *kāma* wedded love) are to be pursued by all human beings. It is only *dharma* (the practice of righteousness) which goes with one even after death, not relations or kinsmen. Everything is subordinate to *dharma*. All the worlds are got by it. All things are accomplished by it, even the attainment of heaven. Only the righteous can attain kingship and enjoy all its pleasures. The signs of virtue, O Dharmarāja, are acetism and humility the giving of charity, the carrying out of sacrifices, reading the Vedas, serving good men, worshipping God and revering gurus and respecting *brāhmins* [i.e. wise men]. One should always be engaged in these, for who knows when death may come snapping life's thread. Death does not wait for one to do these things first. So one should start the practice of virtue from very childhood. How stange that even knowing that death is certain, one behaves as if he will never die! Everyone fears death, but the virtuous saints are free from such fear'.

Yama said, 'Your words please me very much. Ask for some boon, other than your husband's life. Hurry, you have already delayed me much. Sāvitrī said, 'O Deva, I wish to be get a hundred sons by my beloved husband, as there is no comfort in the next world without sons'. 'All right', said Yama. 'But don't follow Satyavāna. You are troubled and tired, so go back now and rest'.

[*In reality Yama had been cornered. How could he grant Sāvitrī the boon of a hundred sons from Satyāvana if he was dead? Anyway, Sāvitrī did not give any time to Yama to sort this out. She hurried on with a paean of praise addressed to him*].

What Sāvitrī said :

'You are the uphole of *dharma*, the fount of virtue,
Dispenser of destiny, Time, and Dealer of death,
Upholder of the Vedas, Saviour of the righteous,
Protector and pride of the universe.

O Dharmarāja, be merciful to my husband, to his parents and to me.'

Yama was pleased to hear these words and said, 'I liberate your husband. Now you have got all you desired, so hurry back home. Your husband will reign for five hundred years, and you will live happily with him. Both of you will attain heaven. Your hundred sons will also rule for many years. Your mother. Malavī, will have many sons who will be known as the Mālavas'. Saying this Dharmarāja disappeared. Shortly after Satavāna's soul, thus released by Yama, reentered his body. When they returned they found the king, Savitrī's father-in-law, had regained his sight, and along with his army he entered his lost kingdom and ascended the throne. In this way Sāvitrī brought her husband back to life and also got her father-in-law's lost kingdom. 'Such chaste and virtuous women as Sāvitrī,' Matsya said, 'are worthy to be revered. The entire universe is upheld by them. Their words can never be falsified or be unfulfilled.'

WHICH IS SUPERIOR—FATE OR ONE'S OWN EFFORT ?

This million dollar question gives the Paurāṇic view on a very significant and controversial issue. Most people believe that destiny completely governs us. As Shakespeare says, 'there's a destiny that shapes our ends'. Omar Khayyāma's Moving Finger writes the final word and nothing whatever can alter it. But if everything is thus inexorably decreed, what is the place of individual effort? Astrologers, palmists and a whole lot of those who reiterate the unalterableness of fate, seem to think that human endeavour is of little importance and place it on the back--burner. The *Gītā* makes a kind of compromise by saying that our right is to do works, but their result is not in our control. Indeed at one place (18 : 61) Krishṇa says that human beings are helpless tools in God's hands. Against this background, this passage from the *Matsya Purāṇa* (in the two hundred and twenty-first chapter) is interesting.

Manu asked the Lord, 'Which is superior, O Lord, fate, or one's own effort. I am not at all clear on this point. Kindly remove my doubt.' Lord Matsya said : 'Fate is connected with man's works in past lives. Action or effort is allied with his present life. By persevering effort a man can, by righteous acts, turn his ill-luck into good fortune. Even those who are of the quality of purity, and have previously performed good deeds cannot achieve what they wish for without exerting themselves.

'Men of active ambition attain success by their effort and perseverance. Those who are inactive and dull can get their desire with great difficulty. Men achieve success by being energetic and hard-working. It is only the lazy people who make no effort and keep blaming fate for what they can't accomplish. The inactive man keeps bemoaning his fate. His attitude is. "It was fated that I wouldn't succeed, that's why I couldn't make it." It isn't that fate has no role at all in man's life. It is related to the present, past and future. But it is perseverance which gives results in the present. Then again time (*kāla*) has its importance. If, for example, it rains in time, there will be a good crop.[121] A man should therefore persevere in good works. He can even turn adversity to good advantage. Even if he does not get the fruits of good works in this life, he is sure to get them in some future existence. It's only those who are are lazy that depend on fate. They do not gain their objects. Prosperity forsakes those who are always dreaming of fate. It favours those who are active and alert'.

121. ef., Tulsidāsa in the *Rāmāyaṇa—ka varshā jab krishī sukhāny*—'of what use is rain after the crop dries up' [*Bāla-kāṇḍa*, 260 :2]. Again Tulsī says : 'Birth, death, sorrows and joys, loss and gain, meeting and parting from loved ones—all these are controlled by Time and one's own works. They ever keep happening, day and night'. [Ayodhyā-kāṇḍa, 149 : 3].

THE POLICIES OF KINGS

The great diplomat and policy-maker Kauṭliya or Chāṇakya as he is alo called, lived in the time of Chandragupta Maurya, the great monarch of ancient India. Kauṭilya had been insulted by the Nanda king who had turned him out of his court. He was burning for revenge. While on a visit to Pāṭliputra he met Chandragupta who was yet a child. The boy was playing at becoming a king. Kauṭilya was impressed. To test him he asked the boy for a present. Chandragupta said, 'The ideal present is the earth which is for the enjoyment of heroes'. Chāṇakya chose him on the spot for killing the Nanda king. He gave the boy military training and shaped him to become a powerful king. Chāṇakya's doctrine is contained in *Arthashāstra*. He gave the greatest importance to *ḍaṇḍa*, (punishment) and used to say 'No *ḍaṇḍa* no state'. Next he considered *artha* (accumulation of wealth). This he placed above *dharma* and *kāma* ! The *Matsya Purāṇa* treats of this subject in the two hundred and twenty-second to the two hundred and twenty- sixth chapter.

On Manu's wishing to know the policies which kings ought to follow in order to rule successfully, Lord Matsya said as follows :

A king ought to resort to seven expedients according to the situation he has to face : *sāma, bhēda, dāna, daṇḍa, upekshā, māyā and indrajāla*. Further *sāma* is of two kinds – *satyasāma and asatyasāma*.[122] Needless to say, *asatya* should never be practised on saints and good men, for that will only annoy them. The wicked are not amenable to a policy of conciliation. So *sāma* is not to be practised on them. No good is likely to accrue from it. It should be applied to those of a good family and those who are simple, virtuous and truthful. The policy of divide and rule works well with those who are hostile wicked and quarrelsome. Such people can be easily overcome

---

122. *Sāma* is conciliation by means of talking over. *bhēda* is to create differences (divide and rule policy) *dāna* is winning over the enemy by presents or money. *ḍaṇḍa* is punishment. *māyā* means the policy of diplomacy. *indrajāla* is the use of stratagem. *upekshā is* to overlook something or to continue in endurance. *satyasāma* is genuine conciliation and *asatyasāma* is conciliation by falsehood.

by creating division among them. Matsya went on to tell Manu how such division can be created. The weaknesses and vices of one class should be emphasized to the other who are inmical to them. At the same time their own faults and defects should be pointed out. Thus each will be afraid to face the other, and hatred will be created between them. When a number of kings form an alliance, they gather strength from one another and it is very difficult to face them. In such a case creating dissension between them, is very profitable.

A king should find out the score on which there are disagreements between the allies. Then he should play upon these differences. The king should not, however, himself come into the forefront. He should get the division created by some agency of his. He should also make sure that the agents he employs for these persons are not betraying him by siding with the opposite party, and that they are reliable persons.

There are two source from which the ruler of a vast empire can be weakened One is the internal danger arising from plots and intrigues of his own officials, ministers and so forth. The other is danger from external sources, as for example the desire of other kings for waging war against the ruler in order to conquer his torritory. Of these, the internal dangers are far more to be feared. If internally an empire is strong and free from dissensions and intigues it can effectively resist an external attack. But if weakened internally it is bound to fall. A king should try to divide the kinsmen and communities of the enemy. But at the same time he should keep the communites of his own kingdom united. This can be done by granting them favours and giving them gifts. Even powerful enemies can be overcome by a very small force if there is dissension and disunity prevailing in them. So the policy of divide and rule is very effective.

The policy of winning over enemies by *dāna*, i.e., giving of gifts is best, Matsya said. O king, even those who are rich cannot resist the temptation of receiving gifts. They are readily won over in this manner. The giving of gifts not only conquers this world, but also wins the realms of Indra. (That is to say gifts even please the gods).

Those, however, who cannot be subdued by the aforesaid three means, Matsya said, should be overcome by *daṇḍa*. But *daṇḍa* should be used with discrimination. Sages, virtuous persons and other such, should not be harmed. A king who punishes the innocent and lets off those guilty, goes to hell after losing his kingdom. The sovereign should punish the wicked. If he fails to do so the evil and powerful people will oppress those good—the children, the aged and the saints; as the large fish swallow the smaller ones. Everyone transgresses his limits if the fear of punishment is not there. It is *daṇḍa*. which governs all and protects all. It is always alert when everything is asleep. The learned call it *dharma*. Because of its fear sinners do not sin. Punishment has a deterrent as well as a preventive aspect, for fear of *daṇḍa* keeps evildoers at bay.

A king has been created by Brahmā for the preservation of all his subjects, for carrying out due sacrifices to the gods and for inflicting punishment on those who are guilty. He is like the god of Dharma. He gives the people affection so as to gain their goodwill. But he also punishes where punishment is due.

FROM THE BHĀGAVATA PURĀṆA

The *Bhāgavata Purāṇa* is one of the most sacred of the Purāṇas. It contains much of the teachings of the Vedānta and the Pāñcarātra. There exists uncertainty about the date, but it would appear to be either 512–525 A.D. or 453–466 A.D. (according to *The History and Culture of the Indian People'*, vol. 3 p., 415). It is said to have been authored by Vyāsa, Shuka and Sūta, but there have been many revisions. It represents the ancient Vaishṇava cult of Hinduism. The Supreme Lord is Krishna, who is to be regarded as the personal Vāsudeva and also the impersonal Cosmic Absolute. The doctrines of *māyā*, avatāra (divine incarnation) yoga and *bhakti* (devotion), which we have already discussed in the chapter on Fundamental Concepts of Hinduism, all find place in this Purāṇa. The emphasis is on devotion in its various aspects of prayer, *kīrtana* and so forth. Krishṇa's sport with the *gopīs* (cowherd maids) also find place in it. The key-word is surrender. The Lord removes the sins and sufferings of those who surrender completely to him.

THE CIRCULAR DANCE OF KRISHṆA AND THE GOPĪS

[The Rāsa-krīḍa is said to be a dance in which the women join hands and the men place their arms round the necks of their partners. The particular dance in which Krishṇa and the cowherd maids *(gopīs)* took part, was of a mystic kind in which the dancers formed a circle. There was Krishṇa between two girls and a girl between two Krishṇas playing on his flute. This could not have been possible except by Krishṇa's yoga-*māyā* due to which he caused the illusion of various other 'Krishṇas'. Apparently Krishṇa assumed as many forms as the number of maids. A lot of love literature and poetry exists about Krishṇa and the *gopīs,* particularly the *gopī,* Rādhā. But at the time of his sport with the *gopīs* Krishṇa was only about eleven years old. So no sexual motive or such relation could be possible. Krishṇa had triumphed over sex. In fact the entire dance episode is metaphorical. The *rāsa* is the Divine Sport of the favoured devotee and the goal is *moksha,* emancipation. It is the eternal dance of life from the gross to the subtle, from worldliness to devotion, from devotion to liberation. The account is from book 10 chapters 29–35].

Now the charming autumnal moonlit nights came with the perfumes of the fully-blossomed jasmine wafting with the breeze. The stars and the moon were appearing in the sky, cooling heated bodies as a lover putting soothing sandalwood paste on his beloved's countenance, and the sky turned crimson as the face of a blushing girl. Krishṇa saw the moon which makes lilies open their petals, golden as saffron and splendid as Lakshmī. The groves (of Vrindāvana) were lit up by its light. And the sound of Krishṇa's flute filled the air. Those melodious notes fell on the ears of the *gopīs*. They came drawn by it rushing away to that spot, leaving abruptly whatever work they were doing. Some of them were serving food to the members of their families, some taking their meals, some milking cows, some cooking food or boiling milk, some talking to their husbands, some dressing or beautifying their bodies and some nursing their babies. But as soon as they heard those notes, they hurriedly departed in disorderly haste despite the protests of their men-folk. But others could not go because they were unable to leave the inner appartments. They closed their eyes and meditated on Lord Krishṇa and united with him, transcended the *guṇas* (qualities) and the bonds of worldly existence.

When Krishṇa saw them, he said 'You should not have abandoned your duties in this way. Your people will be searching for you and will be anxious at your sudden departure. Leaving your husbands you have come alone to me. Thus seeking a paramour, is not right for a virtuous woman. You could have shown devotion to me by meditating on me, singing my praises and glorifying my deeds. What was the need for my personal company? There are wild beasts here in the forest and it's risky for you to be out. Besides you have experienced the beauty of the moonlit night and the fragrant breeze. So now go back'.

When the *gopīs* heard these harsh words, grief overcame them. Their lips glowing red like the *bimba* fruit, paled.[123] The saffron-paint on their breasts was washed away by the tears mixed with the collyrium of their eyes. With sore and weeping eyes, they falteringly spoke in a choked voice to Krishṇa. 'O Krishṇa', they said 'do not forsake us. We are your unswerving devotees. You are the Soul of all existence. So in you are contained our husbands, children, kinsmen and friends. We have come to the Source of all, so we have really abandoned no one. Our feet are unable to move now, when we have seen you. How can we go back? We bow and prostrate ourselves at your lotus-feet which even the goddess Shrī seeks to adore. Do not send us back, we who have bee drawn by your charming smiles and bewitching glances. Allow us to serve you as slaves. Who is the girl, O darling, who will not swerve from the beaten path, enchanted by your flute and your charming form? Even a glance from you thrills birds and beasts. O, dear, put your lotus-like hands on our breasts and our aching heads'.

Hearing their heart-felt artless love-filled words, Krishṇa laughed. The Lord of Yoga, who is ever-seated in his own Self, agreed

123. A fruit of deep red colour.

to give them the bliss they craved for. The bloom returned to their faces as they gathered round him. With his lovely teeth having the glow of the jasmine and his charming smiles he looked like the full moon midst the stars. All of them sang songs, and Krishṇa adorned with *vaijayantī* flowers led the bevy of hundreds of young maidens through the forest to the cool sandy river bank.[124] There, fanned by the pleasant breeze cooled by the waters of the Yamunā river laden with the fragrance of water-lilies, surrounded by the *gopīs*, he sported with them. He stretched out his arms, embracing them in various parts, the hands, the hair, thighs, waists and bosoms. He marked their bodies with his nails, sent coquettish glances, smiled and joked and gave them great delight.

[The gopīs were filled with vanity. So Krishṇa disappeared from their midst. But when they were disconsolate and regretful, he came to them again and then the rāsa dance was performed].

On the sandy banks of the Yamunā Krishṇa assumed as many forms as there were *gopīs* and entered in between every two of them, his arms place round the neck of the one next to him. The gods and goddesses appeared in the sky to see it. They sounded kettle-drums and rained flowers, The bangles and anklets of the maidens jingled and their waist-band bells tinkled. Krishṇa looked like an emerald between two golden beads. The *gopīs* smiled, their breasts trembled, their eyes sent amorous glances. With their waist sundulating, ear-rings shaking, they danced till drops of sweat bathed them. They sang in chorus. One girl flung her arms round Krishṇa, her bangles slipping and her her braid loosened, with the flowers falling off from it. Another could not restrain herself from amorously kissing Krishṇa's arm which encircled her. One girl rested her cheek on his, and he placed his half-chewed betel in her mouth. Another took hold of his hand and pressed her bosom to it. Krishṇa sported with them as a child would

124. *Vaijayanti* is a flowering shrub yielding lovely flowers. Here the idea is that Krishṇa wears a garland having flowers of five different colours. This is called a *vaijayantī mālā* (*mālā* = 'garland'). Krishṇa is usually depicted as wearing such a garland.

play with his reflection in a mirror. He clasped them to himself, pressed their palms, laughed and made amorous advances. The *gopīs* were so overcome by his presence that they did not even care to tidy their dishevelled hair, or to set right their loosened dresses and brassieres. Krishṇā tenderly wiped their perspiration, the girls thrilling at the touch of his nails. In order to cool himself and the *gopīs,* who were exhausted with dancing, he entered the waters of the river along with them. The girls pressed round him, their breasts squeezed to his limbs so that the saffron paste on them covered his body. They sprinked water on him playfully, all the while casting on him their amorous glances. Seeing this celestial sport even the god of the Moon and his retinue of stars were so greatly affected that they halted in their course. Thus the *gopīs* and Krishṇa sported in the groves of Vrindāvana for several nights without stopping even for a minute.

Hearing this account of Shuka, king Parīkshit was scandalized. 'How is it' he asked the sage, 'that the upholder of ethics, virtue and *dharma*, thus openly and shamelessly seduced married women?'

Shuka said, 'O king, the fire does not get polluted by burning unclean things. The ordinary code of moral conduct does not apply to the Almighty for whom the piety or impiety of an act is of no consequence. Krishṇa dwells in the hearts of all, the *gopīs* as well as their husbands. The husbands of these women always considered their wives to be with them. They were enraptured as much as the *gopīs* were. How could even a trace of jealousy ever enter their minds?'

THE IDEAL HOUSEHOLDER

It has been said in the introduction to the book that the Hindus conceive life as being of four stages *(āshramas)*, the celibate student, the householder, the forest-dwellers and the wandering hermit. In the present times the hermits and forest-dwellers have all but vanished. Instead shikarīs in search of game, dacoits and terrorists infest forests, and there are no hermits, only beggars and frauds who go about as fortune-tellers. The students are no longer celibates. They seek girl-friends and boy-friends and the obsession with sex, drugs and homosexuality has overtaken youth. But in ancient India there were saints and hermits, and celibacy was the pride of our *gurukuls.* However, in keeping with the present times, the ideal householder has been selected for portrayal—though the Purāṇa mentions the others too—and the vanishing celibate has been put on the back-burner! The reader will meet him later in the Veda and the Upanishad. The account is from the seventeenth chapter of the eleventh skandha.

The account is given by Lord Hari to Uddhava. Lord Hari said: It's not necessary that my devotee should go through all the four *āshramas*. If he desires sex he becomes a householder, if he likes to meditate he may go to the forest and if renouncement is his forte, he takes to sannyāsa (become a hermit). The man who wishes to enter family-life should choose a suitable girl as his life-partner. She should be of a good family and of good character and habits and younger than him. She ought to be of the same *varṇa* (class) as he is. But if the girl does not sexually attract him he may take a wife from any other *varṇa* [thus the main thing is sexual compatibility].

The *brāhmin* has special duties. He should perform sacrifices. He may accept gifts, but if he finds this interfering with his austerities he should earn his living by teaching the Vedas and acting as a priest. If he feels these are not suitable for him he should live by picking up the grains of the crop left behind *after* the owner of the field has harvested it. Trivial enjoyments are not meant for him. He should persevere in suffering and practise austerities and thereby strive for emancipation. The twice-born (i.e., *brāhmin, kshtriya* and *vaishya*) should give charity, perform sacrifices and study the scriptures.

Who finds peace? It is the man who is content with taking the grains of corn strewn on the fields after their harvesting and from the market-place after market is over; who is hospitable to guests; who is not too much taken up with his family (even though living with them); and who is wholeheartedly my (i.e. God's) devotee. Like a boat which rescues a drowning man, I come to the relief of one who helps a devotee of mine who's in trouble. [*Here follows a short advice to kings which is omitted as it is a digression*]. A *brāhmin*, continued Lord Hari, may, if he faces penury, take to business but he shouldn't sell things which are prohibited by the *shāstras*, like salt, wine and so forth. In case the business brings him loss, he may earn his living by becoming a warrior. But he shouldn't take up baser occupations. Similarly if faced by poverty, a *kshatriya* may engage in trade, or live by hunting or by teaching the scriptures, but he should never take up menial service. Fallen on bad days a *vaishya* may take up small jobs like weaving mats or working as an artisan. But once he's on his feet again he should leave these and revert to his normal calling.[125]

A householder should carry out worship and make oblations to the gods according to his means. He should make the offerings due to his ancestors, serve guests and give food to the needy. He ought to perform sacrifices but without causing financial hardship to his family. He should carry them out with money which may be inherited by him, and with that earned and got by fair means.

The Lord went on to dilate in greater detail on the detachment a householder ought to have, even though discharging his family obligations. The householders should not be attached to his own family. He ought to worship God at all times. The enjoyment of heaven, too, is as ephemeral as that of the world. Association with one's family is momentary. It is like travellers come together for a few moment to drink water. When, after death, the soul takes another body these— one's wife, children and

125. Thus the idea of *varna* being a watertight classification is entirely mistaken. It should be observed *as far as possible*, but also departed from when the need arises. This debunks much of the false impression politicians and pandits have, and are for their own greed and selfish ends raking up caste and so misleading Hindus and thereby trying to destroy what Hindu *dharma* has long preserved.

relations – vanish like dreams that disappear on waking. Unconcerned and thinking himself to be a guest in his house, neither attached to property nor relations, shorn of concepts of 'I' and 'mine'; the householder achieves liberation even in this very life. But he who is deeply attached to his family, greedy for money, thinking most of the time of the pleasure of sex and of producing children, is an egotistic fool with no discrimination. He is always filled with anxiety. 'Without me my aged parents, my wife and children will be helpless and miserable. Who then look after them ?' With such thoughts that foolish man keeps worried. They pursue him till the end and remain with him at the hour of his death. Such a man goes to hell.

THE ILLS OF THE KALI-AGE

As we have said elsewhere, the *yugas* are the Hindu division of the age of the world. There ae four of them namely the Krita, Tretā Dwāpara and Kali (of 4,800; 3,600; 2,400 and 1,200 celestial years respectively).[126] They are the periods of diminishing righteousness, the greatest righteousness prevailing in the Kria-yuga, and the least in the Kali-yuga which happens to be the one in which we are living, and so of particular interest to us. The ills of the Kali-age have also been related in the *Rāmacharitamānasa* of Goswāmī Tulsidāsa. Though extracts from that book will follow later, the portion about Kali-yuga in it is being given along with this account from the *Bhāgavata Purāṇa* for the sake of continuity. The account in this Purāṇa is also contained in *Skandha Purāṇa* 12, chapter 2.

Shuka spoke to king Parīkshit about the kings who will reign in the Kali-age. Concluding, he said, O king all these rulers will do evil things. They will covet the women and property of others. They will murder women, children and *brāhmins* and slaughter cows. They will be weak and have short lives. Instead of caring for their subjects they will exploit them. Their people will also walk in their ways, and they as well as their rulers will meet with perdition.

Thereafter there will be a decline in virtue, truth, purity, forbearance and mercy. Wealth and brute force will dominate society. There will be love-marriages and ancestry or family will be of no account. Sexual pleasure will be the only aim of the union of men and women. People will not bathe regularly. They will just use cosmetics to appear artificially beautiful. There will be no internal purity. People will instead pretend to be pure by putting on many sacerdotal marks on the body, wearing the sacred thread and so forth. Justice will become weak and the poor will be deprived of it because they won't have money to bribe the judges. Hypocrisy, arrogance and audacity will thrive. Instead of serving their teachers and gurus, people will grow long hair and make pilgrimages. Religious rites will

126. A celestial year comprises 360 of our years.

be performed merely to show off and for publicity. The rule will be, 'might is right' and wicked persons will prosper. Thus cruelly deprived of their women and wealth, the impoverished and grieved people will be forced to find shelter in mountains and forests, living on leaves, roots, meat, honey, fruits, flowers and whatever they can get there to eat. Anxieties, hunger, thirst and disease will cause people to die early. The maximum age will be fifty years. People will be emaciated and unhealtly. They will disregard scriptural injunctions and become heretics. Kings will rob their peoples' wealth. Men will commit theft and economic offences. Violence and mendacity will prevail.

All *varṇas* will be debased. There will be no celibates or recluses, only householders. The word 'relative' (relation) will mean only the relations of one's wife, none else. Cows will become stunted and yield very little milk. Medicinal herbs will cease to effect cures. Trees won't grow tall, nor will they give any shade. There won't remain any hospitals.[127] There will be lightning and thunder in the clouds, but no rain. Houses of the people will bear a desolate and deserted look. After the people have suffered such hardships, the Lord will incarnate himself in his *sāttvika* form to protect religion.[128] He will be incarnated in the village known as Shabhala [near Moradabad in Uttar Pradesh eightly miles east of Delhi, India's capital]. He will be born in the houses of the Vishṇuyashas, the noble *brāhmin* chief [*sarpanch*?] of the village. He will be riding a swift horse called Devadutta. He will go round the whole world mounted on this horse, and will, with his sword slay millions of robbers and wicked persons who pose themselves as kings. Thus when evil men, thieves and robbers

127. We do have them now. But they are almost useless, giving rise to nursing-homes where the main incentive (with exceptions of course) is not caring for patients, but greed. Hippocrates and his oath are buried deep down!

128. As promised by Krishna in the *Gītā,* whenever righteousness declines and unrighteousness prevails the Lord Vishṇu incarnates himself to punish evildoers and reestablish *dharma* (*Gītā,* 4 : 7–8) Kalkī or Kalkīn is to be the tenth avatāra of Vishṇu. It is to come at the end of the Kali-age. The avatāra will be riding a white horse, with a drawn sword.

are annihilated, the fragrant breeze blowing from the Lord will purify the progeny of these vicious beings. When Lord Hari thus descends on the earth the Krita or Golden age will restart, and those who will be born thereafter will be pious and pure.

[The account of Kali-yuga as contained in Tulsidāsa's Rāmacharitamānasa now follows. Kākbhushuṇḍi has given the account to Garuḍa in the Uttara–kāṇḍa]

In the Kali-age, said Kākbhushuṇḍi, there remains neither *varṇa–dharma* nor the four ashramas (stages of life). All persons become antagonistic, to the Vedas. *Brāhmins* do not recite the Vedas as part of their duty but charge exorbitant fees for doing so. No one pays any heed to Vedic injunctions. Kings are bent upon totally destroying their subjects. Whatever pleases one is considered by misguided people as virtue. He who boasts is taken to be a pandit (learned man). The person who is steeped in hypocrisy is believed to be a saint. He who in some way or the other appropriates another's wealth is indeed considered wise in the Kali-age. The arrogant person is taken to be a great teacher. He alone is considered to be worthy who speaks lies and knows how to ridicule others. He is taken to be full of wisdom and renunciation who is devoid of all principles, and has abandoned the way of scriptural-knowledge. He is said to be a recluse of note who keeps his nails long and his long hair matted. They are taken to be the accomplished yogis and worthy of reverence in this Kali-age who wear inauspicious garments and ornaments and eat all kinds of food not caring for its wholesomeness and purity. Those who cause injury to others are given eminence and are considered worthy of honour. They are taken to be orators in the Kali-age, who by their acts, words and thoughts vilify others. O Garuḍa, all men are completely dominated by women and dance to their-tune as monkeys dance in a conjurer's show. *Shūdras* teach wisdom to *brāhmins*. Villains put the sacred thread on themselves [thus pretending holiness] and take charity. All the people are steeped in greed, lust and anger. They are opposed to the saints, the gods, *brāhmins* and the teachings of the Vedas. Misguided women forsake their handsome and gifted husbands and cohabit with other men. Married women are without ornaments, while widows beautify themselves in many ways. Teachers are ignorant and students turn a deaf ear to all they teach. Gurus deprive their students of their money but fail to remove their sorrows. Therefore hell is the place for the gurus of the Kali-age. Parents instruct their children only in that which will bring them money so that they are able to fill their bellies. Men and women talk of nothing save knowledge of *brahman*, but even for a little gain they do not hesitate to murder *brāhmins* and gurus. *Shūdras* argue with *brāhmins* and say to them 'Are we any the less than you?' They scold them, and glaring at them say, 'Can't you recognize a *brāhmin* (meaning themselves) when you see one ?' I have noticed in the Kali-age, continued Kākbhushuṇḍi, that only those men are knowers of the oneness of the soul and *brahman*, who are attached to other peoples' wives, who are replete with cunning, deceit, delusion, affectation and malice.[129] The people of the Kali-age ruin not only themselves but also those who are treading the path of truth. They disparage the Vedas by their cavil. Such as these dwell age after age in various hells. Those of inferior *varṇas*—those who extract oil, potters, *chāṇḍālas, bhīls, kols* and *kalawārs*—shave their heads and pose as *sannyāsīs* after the deaths of their wives and the destruction of their homes. They get themselves venerated by *brāhmins* and deprive themselves of the two worlds by their own deeds. *Brāhmins* take to themselves the adulterous women of men of the who are of low castes, illiterate, greedy, lustful, unprincipled and foolish. The *shūdras* observe many kinds of fasts, austerities and continual holy chantings. They take high seats and recite the Purāṇas [things that they are forbidden to do]. Everyone does as he chooses to. O Garuḍa, the things that are done in the Kali-age against the established norm are too numerous to be recounted. In Kali-yuga there is admixture of castes, and bastards are born. Propriety is set at naught. People commit sins and have consequently to bear sorrow, discase and fear, and are deprived of things they'd love to have. People abandon the path of Veda-knowledge,

129. This meant to be a kind of taunt. It is not, of course, to be taken literally.

renunciation and devotion to Lord Hari, (i.e., God). Instead these deluded persons seek new pathways. *Sannyāsīs* spend lavishly in decorating their houses. They are slaves to desires and are overpowered by the longing of sensual enjoyment. Ascetics become rich and householders poor. O friend, the strange ways of Kali-yuga are indescribable ! Men turn out of their houses their virtuous and devoted wives and becoming characterles, bring kept women to enjoy. Sons care for their parents only till they are unmarried. Then they are attached to their in-laws and become inimical to their erstwhile family-members. In Kali-yuga kings become sinful. *Dharma* (right) no longer guides them. They keep tormenting innocent subjects by punishing them without cause. It is wealth which determines status not family traditions. The only sign of a twice-born is now the sacred thread, and baring the body that of an ascetic. Only those are known to be real saints and devotees who do not have any belief in the Vedas and the Purāṇas. Poets have multiplied, but there is none to appreciate and patronize them. There are many faultfinders, but none without faults. In Kali-yuga there are frequent famines. People are grieved by hunger and die of starvation.

Listen, O Garuḍa, in Kali-yuga deceit, obstinacy, vanity, hatred, hypocrisy, arrogance, delusion, lust, wickedness and so forth, have overtaken everyone. People are too lazy to undertake sacrifices, austerities, fasts, the giving of charity etc. The gods do not give the earth rain and crops dry. Women wear no ornaments. They are never satiated. They remain sorrowful because of various unfulfilled cravings. Foolishly they desire happiness but they have not love for *dharma* [so how can they get happiness?]. Their wisdom is little. And it makes them rough, rather then gentle. People are troubled by diseases, and there is no joy anywhere. Men are arrogant and recalcitrant without cause. Life is short and existence ephemeral. Yet man's arrogance is so great that he thinks he will live on till the destruction of the world (*pralaya*) ! The Kali-age has thrown mankind into disorder Men lust even after their daughters and sisters. People are neither contented, not have they calmness and understanding. Envy, harsh and bitter words, and greed, reign supreme. There is no sympathy. Partings and acute sorrows oppress everyone. The duties of *varṇas* exist no longer. No one has any good thoughts or kindness left in him. Nor is there wisdom or control over the senses. Folly and cheating others are on the increase. Men and women have no other aim except attending to the needs of their bodies. The world is replete with slanderers and everyone is busy reproaching others.

[This account is contained in Tulsidāsa's Rāmacharitamānasa, Uttara-kāṇḍa 97 (A)–101 (5) Gita Press edn. Kākbhushuṇḍi goes on to say that despite Kali-yuga being the abode of sin and evil qualities, yet there is one redeeming feature. Merely by chanting the Lord's name deliverance can be achieved in this age. So to reach God is easy. It seems hard to agree with that. It amounts to saying that since there's an abundance of evil a little good can bring one salvation! It may be creditable, for a rare thing is always prized. But salvation is another matter. And it is not easy either. Everything works towards it as the Gītā says – devotion, doing one's duty, good works and wisdom which relalizes the Soul's nature. However our objective is not to comment but only to quote. So this may be taken to be just an aside].

FROM THE SHIVA PURĀṆA

The *Shiva Purāṇa* is also a Mahāpurāṇa (i.e. a 'great Purāṇa') The Purāṇa gives the genealogies of kings, as other Purāṇas do. However the main emphasis is on the Shiva-ritual. Shiva is said be the supreme god, the Cosmic Soul and from whom all existence proceeds. The Shiva Purāṇa gives us various forms of worship and meditation on Shiva, based on Tantra, Yantra and Mantra. A course of devotion having three aspects is given. They require the same steady application as in sex-play. The devotee should control the six *chakras* in the spinal column. This is possible only by yogic and other spiritual rites. Finally the Shiva-devotee, after stern devotion, finds refuge in Shiva and attains him. Above all, this Purāṇa is an account of Shiva's legends and rituals. It eulogizes Shiva just as the *Bhāgavata Purāṇa* sings the glories of Vishṇu. It is of particular significance for Shiva–worshippers.

WHAT GOOD CONDUCT IS

[The Purāṇa concentrates on the correct way of doing things, with particular reference to brāhmins. Most of the things commented on are items of daily ritual and routine. Very little of it deals with ethics or spriritual goodness. The extract which follows is from chapter 13 of the Vidyeshvara saṁhitā].

A *brāhmin* who follows only some of the *shāstric* rules and has just a little knowledge of the Veda is really of the nature of a *kshatriya*. If he is very careless he is more less a *vaishya*. If he himself ploughs a field he is a *shūdra–brāhmin*. A *brāhmin* should endeavour to realize *brahman*. Wealth comes from virtue. It gives a man pleasures. After the man has enjoyed to the full through wealth, he gets fed up it and seeks detachment. But wealth should be got only by rightful means, otherwise is increases passion. He who renounces desires, becomes pure. Then he acquires knowledge. In the Krita-age one gets wisdom by meditation, in the Tretā, by austerities, in the Dvāpara by performing sacrifices and in the Kali-age by the worship of images.

All those who earn wealth should divide it into three parts for its disposal. A third should be for acts of *dharma*. Another one- third for increasing whatever wealth he already has. With the last portion he may enjoy himself to the full, but not in wrong or lecherous pursuits. When wealth is got by agriculture one-tenth of it must be first given in charity and then the remaining used as aforesaid. This removes sin. Traders should similarly give one-sixth of their wealth in charity. Good *brāhmins* should give a fourth of what they get as gifts etc., in charity. And if the *brāhmin* gets a lot of money unexpectedly he should give away half. One should give what another begs for, according to his ability. If he does not, he will have to do so in his next life. The faults of others should not be pointed out to all. Nor should one do any scandal mongering or speak words which may cause hurt to others. He should carry out sacred rites in the fire both early morning and in the evening. Virtue should be practised and violence eschewed, for virtue brings a man happiness and evil, misery. One gets salvation by acquiring wisdom through a guru. Salvation means realizing what one really is and achieving perfect bliss. One who desires his own continued welfare should give *brāhmins* fruits. grain and other things they need. A householder should give gifts in charity. He who is thirsty must always be given water to drink. The sick and the hungry should be given food. The giver of food gets half the merit of the receiver of it. This accumulates till such time as the food is digested. The person who receives gifts must make up by practising austerities or by similarly giving gifts to others. If he fails to do so he will surely go to hell.

SHIVA'S DALLIANCE WITH SATĪ

[After his marriage with Satī, Shiva proceeded to the Himalaya mountains with her. This is a description of their lovemaking. The account is from chapter twenty-one of the Rudra-Saṁhitā section 2. Narrative of Satī].

Shiva dismissed his attendants and asked them to come only when he desired. Then he was alone with Satī. He gathered flowers made them into a garland and put it round her neck. While she looked at her face in the mirror he came from behind and peeped into it. He played with her ear-rings, applied red dye to her feet and whispered sweet nothings into her ears. While she was engaged in some thought he would come from behind and blindfolding her eyes with his hands say, 'Guess, dear, who it is'. He would at times make himself invisible and embrace her. Then she would get frightened. Sometimes he'd make nailmarks on her breasts in the shape of lotus-buds. He'd take her necklace off and then press her breasts. He caressed her big breasts and lingered at the black mole on them. He decorated her body all over with lotuses and lovely flowers. He sported with her among hedges and caves. Then going to the high hills he desired the presence of Kāma, love's god. When Kāma came, the creepers burst into bloom. Bees hovered round lotuses. Gentle and cool breezes began to come from all sides. The *palāsha* flowered, lotuses bloomed, fragrant breezes fanned the lovers, the mango trees blossomed and everything became lovely to excite passion. The water of the lake shone like the minds of saints in which the *ātman* is reflected. The whole place was lit by soft moonlight. Shiva dallied with Satī thus for long amid groves, hedges and streams. Then passion woke up strongly in Satī. She embraced Shiva so tightly that she seemed to enter his body, and his juice flowed into her. He put flower-garlands on her body and limbs. They tasted renewed pleasures. He talked sweetly, joked and drank the nectar of her moon-like face. He experienced great pleasure in her. He loveliness, the fragrance of her limbs and of her face like a lotus, charmed him, and he was their prisoner even as an elephant is bound with ropes. Thus for twenty-five celestial years Shiva dallied with Satī in the Himalayas.

Apparently the lovers had not had their fill. The Purāṇa goes on to tell us that the two then went to the summit of the mountains, where there was 'the city of the Himalaya'. This was a very beautiful place with grassy plains and trees where the sky seemed to touch the mountain-top. It abounded in all kinds of flowers and birds, beautiful lakes and groves. Celestial women played on musical instruments. and danced. In that spot the two sported for ten thousand celestial years. They went to many places before settling down in a ome. Shiva found pleasure only with Satī. He abjured sacrifices, austerities and scriptural study. The two kept only staring at each other's face. Thus they lost themselves in lovemaking.

(C) FROM THE VEDAS

WHAT THE VEDAS ARE ABOUT

The word 'Veda' is from the root *vid*, 'to know'. The Vedas imply 'divine knowledge', and are the scriptures that are the basis of Hindu religion.

They are full of vibrant life and give a vivid account of the society then existing. They narrate legends, customs and manners, as for example marriage customs, funeral ceremonies, drinking, gambling, spells and incantations. They tell us a lot about village life. They are not for ascetism. Rather what they praise is a full life of domestic happiness, knowledge and activity. Renunciation comes at the end, after living such a life. A very significant principle advocated in them is that of friendly coexistence. In the *Atharva Veda* we are told that there should be unity not only in the country, but throughout the world. Varuṇa [god of the sky and ruler of the firmament] it says, 'belongs not only to our land, but to foreign lands too'!

The Vedas are believed to have been revealed by the Almighty to sages (*rishīs*) whose names they bear. So they are reverered as *apaurushēya* i.e. 'not of human origin (from *purusha*–a human being). The oldest Veda, the *Rig Veda* dates back to 3000 B.C. The *Atharva Veda* is comparitively recent. The Vedas are among of oldest literatures of the world. For long they were transmitted orally from teacher to pupil. The sage, Vyāsa, is said to have arranged them in the four divisions which we know of today. He taught the *Rig Veda* to his disciple, Paila, the *Sāma Veda* to Jaimini, the *Yajur Veda* to Vaishampāyana and the *Atharva Veda* to Angiras. These are the four existing. Of these the *Rig Veda*, having 11,000 hymns contained in ten books, is the longest and the most outstanding. The stanzas have four lines each, containing usually eight, eleven or twelve and sometimes five or four, syllables. The metre varies. There is no rhyme. Some western critics have made uncharitable remarks about the literary quality of the Vedas.[130] It is forgotten by them that the Vedas are scriptures, not poetry. For Sanskrit poetry one has to go to Kalidāsa not the Vedas, just as for Enlish poetry, it is to Milton, Keats, Eliot etc., that we have to turn, not to the Bible.

Contrary to the observations of such critics, the Vedas have felicity of language. The Vedic poets were expert craftsmen. The Sanskrit they wrote is simple, spontaneous and rich in figures of speech, particularly comparisons. For example, the bow which a warrior presses close to his ear is like his sweetheart held in his embrace. The twang of the bowstring is like love's secrets which she whispers to him.[131] A lover casts a spell on his girl in order to 'make her long for his body, his feet, his eyes and lips and swiftly go and lie on his bosom'. A gambler loses his fortune in the game after which he finds himself shunned by all. He bemoans 'My mother-in-law hates me now, and everyone is averse to me. They say there's no more use of a gambler who is penniless. He's like an aged horse that his owner wants to sell, but there are no buyers!' Hard work on the field is extolled in the Vedas. 'My plough which is sharp-edged and smooth to handle, enables me to make neat furrows in my field' says a farmer. 'Thus the crop is good and I can sell the wheat at a decent price. This gets me a sheep, a horse to draw my cart and a plump lass too!' Emphasis was placed on character. The goddess of learning tells a teacher to fetch her those who are pure, learned and chaste, not crooked people who are full of hatred and jealousy, carnal and lascivious.

Bhagavad gītā. 2. 42–43.

Atharva Veda. 36. 18.8 and 4. 16. 8.

130. For example Professor Cowell says, 'The poetry of the Rig Veda is remarkably deficient in that simplicity and natural pathos or sublimity which we naturally look for in the songs of an early period of civilization . . . as a rule we find few grand similes or metaphors'. Professor Williams says, 'they (the Vedas) abound more in puerile ideas than in striking thoughts and loty conceptions'. Quoted in J. Dowson. *A Classical Dictionary of Hindu Mythology and Religion* etc. London : Routledge & Kegan Paul. 1961, p., 347.

131. *Rig Veda.* 6. 75. 3

Each Veda has two parts, the *mantra* and the *brāhmaṇa*. The *mantra* is usually a prayer or praise contained in metrical hymns. The *brāhmaṇas* are in prose and are explanations of the hymns. There are various legends also interwoven with them. To these are also appended the Āraṇyakas and Upanishads which speak of God (*brahman*) and the Soul (*ātman*). There are two divisions of all the Vedas. One is the *karma-kāṇḍa* dealing with works and ceremonies. The other is the *jñāna-kāṇḍa* the subject matter of which is knowledge. The Vedas are classed as *shruti* because they are direct revelation. The *mantras*, which are more ancient are grouped a Sanhitās. the *Rig Veda* and the *Sāma Veda* have one Sanhitā each, the *Yajur Veda* has two.

While quite a few hymns of the Veda are in praise of various gods like Indra, Agni, Sūrya, Aditi, Varuṇa Ushas, and so forth, we find in the *Rig Veda* the idea of the one *brahman* taking shape: Some writers dismiss this as vague and nebulous. But it isn't really so. There is the concept of *ṛita* or order in things and the uniformity of nature. There is a definite trend towards monotheism. The *Rig Veda* says, 'The worshipful divinity of the gods is one' [*mahat devānām asuratvam ekam*].[132] 'What is one, people call by various names'[133] is another such observation. The gods were collectively called by the term *vishva-devas* (i.e. 'all the gods') One deity was designated as the Supreme God, as for example, Visva-Karman 'the Maker of everything' and Prajāpati, 'the father god' or 'lord of all beings'. In the 'Song of Creation' contained in the *Rig Veda,* we are told that the entire world was perhaps created by one Divine Being.[134] Doubt has not been eliminated, yet the root of monotheism has positively sprouted. There are various accounts of creation in the Vedas. Sacrifice is regarded as a duty and debt due to God (*riṇa*). Virtue is emphasized. The *Rig Veda* says 'He who cooks food for himself alone eats nothing but sin'.[135] Though mainly worldly life like war, farming, domestic bliss etc., is given prominence, there is a

132. *Rig Vēda.* 3. 55. 46

133. ibid. 1. 164. 46.

134. ibid. 10. 129.

135. ibid. 10. 117. 6.

strain of ascetism too at times The *Rig Veda* speaks of long hair and coloured dress (as of a hermit).[136] The belief that one can have a happy life in heaven shows that the Vedic seers believed in life after death.

The *Yajur Veda* consists of some hymns from the main *Rig Veda*, but has also many new prose passages. It lays down the ways of the performance of sacrifices, and so is of great significance for priests. It has two *sanhitās*, the Taittirīya and the Vasjasanejī, commonly known as the Black and the White Yajurs. The Black Yajur is the older, while the White is more systematic. *The Sāma Veda* consists of metrical hymns for being chanted at sacrifices or offerings of Soma. They are mostly addressed to Soma, Agni and Indra. The *Atharva Veda* is of later origin. The hymns in it are partly metrical and partly not. There are about 760 hymns and 6000 verses. This Veda also contains many incantations. These are for some end like long life, recovery from disease, the vanquishing of foes, attainment of wealth or power, success in love or in play, the removal of pests, even for growing hair on a bald head! Lucky talismans, necklaces and herbs effecting miraculous cures are mentioned in it. Occasionally there are hymns which achieve great sublimity, as the one to Varuṇa who rules over the three worlds and sees all that is within and beyond heaven and earth.

136. ibid. 10. 136. 2.

READING LIST

Translations of the individual Vedas are given below :

Rig Veda

1873 Max Müller, Trübner.

1872 Sayanācharya's commentary. Oxford 4 volumes.

1889–91 R.T.H. Griffith. 4 vols.

1922 Martin Haug.

1861 Aufrecht 4 vols. (German).

Sāma Veda

1842 Dr Stevenson ed. Wilson.

1848 Benfey.

1874–78 S. Samasramin (Bibliotheca Indica).

8981 R.T.H. Griffth.

Atharava Veda

1899 M.A. Bloomfield.

Consolidated Editions of the Vedas

1933–Sl Vedic Sanshodhan Maṇḍala Poona 5 vols. Sanskrit text, Sayanācharya's commentary.

1939–55 Dr Lakshmana Swarup. 4 vols. Sanskrit text with Mādva's commentary.

1963 Ramagovinda Trivedi 8 vols. Sanskrit text with Hindi translation.

1973 Dayananda Sansthan New Delhi. 4 vols Sanskrit text with Hindi translation and commentary of Maharshi Dayananda Sarasvati.

Other Books (Text and Criticism)

Anandashrama, Poona. *Yajur Veda*, 1940.

Arvinda. Hindi Veda Rahasya. Sri Arvind Society, 1972

Arya Sahitya Mandir, Ajmere. *Sāma Veda*, 1954

Aufrecht, Th., *Dic Hymen des Rigveda*. Berlin : Ferd. Dummler's *Verlagsbuchhandlung* 4 vols. 1861.

Bloomfield M. *Atharva Veda*. Strassburg, 1899.

The Religion of the Veda. New York, 1908.

Das, A.C. *Rigvedic India* Calcutta, 1947

Deshmukh, P.S. *Religion in Vedic Literature*. Bombay, 1933.

Giri, M. *Vedic Culture*, Calcutta, 1921.

Gopalacharya, M.R. *The Heart of the Rigveda*. Bombay : Somaiya Publications Pvt. Ltd., 1971.

Haung, Martin. *The Aitereya Brahmanam of the Rig Vēda*, 1922.

Hillebrandt. A. *Vedic Mythology* (tran. from German into English by Sarma, Dr S.R. 2 vols Delhi : Motilal Banarsidass, 1981.

Kaegi, Adolf. *The Rig Veda*, 1886.

Kapoor, D.K. *Selected Hymns of the Rig Veda*. Bombay : Deva Vedic Prakashan, 1978.

Machdonnell, A.A. *Vedic Mythology*. Strassburg, 1898.

Maurice, P. *The Teaching of the Veda*, Delhi : Seema Publications. (Reprint) 1976.

Mee. Jean Le. *Hymns from the Rig Veda* (English translation). London : Jonothan Cape, 1975.

Müller, F. Max. (ed.) *Rig-Veda-Samhitā* (commentary of Sayanāchārya) Oxford University Press. 4 vols., 1892.

Pendeya, S. *Vedakālin Rajyavyavasthā*. Lucknow : Hindi Samiti, 1971.

Pillai, G.K. *Vedic History.* Allahabad, 1959.

Prabhānanda, Swami. *Vedic Religion and Philosophy.* Mylapore, 1940

Rai, Raja Rammohun. *The Vedas.* Delhi : Nag Publishers, 1977.

Roth, R. *On the Literature and History of the Vedas*, 1880.

Sarasvati, Swami Saty Prakash and Vidyalankar, Swami. *Rig Veda Samhitā* (English translation) New Delhi : *Veda Pratishthāna* 10 vols. 1980.

Satyavalakara, P. *Sāmaveda.* Surat : Svadhyaya Mandal.

Rigveda Samhitā (commentary Sayanāchārya). Poona : Vedic Sanshodhan Mandal. 5 vols. 1933–51.

Sāmaveda (commentary Sayanāchārya) Asiatic Society of Bengal. 5 vols., 1974.

Swarup, Dr Lakshmana. *Rigveda Samhitā* (commentary Mādva). Lahore : Motilal Banarsidass. 4 vols., 1935–55.

Trivedi, R. *Rigveda Samhitā* (English translation). Allahabad : Indian Press, 1945.

Rigveda Samhitā (Sanskrit text with Hindi Translation). Bhagalpur : Vedic Pustakmālā, 1963.

FROM THE RIG VEDA

As has been said, the Vedas have a spirit of optimism. The Rig Veda praises a full life of happiness both for the husband and his wife and for everyone. The selection is from the eighteenth section of the tenth book of the Rig Veda (based on Dayananda's commentary).

GLORIOUS EXISTENCE

When death comes to you, may you take the way of the Fathers (*pitryāna*) not that of the gods, for then you will rejoin your parents, who have gone there before. O you, who carry out sacrifices, live a pure life, begetting sons and full of wealth and prosperity. When you will depart from the earth after warding off the troubles and ills of life so long as you have lived, you will again get a good life (on rebirth) and live long. May we remain away from death and the dying. May we ever have the opportunity of hearing auspicious and wise words; so that all through the years, living most excellently, we may pass the days in laughter, dance and merriment. May all persons be protected (from all misfortunes), and ponder not on death. May they live for a hundred years and even longer and keep death, the foe, away. As days keep following nights and the seasons follow close upon one another, so too, O God make the lives of these men long, without break. O human beings, may you, climbing the ladder of life, endeavour to go the way of your wise and noble predecessors. May the Lord of all beings be favourable to you and bestow long life on you. May the virtuous wives anoint themselves with fragrant unguents and enter their inner apartments. May these women free from grief and disease, and capable of giving birth to lovely and accomplished children, live in their houses receiving all honour and consideration.

O girl, be full of good spirits and lively. Arise, seek one who will wed you and look after you well. Live with him and give birth to virtuous progeny. And if you are unable to bear children, you may enter into the *niyoga* union in order to have them.[137]

Succeeding to the inheritance of your dead father, may your son prove worthy, strong, powerful and courageous, so that he may be able to defeat the armies of his foes. May you live on this pleasure-yielding earth, vast as the sky, which is like the bride of a generous, strong, wealthy and enterprising husband. May this virtuous earth keep you away from the path of evil.

137. *Niyoga* means the marriage of a widow with the brother of her deceased husband. Early marriages were prevalent. It could thus happen that the husband of a woman may die before any children were born. Niyoga marriages were particularly advocated by Swami Dayananda whose commentary is the basis of this translation.

DOMESTIC BLISS

[The ancient Āryans gave high honour to women who were virtuous. The attitude of considering them as inferior to men has its origin in the Purāṇas. which came later. The *Rig Veda* conceives a homely life of domestic bliss in which the newlywed bride is loved by all the members of her husband's family, and is in fact given a place of honour above them all. The passage is from the 85th section of the tenth book of the *Rig Veda*].

Truth is the support of mankind, and human beings should follow the path of truth in their relationship with each other. It is thus only that peace and happiness can be attained. It is the sun which lights up and upholds heaven, and Soma is its support. The laws of Nature also follow truth. The moon gives strength to the years, to the earth and to the asterisms. Soma is not an alcoholic beverage as men wrongly think. It is the herbal plant which gives life-giving juice, but in its real sense it yields one *brahman*-knowledge. This Soma is guarded by God as the ramparts protect a fort. It is contained in the creative arts (like song and literature) and in holy chants. Only enlightened and wise persons can savour it, not worldly men or kings. Vāyu (the wind) is its protector and it is obtained by the gods. The months pass into years, and the months are determined by the moon. Vāyu is the protector of the worlds and also of the moon.

The words of the wise are a gift to men. The praise of people for such wisdom is like a mantle and the sun's light is as a bride's dress. Thus wisdom purified by the men of enlightenment is doubtless auspicious. The union of mind and wisdom is like a husband and his wife. The mind's determination and discrimination is as a cosy cushion and knowledge is as the collyrium applied to eyes. The heaven and earth are like lovely hair.

[We go on to the later part of this section from verse 33 onwards].

This girl is of auspicious signs. Come with your relations to see her and after giving her your blessings go back home.[138] Some girls give a man agony so great as one feels when, tormented with thirst, he gets no water. They are acrimonious and one should keep away from them as from poison. They are not fit for conjugal bliss. That person alone is qualified to select a bride who is wise and learned in the Vedas. Only such a discriminating person can recognize evil qualities in the prospective bride—defects such as disease of the body, physical defects and deformities, disregard and lack of respect. At the time of the wedding ceremony the bridegroom pledges to fulfil all the desires of his bride and to give her a trouble-free life. He is bound to her lifelong. This is the marriage sacrament ordained by God and enjoined by the wise : 'O Almighty, bless my union with this man (prays the girl) so that this husband of mine who puts his semen in me may be able to satisfy me sexually, and we may get mutual satisfaction. O God bless this woman so that she may have worthy children. Bestow her strength and splendour. Grant her husband long life, even to a hundred years'. To start with, God gives the newlywed bride gentleness and simplicity, then entertainment, music, song and adornment, third, after attaining puberty the desire for congress with her husband and thereafter the birth of children. O husband and wife, stay in the home as householders. Never be separated from each other. Live a full life, happy in your home, delighting in the company of your children and grand-children. May the Lord of beings give you children, keep you united and give you his protection all through life till old age. May he keep you away from the inauspicious, (i.e., protect you two from misfortunes), favour the husband in all his endeavours, and make him kind to all men and animals. May the married woman be loving not harsh; may she keep her husband happy, not troubled and be attentive to the house-pets. May she be cheerful, lovely and strong and the bearer of progeny, considerate to her husband's brothers both younger to him and elder, good-natured, pious and kind to all creatures. May God give her wealth and strong, healthy,

138. This concerns the ceremony of *mukh–dekhāi* or 'seeing the bride'. The bridegroom's people come to see the girl and give her a gift to cement the alliance. A kind of engagement preceding marriage.

children. May she have at least ten children or even more. May she be the darling loved one of her mother-in-law and her father-in-law. May her husband's sisters and brothers acknowledge her authority as housewife and act according to her wishes [so that she gets as much love and consideration as she used to get from her own parents.]. May they (husband and wife) be one, as the one water, (i.e., be ever in accord), and compatible to each other. May God protect them and keep them united, free from all differences and misunderstandings.

THE DISAPPOINTED GAMBLER

[This account of the fascination of a gambler for gambling and his feelings on becoming broke after indulging in it is from the thirty-fourth section of the tenth book of the *Rig Veda*. We have given an account of the gambling match between Duryodhana and Shakunī on the one side (the Kauravas) and Yudhishṭhira (the Pāṇḍavas) on the other, in the extracts from the *Mahābhārata* ante. But in that case the stakes were unusual and Shakunī cheated in the game. Here the gambler's own folly led him to lose all his money. Apparently the game of dice with which gamblers played was a very ancient one as the *Rig Veda* too mentions it as one of the pastimes].

These pieces of dice obtained from the tree of the barren area without manure or even water, and like the fruits of a huge tree make me glad (because I can gamble with them).[139] These bits of dice produced from the *baheṛa* tree *(belleric myrobalan)*, found on the slopes of the Mujjavān mountain are pleasure-giving as the juice of the Soma plant. They beckon to me to play. These dice meant for gambling have won over a man like me, greedy for money. My wife never disrespects or disregards me. She looks well after me and my friends too. Yet because of my addiction to gambling I frequently leave her lonely and keep away from home. The result is that due to my constantly losing my money in gambling my wife hates me and my mother-in-law has only contempt for me. Even when poverty (caused by loss of money) torments me, friends forsake me and do not lend me any money. Alas such is a gambler's lot, and I have brought it upon myself. I am bereft of all protection and happiness, and as unwanted as an old horse, or as worn out discarded clothes! See the evil consequence of gambling! When a man gets habituated to it, his wife leaves him and cohabits with others. Even his parents and brothers disown him, saying 'take him away,

139. Apparently the pieces of dice were cut out from the wood of a tree which could grow on any kind of soil, and the tree did not need watering.

we don't know who he is'. Realizing this I determine firmly that I will gamble no more. But my fellow gamblers come and entice me away again to play And as a lustful woman running after her lover, I follow them helplessly.

[The above depicts the anguish of a gambler who loses all his money and is shunned by everyone, yet is irresistibly drawn to it and can't abandon it. Now is narrated the evils of gambling].

The gambler brings his wife sorrow and suffers the misery of extreme poverty. When he sees the families of others (who do not indulge in gambling) happy and prosperous, he repents and feels sorry for himself. When the night is spent [after having gambled] he also earnestly prays to God to come to his rescue and be graceful to him, [i.e., save him from this evil].

O gambler! when your sorrow is full and you are thoroughly disgusted this evil habit, you ought to go the headman of the village and before him and all your co-gamblers, solemnly declare that henceforth you will refrain from this despicable game. This is the only way by which you can escape this evil. O man attached to gambling! leave off casting the dice. Instead, take to farming and considering that adequate for your sustenance, cultivate your land with hard labour and earn from it. With such wealth gained honestly and by the sweat of your brow, you will be able to remain happy and keep your family prosperous and your cows well-fed. Then God will also give you his blessings.

O my fellow-gamblers, the gambler says, do not detest me for abstaining from gambling. Keep your anger to yourself (don't vent it on me). I am your well-wisher, and my advice to you too is to keep away from these deceitful shining pieces of dice.

[We find in the Rig Veda that bud of monotheism which blossoms out in the full blown flower in the Vedānta. We give here two extracts one from Rig Veda 1. 64. 46 and the other, the 'Song of Creation', from the one hundred and twenty-ninth section of the tenth book, to bring this out].

Wise people call the one great *brahman* and Īshvara (God) by many names, as Indra, Varuṇa, Yama, Vāyu and such hundreds of names. These represent the qualities, working and nature of that One Almighty Supreme Being.

At that time, before creation there was neither existence nor non-existence, nor atoms nor ether which are the subtlest of the subtle. Was there anything which covered all? Where and what was the habitation? Were there deep waters difficult to fathom? There was then neither life nor death. There was no distinguishing feature marking night and day, [i.e., one could not say what 'night' was and what was 'day']. Sun and moon were not there, nor was there any division of time [into seconds, minutes, hours, days, months, years centuries and so forth]. There was only the One without breath, endowed only with his own power and his own subtle Nature. Apart from him there was nothing, neither gross nor subtle; no, nothing at all. Before creation everything was shrouded in darkness. There was nothing with any form or movement. It was covered by the subtle ether from all sides. By means of austere wisdom the One arose. He, the First, the Seed of existence, resolved. The men of wisdom from whom nothing was hid, then came to know truth which gives orderliness to chaos. The rays of the light of knowledge were diverse. Some went up. Some perhaps down, [i.e., people had different concepts of truth]. The all-powerful Lord was of great majesty. Nature was too little to contain within it the vast scheme of creation. Who knows really what this creation is? Who is there who can speak about it? From where was all this [these creatures and all else] produced? What is the origin of this myriad creation? Who knows from where this world originated? Creaton came into existence before, and the knowers of it later; so how could they know? Who is the source of this vast creation, who is its upholder and Lord? O friend, O inquirer, is there one who knows it, or is it known to no one?[140]

140 Swami Dayananda gives a different interpretation. He says : 'O friend, he knows, he surely knows'. But this is not borne out by the text – *vēd yadi vā na vēd*. This does not however imply that the idea of the one Creator is not contained here. The passage read as a whole does convey the sense of a Cosmic Absolute which the Upanishads later came to know as *brahman*.

[This passage of the *Rig Veda* has become very famous. It has been translated into English verse by J. Muir, and is believed to contain the quintessence of monistic thought in the Veda. Muir's verse translation is doubtless meritorious and good poetry. Nonetheless in some parts it is not faithful to the original. For example speaking of the Creator, the 'One' he says 'within it first arose desire'. Desire is not exactly the sense here. *Kāmaḥ* means here *sankalpa* i.e. 'resolve'. The word 'desire' implies attachment. But how can God have attachment? Similarly Muir's concluding line is 'its Lord in heaven alone can tell, if even he can show?' This too is not appropriate, for if the Lord desires he can reveal himself to one who is worthy. He cannot be bound by any such limitation].

FROM THE ATHARVA VEDA

THE ETERNAL BRAHMAN

[Here again we find positive mention of the One Cosmic Absolute, thus debunking the view that the Vedas did not conceive the eternal brahman. The extract is from the second book (kāṇḍa) of the Atharva Veda]

That great Lord, *brahman* is so subtle that he resides in the hearts of beings and is their Knower. He is so large that the entire universe is contained in him. Sages sit calmly in meditation and chant his name. They rejoice in him and in his creation and are always singing hymns in his praise. These learned māhatmas realize the greatness of *brahman* and are always discoursing of it. He is the subtlest of the subtle and the mightiest of the mighty. He is the Creator, the Preserver and the Destroyer. He is the Lord of the past, the present and the future and the Maker of three qualities of purity, activity and dullness. That wise man who knows about these attributes of the Lord in all their individual and sundry aspects, [i.e., in each and every way] is of all learned persons, the most knowledgeable. That same Īshvara is our Sustainer our Father and our Relation, [i.e., everything]. He knows all the worlds and all beings. It is he who classifies all beings and objects, [i.e., he designates a cow as 'a cow', a river as 'a river' and so on]. All learned beings worship him, and it is to him that they go. The knowers of the real truth understand that there must be the Maker of the world and everything in it and that therefore there is the Almighty God, just as the hearers of those who give discourses, absorbing their import, give credence to the orginator of those words. That very Lord has laid down the law of *dharma* (righteousness) which governs creations. He is the Sustainer of all—as the heat cooks food which nourishes the body and makes the blood course through it, and gives it life and strength. Those who are drawn to the divine, see the universe as pervaded by that great Lord, the Father of all beings on earth. They remain blissful and relinquishing all selfish desires, take refuge in him. Those courageous and calm, the saints and sages see with the eyes of wisdom that same God in everything and in all creatures and relinquishing vanity, purify and strengthen themselves and achieve happiness. He is the maker of the sun and gives it light. May that Lord of beings give me strength to overcome anger. May he save me from the three sorrows.[140 a] By worshiping that Lord of all creatures one gets intense joy and peace. He is ever present with all his powers in everyone and everywhere and in the atomosphere and waters and everything arising from them. These wondrous powers are present in the greatly vast sky and exist in the form of atoms in the bodies of beings. When these bodies cease to be, they vanish and can't be seen. These powers are the agents of the Almighty Lord. Everything in the world and all substances, are seen to be affected by them. They are subordinate to the Lord and are the cause of the arising, maintenance and ending of the entire creation.[140 b] All creatures great and small, accept these powers as being of the Lord, their Master and thinking of his beneficence rejoice. That Lord chastises the wicked and blesses those who are gentle and virtuous. He is all-powerful and of gracious nature. he loves those who do good deeds in the world. All creatures obey that Almighty Lord and remain happy.

The Himalayan rivers (having their source in the Himalaya mountains) remain full of water even in summer. They keep the crops and the grain alive and green and in this way sustain the people of the land. In the same manner *brahman* resides in the hearts of all creatures and preserves them. All men should acquire knowledge, maintain celibacy, (i.e., purity of mind) and live in bliss. He, the Lord, has given all medicinal herbs the power to cure diseases and thus end suffering. As wise men, (i.e., men who know the virtues of medicinal herbs), dig the earth by spades and take out the roots which can cure diseases and use them to alleviate suffering, even so

140a. For the three sorrow, see., The Fundamental Concepts of Hinduism–Sorrow and how to Remove it. The three sorrows are those coming from a divine agency. those from other creatures and mental grief.

140b. We see here a pointer to the *māyā* of the Lord. We have dealt with *māyā* in the introduction – Fundamentals of Hindu Philosophy – In the *Rig Veda* *māyā* meant supernatural power. mysterious will power or wondrous skill. In the *Atharva Veda* it meant magic or illusion (P.D. Shastri. *The Doctrine of Māyā*).

that Almighty Lord has, ever since the beginning of creation, made provision for removing mental and physical tortures. Those who have faith in God see him in every substance and by his divine glory and grace are able to overcome all their suffering and rejoice. This *brahma*-like (godly) spirit resides in all creatures. People should realize this *brahman* and enjoy peace and calmness of the mind. Praying for the grace of God, we should keep engaged in the tasks of life, so that water, fire and so forth, all things remain pure and keep us disease-free. Thus we ought to drive away evil from us and remain joyful, even as a king punishes dacoits thieves and other vicious people so that they leave his kingdom and stop vexing his subjects.

To live long one ought to achieve glory in this world. One should have continued joy by achieving *brahman* (striving for God) and at the same time keeping the body healthy and free from disease. In this way by the knowledge of truth obtained from sages one profits himself and does good to the world too. He should have faith in the Lord who is the preserver of all and all-powerful. Abandoning laziness, he should engage in the aims of life he has set before himself. May God protect such a man from evil, demons, destruction, those out to injure him and the like. The enterprising and discriminationg person should have faith in God. He should be able to tide over mental and physical hindrances, keep fit and remain happy. People can protect themselves and others, by industry, a healthy regimen, selfless service and belief in God. Such yogis, austere persons and seekers of wisdom who are devoted to the Almighty, can surmount all hindrances and gain strength and be happy. Those wicked persons who do not take the rightful path and do not make the practice of virtue and truth their aim in life, reap great sorrow for so it is divinely ordained. Truthful, hardworking perons who care for their health and take nourishing food, obtain the blessings of that Almighty Being, and progress in the world achieving success. They find real happiness and lead a fruitful existence.

[*Atharva Veda*, *kāṇḍa* 2, *sūkta* 1–4].

PRAYER FOR A BARREN WOMAN

In Hindu society, particularly in the old days, a barren woman was considered inauspicious. So much so that people would not cast their eyes on her in the morning. She was despised by her her relations, friends and even by her own family. In some respects her position was worse than a Hindu widow. In one of the traditional rural songs of India we are told of the wretchedness of such a woman. She wants to die, but a tigress whom she invites to eat her won't do so, nor will a she-cobra bite her for fear of going barren themselves. Her mother too drives her out. Then she goes to Mother Earth for support. But even *she* won't accept her and says : 'Go back, O barren woman, if I sustain you I too will become barren'! (*One Hundred Rural Songs of India* by the author. UNESCO/Motilal Banarsidass). It is heartening to find that the Vedas have encouragement for such innocent victims of Hindu society. The passage is from the third *kāṇḍa* of the *Atharva* Veda, *sūkta* 23].

O barren woman, I will remove your barrenness. I will remedy that which is the cause of your being barren, and absolve you of it, so that you may have children. O gentle woman, may the life-giving embryo enter your womb, as the arrow in tis quiver. May the foetus of a son grow there and may you give birth to a son after ten months [obviously the calculation of the period was on somewhat different basis]. May your son prove a worthy scion of your family.

I pray that you give birth to a valorous son who may protect you. Thereafter to another. May they revere you and always practise virtue, so that they may never come to evil in afterlife and keep away from hell. Tend your children, O mother, and nurse them when they are babies, as wise, *ṛishīs* prepare the sustaining juice of herbs, (i.e., tonics) for children. I will offer oblations to the gods for the protection of your children. O woman who gives your husband succour, may you be pregnant and give birth to sons who give birth to sons who may be the pride of your clan. May they keep you happy and may you too be a source of happiness to them. May those medicinal herbs whose growth the sun accelerates, and which the earth produces and whose roots are made strong by water – may these heavenly herbs of divine nature assist in removing your barrenness and giving you children.

THE CALL OF A LOVER TO HIS GIRL

[This extract is from the 25th *sūkta* of the third *kāṇḍa* of *Atharva Veda.* Dayananda has taken it to be a prayer to knowledge (*vidyā*) which destroys ignorance. But that is unnecessarily trying to make every passage of the Veda a paean of virtue. We therefore take the plain and straightforward interpretation. Hindu philosophy does not discard love or even passion, as we have explained in the introduction. Khajuraho is a living proof of this].

O sweetheart may you become restless with love [for me]. Do not desire to stay in your bedroom [alone]. I pierce your heart with the sharp arrow of love. May this arrow of my love and longing, whose sharp point is desire and whose wings are the yearning for satiation, find your heart as its target and fly straight to it. I will pierce your heart with this well-aimed arrow of love which will create in you burning passion and awake in you the fire of love. Fly into my arms quickly, darling, for your mouth is parched with ardour. Leave your arrogance. aside, O sweet-tongued girl of gentle nature and amiable temperament. I will obtain you by asking your parents for your hand. Then you will ever remain mine in body, as you already are in my heart. May the gods (Mitra and Varuṇa) remove all other thoughts from my beloved's mind [except for me alone] and rendering her powerless to resist me, make her mine.

A HYMN TO VARUṆA

[Varuṇa—equivalent to the Greek god *Oúgavós*—is one of the oldest of the Vedic deities. He is the king of the universe, of gods and men and the supreme deity of greatest honour. According to Professor Wilson there is no passage in Vedic literature which is so sublime as this hymn to Varuṇa. It occurs in the 16th *sūkta* of the fourth *kāṇḍa* of the *Atharva Veda*].

Varuṇa, the great Ruler of the universe sees the future in the present, (i.e., nothing is hid from him). He is the Protector of all and makes creation go forward. He is the Knower of all there is in the universe. The wise gods know him to be so. He is the Onlooker from whom nothing can remain concealed. He knows who is standing and sitting, (i.e., active or idle) who goes in, who comes out, (i.e., what's happening in all places). He knows who is cheating and doing other such misdeeds and he even knows what one man is whispering into another's ear. The entire earth and the bright sun afar is ruled by King Varuṇa. The seas and the sky are contained in him. He lives in all the waters, great or small. Varuṇa belongs to every country under the sun. His majesty spreads throughout the world. Wherever a man goes, whatever he does, in whichever of the hundreds of works and relationships he is involved; Varuṇa is his protector and is always with him.

Varuṇa sees and knows whatever there is between the sun and the earth, and also what is beyond. Even the wink of a person's eye cannot remain hid from him. As gambler who has lost, flings down the pieces of dice in despair, so too Varuṇa dislodges the evildoers (chastises them). O Almighty Lord, destroyer of the wicked, your nets and traps are spread out everywhere. They encompass the seven regions[141] and the three divisions of time namely the past, the present and the future. The wicked and sinful creatures cannot escape. Wherever they may be, you catch and destroy them. O Varuṇa, scatter those who are liars and deceivers and punish them. But spare

141. The seven regions are : the earth, water, air, the gross world, the atoms and molecules, and Nature.

those who follow the truth and bestow honour on them. You are the All-knower. Bind these canting hypocrites in a hundred bonds. May they never get emancipation. Cast down these vicious, unjust and quarrelsome persons so that they drop as severed buds from a flowering plant.

Varuṇa, the great Lord, is in all beings and the same to everyone. He is the comforter, and remover of misery. He is the Ruler and Controller. Meeting and parting are at his will. *He belongs to all countries not merely to this (the Āryan land or Āryavarta).*[142] He resides in the hearts of godly persons of divine disposition, and in those who are of calm and gentle nature and meditate on God. He is the Giver. O sons of fathers and mothers, (i.e., all men and women), Varuṇa thus teaches the ways of rightfulness thoroughly. Understand, and act according to them.

142. Thus we see the catholicity and universality of the Vēdas. Where is the religion, apart from Hinduism, which has such a high degree of accomodation? We will see that this is the spirit of the *Gītā* too. And how absurd it is for Hindus themselves to castigate Hinduism (or *Hindutva*) in their own country! Such people should hold their heads in shame.

FROM THE YAJUR VEDA

THE EDUCATION AND MARRIAGE OF GIRLS

[The ancient Āryans gave great importance to the education of women. Unfortunately the foreign rule of the Moslems and thereafter of the British put the clock back for education. Some efforts mostly half-hearted, were made to put it back on the rails, when freedom came. But now it has been placed on the back-burner. The passage is from the twelfth chapter of the *Yajur Veda*].

O mothers and fathers and teachers, you should instruct your children to follow righteousness, observe celibacy and acquire knowledge of the highest kind. Girls should be given the best posible education. It is only after completing their education that they should enter wedlock with a husband suited to them. Then only will the children they give birth to, be happy. Parents should give their daughters a spiritual education so that they may be free from worry and be happy and carefree housewives. When young girls are well-educated, there is happiness in the family. Worthy sons are born. Unless the women are so educated they can find no joy in life, and after death, emancipation cannot be achieved by them . . . That household is prosperous and free from diseases, in which the wife and husband, using their power of discrimination got by education, live in harmony and love; have mutual accommodation and eschew all differences. If they oppose each other they will always be drowned in grief and misery. They should live cheerfully wearing nice dresses and ornaments. Teachers should ensure that the education they impart is according to the aptitude of their pupils. They should take into account their capacity to absorb what is taught, their mental makeup, their beliefs and the tasks they are called upon to perform. It is necessary for all boys and girls to choose worthy and trusted persons as their teachers and then to learn from them and serve them. Teachers ought to increase the ability and mental power of their pupils. *And all the people should be of the same faith, as without that they can't be friendly to one another, and if they are not in harmony they can't remain happy.* Kings and the heads of states should appoint teachers who are enlightened, broadminded, virtuous, wise and keen to do good to others, and teachers should give good education with care and diligence and teach the same *dharma* (scriptural learning) to all their pupils without any discrimination. Family men, husbands and wives, should constantly serve and respect persons who are free from deceit.

THE DUTIES OF HOUSEHOLDERS

[Like the *Gītā* the Vedas too *emphasize* the performance of duties. Here, the *Yajur Veda* gives the duties to be performed by family men and men in general. The passage is from verse 29 onwards (omitting a few verses which are off the point). What is significant is that, as the very first (twenty-ninth) verse says, householders should respect *shūdras* also—the interpretation is according to the commentary of Dayananda. Thus all classes or *varṇas* are worthy of respect according to the Veda].

Family men should give respect to the following persons : celibates with matted hair, shaven *sannyāsīs* and those who are on the path of *sannyāsa* (i.e. hermits), wise *brāhmins*, *kshatiriyas* trained in the use of arms, dwellers in the forest who seek wisdom there amid the peace and silence of the hills and woods, *vaishyas* who are the owers and rearers of cattle and engaged in allied works, and *shūdras*. All these should be honoured and given food whenever they need it. The householders ought to give consideration also to farmers who irrigate their fields well and those who tend plants in gardens (gardeners) and also valorous people who are gentle in speech. They should feed children, praiseworthy wise men, students, old people, their friends and those with whom they associate. Householders should thus assist such persons in their hour of need.

When you meet people and wish to show them regard, you should greet them by saying '*namaste*'. In this way you should greet men of greatly advanced years, (i.e., who are very old), your elder brothers and the younger ones too, relations, *kshatriyas* and *vaishyas* and those of gentle nature who aren't arrogant. *You should also salute the lowly shūdras and mlecchas and so forth.* Revere and please those who excel in glory, those who belong to the families of virtuous and pious people, who are just, protectors, learned in the Vedas, of good behaviour, dispensers of justice, good organizers, those who are careful in money matters and skilful farmers. All these are worthy of honour.

Effort should be made to provide sources of irrigation by means of canals, hand-pumps, well, dams, (i.e., small embankments) and so forth. The water contained in rivers, large lakes, ponds and tanks should be exploited for this purpose. By these means crops, trees, plants and shrubs should be nurtured and preserved. Creatures of the water such as fishes etc., beasts of the jungles and those which thrive on rain, ought to be cared for. People *who live in various types of countries* either starved of rain or receiving excessive rain, those who harness the lightning or sunlight to produce energy and those having knowledge of light (*vidyutāyacha*) should be given recognition and honour.[143] Those also should be honoured who have skilled knowledge about the wind, who protect homes from destruction, who destroy the wicked, who produce useful articles and abstain from base works. *All honour is due of course to one's own countrymen. But we should esteem those who come here, (i.e., in the India of those times– Āryavarta) from abroad, from across the seas; and also those who go out on ships to foreign lands.* They are also praiseworthy who have built ships which can take our men across the oceans and bring them back. They have enabled us to have trade and commerce with other countries by which many desired things from abroad can be obtained and the wealth of our country increased.[144] There are two desired objectives. The first is to improve our spiritual state by serving gurus, observing celibacy, learning and teaching the Vedas, the company of holy men, worship of God, following truth and so forth. These uplift men and take them across the sea of sorrow. The other objective is to cross not the sea of sorrow, but the mundane oceans. It is the capacity and the wherewithal to construct ships which can thus accomplish this goal.

143. Thus in those distant times, hundreds of years before the Christian era, scientfic knowledge had made such progress as leaves one amazed. The use of light for energy. canals and so forth were then in existence.

144. Thus the Āryans built ships and ventured out to other lands, But by the time of the decline, of Hindu India and its conquest by the Moslems, Hindus had become insular and stay-at-homes.

FROM THE SĀMA VEDA

IN PRAISE OF INDRA

[The Sāma Veda is full of hymns to the various gods, particularly Indra, the ruler of heaven. Here we give a hymn about him contained in the second chapter of the Sāma Veda].

Let us sing together the praise of Indra
Who is as beneficent to us as the earth,
Let us adore mighty Indra heaven's king
Who slays in a trice all his enemies.

O Indra, of many valorous deeds,
Godly and of great splendour;
You are the source of all happiness
Make our lives cheerful and joyous.

Chant Indra's name near the sacrificial-square[145]
To sanctify the place of the sacrifice
So that melodious songs of praise
May delight all those who hear them.

O Veda-knower, sing of Indra's lightning flashes,
His bow, and bowstring as the thunder-clap;
Sing of his brilliance that lights up the sky,
That light divine that shines forth from heaven.

May the sacrificial flames rise up to him
And make him powerful, so that he sends
Life-giving rain. May Indra, king of the gods,

145. A *havana–kuṇḍa* or *yajña–kuṇḍa* is a kind of square enclosure made by bricks. The ceremony is held inside it as it involves lighting a fire by piling bits of firewood.

Slay the demons and gain victory,
O mighty Indra, by your great vigour,
Your sway divine and your constancy,
Rain from the heavens, make green our fields,
O Indra, be gracious, grant us our desires.

O sacrificial smoke, convey our prayer
Spread over the vaulting sky touching the feet
Of the divine Lord of heaven; get his blessing.
So that the reviving rain makes verdant the earth.

O Rain-giver, fill the sky with clouds
So that the friendly rain falls on the earth.
And gives us, who sacrifice unto you,
Plentiful cows, wealth and prosperity.[146]

O maker of Soma, prepare the choicest one[147]
For heaven's valiant king, mightiest of all,
So that he may be pleased with the offering
And fill our homes with cheerfulness and joy.

O fearless Indra, giver of hearth and home
We offer you this Soma, O mighty Ruler
Of the vast heavens, Guardian of the skies;
Accept our humble offering, take your fill.

146. Cows were a measure of a person's wealth as they yielded milk, a nourishing food, from which cream, butter and curd (yoghourt) could be made.

147. Soma is not, as some writers mistakenly suppose, an intoxicating drink. It is a herb with wondrous and invigorating qualities. The *Nirukta* [11 : 2] says : 'Soma is the name of a medicinal herb containing a lot of sap because it yields juice when pressed. The qualities of this herb are said to be of many wondrous and diverse qualities as mentioned by *vaidyas* (physicians).

Your splendour and glory are from God alone
O Destroyer of your foes, giver of wealth,
O Indra, of heavenly prowess divine,
O Ruler, who gives us reviving rain.

By your command the rain stops, sins are destroyed,
By your light, O Lord, all the worlds are lit;
You the Controller, in you are contained
These worlds; by your glory they exist.

On Indra, even though we are far from you
You bring us to yourself by your grace
And favour us e'en though we are unworthy,
O helper of mankind, be our friend.

O Indra, keep us away from darkness,
From blinding rage and deceitful desire,
Slay these foes of ours, O mighty Indra,
Protect us all around and from all sides.

As a king protects his subjects from assault
By accumulating wealth and having able warriors,
Even so protect us, Indra, from all that harms us,
From all woes, and all the ills of life.

O Indra, drink this cup of Soma
And gaining strength, make the yellowish clouds
That lie thick in the sky, fall down as rain
And nourish the earth, making it fresh again.[148]

---

148. The leaves of the Soma plant are boiled. The juice is then squeezed out of them. Then it is offered in the sacred fire of the *yajña,* When through this ceremonial offering Indra is pleased, he causes the amassed clouds to rain down on the earth.

O Indra, divine king, we sing your praises
From all sides. O bringer of the rain
So much desired by us. Let it pour down
And make the grain grow plentiful for us.

Those who hasten to offer you oblation
Kindle the fire in the sacrificial-square,
So that, O Indra, mighty lord of heaven,
You may send refreshing showers from the skies.

As a king chases away his opponents
From the field of battle, making them flee,
Even so, O Indra, scatter away the clouds
And make them fall as rain upon the earth.

One speaks, the other hears; isn't it wonderful!
As though the wind is the rope that binds
The word spoken and listened to. Thus forever
Speech is the bond that binds the human souls.

O Indra. the Soma-juice offered as oblation
Is carried to you by Vāyu, your friend.[149]
Even as the fodder carried to the cow
By the cowherd to give her sustenance.

We thank Indra, Vāyu and the other gods
They are our saviours and our protectors;
The givers of rain which keeps fresh our fields
Saving us from hunger and from misery.

---

149. Vāyu is the god of the Wind.

IN PRISE OF SOMA

[Soma ('o' as in 'home') is the juice of a milky creeper (*asclepias acida*). The juice of this plant was extracted and offered in libations to the deities. The concept, that it was a kind of exhilarating drink like alcohol is not correct. For example Whitney says that 'it had the power to elevate the spirits and produce a temporary frenzy. . ...' This is not correct. It was just a plant, the juice of which was used in oblations. Soma was also used to designate the Moon. The Purāṇas say that the chariot of Soma has three wheels and is drawn by ten horses of the whiteness of the jasmine, five on the right half of the yoke and five on the left. The hymns given here are from the fifth chapter of the *Sāma Veda*].

O Soma, those who offer your oblation
Enjoy great bliss, glory and renown;
Therefore the pious offer to the gods libation
Of this holy plant and obtain their blessings

O Soma, in the sacrifices offered
To Indra and other gods, your savoury juice
The drink of the gods, gives them pleasure,
So offer them libations of the choicest Soma

May Indra receive the Soma-oblation
Which gives strength and is greatly pleasing,
May it flow to him as a steady stream
For Soma gives happiness and power and wisdom.

O Soma, by you gods are protected
And demons fly away from fear of you,
You are worthy to be prized by everyone,
O Soma, of great value and priceless worth.

The *rik, yajus* and *sāma* are chanted by the priests,
Milk-yielding cows given away as gifts;
The juicy Soma poured in the holy fire
Crackles as it meets the orange flames.[150]

The Vedas are kept near from which hymns are sung,
The priests sit closeby; Soma-juice is poured –
That sweet Soma from the rain-nurtured plant,
Delicious Soma that is treasured by the gods.

Growing in the cold climate of the hills,
Nurtured by rain that pours from the skies,
Soma offered in oblations rises to the heavens
And the rain-god returns it to the mountain-sides

May this strengthening Soma which nourishes all
This Soma, source of all joy and bliss,
Be offered by the priest in sacrifices.
Which please the gods and obtain their favours.

The Soma-juice squeezed from the hillside plant
And placed in clean, pure wooden jars
Is the juice celestial worthy of the gods
And the giver of all heavenly pleasures.

The priests and those conducting the sacrifice
Men of deep knowledge, those who do good,
Live on the earth happy and contented,
And attain long life, blest by the gods.

---

150. The conducting of the sacrificial oblation by priest is described in this verse. First the chanting of the hymns, then the giving away of cows in charity and therafter the pouring of the Soma-juice in the fire.

This Soma which yields juice in plenty
Got by boiling over the holy fire
Is poured into the flames as oblation
For obtaining glory and life-giving grain.

May lord Soma, who fulfils all desires,
Reside in our hearts and make us powerful;
Drive away anger make us valorous
So that we may vanquish our enemis.

O Soma, purifier, giver of all happiness,
Bright and brilliant, we beckon to you
And offer you as oblation to the gods,
You make us strong indeed and fulfil our desires.

You encourage us, increase our wisdom,
Therefore wise men prize you; O Soma,
Come to us quickly we implore you
As a warrior on a chariot swiftly driven.

You give us milch cows and stately horses,
Brave sons, and all else we desire,
We will make oblations as are prescribed
By the scriptures, we will seek your favour.

O Soma, your fumes borne on the wind
Rise to the sun and the clouds charged with lightning,
We adore you and offer you as libation,
So that the gods may bestow on us their favours.

(D) FROM THE BRAHMA-SŪTRAS

WHAT THE BRAHMA-SŪTRAS ARE ABOUT

The *Brahma-sūtras* are believed to have been conceived by Bādarāyana, about whom very little is known, as the ancient seers were self-effacing and demurred in taking credit for what they wrote. In fact the compilation of such works of wisdom forming the vast canvas of Hindu philsophy came much later. The scriptures were orally conveyed by teacher to disciple and thus faithfully memorized from generation to generation. Their systematization came much after and putting them into writing even later than that. *The Brahma-sūtras* were authored by Bādarāyana and complied and written by Vyāsa, the author of the *Mahābhārata*. It is difficult to say whether Vyāsa just wrote them down according to Bādarāyana's version of did some editing on his own. The *sūtras* are of very ancient origin, earlier than the *Gītā*, and perhaps dating to the sixth century before Christ. They are condensed and cryptic in style, so that it is almost impossible to get at the meaning without a commentary. The word *sūtra* means 'a thread or a string'. It is a kind of key sentence, the nucleus of thought. The *sūtras* could thus easily be memorized. They weren't really meant to be so terse. Madhvāchārya quoted from the *Padma Purāṇa* what a *sūtra* should be. He wrote that it ought to be concise but unambiguous. It should give the essence of what it meant to convey, but should deal with all aspects of the topic. It should be faultless and not repetitive. But the stress on brevity drove out all the other qualities and so the *sūtras*, particularly the *Brahma-sūtras* (or the *Vedānta-sūtras*, as they are also called, are unintelligible with- out a commentary.

The terseness of the *Brahma-sūtras* led to there being many commentaries on them. But terseness was not the only reason. They were considered very sacred, and the foundation of Hindu philosophy. So any sage or scholar worth the name considered it his bounden duty to write a commentary on the *Brahma-sūtras*. The prominent commentators were Shankarāchārya, Rāmānuja,

Nimbārka, Mādva and Vallabha. All of them gave different interpretations according to the school of thought of which they were exponents.[151] However, Shankara's commentary is the one most universally followed. It is said that Vedavyāsa himself appeared in disguise before him when he had completed it while staying at Badrinath. On seeing Shankara's commentary on the *Brahma-sūtras*, Vyāsa blessed him and was so pleased that he said 'Your span of life will be doubled (from the destined sixteen years to thirty-two)'. Shankara's commentary has been adopted in the extracts given in this book.

The *Brahma-sūtras* are the foundation of the Vedānta philosophy. This, in the light of Shānkara's interpretation, implies the non-duality of *brahman*. The nature of *brahman* has already been narrated in the introduction in the section on the essentials of Hindu philosophy, so it is not being repeated here. In brief, the world is only a projection of *brahman*. It has only a limited reality. As for example one who mistakes a rope for a snake thinks the 'snake' to be there till the illusion exists. But as soon as he realizes that it isn't a snake the 'snake' exists no more for him. Of course others who pass that way may fall into the same error. But to him it's no longer so. Even so the world exists as significant reality for one who has not realized *brahman* (or God). Once *brahman*-realization comes, the world does not vanish. It goes on existing as before. However, its worldliness does not have any effect or importance for one who has known God. How should one reach God? There are many ways – devotion, wisdom, desireless works and so forth. But primarily it implies (a) knowing one's own soul, (b) realizing that the soul is of the nature of *brahman* (not *brahman* itself but *of its nature*), and (c) realizing that the souls of all living creatures are the same as one's own soul, so that if a person harms another creature it's like harming himself. The soul is eternal. It does not die with the body, but transmigrates into another. Man is endowed with understanding higher than that given to other creatures. So he is expected

151. Monism (Shankara), qualified monism (Rāmānuja), the theory of difference and non-difference (Nimbārka) dualism (Mādva) and the creed of devotion (Vallabha).

to understand this oneness of creation, to do good and virtuous works, to love all creatures and to serve them as fellow-beings. He ought not to waste the limited years of his life in material and evanescent pursuits like earning money by fraud and deceit, indulging in lasciviousness and so forth. Instead of that he should engage in spiritual pursuits like the acquisition of knowledge, prayer and worship etc. It is by exercising the right choice, i.e., by his works (karma) that his life's achievement will be judged.

The soul is the Eternal Witness. When the man in deep sleep, and is oblivious of everything, the soul in him keeps awake. It is the proof of the man having slept. If the soul too was asleep, who would tell the man that he had slept? The breath may fail, the heart may stop ticking, the brain, starved of blood, may cease to function, the body-heat may go; but the soul is ever there like the sun. People obsessed with the body may not see it or know it, as in one part of the world the sun may not be visible, while it is shining in the other.

The world has its joys and sorrows. How nice it would be if it had joys alone. Everyone wishes to be happy, but happiness remains a will-o'-the-wisp. So almost all religions conceive a heaven, a kind of Utopia where there is unalloyed joy. Vedānta, however, is not satisfied with this. There is heaven all right. But although long in years, it is still a temporary respite. As Krishṇa says in the *Gītā*, after exhausting their good works in heaven, people come back to the world, that *mrityuloka* or world of death, that vale of tears. So Vedānta conceives something higher than heaven. This is that which gives permanent unbroken bliss. There is no more coming back to the world. The soul that has achieved this state, which the Vedānta calls *moksha*, has freed itself from the cycle of births and deaths.

The Vedānta also speaks of *māyā*. This has been discussed in great detail in the section of the introduction dealing with the fundamentals of Hindu philosophy and needs no repetition. It is that which veils the truth and misrepresents it, which emphasizes the separateness of mankind, not the oneness, and that which evokes feelings of 'I' and 'mine' and 'you' and 'yours'.

READING LIST

Bahadur, K.P. *The Wisdom of Vedaanta* : New Delhi : Sterling Publishers Pvt. Ltd., 1983.*

Barth, *A. Les religion de l' Inde.* Paris 1979, 1914. English translation, 1921.

Bühler, G. *The Sacred Books of the East*. Oxford : the Clarendon Press, 1882, 1897.

Crooke, W. *Hinduism. Encyclopedia of Religion and Ethics*

Dasagupta, Surendranath. *A History of Indian* Philosophy. Cambridge, 1951 vols 1-3.

Deussen, Paul. *The System of the Vedanta*. Open Court Publishing Company, 1912

Farquhar, J.N. *An Outline of the Religious Literature of India.* Oxford, 1920.

Gonda, J. *Die Religionen Indien*. Stuttgart, 1960.

Hopkins, E.W. *Religions of India.* London, 1902

Muir, J. *Original Sankrit Texts.* London : Trübner & Co., 1872.

Müller, F. Max. *The Sacred Books of the East* Oxford, 1890. vols. xxxiv and xxv. The *Vedānta-sūtras*. Shankarāchārya's commentary. Transtated by George Thibault.*

Renou, L. *L' Inde classique.* Paris, 1949.

Vireswarananda, Swami,

Brahma-Sutras Almora : Advaita Ashrama, 2nd edition, 1998.*

Zimmer, H. *Mayader indische*, Zurich, 1992.

Note : * The asterisk mark denotes that the book is a translation

ABOUT *BRAHMAN*

[*We have discussed about Brahman in detail in the section dealing with Fundamentals of Hindu philosophy. The Brahma-Sūtra declare Brahman to be the origin of the world*]

Chapter I of the Brahma-sūtras—of the Nature of Brahman.

That from which proceeds the origin and the dissolution of the world should be taken to be *brahman*. The scriptures which are a record of right knowledge also corroborate this. The Vedāntic texts have *brahman* as their main topic, and they clearly say that rituals and performing sacrifices and so forth cannot get one knowledge of *brahman*. *Brahman* is the First Cause of the universe. He is complete bliss. In other words *brahman* is bliss unalloyed. There can't be even an iota of misery in him. The soul is of the same nature as *brahman*, It is *thought* to be different, but this is not really so. However apart from this similarity, the soul cannot be equated with *brahman*. The air which is outside and in the atmosphere is that which is enclosed in a jar. Can we say then that the 'air-in-the jar' is any different from the air outside? Certainly not. So are the embodied soul and *brahman*. Their nature is the same. The Being within the sun and in the eye is *brahman*. Ether is *brahman*, breath is *brahman* (because life ends when breath ceases) and so is the light which shines above heaven and the higher worlds.

That which constitutes the mind is *brahman*. The minuteness of *brahman* is brought out by the Upanishadic texts only to signify that it is the subject of meditation. *Brahman* is the 'eater' in the sense that all things arise from him and return to him. As such he is the creator as well as the destroyer. The soul and *brahman* reside in the cavity of the heart. The fire within a human being (or other creatures) which digests food is known as *vaishvānara*. This fire is also none other than *brahman*. According to Jaimini, *vaishvānara* means the world soul (*vishva* = the world; *nara* = man). In this way too it is *brahman* which is meant.

Brahman is the abode of heaven, earth and everything. In other words all there is, is contained in *brahman*. The *Muṇḍaka Upanishad* says: 'In him the heaven, the earth and the sky are woven. So too 'in him are the mind and the senses. Know him alone as the Self and leave off all other talk. He is the bridge to immortality.'[152] So too the *Īsha Upanishad* says, 'whatever there is – this world or the other worlds – is enveloped by God.'[153] The only goal of life is the attainment of *brahman*. Wealth and sense-pleasures bind a person. How can they liberate him? It is only by realizing *brahman* that a man can escape the round or rebirths and thus avoid the misery of existence. The Infinite is *brahman*. This infinite is that which is beyond the world and everything that is material. It lies beyond both dream and sleep, for it is that which keeps awake through all the states of consciousness namely, the waking, the dream and the dreamless sleep.[154] The Upanishads describe *brahman* as 'neither coarse nor fine, neither short nor long', and as being without qualities, supreme and eternal. So it is obviously not finite.

The Imperishable is *brahman*, because it is the support of everything, right up to the ether. *Brahman* is to be meditated upon. This *brahman* who is the subject of meditation, is the higher *brahman* (not the lower *brahman*).[155] *Brahman* is ether in the sense that it is that in which the air, sun, moon and lightning is contained. Whatever is in this world and whatever is not – all lies in him. The Upanishads say that the Self 'is not affected by sin, age, grief, death and thirst. Truth is his desire and truth is his resolve.'[156] The Upanishads' meaning of the 'small ether' which is sometimes spoken of

---

152. *Muṇḍaka up.*, 1:2.5.

153 *Īsha Up.*, 1.

154. This *turīya* or the Eternal Witness, has been described in the Introduction – Fundamentals of Hindu Philosophy.

155. The Upanishads speak of two forms of *brahman*. In the *Muṇḍaka Upanishad* says that the lower knowledge is the Veda, phonetics, ritual, grammar etymology, metrics and astrology. And the higher is that by which the undecaying is known (*Mu. Up*, 1.1.3.5).

156. *Chhāndogya Upanishad*. 5.1.5.
Muṇḍaka Upanishad. 2.2.10 & *Kaṭha Upanishad* 5.15.

by it, is therefore really this. The word 'small' should not be taken literally.

Everything shines after *brahman*. The Upanishads say 'The sun does not shine there, nor the moon and stars, nor these lightnings, much less the fire. Everything else shines when he (*brahman*) shines. It is his light that lights all this.' Does this mean that *brahman* is some kind of luminous object? It isn't, the author says. True, it is light, but not in the sense of a torch or firebrand which keeps lighting everything. What this means is that it is *because* of *brahman* that the sun, moon, stars etc., even the ordinary fire, receive light. It's like a lamp. The lamp does not keep lighting other lamps. But it gives light to everything in the room.

Who are entitled to study the Vedas? The gods are, says Bādarāyana, and so too are the upper castes. But *shūdras* are not entitled. An imaginary objector to this says, the *shūdras* may show an inclination to study the Veda.[157] So why should they not be allowed? The objector tells about Raivaka, whom king Jānashruti asked for instruction. He sent Raivaka gifts, but Raivaka got angry because he thought them to be very meagre. 'Take away this *shudra's* gifts', he shouted at the king's messengers. But later the king sent him more and, being mollified, he taught the king. So ultimately he did teach Jānashruti, though calling him a *shūdra*. The author, Bādarāyana, says the etymological meaning of the word '*shūdra*' must be taken here. It means 'He rushed into grief' That is to say that the king was greatly grieved.[158] So this objection doesn't hold water. The objector then goes on to another incident in the same Upanishad in which one Satyakāma Jābāla approached sage Gautama for being taught. On inquiring his parentage the man said he didn't know. When his mother was young

157. The sūtras often adopt the method of Socrates in as much as an imaginary objector or objection is interposed. The author 'answers' the objection and then gives his view. Dayananda also adopted this style in his *Satyārthaprakāsha.*

158. The *Chhāndogya Upanishad* in which the incident is mentioned, says that the king thought himself very wise. But he overheard two swawns flying in the sky say, 'Phooh, the king's wisdom is nothing beside Raivaka's. This had grieved him.

she served in many houses as a maid. One of her masters cohabited with her, and so he was born. Why did the sage instruct Jābāla despite this? Bādarāyana replies, Gautama was convinced that none but a *brāhmin* could be so candid.[159] So really Gautama gave Satyakāma instruction, taking him to be a *brāhmin*. The scriptures are of the unanimous view that only those who wear the sacred-thread (*janēyu*) can study the Vedas. Only *brāhmins*. *kshatriyas* and *vaishyas* can wear it, not *shūdras* so *shūdras* cannot study the Vedas.

It is *brahman* who is the maker of the sun, the moon, the earth and the author of all existence. It cannot be any other, neither the vital breath nor the soul. The Self which is to be seen, heard and reflected on, is *brahman*. In the *Brihadāraṇyaka* Upanishad Yājñavalkya tells Maitreyī that all relations like husband, wife sons and so forth, and wealth, learning and possessions are dear to one not in themselves, but for the sake of the Self. So one should know and reflect on the Self. When the Self is known all else is known also.[160] Bādarāyaṇa says that the Self here means *brahman* The reason is that Maitreyī wished to know that which conferred immortality. It was in reply to her that Yājñavalkya says this. So it must refer to *brahman*, for it is only knowledge of *brahman* that can give immortality.

Brahman is the maker the universe which issues from him as the web from the spider. Many scriptural texts bear this out. *Brahman* is referred to as the Lord. A householder asked the sage Angiras 'Sir, what is that through which everything else is known?' The sage told him it was *brahman*.[161] Another Upanishad says, 'In the beginning all this was non-existent. From it was born what exists. That made itself its Self. Therefore it is called self-made.'[162] Thus *brahman* created the world out of himself. Many other texts of the Upanishads support this view also.[163]

---

159. *Chhānd. Up.* 4.4. 1-5.

160. *Brihad Up.* 4.5.6.

161. *Muṇḍaka* Upanishad : 1.1.3.

162. *Taittīrya* Upanishad. 2.7

163. ibid.. 2.6. *Muṇḍaka* Up.. 3.1.3 and 1.1.6. *Shvet. Up-6.19; Chhānd.* Up 6.19: *Chhānd Up.* 6.1.3: 6.1. 4-6 *Mu. Up.* 1.1.3: *Brihad. Up.* 4.5.6.

THE SOUL'S JOURNEY AFTER DEATH

[Hindu scriptures describe vividly the soul's journey after the body's death. The *Gītā* mentions two ways taken by it – that of the father and of the gods. One is for ordinary men the other for men who have achieved enlightenment. The *Vedānta-sūtras* give a more detailed description. They also tell us the manner in which the soul takes rebirth. What is significant, however, is that Bādārayana clears by his argument much of the misunderstanding caused by some writers who take a too literal meaning of the Vedāntic texts.]

About the Soul

The soul is highest entity and worthy to be meditated upon. the *Kaṭha Upanishad* says 'Beyond the senses are the objects, beyond the objects there is the mind, beyond the mind there is the intellect, beyond the intellect there is the great Self. Beyond it there is the undeveloped. Beyond the undeveloped there is the Person (purusha). Beyond the Person there is nothing – this is the highest road, the goal.'[164] This passage shows the soul's superiority. And since the *ātman* (soul) is of the same nature as *brahman*, it follows that *brahman* is the uttimate Reality. The Self (*ātman*) can be known through meditation only. When a knower of *brahman* dies, does his soul get rid of good and evil deeds at the moment of death or when it is on the way to Brahmaloka (the abode of Brahmā)? Bādarāyana says that the accumulated (*sañchita*) karmas of a man are destroyed the moment he attains *brahman*-knowledge, and the *prārabdha* karmas (works, the consequences of which cannot be avoided) are destroyed on death of the man.[165] So no fruits of the deeds remain. The question of casting off the consequences of deeds by the soul on its way to Brahmaloka, thus, does not arise. Morever, only the souls which have realized *saguna brahman*, (i.e., God with form) journey to Brahmaloka. For those who have realized the formless God

164. *Kaṭha Up.*, 1.3.10-11

165. The different kinds of karmas (works) as defined in Hindu philosophy (*prārabdha*, *sañchita* and *āgamin*) have already been described in the Introduction – Fundamentals of Hindu Philosophy (Karma).

(*nirguṇa brahman*) the question of such a journey does not arise, for when the darkness of their ignorance is removed by such knowledge, their souls become one with the infinite.[166] Even in ordinary life there is such differentiation. A man who goes to a certain village has to make a journey to it. But no such journey is needed for one who wishes to get rid of an illness. All worshippers of *brahman* with form (*saguna-brahman*) go to Brahmaloka by the path of the gods, whatever their mode of worship is. A person who has attained knowledge of *brahman* may come back to the earth of his own accord for fulfilling some divine mission, as in the case of sages like Vyāsa, Vashishṭa, Nārada and so forth. But they do not come under *māyā's* sway, i.e., they do not partake of ignorance.

The Self (soul) is an entity quite apart from the body. Consciousness in not the distinguishing feature of the body. If it were so, it could not disappear at death, for the body exists after death too (till its disposal). So consciousness must belong to the soul. Knowledge is not subsidiary to works. In fact those who renounce the world do not perform works, but they are the *brahman*-knowers. As the *Brihadāraṇyaka Upanishad* says, 'Desiring the Self alone, monks renounce their homes.'[167] Bādarāyana's view is that the stage of *sannyāsa* is compulsory as it is mentioned as one of the four *āsharama* (stages of life). Nonetheless works prescribed by the scriptures are of use, though liberation is possible only by knowledge. Work is like ploughing by oxen, while knowledge is like the horse-driven chariot which speeds on. You can't yoke the horse to the plough! One who has undertaken lifelong *sannyāsa* cannot revert to the other stages of life.

The Soul at Death and After [Chapter 4, Sections 2-3]

166. This is food for thought for those who condemn Hindu religion as being polytheistic and mere idol-worship. Believers in the formless God (as the Moslems and to some extent Christians) often consider Hinduism as inferior becuase it is said to advocate image worship. They should understand that Hinduism is *both* monotheistic and polytheistic, as the Vedānta clearly shows. Not only that, realization of the Formless God is considered superior.

167. *Brith. Up.* 4.4.22

At the time of a person's death the function of the various organs merge into one another. The *Chhāndogya Upanishad* says, 'when a man dies, speech merges in *prāṇa* (life-breath), *prāṇa* in fire and fire in the Highest Deity.'[168] When the physical body dies, the subtle body, minute and transparent, comes out (covering the soul). This subtle body is transparent and so invisible. It is ethereal and so not obstructed or impeded by gross bodies, (i.e., it can pass through a wall, a roof or a closed door).[169] What actually happens at the moment of death? The *Brahma-sūtras* say : The top of the heart begins to glow. The soul (which resides in the heart) senses this as a kind of signal for its departure and prepares to go [it's like the green lamp flashed to the engine-driver as a signal for the train's departure]. The Being in the heart reveals to the soul thereby (by this light) the kind of afterlife which will be his according to the man's knowledge, meditation and the kind of life he has lived. Till here the process is common to all beings. But thereafter, the soul of the knower of *brahman* with form (*saguna brahman*) goes out by the *sushumna* nerve which is the one hundred and first nerve situated in the head, while the souls of others go out from various others parts of the body. The *saguna-brahman*-knower's soul goes along the rays of the sun, wherever the sun may be, (i.e., even if the man dies at night the path is the same – the sun's rays). The soul of a knower of *saguna-brahman* goes from the deity of the year to that of the air then to Varuṇa, Indra, Prajāpati and finally to *brahman*. These deities are not exactly guides. They only help the soul to get through without hindrance. When the soul reaches the moon and then to lightning, a Being who is not human, leads it to the world of *Brahmā*. But only those souls go to Brahmaloka who meditate on the *saguna-brahman*, without the aid of symbols. [Apparently meditation is more prized than image-worship].

The Return of the Soul for Rebirth [Chapter 3; Section 1]

When the soul's good works are exhausted, it returns to the earth with its residual karma. The route of descent is slightly

168. *Chhānd. Up.*, 6.8.6

169. See also Introduction – Fundamental Concept of Hindu Philosophy.

different from that by which it went up from its previous body—the night, the dark fortnight and the half-year when the sun moves south being omitted. The souls of those who have lived lives of unalloyed evil and so do not go to the moon and Brahmaloka, are reborn as flies, gnats, mosquitoes and such insects. But those of virtuous people acquire a new human existence, for once human life is attained (after eighty-four lakh births) the person, if he does not stoop to evil deeds, will be reborn as a human being. Does the soul actually *become* the substances through which it is said to pass [viz. ether, air smoke, mist, cloud and rain] ? Certainly not, says Bādarāyana. How can the soul become all these things, seeing they are so different from one another? In truth the soul only *acquires the nature* of these substances, that is to say it becomes subtle as ether, light as air, and mobile as mist, cloud and rain. The time taken for the soul's descent is not long. But once it descends it might take much more time for rebirth. The entire period from the moment it starts its descent to the moment of its rebirth would not exceed about a year. After the soul reaches the earth, it enters some plant, like rice or barley stalks, herbs, trees, sesamum plants and beans. From then onwards its rebirth becomes rather difficult, for it enters whatever human being eats the food. Entering him it turns into semen and goes into the womb of the woman with whom the man has sexual intercourse. But it should not be understood thereby that the souls actually enter the plants as an extension of experiencing the result of their deeds. The souls' connection with the plants is just as it was with smoke, mist air, ether etc. The souls are only like guests in a house. As a guest comes for some work in a person's house and after having done it, goes away, so too the soul only lies waiting for acquiring a new body. So is the case with the man in whose seminal fluid the soul enters, and who cohabits with the woman in whose womb he is, as a consequence, born. Just as the plant serves only as a medium, so too is the soul's association with the man and the woman. They are mere agents in providing the soul with the body it has got as a consequence of its residual karma. It is the works and merit of the soul's previous life which are significant. The other factors are mere adjuncts.

THE SOUL IN DREAM AND SLEEP

The point which is here under discussion is whether the dream state is real. In other words whether there is a difference or not between the two states. Bādarāyana says the two are different. The waking world, or let us say just the world, is the handiwork of God, while dreams are conjured up by the soul. The *Brihadarānyaka Upanishad* supports this view. It says, 'When he falls asleep then having taken with him material from the whole world, destroying and building it up again, he dreams by his own light.'[169 a] Nevertheless dreams do have a significance. They portend future events. Those who can interpret them, can tell what's about to come. Dreaming of a black man with black teeth portends death. Dreaming that one rides a donkey portends misfortune, while seeing oneself riding on an elephant is believed to bring luck. It is said that what is told to one in a dream by a *brāhmin*, a bull, a king or a god, will come out true. However, irrespective of the interpretation of dreams, the view of the *Brahma-sūtras* is that dreams are illusory and not of the nature of the waking state.

Next, the soul in the state of deep sleep is considered. According to one Upanishadic text the soul rests in this state in the nerves or *nāḍīs*, or the Self. Another text says that it goes through the nerves and rests in the region of the heart. Other texts have it that it rests in the ether within the heart or is embraced by the highest Self or by the real Self (ether) within the heart, or that it becomes one with the life-breath.[170] The opponent says these are different places, so the soul does not rest at any one place, but wanders about. Bādarāyana says, no, the three places pointed out in these texts are the nerves, the region around the heart, or the Self, (i.e., *brahman*). So it would be right to say that the soul goes through the nerves, into the region of the heart and there rests in *brahman*.

169a. *Brihad. Up.*, 4.3.9.

170. The Upanishadic texts respectively are—*Chhānd. Up.*, 8.6.3 & 6.8.1; *Brihad. Up.*, 2.1.19, 4.4.22,4.3.21 & 2.1.17; and *Kaushītaki-Brāhmaṇa* Up., 4.20.

The next question is that when the soul returns from deep sleep, is it the same soul or another? The author says it is the same soul. The waking man remembers all the work he left half-finished. He remembers all past events. If it were another soul he couldn't do so. The scriptures too confirm this, as for example 'He hastens back again as he came to the place from which he started, and so wakens.'[171] And again, 'Whatever these creatures are here, whether tiger, lion, wolf, boar, worm, fly, gnat or mosquito; that they become again on coming back from *brahman*.'[172]

What is a swoon? We know that there is a state which is neither deep sleep nor dream in which temporarily consciousness is lost, as on being given general anaesthesia, in a coma and so forth. The author says this is not a fifth state, for only four are known, namely waking, dream, deep sleep and death. He concludes that a swoon is a mixture of the states of deep sleep and death, for in swoon or coma the person experiences misery not happiness. Besides, he may come back to life, or maybe he doesn't, and dies.

Here the discussion on the soul in dream and sleep ends. A short bit about *brahman* follows, but as we have spoken about Bādarāyana's view on *brahman* already, it is omitted. The section concludes with the topic : 'Who is the giver of the fruits of works?' Is it karma (a person's deeds) or God, (i.e., *brahman*)? Bādarāyana says it can't be karma because it is shortlived and insentient. So it is God. *He* gives the fruits of works. The scriptures too say that he whom he wishes to raise, he makes him do good work and he whom he wishes to lead down, he makes him do bad works.[173] Thus God is the final dispenser of the fruits of works.

[From chapter 3, section 2].

171. *Brihad. Up.,* 4.3.16.

172. *Chhānd, Up.,* 6.10.2.

173. *Kaushītaki-Brāhmaṇa Up..* 3.8.

(E) FROM THE BHAGAVADGĪTĀ

WHAT THE BHAGAVADGĪTĀ IS ABOUT

The *Bhagavadgītā*, or *Gītā* as it is usually called for short, is the most sacred scripture for Hindus and the best known the world over. It is part of the *Mahābhārata* epic, but it doesn't narrate stories as the epic often does. It is purely spiritual and philosophical. The *Māhābhārata* provides only the setting for it and this consists of the first of the eighteen chapters. The *Gītā's* literary quality is perhaps unequalled. The Sanskrit verses are simpler in structure than those of other Hindu philosophical works. It has a mixed metre called the *upajāta*. Some lines are in the *indravajrā* form. Other in the *upendravajrā*. Both of them have eleven syllables each. The first chapter describes the two armies of the Pāṇḍavas and the Kauravas facing each other. We are told the names of some of the prominent warriors on each side. War-trumpets, drums and conches are sounded. Missles are about to fly. Just then Arjuna, whose charioteer is Krishṇa himself, asks that his chariot may be driven nearer the enemy forces so that he may have a look at them. The sight fills him with dismay. He sees his kinsmen and even some of his revered teachers among the Kaurava warriors. Grief overpowers him. His bow, Gāṇḍīva, slips from his hands. Forgetting that he is a *kshatriya* and so duty-bound to fight when challenged, he tells Krishṇa that he won't fight and thus kill his own relations. Krishṇa upbraids him for his cowardice. He says 'Look, there is no greater glory for a warrior than to fight a righteous war. Besides, you fear to kill. But death comes to all. It is inevitable. And he who dies will be reborn. The soul never dies. It keeps changing bodies just as a man discards old and worn out clothes and wears new ones.' He gives Arjuna instruction in the philosophy of Yoga and Sāṁkhya. 'You have the right to works' he tells him. but the result of acts is not in your hands.' Arjuna is confused. 'You say that I should follow the path of knowledge, but then why do you ask me, in the same breath, to spill blood?' Krishṇa said, There are two paths, one of knowledge the other of action, (i.e., works). One should follow the one suitable to him. But action should be desireless. In fact it must be so, otherwise if a man is attached to action, he'll be frustrated and disappointed if the action does not yield the result he wants. Every action and even a thought, whether good or bad, has five constituents one of which is the divine will. So everything can't be in our hands. When works are purified by taking away desire from them, they get strength. Everyone must work. One can't even live if he does not work (for his livelihood). Even I work, Krishṇa said. Firstly to keep the worlds in order, secondly to be an example to human beings. One should faithfully perform his own duty without bothering about that of others. If everyone did that, goodwill prevail.

Krishṇa went on to speak about yoga and renunciation. The mind ought to be controlled by effort. There ought to be moderation in one's life and habits. It's best to surrender everything to God. The man who does that rids himself of all worries. Unswerving devotion, desireless works and acquisition of spiritual wisdom are the three paths to God-realization. Anger, hate, running after sense-pleasures, jealousy and other evil qualities should be abandoned. One should serve humanity and do good to others, not just keep thinking of his own good. He should feel for the sufferings of others as if they were his own. Although the *Gītā* is not for *sannyāsa* or austerities which only weaken the body, it advocates both detachment and renunciation. In fact *sannyāsa* means just renouncing the fruits of action. One should be detached even while living in the world. He shouldn't have attachment to home, sons, family and so forth. He ought to have love for solitude and avoid crowds. Peace and meditation are best attained in such a quiet atmosphere.

The *Gītā* embodies the thought of both the Sāṁkhya and the Yoga philosophies but with modifications, emphasising the supremacy of God. Krishṇa draws a distinction between those whose nature is godly and those who are thoroughly wicked, and tells Arjuna of the miserable fate which awaits the wicked. Persons who are the same in joy and grief, who are not obsessed by wealth and to whom praise and blame, foe and friend are the same, are praised. Though one must do his duty and keep doing desireless works, it is God who, seated in the hearts of all persons, makes them helplessly go round and round. He is the Controller. After Krishṇa has given Arjuana the teaching of the *Gītā,* he says, now think well over what I have told you and do as you feel proper. Arjuna agrees to fight and follow Krishṇa's advice. He has at one place been shown Krishṇa's cosmic form. So he realizes the Lord's divine nature. Krishṇa then gives Arjuna his final message. Worship me, he says, adore me, pray to me, be my single-minded devote. Fear not, I will rescue you from all sin and evil. It is Saṁjaya who narrates the Mahābhārata war and also the *Gītā* to the blind Dhritarāshṭra, for Saṁjaya had the gift of seeing exactly what was happening in the field of Kurukshetra where the war was going on.

READING LIST

There are over eight hundred editions of the *Gītā* in more than twenty-five languages including eight non-Indian languages, and still every year someone or the other is bringing out his own translation and commentary. The classic commentaries are of Shankarāchārya, Ānandgiri, Shridhara, Madhusūdhana, Tukārāma, Jñāneshvara, Rāmānuja, Madva, Nīmbārka and Vallabha. In recent times commentators were B.G. Tilak, Shri Aurobindo, Mahātmā Gāndhi, S. Rādhākrishnan and others. The Gītā Press Gorakhpur, Shri Rāmakrishṇa Maṭh, Mylapore and Ānandāsharama, Poona have brought out useful editions of the text in Hindi and English.

The more outstanding books are given in the list below. The ones dealing with the text (translations) are marked with an asterisk.

Aurobindo. Shri. *Essays on the Gita*, 1928.

Bahadur, K.P. *Shrimadbhagavadgītā*. (Transliterated text in English. Word for word meaning. Translation into English and Hindi verse and Commentary in English). New Delhi : Ess Ess Publications, 1993.*

Barnett, L.D. The *Bhagavadgita*, 1905.

Besant, Annie and Das, Bhagawan. *Bhagavadgita*, 1905*

Bharadvaja, M.S. *Gita*. Jaipur : The New Asiatic Research Society (Hindi).* Bhattacharya, K.K. *Shrimadbhagavad Gita* Bombay : Gujarite Press, 1972 (Sanskrit text and commentary).*

Bhave, Acharya Vinoba, *Talks on the Gita*. London : George Allen and Unwin, 1960.

Chidbhavananda, Swami *Shrimad-Bhagavad-Gita*. Madras : Shri Ramakrishna Math (English commentary).*

Dsagupta, S.N. A *History of Indian Philosophy*. London : George Allen and Unwin vol. 2.

The Gita in World Literature. ed. Verma, C.D. (Papers read at the International Seminar held at New Delhi) New Delhi : Sterling Publishers, 1990

Goswami, L.P.T. *Shrimadbhagavad Gita* Calcutta : Gaudia Mission, 1948.*

Hill, Douglas. *The Bhagavad Gita*, 1928.

Nayayanaswami, R.N. *Shrimadbhagavad. Gita*. Lucknow :

Rama Tirtha Publications, 1936 (English translation).*

Prabhananda, Swami and Isherwood, Christopher. *The Bhagavadgita*, 1945.*

Radhakrishnan, S. *The Bhagavad Gita.* London : Allen & Unwin

Sarma, D.S. *The Bhagavadgita*, 1937.*

Shivanand, Swami. *Bhagavadgitasara*. Rishikesh :

Yogavedanta University, 1956.*

Swarupananda, Swami. *Shimad-Bhagavad-Gita.* English translation and Shankara's commentary. Madras : Shri Ramakrishna Math.*

Telang, K.J. The *Bhagavadgita*, 1882.*

Tulsiramaswami *Shrimadbhagavad Gita* (Sanskrit text). Ramlal Kapoor Trust, 1977.*

Vireshvarananda, Swami. *Shrimad-Bhagavad-Gita* (with the gloss of Shridhars Swami). Shri Ramakrishan 2, Math, Madras.*

Yogi, Mahesh, *Gita* (Sanskrit text with English translation. London: International Press Publications. 1967.*

THE ENLIGHENED SAGE

What Arjuna said

Tell me, Kṛishṇa, about the man who is established is *brahman* (i.e. who has attained God). and whose intellegence is firm. What's his manner of speech? How does he sit? How does he walk?

What the Blesssed Lord said+

Such a man desires nothing. He remains satisfied in himself. He neither grieves in sorrow, nor revels in joy. He has no attraction or repulsion to anything. He has got over fear and rage. He is not attached to any person or thing. He doesn't gloat over his good fortune, nor turns gloomy when the going's not good. He weans all his senses from the objects of their enjoyment, as a tortoise withdraws his legs within his shell. One 'may keep away from things of desire, but the craving for them remains. When however, the Supreme is seen, that too goes away. For, O Arjuna, the powerful senses carry away by force the mind even of that person who tries hard to restrain them. But if he is a man of firm wisdom, he takes refuge in me. Then he will be able to bridle his senses. When one turns his mind towards sense-enjoyments he becomes attached to them. Longing for them awakens in him. And when, because of some obstacles, he cannot have what he desires, he becomes frustrated and angry. Rage causes confusion of the mind, for an angry man acts stupidly. His memory is affected and he can no longer remember what's wrong and what's right, and when he is not able to discriminate, that person is as good as lost. The man who has, on the contrary, tamed his mind and has freed himself from both attraction and aversion, can be happy even if he dwells on the objects of enjoyment. He who has thus made himself detached and happy, knows no sorrows. His wisdom becomes firm and steady. Without self-control one's mind cannot be sharpened enough to meditate. Without meditation he cannot have peace,

+ Krishṇa is called 'the Blessed Lord' throughout this translation because he is the incarnation of Vishṇu and so Īshvara or God himself.

and how can there be happiness without peace? When the mind runs after the elusive senses, it is helplessly carried away by them as a boat is by strong winds. Therefore, O Arjuna, the mind of that person alone is firm who has wrenched all his senses away from their objects. Ordinary people do not find any joy in spiritual enlightenment. It is as dreary for them as the darkness of the night. But for the yogīs (sages) it is as revealing as daylight. And on the contrary sensual enjoyments give no pleasure to yogis. They are for them like the friendless night's darkness, while to the men who indulge in sense-pleasures they have the brightness of day. As rivers from all around pour into the sea which, being itself full, does not need their waters, even so that person finds peace in whom all desires enter and die away, not he who keeps hugging his desires. That person finds peace who rids himself of craving; who has neither affectation, nor longing, nor arrogance. Arjuna, what I have told you is the way which leads to *brahman*-realization. One who follows it can never be deluded. And he is emancipated when death overtakes him.

[*Bhagavadgītā*. Chapter 2, Verses 54 to 72]

WHO TRANSCENDS THE GUṆAS ?

As we have said in the introduction, the Sāṁkhya philosophy speaks of guṇas or qualities. These are purity or *sattva*, passion or activity–*rājasa* and sloth or *tāmasa*. The *Gītā* believes that actions, which carry forward existence, are caused by these *guṇas* alone. Every person has these three *guṇas* in him in different proportions. In some purity is predominant making them do virtuous works, in others activity, prompting them to be business executives and so forth. And as for the lazy kind, they just rest and sleep and abhor activity. Thus it is the *guṇas* which are the doers. But the sages and wise men who are near God are not affected by these guṇas. The *Gītā* calls them *guṇatīta—atīta* = 'beyond' or freed *(virakta)*. Here Krishṇa tells Arjuna about those who have transcended these *guṇas*.

What the Blessed Lord said

When the embodied soul knows there is no doer apart from these *guṇas* and realizes that the Supreme Being is far removed from them and is untouched by them, then he becomes aware of my nature, (i.e., has attained God). Such a person gets rid of old age, birth and death, and all sorrows, and achieves emancipation.

What Arjuna said

Lord, how is such a person (who has transcended the *guṇas*) distinguishable? What is his behaviour? How does he go beyond the *guṇas*?

What the Blessed Lord said

I have told you that *sattvaguṇa* produces the light of awareness, *rājasa* results in ceaseless activity and *tāmasa* in the delusion that laziness is good for one. That man, Arjuna, who neither resents these *guṇas* when they are there in him, nor longs for them when they aren't, has triumphed over them. Such a man is indifferent to the *guṇas* and unconcerned with their presence. He realizes that what's going on around him is only due to the interaction of the *guṇas*. And this realization makes him remain steady in the Lord. Nothing can agitate him. He is the same in sorrow and joy, and content in himself. To him gold is just as valueless as a clod or a stone. The pleasant and the unpleasant, praise and blame are for him alike. He has patience and calmness of the mind. Honour and dishonour are the same to him. He regards equally a friend and a foe. He doesn't have the vanity to think that it is he who is the initiator of actions.

Whoever worships and serves me, who am the Supreme Lord, with unswerving devotion and in the spirit of yoga, also transcends the *guṇas* and becomes qualified for *Brahman*-realization: for it is I who am the source of the eternal nectar-like *brahman*, of the ever-abiding *dharma* (righteousness) and of the infinite and everlasting bliss.

[*Bhagavadgītā* Chapter 14, verses 19-27].

KRISHṆA AS THE LORD'S INCARNATION

What the Blessed Lord said

I told Sūrya the eternal doctrine of Yoga. Sūrya told it to Manu and he to Iksvāku. In this way this knowledge continued, and the royal sages knew it. But after continuing a long time, this wisdom was lost to this world. You are my devotee and my friend. So I am telling you today this ancient and very beneficial secret knowledge.

What Arjuna said

Your birth is recent, and Sūrya's much earlier. How can I believe then that you told this knowledge (to Sūrya and others) in that far off time?

What the Blessed Lord said

Both I and you, Arjuna, have passed through many lives. I know them all, but you do not know them. Although I am the eternal *ātman* unborn and imperishable and the Lord of all creatures, I control *prakriti* (Nature) and take birth through my *māyā* [in other words I cast the veil of delusion on the eyes of people, so that they take me who am the Lord, to be a human being]. Whenever righteousness declines and evil increases, then, Arjuna, I appear on the earth to proctect the good people, destroy those wicked and to restore *dharma*. I incarnate myself age after age this purpose. Those who in truth know this birth of mine and its intention, Arjuna, do not have to take rebirth after they die. They come to me.

Many persons who have freed themselves from desire, fear and anger, who delight in me and seek my support, purify themselves with the austerity of wisdom and attain me. I confer my grace on all who seek me, whatever their manner of approach. For, Arjuna, all paths lead to me. Those who desire to obtain the fruits of their works soon, (i.e., material desires) worship the gods. They are able to obtain such desires in the world itself, for material things are quickly got.

I have made the four *varṇas* on the basis of the nature and occupation of each class. Though I am their Maker, you should know that I am indestructible and beyond action. I am not attached to works, nor do I have any desire for their fruits. Works do not bind the man who knows me to be of such nature. Those ancient men of wisdom who desired salvation, worked in this manner. You should also act likewise.

[*Bhagavadgītā*. Chapter 4, verses 1 to 15].

ON DEVOTION

What Arjuna said

Of those who worship you and those who meditate on the fromless *brahman*, who are the greater knowers of Yoga?

What the Blessed Lord said

I consider them to be best yogīs who constantly worship me with single-minded devotion and complete faith. But they also attain me who, having brought all their senses under control, meditate on that *brahman* which is beyond the reach of thought speech and understanding, omnipresent, ever the same, eternal, immovable and formless. Such persons who, remaining engaged in the good of all creatures and looking on them all alike, meditate deeply and constantly on that indestructible Cosmic Absolute, also come to me. But for one who has acquired a human body the quest of the formless *brahman* is rough going, for it is fraught with sorrow, (i.e., is very difficult). O Arjuna, I quickly rescue from this Ocean of Death, (i.e., from repeated rebirths on the earth) those who surrender all works to me, and having faith in me, direct their thoughts to me and, meditating on me, worship me with unswerving devotion. Resign your mind and your wisdom to me. Having done so you will doubtless attain me, If you can't steadily meditate on me, then, O Arjuna, strive to attain me through the practice of the yoga of devotion. If you are unable to do that too, do desireless works, surrendering them completely to me. And if that also is not possible for you, practise control of mind, and surrender to me all the fruits of works. For wisdom is superior to mere works, (i.e., works with hope of reward), meditation is above wisdom, and the surrender of the fruits of works excels them all. Such renouncement of fruits brings eternal peace.

Ans now I will tell you, Arjuna, the kind of person who is my beloved devotee and whom I greatly love, He is the person who bears no one any malice. He is friendly and compassionate. He is free from affectation and arrogance, forgiving, always satisfied, and engaged in yoga. He is the same in sorrow and joy, of firm determination and self-controlled. He surrenders his mind and wisdom to me. He has relinquished pleasures, fear and agitation, and is not distressed when he sees other people flourishing. He does not affict anyone, nor is himself troubled by the acts of others. He has abandoned all desires, and all works which seek reward. He is pure, skilful, fearless and unbiassed. he neither rejoices nor retains any rancour, nor any longing nor sorrow, and is unconcerned with the auspicious and the inauspicious. Friend and foe, honour and dishonour, heat and cold, sorrow and joy, praise and blame, are all one to him. He does not cling to the world, speaks little and is satisfied with whatever comes his way. He is of firm understanding and is not attached to home and family.

Those persons are extremely dear to me who follow what I have said and conduct themselves according to the nectar-like righteousness of which I have spoken to you, Arjuna; and who have faith in me and reverence for me.

[This is the twelfth chapter of the *Gītā* containing 20 *shlokas* (verses)].

THE LORD'S PROMISE TO HIS DEVOTEES

What the Blessed Lord said

To the person who, meditating on me, worships me with unswerving devotion, I myself give all that he needs and protect it from harm.[174] Those devotees who worship other gods with faith, they too, worship me, O Arjuna, though not in the proper way. For I am the Enjoyer of all sacrifices and their Lord. But these persons do not know my nature, and so keep being born again and again on the earth. Those who worship the gods go to the gods, those who worship the ancestors go to them. The worshippers of the elemental spirits go to those spirits. My devotees come to me, (i.e., they achieve emancipation and are not reborn). Whatever a devotee offers me with love, even though it may be just a trifle like a flower, a leaf, a fruit or even water; I accept that offering of devotion of the man of pure soul. Whatever works you do, whatever you eat, whatever gift you give in charity, whatever oblations you make and whatever, sacrifices you perform; consecrate them all to me, O Arjuna. By doing so you will be freed from the bonds of all works, good or bad, and being firmly established in the yoga of renunciation, you will come to me. All creatures are alike to me. I am not partial to any of them. But my devoted worshipper is enshrined in me and I too am in him. Even though a person may be of the most evil conduct, if he adores me with single-minded devotion, he should be considered to be a virtuous soul, for he has rightly resolved. He speedily becomes a saintly person and gets eternal peace. O Arjuna, know for certain that my devotee never comes to grief. Even women, *vaishyas* and *shūdras* are liberated from the bonds

---

174. The expression used in the text is *yoga-kshema* which implies 1. The giving of whatever a man needs for himself and 2. The preservation of what is given.

of existence, not to speak of sages and pious *brāhmins*. Having taken birth in this evanescent world of misery, you should worship and pray to me. Direct your thoughts to me, be my devotee, chant my name, bow to me. Thus adoring me with your whole soul and taking refuge in me you will become one with me.

[*Bhagavadgītā*. Chapter 9, verses 22 to 34].

THE DIVINE AND THE DEMONIACAL

What the Blessed Lord said

I will tell you now, Arjuna, the qualities of godly persons. Their minds are pure, they are fearless, eager to attain knowledge and to reflect on it. They are self-controlled, austere and straightforward. They perform sacrifices, give charity and study the scriptures. Such men speak the truth, never show violence, or anger and are kind to all creatures. They are tranquil, gentle, modest and firm. They are of a renouncing nature. They covet nothing and do not indulge in cavil. These godly persons are vigorous, forgiving, brave and blameless. They are neither malicious nor conceited. The godly persons are qualified to be emancipated, while the ungodly are ever in bondage. But do not fear, Arjuna, your nature is godly.

I have thus described the godly kind of persons in detail. Now I go on to tell you of what kind the ungodly are. They are vain, arrogant and boastful. Anger, harshness and ignorance are their marked qualities. They cannot discriminate between what should be done and what shouldn't. They aren't pure, good or truthful. They say the world is unreal, without any basis, or a Creator. It comes about only by men and women carnally copulating with one another. Convinced thus, these fallen souls of feeble understanding and wicked deeds, are set against the world and are bent on destroying it. These boastful arrogant, conceited and impure people, tread vile paths, delude themselves with false resolves and hold fast to material desires which are hard to get. They are weighed down with endless cares, which cease only when they die. They love sense-pleasures most, and their whole mind is engrossed in them. Beset by hundreds of desires, these evil men in whom lust and rage abound, crave for heaps of ill-gotten wealth to gratify their sense-pleasures. These deluded and ignorant persons keep thinking thus : I have got this and soon I'll get that too. This wealth is already mine, that too I'll soon get. I have killed this foe and will slay the others too. I am the master and enjoyer of everything. I am perfect, powerful, happy, rich and wellborn. There's no other like me. I will perform sacrifices for showing off, give gifts so that people may be deceived into thinking me to be charitable, and I will make merry. Such deluded men, Arjuna, bewildered by contrary thoughts and given to carnal pleasures fall into a foul hell. They are haughty and conceited. Wealth makes them heady and vain. They carry out religious rites for mere show without following the prescribed procedure. They arrogantly flaunt their strength, and are given over to lust and rage. These malicious person despise me, who dwells in them and in other creatures, (i.e., they despise God). I constantly hurl these most wicked persons who are full of vicious hatred, into inauspicious and demoniacal wombs. These deluded persons, O Arjuna, failing to attain me birth after birth, go to the lowest state of existence.

Lust, anger and greed are the three posterns of hell, which ruin a soul. So you should shun these. He who avoids these three evils. does what is beneficial for his soul and so reaches the highest state.

The scriptures should be your guide in everything you do. If you ignore their injunctions and do whatever you wish at your sweet will, you will neither be happy nor get salvation.

[*Bhagavadgītā*. Chapter 16, verses 1 to 24].

THE NATURE OF RENUNCIATION

What Arjuna said

I wish to know from you the separate natures of *sannyāsa* and renunciation.

What the Blessed Lord said

Wise men consider *sannyāsa* to be the abandonment of all works performed with desire. And they think renunciation is the giving up of the fruits of all works. Some wise men say that all works should be given up because all are fraught with some blemish, while others say that sacrifices, charities and austerities should not be abandoned. Now listen to my view about this, O Arjuna. Renunciation is said to be of three kinds, (i.e., *sāttvic, rājasic* and *tāmasic*). Sacrifice, charity and austerities should not be given up, for they purify wise men. But these too should be done without desire and without expecting a reward. This is my firm belief. Prescribed duties are not to be renounced, for such renouncement proceeds from delusion and laziness. The man who relinquishes works because they are troublesome and because he fears they may tax his body, doesn't get the fruit of such relinquishment, for it is *rājasic* in nature. That work which is done without attachment and not desiring any reward, but taking it to be an obligatory duty, is of the *sāttvic* kind. That person yoked to truth, who is neither repulsed by works which are uncomfortable nor attracted to works which are congenial, is wise, pure of heart, free from doubt and a real renouncer. Because a human being cannot possibly relinquish all works, so it is enough if he renounces the fruits of works. Those who do works hoping for reward, get, after death, three kinds of fruits – pleasant, unpleasant or a mixture of the two, (i.e., partly pleasant and partly unpleasant). But the person who has renounced the fruits of works is emancipated.

There are five factors constituting action as the Sāṁkhya says. I will tell you these now, Arjuna. The first is the body in which all that happens, takes place, second, the doer of the works, third the various senses through which works are possible, fourth the different kinds of endeavours a person makes, and fifth the divine (the final arbitrator of works). Whatever a man speaks, thinks or does by exerting his body, whether it is good or bad, these are the five factors constituting it. This being so, the person of poor understanding who thinks himself to be the doer, commits a grave error.

[*Bhagavadgītā,* Chapter 18, verses 1 to 16]

HOW TO ATTAIN BRAHMAN

What the Blessed Lord said

I tell you now, Arjuna, in brief, how the seeker obtains *brahman* which is the ultimate goal of all wisdom. He acquires spiritual wisdom and calm, abandons vain talk and sense-pleasures, remains free from attraction and aversion, loves solitude, eats little, is controlled in mind, body and speech, keeps meditating and practises renunciation. That seeker of *brahman* is gentle, humble and free from egoism. He has in him no desire, rage and possessiveness. He is tranquil and detached. Such a person is worthy to attain *brahman*. He becomes one with *brahman* and experiences endless bliss. He neither grieves nor desires, and seeing all existence as one, he becomes my supreme devotee. He comes to know my real nature and having known it, is united with me. He takes my refuge and obtains my grace. He thus reaches my eternal abode, (i.e., attains me).

[*Bhagavadgītā*. Chapter 18, verses 50 to 56].

[Krishṇa went on to tell Arjuna that he should surrender to him, (i.e., to God) completely. But if he persists in not listening out of self-conceit, he will perish. Even if he refrains from fighting, his kshatriya nature will spur him on to do so. For the Lord abides in the hearts of all creatures and makes them go round and round as the worker of a machine works it. Arjuna listened to all this, but kept quiet. Then Lord Krishṇa spoke to him, giving him his final message].

THE SUPREME PATH

What the Blessed Lord said

I again declare my supreme and secret words to you, Arjuna, because you are very dear to me, and I want your good. Fix your mind on me, worship and adore me with folded hands. Be my devotee. I promise you will thus come to me for I love you much. Don't bother about duties, just take refuge in me, and leave all other paths. I will absolve you of all sins, grieve not.

[*Bhagavadgītā.* Chapter 18, verses 64 to 66.].

Then Arjuna surrendered himself to the Lord. 'My delusion is destroyed'. he said. 'My doubts have been removed. I have known my inner Self. I will do as you say'. [That is the ultimate wisdom of the human mind; the wisdom which all religions teach–Thou, O Lord not me. Thine will be done, not mine.]

(F) FROM THE UPANISHADS

WHAT THE UPANISHADS ARE ABOUT

The word 'Upanishad' is from *upa* 'near', *ni* 'down' and *sad* 'to sit'. Thus it means literally 'sitting down near'. The pupils who wished to learn the Upanishads sat down and listened to their teacher expounding it to them. Thus, as other ancient Scriptural texts, the Upanishads too were transmitted verbally, and are classed as *shruti*, i.e., revealed literature. They are of very ancient origin, going back to 800 B.C., and are said to have been revealed by God to the *rishīs* (sages) who went to the forest. Though some put their number as one hundred and fifty, the genuine ones are believed to be a hundred and eight and of them the classical ones are eleven.[174a] These are the ones on which Shankarāchārya commented.

A detailed study of the Upanishads is not necessary here as their philosophy has already been given in the Introduction – Fundamental Concepts of Hindu Philosophy. Besides the *Brahma-sūtras* too embody much of it. The main concepts are the oneness of the soul (*ātman*) and the Cosmic Absolute (*brahman*), transmigration, karma, *moksha*, and the nature of the soul in dream and sleep. They do not take a gloomy view of life, although they deal with both life and death and the hereafter. The *Īsha Upanishad*, for example says, 'One should live a hundred years and do the tasks allotted to him'.[175] There is certainly much wisdom in them. Like the *Gītā*, they are concerned with the more important and spiritual questions of existence. There is little narrative and whatever there is fits so unobstrusively into the philosophical discourses that it is hardly noticed. Five of the Upanishads are almost wholly in Sanskrit verse. The others are in prose, with only occasional verse. Schopenhauer had the Upanishads on his table and read through some of it daily before going to bed. 'They are the products of the highest wisdom, he said 'destined soner or later to become the faith of the people'.

174a. These are *Īsha, Kēna, Chhāndogya,* Brihadaraṇyaka. Aitareya. *Taittīrya,* Muṇḍaka. *Māṇḍukya, Svētāshvatara. Kaṭha* and Prashna.

175. *Īsha Up.* 2.

READING LIST

Commentaries

The clasical commentators are Shankara, Madhva Rāmānuja and Bāladeva. Nārāyaṇabhaṭṭa, Professor R. Tarkaratna, H. Vidyā bhushana and V. Shāstri wrote commentaries for the Bibliotheca Indica. Other commentaries were written by F. Max Müller, G.R.S. Mead and J.C. Chattopādhyayā, S. Sitārāma Sāstri and Gangānātha Jhā, Sītānath Tatvabhūshana, S.C. Vasu, R.E. Hume, Swamei Prabhānanda and Fredrick Manchester, Swami Nikhilānanda and S. Radhakrishan.

Translations

Most of the principal Upanishads have been published by Shri Ramakrishna Math, Mylapore Madras. These have word for word meaning in English with commentary in English also. Some have been published by Chinamaya Publications Trust, 175 Rasappa Chetty Street, Madras with Sanskrit text, English meaning and commentary.

Other translations in English are :

Brihadāranyaka (E. Roer; S.C. Vasu).

Chhāndogya (R. Mitra).

Aitarēya (Bhadkamkar)

Taittirīya (A.M. Shastri, S.C. Vidyarnava, M.L. Sandal).

Kena (M. Hiriyanna, S.C. Vasu, A.C. Thirlwall).

Kaṭha (W.D. Whitney, S.C. Vasu, Rawson, Krishna Prem).

Īsha (Sir William Jones, S.C. Vasu, A.C. Thirlwall).

Māṇḍukya (Swami Nikhilananda, M.N. Dvivedi).

Kaushitatī (E.B. Cowell, SC. Vidyarnava, M.L. Sandal).

Maitrī (E.B. Cowell).

Books (including texts, translations and commentaries).

Aiyar, N.K. *Thirty Minor Upanishads*. Madras, 1914.

Bahadur, K.P. *The Wisdom of the Upanishads*. *New* Delhi : Sterling Publishers, 1989.

Hume, R.E. *The Thirteen Upanishads*. London, 1931.

Mahadevan, T.M.P. ed. The Upanishads. London, 1931.

Mead, G.R.S. and Chattopadhyaya. *The Upanishads.* 2 vols. 1896.

Müller, P. Max. *The Upanishads.* 2 vols. Oxford, 1879-84.

Nikhilananda, Swami. *The Upanishads.* 4 vols. London : Phoenix House, 1951–59.

Prabhananda, Swami and Manchester F. *The Upanishads.* Madras : Sri Ramakrishna Math.

Radhakrishan S. *The Principal Upanishads.* London : George Allen and Unwin Ltd., 1953.

Shastri, J. *Collection of Upanishads.* Delhi : Motilal Banarsidass, 1980.

Tattvabhushan, S. *The Upanishads.* 2 vols., 1900–104,

Vasu, S.C. *The Upanishads* (with commentary of Madhvācharya). 3 vols. Allahabad : Panini Office, 1909–16.

ABOUT GOD

Vishvakarman is the source of the universe. It arose from him though the elements like water, fire and so forth. He is greater than the other gods. The sun shines with the glory of Paramātman (God). It dispels the gloom in which the earth is shrouded. There is no other way to emancipation except the knowledge of Paramātman. He is beyond ignorance and darkness. To know him him is to conquer death. The wise man who knows the Supreme is even above the gods. He supports heaven and earth. He dwells in all living creatures and is their Lord. The mountains– Himalayas and all others, the rivers, heaven, earth, sky and all things testify to his majesty. He is the ultimate dispenser of justice. He gives release from existence to virtuous souls. He fills the heavens. From him is creation. He is the inner spirit of all beings, facing in all directions. He in One without the second and controls all creatures by *dharma* and *adharma*.[176]

The universe originates from the Lord and is absorbed in him. He is the warp and the woof of all creation. It is he who causes the three states of consciousness–waking, dream and sleep–to exist. It is in him that the entire universe rests. He is our father and friend. He ordains destiny and gives a suitable place to every creature, for he understands them all. As cloth is woven by thread so the entire universe is the Lord's handiwork. Whoever knows him by meditation attains *brahman*. He is the Ruler and Protector of all souls.

The soul is indeed the Supreme Light which shines on the water. it is that which is the inmost essence of all creatures. While embodied in the body it becomes subject to ignorance, but it is really the eternal *brahman*.

He who repeats the following *mantras* (sacred verses) is released from sin : I am the ground of sins, destroy them, O Varuṇa, for you absolve all who go against the scriptures, who are thieves and all those who treat their teachers with contempt.[177]

---

176. In other words, there are some beings in the world who are virtuous, others who are wicked, but of all these God is the controller.

177. The *mantra* is chanted while one is bathing.

As the ocean covers all, so too the Supreme pervades all creation. He creates beings on the basis of their past deeds. He rules the universe and is gracious to his devotees in whose hearts he dwells. He is the dewller of all souls.[178]

WHAT GIVES LIBERATION?

Prajāpati's son, Āruṇi, went to his father and asked him what the supreme means of liberation was. Prajāpati said it was truth, for by it the wind blows and the sun shines, and in it all life has its support. Truth is the foundation of speech. So by truth one is liberated. Other means to liberation are religious austerities, sense control, calmness of the mind, the giving of gifts to priests and others as a sacred obligation,[179] following *dharma* (the moral laws), the performance of sacrifices and prescribed religious rites, meditation, and *sannyāsa* (renunciation).

The Person in the sun, Hiranyagarbha, is the *ātman* or Self of all creatures, and the Protector of the universe. The sun gives heat which makes vaporizes water and makes it take the form of clouds. The clouds shower rain, and rain causes trees, herbs and crops to spring up. From these comes food which nourishes life and makes people strong so that they are able to practise self-control, observe religious rites and so forth. From such practices one has belief in religious and spiritual books and knows truth. He develops faith and controls his senses, and so is able to get mental peace.[180] He knows the *ātman*, the Supreme, and attains to *brahman*. That Person, O Āruṇa said Prajāpati, can be realized through *sannyāsa* (renunciation). So *sannyāsa* is the greatest means of liberation. The *sannyāsi* should meditate on *brahman*, uttering the sacred syllable '*Om*'. He who meditates thus attains *brahman*.

[The above two passages are from the *Mahānārāyaṇa Upanishad*, sections one and seventy-nine respectively'].

---

178. This verse is chanted after the bath.

179. The word is *dakshiṇā*, of which in English only an approximate equivalent can be given.

180. Cf., *Bhagavadgītā* 3. 10–16.

RIGHTEOUSNESS

[Most scriptures, of whatever religion they may be, give accounts of how creation came about. Despite the advances of modern science, creation still remains a mystery, and at the most we can have surmises and theories about it. At that distant time it was even more a mystery. The *Brihadāranyaka Upanishad* gives an account of the origin of creation. We will give only one verse from this account. We see today strong and powerful persons exploiting, bullying and looking with contempt on the weak. Everything is for those with power and money, nothing for the poor, not even justice, which is a costly luxury. Let us see what the Upanishad says about it].

Brahman was alone, so he created the *brāhmin* caste and then the others–*kshatriyas, vaishyas and shūdras*. But he did not think that enough, i.e., he felt there was something still lacking. So he created that best of things–righteousness (*dharma*). It is righteousness which rules even over the rulers. Therefore there is nothing greater than that. So even a weak person can stand against one who is powerful, because he has the support of righteousness, even as a weak subject can have the king's support. So when a person speaks what is true, they say he speaks what is right, and when one says the right thing, they say he is speaking the truth.

[*Brihadāranyaka Upanishad.* 1. 4. 14].

THE ONENESS OF BRAHMAN AND THE SOUL

[Yājñavalkya, a householder, had two wives, Kātyānī and Maitreyī. Kātyānī was wordly-minded, but Maitreyī was spiritual. It was the practice those days to leave the world and family life and go away to the forest to meditate on God and the mysteries of life, death, afterlife, the soul and so forth. This was the third stage of life, that of a forest dweller. So when Yājñavalkya decided to leave home he wished to make a final settlement of his property].

Yājñavalky said, 'Maitreyī, my dear, I am going away to live as an anchorite. Let me make a settlement of my property between you and Kātyānī'. Maitreyī said, 'Suppose I were to get the wealth of the whole world, would I be able to get immortality through it?' 'Ah no, not at all', Yājñavalkya said. Having got wealth you will live the life which a rich person lives. But as for immortality, that can't be got through wealth'. 'Well, what shall I do with that which can't give me immortality', said Maitreyi. 'Venerable sir, tell me that alone,—knowing which I may achieve immortality'. Yājñavalkya said, 'Ah, my beloved, you have always been dear to me. And now what you say pleases my heat. Come, dear, sit beside me. I will tell you what you wish to know. but ponder well over what I say'.

Yājñavalkya said, 'Look, whatever relations there are—husbands, wife, or sons—whatever wealth one has, whatever people there are of whatever class; all things, beings and worlds, even the gods; are not dear in themselves, but for one's own sake, Therefore, Maitreyī, it is the Self which should be meditated on, reflected on, heard and understood. Only by realizing the Self thus, can one know all this.

'One cannot know what musical instrument is being played, whether a drum, conch or lute, by listening to just one note. He can only distinguish them if the knows what that instrument generally sounds like. So too the waking or sleeping world has no existence apart from *brahman*. As smoke, sparks, flames and so forth, originate from the one fire, so too, my dear Maitreyī, all branches of knowledge, like the Vedas Upanishads, history, mythology, the arts and so forth, are the mere breath of *brahman*.

As all waters merge in the sea, all kinds of touch in the skin, all odours in the nostrils, all savours in the tongue, all sights in the eye, all sounds in the ear, all resolutions in the mind, all knowledge in the intellect, all activity in the hands, all pleasure in the organs of generation, all excretions in the anus, all walking in the feet and all the scriptures in speech; as when a lump of salt is thrown into water is dissolves and ceases to exist as a lump, but from wherever the water is tasted it is salty; so too, Maitreyī, when one realizes that all is *brahman*, separateness is destroyed and only that One Reality, which ever was, ever is and ever will be, exists'.

[Maitreyī did not understand this because she fell into the same error as many people fall, when they believe moksha (emancipation, or merging of the soul with brahman) as implying loss of its consciousness, and so look with horror on a state in which a man is deprived of, what they term, his 'personality'].

Maitreyī said, said, 'Venerable sir, I am confused. When you say that the soul has no consciousness'. Then Yājñavalkya said. 'I say nothing which is confusing. What I have said is enough to give one knowledge. For when there is duality, it is as though one sees, hears, speaks of, thinks of and knows, another. But when one has attained *brahman*-knowledge and has known *brahman*, what should one smell, see, hear, speak of, think of and know? And through what? Because it is then by *brahman* that all is known. He is the Knower. How can one *know* the Knower?[181]

[Having said this Yājñavalkya, having made arrangements for his property, and having given what each of his wives wanted – wealth to Kātyānī and wisdom to Maitreyī, departed for the forest].

[*Brihadāranykaka Upanishad.* Chapter 2, section 4. 1–13].

181. It's as fire can't burn itself. It can burn other things but not itself. So too, while there is duality there are two, the Knower and the known. But when there is only One no difference remains.

THE FATE OF HUMAN BEINGS

[*King Janaka, himself a wise man, was a true seeker of knowledge. Here he is instructed by the sage Yājñavalkya about the man who desires worldly things and he who wishes to attain brahman].*

The soul is indeed *brahman*. When it is associated with the gross body (as *jīva*) it is identified with various things – the mind, the intellect, sight and hearing, the elements earth, water, fire, wind and ether, light and darkness, desire and desirelessness, anger and calm and right and wrong. Thus the soul is connected to what is experienced in existence as well as what is unperceived, for one can know by a person's outer demeanour what emotions are swaying him. As a person conducts himself so he becomes. He who does good acts will become good. He who does bad acts will becomes bad. He is made pure by good works while bad works debase him.

Others, however, say that a person consists of desires. As his desire is so is his will. As he wills, so he acts. And as he acts so are the fruits of his actions.

On this there is the following verse : The person who works for an end, gets the fruits of his works when he dies. And when he has exhausted these fruits he is reborn on the earth to do nore works.

So much, O king (Janaka), for the man whom desires enslave. but he who does not desire, who being satiated with desires, becomes freed of them, who longs for the Self alone; attains *brahman* in this very life.

Further, there is the following verse : When the heart is freed of all desires, the mortal man becomes immortal. For he attains *brahman* even in this life.

This lifeless body, your majesty, is then of no account. It is as the cast-off slough of a snake lying on an anthill. And the soul which has left it shines with the light of the Supreme *Brahman*.

[*Brihadāraṇyaka Upanishad.* Chapter 4, Section 4 : 5–7]

ON THE NATURE OF THE SOUL

There was a boy of twelve years called Shvetaketu Āruṇeya whose father Uddālaka Āruṇi, a very wise sage, once called him and said 'You should live the life of a religious student, for it is our family tradition that we should be adept in the scriptures'. The lad went to a teacher and stayed twelve years, learning the various branches of knowledge. He came back rather arrogant and conceited, believing himself to have become very learned. His father noticed this. 'You seem to consider yourself very learned now', he said. 'I wonder if you asked your teacher about that by which one can know what can ordinarily not be known?' 'What's that?' the boy asked, 'That is *brahman*', his father said, 'It reveals everything. As by knowing a clod one can know clay, by knowing a pair of nail-scissors one can know iron and by knowing a piece of gold one can know gold, So too by knowing *brahman* one can know everything there's to know'. 'My teacher couldn't have know about it' the boy said. 'If he had, he'd surely have told me. Why don't you tell me about it, father?' Uddalaka then instructed Shvetaketu.

'When a person dies', he said, 'his speech merges in his body, his mind in his breath, his breath in the body's heat and his body's heat in the highest Being. the inner spirit of this is the subtle essence, which is your soul and the soul is what you really are, son'. Shvetaketu was puzzled. He had been taught that the soul went to the Being when the man slept, but the sleeper wasn't aware of it. So he expressed his doubt to his father.

Uddalaka said, 'Bees prepare honey by gathering nectar from flowers. Does the nectar say, I am from such and such a tree? So too the souls of different creatures—humans, beasts, insects etc.—reach the Being, but the creature does not know, for the souls are the same. On rebirth they again become differentiated. Rivers pour their waters into the sea, but while their waters form the sea, do the rivers know which part is theirs? If one struck at a tree-trunk with an axe the sap may ooze out, if one broke a branch that branch would wither.

But the tree would still survive. If its nourishment ceased, however, it would dry up and die. So too the soul is the body's nourishment. Without it the body can't survive. You are that soul, Shvetaketu'.

The lad wondered how the vast universe and all it contained could be produced by the subtle Being which one couldn't even see. So he asked his father how could that be. Uddalaka said, 'Bring me a fruit of the bunyan tree. Now split it open. What do you see inside?' 'I see tiny seeds', the lad said. 'All right, now break one of these seeds. What do you see inside it?' 'Nothing at all, father', Shvetaketu said. 'From this subtle essence, which you don't see', Uddalaka said, this whole tree arose. This subtle essence is the soul of all beings. It is true son. That indeed, is what you are, Shvetaketu'.

[*Chhāndogya Upanishad*. Chapter 6. Sections 1–12–part of the chapter].

MORE ABOUT THE SOUL[182]

Prajāpati said, one should seek and desire to understand the soul which is free from evil, old age, grief, hunger and thirst. He who is able to do that attains all the worlds and all desires. The demons and the gods both heard this. Indra representing the gods and Virochana for the demons came to seek this knowledge. They stayed with Prajāpati thirty-two years. Then Prajāpati said, The soul is the Person seen in the eye. What he meant was the Seer of the image in the eye. But they thought it meant the reflection one sees when he sees himself reflected in the water or in a mirror. They went away convinced that what they saw thus was indeed the soul. Prajāpati, of course, knew they were in error. Whoever

182. This is based on the author's book *The Wisdom of the Upanishads*. New Delhi : Sterling Publisher, 1989, pp., 134–6.

understands the soul thus will surely perish, he said. Virochana went and told the demons that the body was the soul and he who worships and attends to it would gain this world and the next. That's why even today then say of a man who has no faith, gives no charity and performs no sacrifices, He's a demon. For this is the belief of demons. They deck the body of the dead with clothes and ornaments, and things they have begged for, and think thereby they'll win the world beyond.

Indra, however, had his doubts. If I accept this, he thought then if the body is blind, lame, or crippled, and I see it thus in the mirror and water, it would mean the soul too is blind, lame, or crippled. So he came back to Prajāpati. After he lived another thirty-two years, Prajāpati said, The soul is that which moves about happy in dreams. That is the immortal and fearless. That is *brahman*. Indra went away, but he thought, the person who sees dreams is grieved and even weeps when the dreams are bad. I don't see how that can be soul. So he came back to be reinstructed. Prajāpati said, your doubt is justified. Live with me thirty-two years more, then I'll tell you. Prajāpati then said, When a man is sound asleep, with his senses withdrawn and serene and sees no dreams that is the soul, immortal and fearless. Indra went away, but on the way he thought, In dreamless sleep the soul does not know itself as 'I am'. Nor does it know any other thing. Everything is a blank. I see no good in this. So he went to Prajāpati again. This time he lived there five years. Thus his stay was a hundred and one years in all. Prajāpati then said as follows:

Indra, this body which is mortal and liable to perish any moment, is the abode of the deathless and bodiless soul. So long as a man is thus yoked to the body, he is subject to pleasure and pain. But these cannot even touch one who does not identify himself with the body. The wind, cloud, lightning and thunder have their root in the incorporeal. Yet they acquire a form when they arise out to the sky. The wind rustles, the clouds mass in the sky, the lightning streaks across the sky and the thunder roars. Just so, the serene soul, the highest light, takes form when yoked to the body. It appears to move about, laugh, sport and rejoice whether it be with women, chariots, or relations; but disinterestedly, not remembering that it is part of the body. It's attached to the body much like a beast is attached to a cart which it draws. It is the soul which is the person shining in the eye, whereby they can see, the smelling power of the nose, and that which resides in speech, hearing and thought. The mind is indeed the divine eye, for it cognizes not only what is present before it, but also what is not present (the past, future and distant subtle objects). With this divine eye the unconditioned soul sees all objects it desires and rejoices in them. They who are in the Brahma-world meditate on that soul and therefore all the worlds and all desires are gained by them.

[*Chhāndogya Upanishad.* Chapter 8, sections 7–12]

HOW TO KNOW BRAHMAN

The Vālakhilyas were virtuous perons who had no evil in them. They approached Prajāpati Kratu and asked how the soul after leaving the body, could obtain union with *brahman*. Prajāpati said: Death comes suddenly and is unavoidable. It is like the waves of a large river or like the tide, hard to stem. Men who are obsessed with sense-pleasures are bound with the fetters of good and evil. They are like cripples handicapped by their infirmity, or as a man in prison. To them delusion is like heady wine, and they run about as though pursued by evil spirits. They are bitten by the world as though by a big snake. The darkness of passion casts a veil round them. They are full of vanity as one changing dresses, and artificial like a painted wall. They have no substance in them. They are always fearing death. People like these do not know the Self.

Now I will tell you, said Prajāpati Kratu, how that Self can be acquired. It is by knowledge of the scriptures, and the performance of one's own duty (according to his *varṇa*) which is more important than the duty of another, even as the tree is much more significant than its branches. Through the performance of his duty a man rises, otherwise he falls. Everyone must follow the rule of the *āshramas* (stages of life). An ascetic too must pass through them, before renouncing the world. Nonetheless an ascetic alone can get knowledge of the Self. He obtains goodness by his austerities, from goodness, enlightenment, and then the Self from which there is no return. Meditation of '*Om*' makes one realize the greatness of *brahman*. Thus by knowledge, penance and meditation one achieves *brahman*. Freed from the body, senses and all to which he was attached, the ascetic attains *brahman*.

[*Maitrāyaṇa–Brāhmaṇa Upanishad*. 4 : 1–4]

NACHIKETAS AND YAMA[183]

The performance of sacrifices (some being those in which animals were also offered) was an ancient Hindu religious rite. A sage named Vājashravasa was performing the *vishvajit* sacrifice. It was usual to give gifts to priests and *brāhmins* on such occasions. So the sage was giving away cows. His son, Nachiketas, noticed that all the cows being gifted were useless, for they were old and unfit to give milk. So Nachiketas was very angry and said to his father, 'to whom will you give me?' When he repeated his question three times, Vājashravasa was annoyed and blurted out, 'Boy, I'll give you away to Death!' It was, of course, merely an expression of the sage's anger. But the lad took it in all seriousness. His father's words had to be kept, come what may. So, though he didn't consider himself so bad as to merit what his father had said, he decided to go to Yama, the god of Death, for it was to Death that his father had consigned him.

When he reached Yama's house it found it locked. Yama had left town and would not be back before three days. So Nachiketas, who was weary with travel lay on the doorstep. When Yama returned he was aghast to find a guest lie outside for three days without food or water, and that too a *brāhmin* boy. So to make up for his fault he promised to give Nachiketas three boons. The lad asked as his first and second boons that his father may shed his anger against him, and that Yama tell him (Nachiketas) the way of performing the fire sacrifice which enables the sacrificer to go to heaven. The boons were given. Then Yama said, 'Now ask your third boon'. Nachiketas said, 'When one dies, some say that's the end of everything. There's nothing after that. Others say, some part of him does exist even after death, and that's his soul. Tell me, what the truth is'. Yama said, 'Look, dear boy, even the gods had their doubts on this. It's a knotty matter. So don't press me for this boon. Ask another'. Nachiketas said,

183. This passage is form the *Kaṭha Upanishad.* Max Müller says about it that it is one of the most perfect specimens of mystic philosophy of the ancient Hindus.

'You yourself say it's hard to explain this. And now I have you as my teacher. Where can I find a better one? So I feel I must learn this from you'. When Yama saw the lad was adamant, he promised to give him longlived sons and grandsons, cattle, horses, elephants, gold, territory, eternal life, (i.e., as long as he chose to live), the earth's treasures, fair girls, musical intruments and every other thing he wanted; in other words he promised him the moon, provided he didn't ask about death.[184] Nachiketas said 'What you're offering is transient. They only make one weary. Life is too short for indulging in such profitless things. How can wealth bring contentment? Pleasures last but a moment. What joy can they give? Your shadow, (i.e., the thought of death) is always with us. No. I wish to know only about that hereafter which remains a mystery to us. Tell me, Yama, about that. I seek no other boon'.

What Yama said

The good is one thing, and quite another is the pleasant. He who pursues what's good, fares well. He who runs after the pleasant misses the aim of living. Nonetheless both are bondage. Both the good and the pleasant are there to choose from, The wise man ponders well and, discriminating between them, chooses the good. The fool chooses the pleasant because of greed and avarice. You, Nachiketas, have wisely rejected wealth and pleasures which lead to perdition. You aspired for knowledge and even many pleasures did not tempt you. Ignorance. and knowledge are wide apart and they lead to different ends. There are many persons who live in the midst of ignorance, but still think themselves to be learned. They are fools.

They are like blind men led by those who are blind themselves. They keep being bound to the chain of births and rebirths. The childish man is fooled by the lure of wealth. He thinks there is only this world and no other. He is completely unaware of the hereafter. So he comes again and again in my hold.

184. Really these were not offered as temptation. Yama wanted to test the lad whether he was sincere in his quest. If he yielded and accepted wealth and pleasures instead, it would be clear that he wasn't fit for spiritual instruction.

Very few people in the world even hear about the soul. Of those whose mind is directed to it, few can comprehend it. The man who teaches about it is indeed praiseworthy. And so too he who learns about it from an able teacher. It's not anybody who can teach what the soul is. It can be taught only by one who has himself known it. For its knowledge is communicable by experience, not by argument. It can't be reasoned out. As I have said, it can only be taught by another. You, Nachiketas, acted wisely. Many people here carry out rituals to gain heaven. That's their highest aim. But you weren't so tempted. You wanted to have that knowledge which leads to emancipation.[184a] The man who knows the ancient soul through meditation is free from the dualities of joys and sorrows. This soul lies within the heart's cavity. It is radiant, hidden, immanent and hard to see. He who hears about this soul and knows it, is full of bliss, for he has discovered the very source of joy. The abode of *brahman*, O Nachiketas, is open to you.

What Nachiketas said

What is that deepest Reality which is beyond right and wrong, cause and effect and beyond the past and the future?

What Yama said

It is the sacred syllable '*Om*' (or *Aum*). This is the goal laid down by the Vedas, the culmination of all austerities. Religious students desire it. It is both *brahman* with form as well as the formless *brahman*. Whoever knows it gets all he desires. The soul never dies. It is is eternal, everlasting, without end or beginning and unborn. It does not die with the body. It is smaller than the smallest and greater than the greatest, it dwells in the heart of every creature. Though actionless, it takes part in all actions. Though still, in dreamless sleep, it moves about everywhere. Only that man can know it who's calm, desireless, free from grief, not bound to sense-plaeasures, discriminating, content, virtuous and

184a. Nachaketas had asked to be tdd how to carry out the Fire sacrifice which led to heaven. But he didn't stop at that. He went on to inquire about afterlife and spiritual things. That shows his aim wasn't to get heaven.

contemplative. It can't be know by the study of the scriptures, or by the intellect, or by great scholarship. It reveals its true nature only to him whom he chooses to. The castes do not have any significance for it. They are as mere food for it (what has the soul to do with food?) Death is a trifle for it, (i.e., of no significance, for it means only a change of bodies).[185] It's as sauce for a dish. How can the ignorant man who is lost in the maze of the senses ever know this soul?

The Supreme Soul and the individual soul, both dwell in the inner cavity of the heart. The Supreme Soul merely looks on. The other experiences the results of its actions. The former is light, the other its shade.

The body is like a chariot. The soul, the owner who sits on it. The intellect is the charioteer and the mind the reins. The senses are the horses and the sense-objects the road. When the horses are unruly and the charioteer can't hold fast to the reins, the chariot will become uncontrollable and run amuck. So too the man whose intellect is poor, whose mind is corrupt with ignorance and who indulges in sense pleasures; is carried away by his senses. He lets down his soul which is seated in his body. But the man of pure mind and intellect keeps his senses in control and his soul, inside the body keeps serene. He goes on life's road smoothly and quickly reaches the goal. The subtle objects are beyond the senses. Beyond the senses is the mind. Beyond the mind is the understanding and beyond the understanding is the soul. Beyond the soul is the Unmanifest and beyond it the Spirit animating it. This is the higest goal.

The soul remains hid. It generally can't be seen. But he who has a sharp intellect and meditates on it can know it. Arise, awake and learn about this soul from able teachers. This path, (i.e., the path of soul-knowledge) Nachiketas, is not easy. It is hard to tread. It's as though one were to walk on a rajor's edge.

---

185. cf., *Gītā*. 2 : 22.

That man knows the soul who knows it as being without touch or sound, without form, taste or smell, without beginning or end, undecaying and beyond *mahat* (the first product in the evolution of Nature). He who hears this ancient teaching given to Nachiketas by the god of Death and conveys it to others, receives glory. He is greatly rewarded who relates this supreme secret to worthy and devoted hearers, or recites these verses during ceremonies for the dead.

[From *Kaṭha Upanishad.* Chapters 1 to 3]

THE UNITY OF EXISTENCE

Whatever there exists in this changeful world is enveloped by God alone. So make renunciation your support. Do not covet the wealth of others.[186]

If you can't renounce, live a hundred years in this world, doing good works. There is no other way to escape the taint of evil deeds.

The wicked life of sensual enjoyment is indeed shrouded in blinding darkness. Those who live such lives destroy themselves. They remain bound to the chain of births and deaths in this world.

The Self is changeless. It does not take part in action. But it makes life's wheel move by its very presence. In this way it outstrips all activity. It is swifter than the mind and even more so than the senses.

Thus the soul is in truth unmoving but it appears to be involved in works. It is near to those who make an effort to know it while from others it is far. It is the pivot of the individual and also the Supreme World Soul.

The wise man knows that it is the same soul which dwells in all creatures. Knowing this he bears no animosity to anyone. The man who thus sees the unity of all existence, finds no difference between himself and other beings. What attachment or sorrow can there be for such a wise man?

It is *brahman* who assigns everyone his place in the world. This *brahman* is pure radiant, partless and taintless. It is bodiless and can't be slain or harmed. It pervades all and knows everything. Nothing can remain hid from it.

Those who put their trust in rituals enter into blinding darkness. But those who make empty learning their goal enter into darkness which is still greater.[187]

---

186. Shankara thinks this verse is for recluses and the next one for householders.

187. Compare with this Shankarāchārya's *Bhaja Govindam* : 'O deluded man, surrender youself to the Lord. Chant his name and take refuge in him. When inevitable death overtakes you, never, never, will the grammatical rule *du-krin-karne*, (i.e., mere learning) be your protector'.

Wise men say that knowldege of the scriptures takes the soul to the world of the gods, while those who are ignorant and mechanically perform rituals go to the world of the manes.

He who knows both the scriptures and the proper performance of rituals attains the world of immortals by the knowledge of ritualistic philosophy, and by rituals conquers death.[188]

Those who worship unmanifest Nature fall into blinding darkness. And they who delight in becoming, i.e., venerate created Nature or the world of creation, fall into greater darkness.

The worship of *sambhava* or created Nature, endows one with yogic powers, and by worshipping Nature in the form of *prakriti* (the unmanifested), one is absorbed in that very same *prakriti*.

He who understands both the manifest and the unmanifest, crosses death by the unmanifest and through the manifest he gets eternal life.[189]

[From *Tsha Upanishad.* verses 1–14].

Of the Tsha Upanishad, Shankara says 'He should read this Upanishad who is eager to get rid of the world's suffering and delusion'. Dr E. Röer who has translated the Upanishad says: 'This short Upanishad is composed for the purpose of exalting knowledge of the Supreme Spirit. It appears to address the last advice of a teacher to his disciples after the course of their instruction is completed, or to embody the sum total of human wisdom in a few words for those who have attained it'.

---

188. According to Shankara the world of the immortals does not mean attainment of *brahman*, but the world of the gods, while death means the works and knowledge of the ordinary ignorant person. According to him works and knowledge are opposed as night and day. So they can't be combined to attain *brahman.*

189. Shankara reads *sam-bhūti* in the first line of this verse as *asambhūti* and the second line as *tīrtvāsambūtyā*. Thus he reverses the meaning, i.e., through the manifest one gets eternal life, and through the manifest crosses death.

ONE IS JUDGED BY HIS DEEDS

Yājñavalkya was questioned by Ārtabhāga. 'What are the organs of a person,' Ārtabhāga asked, 'which bind a man to the senses?' Yājñavalkya said, 'They are the nose through which one breathes in and out and by which he smells, the speech by which names are uttered, the tongue which tastes, the eyes which see, the ears which hear, the mind which thinks, the hands which work and the skin which has the sensation of touch'.

Ārtabhāga said, 'All these are as food for death, for when one dies, they are no more. Tell me who is the god for whom these are food ?' Yājñavalkya said, 'It's fire, for he consumes all there is. But fire's death is caused by water. For water puts out a fire. He who knows this is saved from births and deaths'.

Ātabhāga said, 'When a sage dies, do the vital breaths move out of him or not?' Yājñavalkya said, 'No, they do not move out. They are gathered up in him. His body swells up and he's dead. His body lies thus'. 'And when such a man dies, what does not leave him?' Ārtabhāga asked. 'The name', Yājñavalkya said. 'The name of the Lord is in his thoughts. This name of the Vishvedevas is endless and by it the man gains the endless world'.

Then Ārtabhāga asked Yājñavalkya, 'When the speech of this man enters into fire, breath into the air, the eye into the sun, the mind into the moon, the hearing into space, the body to the element of earth, the Self (soul) in ether, the hairs of the body into medicinal plants, the hairs of the head into herbs, and when the blood and the semen are deposited on the waters; where is then that person?'

Yājñavalkya said, 'Take my hand, friend. We will go away to some lonely place and talk about this. Just the two of us. For this matter ought not to be discussed in public'. And so the two went away. What they talked about was karma (deeds). Whatever they spoke was about karma. That, they said, was the cause of the state of one's birth. Whatever they praised was karma. And they resolved in their minds that one becomes good by good deeds and bad by bad deeds. After that Ārtabhāga being satisfied by what Yājñavalkya told him, held his peace.

[From *Brihadarāṇyaka Upanishad.* Chapter 3, section 2, 1 : 13].

THE SOUL IN VARIOUS STATES OF CONSCIOUSNESS

All that which is immortal is '*Om*'. It is the past, the present and the future. All this is really *brahman*. The soul that inhabits the body is also *brahman*. The soul has three states of consciousness, namely waking, dream and deep sleep. The *turīya* is the substratum of these three states and it contains them all.[190]

The first state of consciousness is the *vaishvānara*. The sphere of activity of this is the waking state. All men are from the *vaishvānara,* i.e., it is common to all men. This is seven–limbed [The head of the *vishva* is the heaven, the sun his eys, the air his breath, the sky his body, water his lower organ and the earth his feet]. He is nineteen-mouthed [the five sensory organs, the five motor organs, the five kinds of vital enrgy, and four aspects of the mind. These are called mouths because man enjoys the external world through them]. Thus equipped the waking man enjoys the world.

The second state of consciousness of the soul is the *taijasa*. It cognizes the internal objects and is also seven-limbed and nineteen mouthed. It experiences subtle objects, for dreams are the impressions of the waking state stored up in the memory. The third state is *prājña*. The sphere of the soul in this state is deep sleep. In this state of dreamless sleep one has no desires. The experiences of the waking and the dream states are contained in this state in a latent manner.

190. The *turīya* state has been discussed in the intoduction—Fundamental Concepts of Hindu Philosophy. q.v.

Their diversity is lost. All that remains is a mass of consciousness. It is the state of supreme bliss and is a kind of gateway to the other two states of waking and sleep. This consciousness, known as *prājña*, is the Lord, the Knower and the Inner Controller. He is the source of everything. All beings have their origin and dissolution in him.

The fourth state is the *turīya*. In this state there is neither inward not outward congnition. In other words it knows neither external objects as in waking, nor internal objects as in dreams. Nor does it know both of them together. Nor is it what exists in deep sleep. It cannot be conceived, inferred, imagined or described. All phenomena ceases in it. It is the state of perfect peace, bliss and non-duality. This is the soul which should be known.

This same soul is now being described in terms of 'aum'. The first letter 'a' corresponds to the waking state. As the waking state pervades the whole world so 'a' is the source of all sounds. Being the first letter it signifies the waking state as that first. He who knows this obtains all his desires and is the foremost of beings. 'U' signifies the dream state. It is superior to the waking state as the objects seen in this state are subtle not gross. As the dream state comes between the waking and the sleep states, the letter 'u' is in the middle. Only knowers of *brahman* are born in the family of the person who knows this. The third letter 'm' denotes deep sleep. As the waking and dream states merge in that of sleep, so the sounds of the letters 'a' and 'u' merge in that of 'm' when one utters this sacred syllable. He who knows this realizes the unreality of all the three states. He knows the true nature of the universe. He becomes godly The entire syllable 'aum' corresponds to the *turīya* state. It is without parts and transcends the idea of cause and effect. All phenomena cease in it. It is non-dual and the supreme bliss. Aum is indeed the soul. He who knows this goes beyond birth and death. His soul merges with the immortal.

[*Māṇḍūkya Upanishad.* 1–12].

FROM FIRE TO FIRE

Once when Shvetaketu Āruṇeya arrived in an assembly of the Pāñcālas, king Pravāhaṇa Jaivali, among other questions, asked him, 'Young man, has your father told you how the offering made in the fifth libation in a sacrifice came to be called a man?' Shvetaketu admitted that he had not learnt about this. So he went back to his father, Gautama, and said, 'That fellow of a *kshatriya* asked me a few questions and I could not reply'. 'Son', Gautama said, 'I didn't know or I would have surely told you'. Gautama therefore went to the king to hear the answer from him. The king said, 'This knowledge has never been given to a *brāhmin*. It has always remained with *kshatriyas*. Even then I'll tell you because you are eager to know'.

'The heaven is a kind of scrificial fire. The sun is its fuel, for the heaven shines when fed by the sun's rays. The rays of the sun are like smoke arising from fire. The day is like the flames because of its brightness. The moon is like coals because it glows in the dark as coals do. The stars round it are like sparks. In this fire the gods offer faith as libation. Out of that offering King Moon is born. The god of rain is the sacrificial fire, the air fuel, the cloud smoke, lightning flames, thunder coals and thundering the sparks. The gods offer King Moon as oblation in this and of that offering, rain is born. The earth is fire, the year fuel, space smoke, night the flame, the points of the compass coals, and the intermediate directions, sparks. The gods offer rain as libation in this fire, and from this food arises. Man is the fire, speech fuel, breath smoke, the tongue the flame, eyes coals and ears sparks. In this fire the gods offer food as libation from which semen arises. Woman is the fire, the sex-organs, fuel, the yearning for sex, smoke, the vulva, the flame, the copulation, coals, and the pleasures of lovemaking, sparks. The gods offer semen as libation in this fire and out of that offering the foetus is formed.

'In this way, Gautama', Jaivali said, 'does water come to be called man in the fifth libation. The human foetus lies enclosed in its membrane for nine months or ten, and then emerges as a child. Having been born, the man lives so long as his span of life may be, and when he is dead they carry him to the fire in which he is cremated. Thus from fire he arises and to fire returns.

[*Chhāndogya Upanishad.* Chapter 5, sections 3 to 9. Translation author's in *The Wisdom of the Upanishads. New Delhi : Sterling Publishers.*

THE ORIGIN OF THE UNIVERSE

Those who wish to know about *brahman* ask the following questions : What is the cause of this universe? From where does man come? By what does he live? Where does he go after death? Who distributes joys and sorrows to men? People give various answers. Some say it is time which is responsible for it, others that it is nature or necessity and some think it is chance which governs all. Some think the elements cause all this to happen, others that is is the soul. These act separately, or all together, they say. They are all wrong. How can these act by themselves? Nor can the soul be responsible, for the soul itself experiences the consequence of good and evil deeds.

The sages found, after meditating on these matters that it was God who directs all this. The sages pondered on God from whom this universe proceeds. It is he who makes existence which is shaped as a wheel. The rim of this wheel is illusion, and the vanity of works, whether good or bad, is the moving force which keeps the wheel of existence ever revolving. The wheel moves on three roads – right, wrong and knowledge. It has three tyres, sixteen ends, fifty spokes. twenty counter-spokes, six sets of eight and one rope of many strands.[191]

[*Shvetāshvatara Upanishad.* 1. 1–4].

191. The wheel = God or Īshvara, the rim the world the three tyres = the three *guṇas* (qualities). The sixteen ends = the sixteen products of the Sāṁkhya philosophy (the eleven organs and the five elements). The fifty spokes are ignorance, self-love, love, hate and fears the twenty-eight disabilities which cause misconception, the nine satisfactions and the eight perfections (*siddhīs*). The counter-spokes are the ten senses and the ten objects. The six sets of eight are the eight each of psychic powers, mental states, super-human beings and the soul's virtues. The rope of many strands is love or desire for food, for children, heaven or anything else.

GOD AND THE COSMIC PROCESS

There are some deluded men who think it is Nature which is the working force of existence and its Controller. Others thinks it is Time. They do not know how wrong they are, for it's neither Nature not Time. The Controller of existence is really God. He pervades the entire universe. He is the Knower of Time and the Lord of the *guṇas* (qualities). He is pure consciousness. It is at his behest that creation proceeds and the creatures formed of earth, water, fire air and ether exist. After setting the universe into motion, he withdraws from it. He unites both spirit and matter with one, two, three and eight.[192] No one sees his unseen hand behind the world process.

God starts creation with the interplay of the *guṇas*. When their motive power is exhausted, he destroys it. He stands apart from it all. He is the beginning of everything, the one who unites the soul and the body, beyond Time – the past, present and the future. One attains *moksha* by worshipping that Lord of many forms, and the source of all. God is both beyond Time and existence. He is other than the world's mover. He is the Lord of bliss dwelling in the soul, the immortal and the support of all. He brings good and removes evil.[193]

We should know him as the supreme Lord of lords, the supreme God above the gods, Ruler of rulers, transcendent, imperishable and the Master of the universe. There is nothing left for him to achieve, no act to be performed. No one is equal to him or his superior. He has all power, knowledge, strength and action. No one is his master or ruler, and there is no sign by which his existence can be inferred. He is the cause of all and the Ruler of all souls. He has neither

192. According to Swāmi Tyāgīshānanda, 'one' means ignorance; 'two' *dharmā* (righteousness), and unrighteousness; 'three' the three bodies – the physical, subtle and causal; and eight the eightfold aspect of Nature, namely the five elements, mind, intellect and the I-sense. (Shri Ramakrishna Math, Mylapore, Madras).

193. Compare Tennyson's : 'Oh yet we trust that somehow good will be the final goal of ill.' (*In Memoriam*).

an overlord nor parents. He weaves existence from his own Self as a spider makes the web, and he again absorbs it into himself as the spider draws back the threads of its web into its navel.

The one God inhabits all souls. He pervades all and ordains all deeds. All beings reside in him. He is the Witness, pure consciousness and unaffected by the *guṇas*. He controls all and makes the One manifold. He only is happy who knows him as residing in the soul. He is the Eternal Soul, the intelligence of all that is intelligent, the One who grants all desires. He is realized by the Sāṁkhya and Yoga philosophies. All fetters are removed when he is known.

When he (*brahman*) shines, then only the sun and the moon and the stars shine, not to speak of the lesser lights and the fire. It is God's light which lights them. This Universal Soul dwells in the world like a swan in a lake and as fire on the waters. One can only overcome death by knowing him. There is no other way to do so.

He is the creator and the Knower. He is his own source. He is the All-knowing, destroyer of time and full of goodness. He is the Lord or the sciences, matter, spirit and qualities and the cause of both liberation and bondage. He becomes nature and existence, but remains immortal. He is Lord, Knower, ever-present and the world's Protector. He is the world's eternal Ruler. They who seek liberation, take refuge in him. . . who is partless and actionless, tranquil, faultless, taintless and the highest bridge to immortality; who is like a fire, burning even after its fuel is consumed.[194] It is as futile to end misery without God-realization as for a man to try to roll up the sky as though it was a piece of skin.

[From *Shvetāshvatara Upanishad.* 6.]

194. Compare God's appearance to Moses at Mount Sinai 'and behold the bush burned with fire, and the bush was not consumed.' (*Exodus* 3:2).

(G) FROM THE RĀMACHARITAMĀNASA

What The Rāmacharitamānasa Is About

THE BEAUTY OF TULSĪDĀSA'S LANGUAGE

The *Rāmacharitamānasa* was written by Goswami Tulsīdāsa (1497, or as some believe, 1533,–1624), in the year 1571 at Ayodhyā. The language used is Avadhī, the Hindi dialect spoken in Avadh (Oudh). While the *Mahābhārata* depicts life as it is, the *Rāmāyaṇa* depict it as it should be. There are many other versions of the *Rāmāyaṇa*. The classical one is that of Vālmīka in Sanskrit. Then there is the *Adhyātma Rāmāyaṇa*, also in Sanskrit which incorporates the *advaita* viewpoint, i.e., monism or God as *brahman*. Others are the *Kamban Rāmāyaṇa* in Tamil and the *Krittibāsa* in Bengali. The *Rāmāyaṇa* is known in China, and from Cambodia to Java. It has been translated into the various Indian regional languages, such as Kannada, Kashmiri, Telgu and Malyam. There are versions in English, Latin, French and Italian, and it is considered to be one of the world's classics. The metres used by Tulsī are *doha, soraṭā* (inverted *dohā*), *chaupāi*, *tomara* and *shlokas* (wherever there is Sanskrit). The *Rāmacharitamānasa* it the most popular version of of the Rāma story. Its language is simple but its poetic and literary qualities are supreme. The hymns in it are so musical that they have been sung by prominent singers like Mukesh. In its sacredness for Hindus it is next only to the *Gītā*. Though Tulsī says, swears, even, that his verse has not a single poetic device : *kabit vibek ēk nahiṁ moreṁ/satya kahauṁ likhi kāgad koreṁ*, there is hardly any poetic art which he hasn't used—variations in metrical stanzas, metaphors, similes, attiteration and so forth. Three examples of his felicitious comparisons are given.

1. The treachery of deceit—'See the charming nature of friendship! Water sells at thc price of milk when mixed with it. But the moment the sourness (of guile) is cast in it the two separate'.

2. Sītā is languishing in the Ashoka-vāṭikā where Rāvaṇa has kept her captive. Hanumān (the monkey-god) visits her secretly there. She narrates her miserable plight and asks him to tell Rāma : 'I do admit one fault of mine. Why didn't I die the moment I parted from you, (i.e., from Rāma). But, O lord, in truth it's my eyes which are the culprit, for it is because of them my soul does not depart. Separation is like the fire, my body is like cotton and my breath is as the wind. The fire of separation can burn up my body all in a moment. But my eyes so yearn to see you that they constantly keep raining tears, and so prevent me from being burnt'. (*Sundara–kāṇḍa*).

3. 'There are three kinds of persons in this world, comparable to a rose tree, a mango tree and a jackfruit tree. The rose tree has flowers only, the mango tree has both flowers and fruit, while the jackfruit tree has fruit. Even so, there is one kind of men who say but do not do as they say; others who do what they say; and yet others who do, but do not boast of what they do'. (*Lankā–kāṇḍa*).

These are just a few examples. The *Rāmacharitamānasa* is a treasure-house of poetic and philosophical passages.

The book places emphasis on devotion. This devotional aspect places Tulsī's version quite apart from the others. 'May Rāma be dear to me' says Tulsī, 'as a girl to a lustful man, or wealth to one greedy'. (*Uttara–kāṇḍa*). Then again, 'I seek neither wealth (*artha*), nor *dharma* (righteousness), nor the pleasures of the senses (*kāma*); devotion to the feet of Rāma, life after life, is the only boon I seek'. (*Ayodhyā–kāṇḍa*).

Through his characters, which are very much lifelike, Tulsī shows how men and women ought to conduct themselves – husband and wife, brother and brother, sister and brother, father and son and so forth. He provides a kind of code of ideal behaviour. But he does it very subtly, just by the interplay of his characters. Ethics and philosophy are cleverly interwoven with the story without seeming glaringly didactic.

THE CHAPTERS OF THE RĀMACHARITAMĀNASA

There are seven chapters in the *Rāmāyaṇa* :

1. *Bāla-kāṇḍa*. The Boyhood of Rāma.
2. *Ayodhyā-kāṇḍa*. The Events at Ayodhyā and the Banishment of Rāma following the intrigues of Mantharā.
3. *Araṇya-kāṇḍa*. 'The forest section'. Rāma's life in the forest. His hermitage at Panchavaṭī. The carrying off the Sītā by Rāvaṇa, the demon-king of Lankā.
4. *Kishkindhyā–kāṇḍa*. Rāma's residence at Kishkindhyā, the capital of king Sugrīva. His alliance with Sugrīva. The meeting with Hanumān, the Wind-god.
5. *Sundara-kāṇḍa*. 'The Book of Beauty'. The crossing over the ocean by building a bridge across it, by Rāma's army. Arrival in Lankā.
6. *Lankā-kāṇḍa*. 'The Book of Lankā'. The rival armies of Rāma and Rāvaṇa face each other. The battle resulting in the death (slaying) of Rāvaṇa. Sītā is freed. Her ordeal by fire. Rāma and his party return to Ayodhyā after his victory.
7. *Uttara-kāṇḍa*. 'The Book of the North'. The welcome accorded to Rāma at Ayodhyā. His coronation. Rāma Rājya, the kingdom of Rāma. His discourse on the nature of saints and evil persons. Vibhīshaṇa and the monkey-warriors return to Lankā. Hymns of Shiva and of the Vedas in praise of Rāma. Rāma's sermon.

A SYNOPSIS OF THE RĀMA-STORY

BIRTH AND THE BOYHOOD

The demons, led by Rāvaṇa, their king, began to oppress sages and virtuous people. Evil spread on the earth. Men began to covet the wealth and the wives of others. They would neither respect their parents, nor revere the gods.

The Earth took the form of a cow and went to Brahmā, the Creator, to acquaint him with its troubles. He advised it to go to Lord Vishṇu. 'He knows your sorrows', he said, 'and will surely remove them'. Vishṇu said 'Don't fear, I will take a human form and be born in the family of Raghuvanshīs. I will slay the demons and restore peace on earth'.

Dashrath, of the race of Raghus (Raghuvanshī) was king of Ayodhyā. He was a virtuous ruler, and there was peace and prosperity in his kingdom. But he was sad because he had no son. He consulted his family priest, Vasishṭha, who advised him to carry out a sacrifice (*yajña*). When the *yajña* was performed, Agni, the Fire-god, came out of the sacrificial fire with a pot of celestial *khīra* (milk-and-rice pudding). 'Give this to your queens to eat' he said. 'They will bear you sons'. The king gave half of the *khīra* to his queen Kaushalyā, and a quarter each to his other two wives, Kaikeyī and Sumitrā. In course of time Kaushalyā gave birth to Rāma. He was born with the divine form of Vishṇu, but seeing his mother frightened, and on her entreaty, he assumed the form of a newborn baby. Kaikeyī gave birth to Bharata and Sumitrā had twins, Lakshmaṇa and Shatrughana. The brothers loved one another very much, but Lakshmaṇa was particularly devoted to Ramā and Shatrughana to Bharata. They were trained in the use of arms and taught the way of *dharma* (righteousness).

One day the sage Vishwāmitrā came to Ayodhyā to seek Rāma's help in overcoming the demons who were sorely vexing the sages and holy men. Rāma was a mere stripling and so Dashrath was loath to send him on so hazardous a mission. But Vasishṭha assured him that no harm could come to him. Rāma, and Lakshmaṇa his brother, went to Vishwāmitra's hermitage. There Rāma slew the female demon Tarakā, though after a great deal of persuasion, as he hesitated to slay a woman. He killed other demons too, and one of them, Mārīcha, at whom he shot a blunt arrow, fell 1,600 miles away! The sages were able to continue their *yajñas* in peace thereafter. Vishwāmitra gave many celestial weapons to Rāma, which proved a great asset later on in the war with Rāvaṇa.

THE MARRIAGE OF RĀMA WITH SĪTA

Janaka was king of Mithilā. He had a lovely daughter, Sītā, whom he wanted to give away in marriage. Many suitors were invited from distant places. The condition was that he who could break Shiva's mighty bow would wed her. Vishwāmitra heard about this, and took Rāma and Lakshmaṇa to Mithilā. None of the warriors could even lift the bow, much less string it. Seeing this, king Janaka bemoaned that his daughter would remain unmarried. 'Shame on you all!' he exclaimed. 'Is the world bereft of warriors'. Then Vasishṭha, who had accompanied the brothers, said to Rāma, 'Go, and remove Janaka's grief'. Rāma bowed to the sage and went to where the bow was. As soon as he lifted it, lo! it got stringed of itself and broke in two with a deafening noise. There was great rejoicing, which however, was soon cut short by the arrival of Parashurāma a sage who was a devotee of Shiva. When he saw Shiva's bow lying snapped in two, he was filled with rage. There ensued a heated exchange of words between him and Lakshmaṇa. Rāma tried his best to assuage Parashurāma's anger, but when he found him irascibility incurable he said 'One who has taken birth as a *kshatriya* (warrior) never turns his back on battle. It's not a boast, but I say it as a fact, that Raghuvashīs will even fight Death if he throws a challenge'. Parusharāma suddenly recollected that Lord Vishṇu was to incarnate just at this time. Could it be that Rāma was the person in whom he had incarnated ? He gave his own bow to Rāma and said 'Rama, string this bow and remove my doubt'. The bow belonged to Vishṇu and could be stringed by him, or his incarnation only. As soon as Rāma touched the bow it stringed of itself. Parusharāma was repentant. He sang a hymn in praise of Rāma, and went away. Sītā was married to Rāma amid grand festivities. His three brothers were married to a sister and two cousins of Sītā.

THE FOURTEEN YEAR'S EXILE

One day Dashrath noticed that he was greying on the temples. He called Vasishṭha, the family priest, and said 'I am growing old I feel I should declare Rāma as the heir apparent and leave the kingdom to him'. Vasishṭha lauded the proposal and preparations were made to crown Rāma as king of Ayodhyā.

There was a maidservant, Mantharā, a hunchback, who was Kaikeyī's favourite. She wasn't happy at the turn of events, and brainwashed her to get Bharata installed as king instead of Ramā. Bharata was not in Ayodhyā at that time. Once king Dashrath had given two boons to Kaikeyī, who was his most beloved wife. But he had forgotten all about it and she too had never mentioned them. Now, instigated by Mantharā, she asked him for these two boons, after making the king promise that he would abide by them. She asked that Bharata, her son, be crowned king, and Rāma sent away to the forest to live as a hermit for fourteen years. Dashrath was deeply grieved, for life for him without Rāma was impossible. But he could not break his word. Rāma, Lakshmaṇa and Sītā put on the clothes of hermits and left for the forest.

On the way they were welcomed by Nishāda, a low-caste chief but a devotee. Rāma blessed him and accepted his hospitality. They were rowed across the river Saryu by Kēwaṭ, another low-caste devotee of Rāma. Rāma gave him the blessed gift of devotion. During his wanderings in the forest, they visited many divine sages. Finally the three made Panchavaṭī, by the Godāvarī river their home for the period of the exile.

At Ayodhyā, Dashrath could not bear the grief of parting from Rāma, and died with the name of Rāma on his lips. When Bharata returned to Ayodhyā, he was distressed to learn about his father's death and Rāma's exile. He spoke very hashly to his mother, Kaikeyī, upbraiding her for her villany, and refused to even go to her apartment. Along with a retinue, he went to visit Rāma in his forest abode, hoping to persuade him to return and take his rightful place as Ayodhyā's king. But Rāma politely declined, as that would mean breaking his father's word. Bharata had to return disappointed. However, he reverently carried Rāma's sandals on his head and placing them in a cottage on the outskirts of the city, he would first worship them and then carry out the duties of state.

Wasting with grief on being parted from Rāma, he thus acted as his brother's regent, awaiting his return from the long period of exile.

RĀVAṆA CARRIES OFF SĪTĀ

Rāvaṇa, king of the demons, ruled in Lankā. His sister, Sūrphanakhā, learnt about Ramā's arrival at Panchavaṭī. She went to visit him, and on seeing him instantly got enamoured of him. Rāma evaded her advances. She got enraged and attacked Sītā. Lakshmaṇa cut off her nose with his sword. In order to avenge herself she brought her brothers Khara and Dūshaṇa along with an army of demons to slay the brothers and Sītā. But they were all killed by Rāma. Then she went to Rāvaṇa and related her plight. She extolled Sītā's beauty, and asked him to carry her away and bring her to Lankā. Rāvaṇa thought of a stratagem. He went to Mārīcha and asked him to take the form of a golden deer in order to lure Rāma in pursuit of him. While Rāma chased the 'deer' he himself would carry Sītā away. Mārīcha wasn't happy about this for he knew it meant certain death for him. But Rāvaṇa threatened to slay him if he did not do his bidding. It is better to be killed by the divine Rāma, he thought, than to die the hands of this demon. So he agreed to the plan.

Sītā saw the lovely golden deer and urged Rāma to bring her its skin. Rāma left her in charge of Lakshmaṇa and went after the elusive deer. It was only after a long chase that he could shoot it. Mārīcha loudly called out 'Ah, Lakshmaṇ!' and died. Rāma was amazed to see Mārīcha lying dead before him. Meanwhile Mārīcha's cries were heard by Sītā, and she feared that Rāma had come to grief. Lakshmaṇa's assurances did not satisfy her and she spoke some unsavoury words to him. So he left, leaving her in the care of the spirits of the forest. After he had gone, Rāvaṇa came there in the form of a mendicant and asked her for alms. When she came out of the cottage with alms, he assumed his real form and seizing her, took her away on his flying-chariot (*vimāna*), which was nearby.

THE SEARCH FOR SĪTĀ

When Rāmā saw Mārīcha lying dead instead of the deer, he suspected foul play. He hurried back and on the way Lakshmaṇa met him. That unnerved him even more, for Sīta was alone in the cottage. When the brothers reached the cottage they found her gone. Rāma was beside himself with grief. So much so that he wandered about asking the trees and plants if they had seen Sitā! After a great deal of search they came across Jaṭāyū, the king of the eagles. He was grievously wounded, as he had fought with Rāvaṇa to rescue Sītā. Before dying he told them that the demon-king had carried her off. The search for Sītā was resumed. The brothers saw a headless monster, Kabanḍa, whose disembodied spirit counselled Rāma to seek the aid of Sugrīva, king of the monkeys. Accordingly the brothers met him, and Rāma assisted him in recovering Kishkindhyā, his capital, from his brother Bāli, who had usurped it. Rāmā also met Hanumān, the Wind-god who became his ardent devotee and constant helper. Groups of monkey-warriors (who, as we have said, were gods in disguise), were sent to find out the whereabouts of Sītā. Hanumān headed one such group. He found out that she was held captive in Rāvaṇa's palace-garden. But that was across the ocean. However, he managed to leap across the ocean and, after overcoming some obstacles on his flight, reached Sītā. He comforted her and assured her that Rāma would soon come with his army and rescue her. He also ravaged Rāvaṇa's garden, killing one of his brothers who was sent to capture him. Ultimately Meghnād, Rāvaṇa's son, brought him bound before the demon-king. It was decided to set fire to Hanuman's tail as a punishment. As soon as they put it on fire, he went round the city burning up most of it with his lighted tail. Then, after taking leave of Sītā, he flew back and broke the happy news to Rāma.

THE BATTLE BETWEEN RĀMA AND RĀVAṆA

Rāma's army advanced toward Lankā. The problem however was how to bridge the ocean so that it could get across. Rāma decided to first pray to the Ocean-god to allow it to get across. But even after the three days the Ocean would not stir. Then Rama said, 'It is only fear which can create love, it seems. Fetch my bow so that I may dry up the Ocean'. Seeing Rāma ready to discharge the Fire-arrow, the Ocean-god came out and prayed to Rāma. If the Ocean is dried up, he said, the balance in nature will be disturbed and cause great misery to the world. He told Rāma that there were two monkey-brothers in his army, Nala and Nīla. They had the gift of making even heavy rocks float on water. In this way a bridge could be built. While the monkey-warriors were building the bridge, Rāma made a Shiva-*linga* and dedicated it to Lord Shiva (this place, Rāmeshwarama, is a sacred place of pilgrimage even today). Rāma's army went across. Rāma decided to send a peace-messenger to Rāvaṇa, giving him a chance to make peace and return Sītā, before he launched the offensive. Angad, Bāli's son, was sent. But Rāvaṇa would not listen. Angad put his foot on the ground and challenged any of Rāvaṇa's warriors to shift it. None of them, not even Meghnād the mighty warrior who had once captured Indra, the god of heaven, could move Angad's foot. Meanwhile, Rāvaṇa's brother, Vibhīshaṇa who was a devotee of Rāma was insulted by the demon-king. He went over to Rāma's side.

The war began. One of the main warriors on Rāvaṇa's side was his brother, Kumbhakaraṇa. He was a huge demon who slept for six months at one stretch. Then there was Indrajīt (better known as Meghnād), Rāvaṇa's son. The battle was very fierce. At one stage Meghnād bound Rāma with serpent-arrows. But Garuḍa, the king of vultures ate up the snakes and freed him. Them Meghnād shot a *shaktī* (divine weapon) at Lakshmaṇa, which made him fall into a swoon. But he was revived by the life-giving drug *sanjīvanī* which grew on the Himalayas. For this Hanumān fetched Sushēna, Rāvaṇa's physician. Then he flew to the Himalayas and brought the medicinal plant yielding the drug, flying too and fro in just one night. Kumbhakaraṇa was slain by Rāma, and Meghnād by Lakshmaṇa. Finally Rāvaṇa was slain by Rāma after a fierce combat, bringing the battle to an end.

Sītā was rescued. But before she could be accepted, she had to undergo the ordeal by fire. Long back when Rāma had known that she would be carried off by Rāvaṇa, he had summoned Agni, the the Fire-god and given her in his custody. Then he had created a shadow-Sītā, and this was the 'Sītā' whom Rāvaṇa had carried off. So now when the fire was lit, the shadow-Sītā went into it, and Agni handed back the real Sītā to Rāma. That was all the 'ordeal by fire', meant. Rāma, Sītā and Lakshmaṇa along with Vibhishaṇa (who succeeded Rāvaṇa as Lankā's king' and the monkey-warriors flew away to Ayodhyā on the *vimāna* (flying-chariot). The fourteen years exile were over. Bharata, who had been languishing in sorrow, cheered up. Rāma was crowned king of Ayodhyā in a grand ceremony.

READING LIST

Atkins, A.G. *The Ramayana of Tulsidāsa.* Orient Longmans, 1954.

Babenau, E.J. *Love of God and Social Duty in the Rāmacharitmānasa. The Religious views of Tulsidāsa.*

Bulke, C. *Rāma Kathā.* Hindi Parishad Prakashan.

Carpentet, J.N. *The Theology of Tulsidāsa.* Edinburgh, 1930.

Das, S.S. and Badthoae. P. *Goswāmi Tulsidāsa*. Hindustan Academy, 1931.

Grierson, Sir George. *Notes on Tulsidāsa* (on certain portions).

Tulsidāsa, Poet and Religious Reformer.

Journal of the Royal Asiasic Society.

Is the Rāmāyaṇa of Tulsidāsa a Translation?

Growse, F.S. *The Rāmāyaṇa of Tulsidasa.*

Gupta, M. *Goswāmi Tulsidāsa* Indian Press.

Handoo, Chanura Kumari. *Tulsi Dasa.* Orient Longmans, 1964

Hill, Douglas P. *The Holy Lake of the Acts of Rama*.

Macfie, J.M. *The Ramayana of Tulsidasa.* Edinburgh. T and T Clarks, 1930.

Macdougale, William Charles. *The Way of Salvation in The Ramayana of Tulsidasa.* The University of Chicago, 1926.

Misra, B.P. *Tulsi Darshan.* Hindu Sahitya Sammelan, 1938.

Ram, S. *The Originality of the Ramayana of Tulsidasa.* Journal of the Royal Asiatic Society, 1914.

Shastri, S. *Index Verborum to the Tulsi Ramayana.* Gita Press.

Tessitore, L.P Rama Charit Manasa eil Ramayana. Journal della Societa Asicalica Italiana 1911–12.

Vaudevilla, C. *Etude sur les sources et la composition du Ramayana de Tulsidas.* Paris Librarorie.

Le problime de la composition du Ramayana Tulsidas. 1935.

Whaling, Frank. *The Rise of the Religious Significance of Rama.*

THE GLORY OF THE NAME OF RĀMA

Tulsidāsa says : I worship the lotus-feet of Jānakījī (Sītā), daughter of king Janaka, and the beloved of Shrī Rāmachandra who is the abode of mercy and compassion. She is the Mother of the world. May she, in her kindness, bestow serene wisdom on me. I bow to the glorious lotus-feet Shrī Raghunātha (Rāma), adoring him through mind, speech and works. I bow to that lotus-eyed wielder of the bow who gives his devotees happiness and removes their suffering. I bow to the feet of both Rāma and Sītā by whom the poor and the grieved are greatly loved. As the wave and the water from which it arises, the word and its meaning are different in name only, but are really inseparable, so too are Sītā and Rāma. I adore Rāma who is the source of fire, of the moon and of the sun. He is Brahmā, he is Vishṇu he is Mahesh. He is the life-breath of the Vedas. He is formless, incomparable and the storehouse of virtue. His name is greatly sacred. Shiva himself chants it. Through it those who die in Kāshī (Varansi) are freed from the cycle of birth and death. The glory of Rāma's name is kown to Shrī Gaṇesha, who, because of it is worshipped before other gods.[195] The ancient poet, Vālamīka, knew the greatness of Rāma's name. He was purified even though he repeated it, reversing the syllables.[196] Pārvatī heard from her lord that taking the name of Rāma

195. There's a legend about this. Once Lord Brahmā asked the gods who among them was worthy of being worshipped first. Each one put forward his claim. So Brahmā said he would be worthy of this honour who could go round the three worlds in the quickest time. Everyone went off. But Gaṇesha's vehicle was a mouse so, of course, he'd be the slowest. He sat down disheartened. Just then Nārada came. Learning about it he said, Rāma is lord of the three worlds. So just write his name and go round it. Gaṇesha did just that. ho! on the journey wherever the gods went, they found the mouse's foot- prints. Thus they discovered that Gaṇesha had outdistanced all of them. Thus by the glory of Rāma's name Gaṇesha won the place of honour. All worship and everything auspicious is done by first taking Gaṇesha's name.

196. Vālmīka was initially a dacoit. He would kill wayfarers and loot their property, not sparing even *brāhmins*. Once the *Saptarishīs* came that way. He was about to lay his hands on them too, but he came to know their true identity just in time. They asked him to expiate his sins by chanting Rāma's name. Vālmika could not utter it despite all efforts. So he chanted 'Marā' (lit., 'dead'). Even that made him a great saint.

even once is like chanting all other sacred names many times. She keeps chanting Rāma's along with that of Shiva.[197]

Seeing Pārvatī's great devotion to Rāma's name, Shiva united her with himself. It was Shiva who drank the poison before the rising of the nectar from the ocean which was churned by the gods and the demons. He could do so only by the power of Rāma's name. Says Tulsī, devotion to Rāma is like the rainy season. The devotees who reap its benefit are like grain and the two syllables forming the name of Rāma, namely '*rā*' and '*ma*' are like the lovely months of Sāvan and Bhādom.[198] Both the words (*rā* and *ma*) are sweet and pleasing. They are the eyes of wisdom, the very life of devotees, and are meditated on with ease. They yield great happiness. Both this world and the other is blessed for those who chant it. They are melodious in chanting, hearing and thinking about.

Tulsī says, they are beloved to me as Rāma and Lakshmaṇa. These syllables are inseparable even as *Brahman* and *jīva* (the embodied soul). They are like Nara and Nārāyaṇa, the two lovely brothers (i.e. the devotee and God). They nourish the world and protect the devotees. They are as the lovely flower-shaped ear-ornaments of charming women, and the moon and the sun showering their benediction on the earth. They are like nectar-giving emancipation and are the supporters of the world like Shesha and Kachchhapa.[199] They are like bumble-bees hovering in the lotus-like hearts of devotees, and like Krishṇa and Balarāma for their doting foster-mother, Yashodā.

---

197. Pārvatī was a Vishṇu-devotee. She used to chant his name a hundred at meals. She sent word that she was chanting Vishṇu's name, and when she had chanted it a hundred times she'd come. Shiva asked the messenger to tell her that chanting 'Rāma' once was equivalent to chanting Vishṇu's name a hundred times. So she ought to come rightaway after saying 'Rāma' once.

198. Sāvan and Bhādoṁ are the fifth and sixth months of the Hindu calendar. They are the months of the greatest rainfall. Sāvan corresponds to July–August and Bhādoṁ to August–September. Coming after the sizzling heat of summer, the rains are most cooling. Many Sanskrit and Hindi poets like Kālidāsa and others have sung of the beauty of the rainy season.

199. Shesha (the serpent with a thousand heads) and Kachchhapa (the Tortoise) are believed, in Hindu mythology, to support the earth.

Says Tulsī, these two letters which form the name of Rāma, yield great splendour. They are the chief among letters even as the jewelled umbrella and the crown are insignias of kings.

[*Bāla-kaṇḍa.* Invocation. vs. 17 (4) to 20 (Gītā Press edition)].

THE FIRST MEETING OF SĪTĀ AND RĀMA

[King Janaka of Mithilā was a powerful ruler. He was also very wise and was considered to be a sage even while ruling over his kingdom, fulfilling Plato's ideal of kings being philosophers and philosophers kings. He was holding a swayamvara (a show of skill or strength at which the winner wed the woman). This one was for the marriage of his daughter, Sītā, and the condition was rather hard, for the suitor had to break the mightly bow of Shiva. The sage Vishvāmitra took Rāma and Lakshmaṇa to Mithila. Sītā, accompanied by her friends (sakhīs), had gone to worship Gaurī (Devī) before the swayamvara. On her return they happened to see the two princes who were strolling in the garden just then. Here is Tulsī's narration of the meeting between Sītā and Rāma].

One of Sītā's friends strayed into the garden to have a stroll. Her gaze fell upon Rāma and Lakshmaṇa and, struck by their beauty, she hastened to tell Sītā about them. When her companions saw her hair bristle and tears of joy coursing down her cheeks, they said, 'Dear, what makes you feel so elated?' 'Two young princes have come to see the garden' she said. 'How can I tell of their charm? My eyes have seen them, but they can't speak. And my tongue can't speak of it for it has not seen them,. All of them rejoiced to hear about the princes, and Sītā could hardly conceal her delight. One of her companions said, 'They must be the same princes, who, I am told, have come with the sage, Vishvāmitra. All those who have seen them are charmed by their splendour. They don't tire speaking of it. Let's all go and have a look at them'.

Sītā rejoiced, her eyes were restless for their sight
Her companions led, she followed.
Who can know whose love lies embedded in one's heart?
Remembering Nārada's words, she was enraptured
And stood frozen like a frightened deer, her eyes searching for Rāma.[200]
When Rāma heard the tinkle of bangles and anklets and the jingle of waist-ornament bells
He was all ears and said, 'Lakshmaṇa, it seems to me
Kāma is out to subdue the world
And is proclaiming his resolve by beating his drum'.

Saying this he looked that way and saw Sītā
His eyes were *chakor* birds gazing on the moon of her face[201]

---

200. Once the sage Nārada undertook austerities which made Indra jealous. He sent Kāma (the love-god) to disturb the sage, but Kāma had no effect on him. Nārada boasted about this to Vishṇu. To cure him of his vanity, the Lord created an illusory city whose king had a lovely daughter, Vishvamohinī. Nārada got infatuted with her. Vishṇu gave Nārada an ugly form with a monkey's face. When Vishvamohinī saw him thus, she was disgusted. Vishṇu too went there taking a *brāhmin's* form. The girl chose him. In his rage Nārada, who saw his face in a pool and was aghast, cursed Vishṇu. He said that the Lord would have to be born on the earth and he too would be estranged from Sītā (Lakshmī). So it happened. Therefore when Sītā saw Rāma she recollected the sage's curse and knew that Rāma was no other than her lord, Vishṇu. The story is told in the *Mānasa* in a different portion of it.

201. The *chakor* is the Indian red-legged partridge, which, according to Hindu poetical imagery subsists only on the nectar drawn from the moon. So it keeps steadily gazing at the moon. The female of the *chakor* is the *chakorī*.

They gazed and gazed at each other steadily;
It was as though the ancestor of Janaka being abashed,
left the eyes, so that the eyelids could not close![202]
Enraptured, Rāma gazed on Sītā's face
His tongue could not speak out his heart's delight
Her loveliness was matchless; 'twas as though
Brahmā, with all his skill had revealed the world.
She made Beauty beauteous, her blazing splendour
Lit up each corner of Beauty's mansion :
The poets have made all comparisons stale
With what shall I compare Janaka's pretty daughter?
Thus rapt in Sītā's loveliness and in his own enchantment,
Mindful of time and place, Rāma said to Lakshmaṇa
'This girl who's going about showering splendour on
the garden
Is the one for whom the *swayamvara* is being held,
Her companions have brought her here to worship
the goddess;
God alone knows why my serene mind
Is agitated so on seeing her heavenly beauty,
But, dear brother, it's an auspicious moment
For the right side of my limbs is throbbing.
A Raghuvanshī can never depart from virtue,

---

202 Is is believed that the ancestor of king Janaka, Nim resides in the eyes of all persons. When he saw Sītā and her future husband gazing at each other shamelessly, he was abashed and left the eyes, so that the eyelids could not close. Nim (or Nimi) was Janaka's ancestor and the founder of his dynasty. He was the twelfth son of Iksvāku, and founded the city of Vaijanta. He wished to perform a sacrifice and invited Vasistha as priest to preside. But Vasistha was late as he had been called by Indra at a sacrifice at the same time. So Nimi asked Gautama to take his place. When Vasistha arrived he found the sacrifice was over. In his rage he coursed Nimi to die. Nimi too coursed the sage. Vasistha, however was reborn. Nimi wasn't, but he had to reside in the eyes of all beings. Thus he ever resides in everyone's eyes and his presence causes them to open and close.

I can't even dream of looking on another woman.
Such faultless people are rare indeed
Who never turn away from the field of battle
Whose heart and gaze a woman can't ensnare
And from whose door a hermit ne'er goes empty-handed'.
Thus Rāma spoke on, but his mind was with Sītā,
His eyes drank in her loveliness
As as bumble-bee sucks the nectar from a lotus.
Sītā's avid eyes searched for him in the foliage
Where'er the gaze of that deer-eyed beauty fell
It seemed a row of white lotuses sprang.
Then Sītā's friends pointing to a creeper said
'There are those princes, the dark one and the fair'.
She looked and slaked the thirst of her greedy eyes,
Rejoicing as one who has found a treasure.
Seeing Rāma's beauty her glance remained transfixed
Her eyelids forgot to close; thrilled with love
She was like a *chakorī* staring at the autumn moon
Her eyes were as a doorway through which his form
Entered, and was enshrined in her heart;
Her eyelids were as doors with which, when she closed her eyes
She kept his image imprisoned within them.
When her companions saw her lost in love
They were abashed and could not say a word.
At that moment the princes emerged from the bower
Each as the lovely moon from within the clouds,
Their splendour was matchless, their body's sheen
Was like two dazzling lotuses', blue and yellow;
Their heads adorned with peacock's feathers
In which bunches of flowers were entwined

Tilak marks on their brows, lovely ear-ornaments[203]
Their limbs resplendent with drops of sweat,
Arched eyebrows and curly hair,
Eyes bright as pink new-blossomed lotuses,
Lovely chin, nose and cheeks, winning smile;
Words fail to speak of the splendour of their faces
Putting to shame even the god of Love.
A garland of gems on bosom, conch-shaped lovely neck
Strong arms, shapely as the trunks of young elephants
Choisest blossoms held in their left hands.[204]
One of Sītā's companions pointed to Rāma and said
'Friends, see that dark prince of beauty unsurpassed'.
When they saw the slender-waisted Rāma clad in yellow
silk,
Of unspeakable splendour and gentleness,
The pride of the Sūrya race, they were beside themselves.

One of Sītā's friends gently took her by the hand and said 'Have a good look at the princes while they are there, you may meditate on the goddess later'. Then Sītā shyly opened her eyes [which she had tull now kept closed, thinking all the while on Rāma]. She gazed on Rāma's lovely form from head to foot, and remembering the stern task [of breaking Shiva's bow] which her father had put as a pre-condition for her marriage, she became sad, thinking how could this tender lad break that mighty bow! When her companions saw her overcome with love, they feared Sītā might linger long there. One of them smilingly said to her 'It's about time we left. We'll come at this same hour another day, so you'll be able to see him again'. Sītā was abashed. She thought her mother would wonder what kept he so long, and her father might

203. A vertical mark on the middle of the forehead. Here, a kind of adornment.

204. The princes had plucked these flowers after taking the gardener's permission.

get anxious. So, consooling her mind, she left, Rāma's form embedded in her heart. She would keep turning back, pretending to look at the birds, beasts and trees of the woods, steal glances at Rāma. The more she looked on him, the more her love increased. She kept thinking of the massive bow of Shiva. How could that tender prince break it! The thought saddened her but she remembered Rāma's great might and felt relieved. She went along rapt in him. It was as though she had painted his picture on the canvas of her heart with the oil-paint of her deep love. Thus thinking of Rāma, Sītā went again to the Gaurī temple and clasping her hands prayed to the goddess.[205]

O Daughter of Himāchala who ever gaze
On Shiva's face as the *chakorī* on the moon
O Mother of elephant-headed Gaṇesha[206]
And of six-mouthed Kārttikeya[207]
O shining goddess of billiant face
O Mother of the earth, I seek you refuge.
You have no beginning, end or middle
Even the Vedas cannot know you.

205. Sītā had been once before to the temple. But then she had asked the goddess to give her a handsome husband—*nij anurūpa subhag baru māgā* (227 : 3). But now she had seen Rāma. So she went again to pray to the goddess to give her Rāma as her husband. Her prayer this time was for a specific person.

206. Gaṇesha is the son of Shiva and Pārvatī, though according to one version he sprang from the surf of Pārvatī's body. The legend about his having an elephant's head occurs in the *Brahma Vaivartta Purāṇa.* According to one account his mother. Pārvatī asked Shani (Saturn) to look at him as she was proud of Gaṇesha's beauty. But she did not take into account the effect of Shani's glance. Gaṇesha's head was reduced to ashes. Brahmā told Pārvatī to replace it with the first head she could find. It was an elephant which was first seen. And so Gaṇesha's head was replaced with that of the elephant.

207. Kāttikeya is the god of war. It is said that Shiva cast his seed in the Gangā and Kārttikeya was produced thereby. He was fostered by the Pleiades (Krittikā) and hence his six heads. Pārvatī, and sometimes Gangā, is believed to be his mother. He is shown as riding on a peacock with a bow in one hand and an arrow in the other.

You create these worlds and all there's in it
You are Preserver and Destroyer too.
You cast the net of *māyā* round the world[208]
Unfettered, you do as you choose.
You are the best of those who look upon
Their husband as their god
Thousands of Sarasvatīs[209] and Sheshas[210]
Can't sing your glorious praise
O Mother, you give what your devotees seek
O wife of Bāna's slayer, the great Shiva,[211]
O giver of the four fruits of life[212]
Gods, men and sages delight
In worshipping your lotus-feet.
O Devī, you dwell in all hearts, you are the All-knowing
So what need is there for me to speak?
With these words Sītā clasped the goddess' feet.
Her love won the Devi's favour,
The image smiled, the garland round it fell,
Sītā reverently touched it with her head.
Her heart o'erflowing with love, the Devī said
Sītā, you will get your heart's desire.

---

208. *Māyā* is the illusory power of the Lord
209. Sarasvatī is Brahmā's wife, and the goddess of speech, learning, the arts and the sciences. She is the inventress of the Sanskrit language.
210. Shesha is king of serpents and of the infernal regions. He is believed to have a thousand heads and is said to support the earth.
211. The word in the text is Tripura. This is the name given to a demon called Bāna, because he got as gift three cities from Shiva, Brahmā and Vishṇu. He was slain by Shiva. His full name is Tripurāsura.
212. The four fruits are the four ends of human life. They are *artha* (honest wealth) *kāma* (sex, which is not illicit), *dharma* (virtue or righteousness) and *moksha* (emancipation).

I truly promise you, you'll wed
Him whose heart has captivated you,
Nārada's words are pure and true.

He whom you crave for, will be yours
Dark-complexioned, handsome, wise;
Abode of mercy, gentle, pure
Your love and nature who doth prize.
With rapture then was Sītā thrilled
To hear the goddess bless her so
Says Tulsī, bowing to her low
She went, her heart with pleasure filled.

[From *Bāla–kāṇḍa* verses 227 (4)–238]

SĪTĀ INSISTS ON GOING WITH RĀMA TO THE FOREST

[Giving heed to the evil counsel of Mantharā, Kaikeyī asked Dashrath to send Rāma to the forest for fourteen years: Bound by his promise, the king had to agree. Rāma was to go alone, but Sītā insisted on going with him. Rāma gave many arguments for not taking her with him, but finding her adamant, he had, at last to agree. The passage depicts vividly the feetings of a wife for her husband]

Rāma found it embarrassing to speak to Sītā in his mother's presence, but there was no way out. O princess, he said, hear my advice without taking it amiss.[213] If you desire your good and mine, do as I say and stay at home. By doing so you will be able to attend to your mother-in-law and your father-in-law. In every way it's good for you to stay. There's no greater *dharma* than revering one's father-in-law and mother-in-law. Whenever my mother is saddened by my remembrance, your will be there to console her by narrating in your sweet voice, stories both old and new. I swear by hundreds of oaths that I wish you to stay here merely for my mother's sake. By obeying me you will effortlessly obtain the reward one gets by the study of the Vedas or by serving one's guru. But if you persist in obstinately disregarding my advice, you will, like the sage, Gālab, king Nahūsha and others, suffer much anguish.[214] Time passes quickly. I'll be back soon after fulfilling my father's words.

---

213. Rāma is speaking to his wife before his mother. So he never calls her by her name. Instead he uses objective forms of address like, 'O lovely woman', 'O beauteous one', 'princes' and so forth.

214. The sage, Gālab, obstinately insisted that Vishvāmitra should take *dakshiṇā* (a kind of gift) even though Vishvāmitra refused to take it. Then Vishvāmitra said, 'All right give me 800 white horses, bright as the sun'. Gālab searched all over, but couldn't find them. He had thus to suffer much distress in his own lifetime.

The story of Nahusha is told in the *Mahābhārata*. He got infatuated by Sachī wife of Indra. Indra, who was in hiding to expiate for some wrongdoing, advised her to pretend to satisfy Nahusha's lust on condition that he came to her on a palanquin borne on the shoulders of the *sapta–rishīs* (seven sages). Eager to reach Sachi soon, Nahusha kicked one of the sages, the great Agastya. The sage cursed him to become a python and live as such for countless years on the earth. **(Footnote contd. on next page)**

O lovely woman, listen to my advice. If, due to love for me, you insist on coming you'll have to face endless troubles. The forest is fearful and cruel. The heat, the cold, the rain and the wind there are terrifying. The pathways are full of stones, prickly grass and thorns. You'll have too walk barefoot. How will your lovely and tender lotus-like feet tread those difficult paths? There are many hills on the way, hard to negotiate, and many rivers, rivulets and drains which are very deep and difficult to cross. Even to look at them makes one tremble with fear. There are numerous frightening mountains, caves and caverns. Wild beasts like bears, wolves, elephants, lions and tigers roam about, their blood-curdling cries striking terror in the heart. You will have to sleep on the ground. Your dress will be the barks of trees. Your food will be roots, fruits and herbs, whenever you can get them. And that won't be always. Demons, who devour human beings roam about the forest too. They assume millions of deceitful forms. The water of the forest is disease-borne and makes on sick. There are so many hardships there that it's difficult even to narrate them, to say nothing of actually facing them. There are deadly serpents in the forest, and fearful birds. Terrifying hordes of demons go about, who carry off men and women. Even dauntless persons fear to tread there and you, O lovely one, are by nature timid. O deer-eyed one, the forest is not for you. Those who hear of you going to the forest will castigate me. Can the female swan reared in the nectar-like waters of the Mānsarovara, ever survive in the salty water of the sea?[215] Will a cuckoo living in a grove of young mango plants look glorious in a forest of thorny shrubs and trees.

The two examples given are appropriate inasmuch as Gālab suffered in his very lifetime and Nahusha in a future life. So too, Sītā had to suffer mentally (as Gālab did) because of Sūrphanakā, Rāvaṇa's sister and during, her stay in the forest. Then she had to suffer in body as well because Rāma made a shadow-form of her, which was the one Rāvaṇa carried away. She had to be parted from Rāma and remain in the care and custody of Agni the Fire-god, till Rāvaṇa's death.

215. The *hamsa* (swan) living in the Mānsarovara (lake) is believed to eat only pearls, and to glide on lotus leaves. Sītā, who lives like a princess in the palace at Ayodhyā has dainty dishes and walks on velvet-carpeted floors. How can she stand the rigours of forest life?

O moon-faced woman, thinking so, you should remain at home? The forest is full of troubles. He who does not heed the good advice of a saint or a teacher, bitterly repents. He will surely come to grief.

Hearing Rāma's gentle and consoling words
Sītā's eyes were filled with tears,
She was distressed by his wise counsel
As a *chakorī* afflicted by the autumnal moon.[216]
Words failed her, the thought of parting
From her beloved made her restless with grief.
Suppressing her tears and calming herself
She touched her mother-in-law's feet
Seeking her pardon for her outspokenness
And said, 'tis true that my beloved lord
Has spoken for my good; but to my mind
There's no greater sorrow in the world
For a wife than separation from her husband.
O lord of my life, Ocean of love, giver of joys,
O heart of my heart, O master of my soul
Without you heaven is like hell to me.
Mother, father, sister, loved brother,
Fond family members, faithful friends,
In-laws, teachers, kinsmen, helpers,
And handsome sons, loving and devoted :
O lord, these, and everything lovely and precious,
Are, without a woman's husband more tormenting
Than the broiling heat of the burning sun.
The world, home, kingdom, domain and wealth,

216. The night of the full moon in autumn is particularly cool and comforting. But the *chakorī* is agitated because her mate, the *chakor*, is not there with her. So she burns with the fire of separation, even though the night is cool.

Yes, even life—are like a house of sorrows
For a woman of her husband bereft.
Pleasures please not, they're a painful disease
Ornaments seem a burden, the world is as hell.
Lord of my life, there's no happiness
Anywhere at all when you are not with me.
As a soulless body, a dried up river
Is a woman, O lord, without her husband.
When I'm with you I'll gaze and gaze
On your face lovely as the autumn moon
And all the world's happiness shall then be mine.
The birds and beasts shall be my family
The forest a city, tree-barks my grand attire
And the humble cottage made of leaves shall be
As pleasure-giving as a palace in heaven.
The spirits of the forest shall care for me
As my in-laws; *kusha* grass and soft new leaves
Of forest trees shall be our bed
Cosier than the touch of the god of Love.
Seeing each moment your lotus-feet
Like the *chakavi* bird I'll remain daylong enraptured,
All the hardships, fears and woes of the forest
Of which you speak, lord, are not e'en a jot
Of the deep anguish of your separation.
Therefore, O beauteous lord, take me with you
What more need I say you are all-merciful
O Knower of hearts, what is there for me to hide?
O friend of the poor, O giver of bliss
O abode of kindness and love, remember this
If you leave me behind I won't survive.
The sight of your lotus-feet will banish all fatigue

O beloved, I'll attend on you in every way
And steal the weariness of the forest path;
I'll sit under the shady trees, I'll lave your feet
With a heart full of gladness I will fan you.
How can grief ever come near me, O lord,
When I see your dark body glistening with sweat?
I'll spread leaves on the level ground and sit
The night through, O beloved, pressing your feet,
I'll not be distressed by the burning breeze
When my eyes dwell each moment on your lovely form.
Who can dare to cast his covetous eyes on me
While you're at my side? Can wolves and hares
Ever look a lioness in the eye?
I'm tender, ha! and you're fit for the forest
The very thought did not break my heart :
It seems to me then that my wretched soul
Will be wrenched away from me when we part.

Having said this, Sītā was agitated beyond measure. The very thought of parting from Rāma was unbearable to her. When Rāma saw the troubled state of her mind, he knew that if he insisted on leaving her behind in Ayodhyā she would surely die. Then the kind-hearted lord of the Raghus[217] said to her, 'Think no more about it and get ready to come with me to the forest. Do not distress youself'.

[From *Ayodhyā–kāṇḍa*. 60–67 (2)]

217. Raghu was a king of the Solar race. According to the Raghuvansha he was the son of Dilīpa. and the great-grandfather of Rāma. Therefore Rāma is known as Rāghava or Raghupati (the chief of the race of the Ragus).

DEVOTION

The pivot of Tulsi's *Rāmayaṇa* is devotion. He himself says that he desires only to worship Rāma's feet life after life. He wants neither wealth, not enjoyments nor *dharma*, nor even *moksha* (emancipation). Various passages and the narration of some of the outstanding devotees of Rāma, are mentioned in the book. Quite a few of the devotees are of the low-castes, the scheduled castes as we now call them. These are, for example, Kewaṭ the boatman, Nishāda, Shabarī and others. Prominent among Rāma-devotees is Hanumān or Māruti, the Wind-god. There are many songs and prayers addressed to him in Hindi devotional music. Tulsi's *Rāmāyaṇa* has many devotional passages. We give here some of them as also the accounts of the meeting of the devotees with Rāma.

Rāma and Kewaṭ

Rāma called Kewaṭ, the boatman, to take him across the Gangā.

Kewaṭ would not bring the boat
He said, I hear the dust of your feet
Gives life by its very touch.
A block of stone became a lovely woman,[218]
My poor boat is of wood
'Twill turn into a sage's wife
And fly away! by this I earn,
'Tis my family's daily bread
I've not other occupation.
If you wish to get across
Let me wash your lotus-feet

218. The reference is to Ahalyā, wife of the sage Gautama. Indra was infatuated by her. He assumed Gautama's form and went to her in the sage's absence. By chance Gautama returned just a few minutes later, when Indra was going out after ravishing Ahalyā. Gautama cursed Indra saying he would become impotent. He also turned Ahalyā into a block of stone, saying she would remain like that till the Lord himself redeemed her. Rāma touched her with his feet and she got back her form and flew to heaven. The incident is narrated in another part of the *Rāmacharitamānasa*.

Then I'll take you, lord, I'll charge
Nothing as the fare; I speak
Truthfully, I swear by you
And I swear by Dashrath too!
Lakshmaṇa may shoot his shaft
And kill me; but, O lord
Till I've washed your hallowed feet
I'll not take you across.
At these words heartfelt and true
Artless but with love imbued
The Lord of mercy threw a smile
At his brother and his wife.
And smiling said, Do that by which
Your boat will not be whisked away!
Bring water to wash my feet
But be quick, it's getting late.
By remembering once whom people cross
The dark ocean of births and deaths
For whom the three worlds were not
Enough to measure his three steps.[219]
To cross a mere river that Lord
Is now at a boatman's behest!
Gangā's mind with doubt was vexed
Was the one who thus pleaded

---

219. The reference is to the Vāman avatāra (incarnation) of Lord Vishṇu, in which he was born as a dwarf. The *Rig-veda* mentions it, calling it 'the three strides of Vishṇu'. In the Tretā-yuga the demon king Bāli had by his devotions acquired the rulership of the three worlds. Being shorn of their power and dignity, the gods became uneasy and approached Vishṇu, who incarnated himself as the diminutive son of Kashyapa and Aditi. The Dwarf went to Bāli and begged of him as much land as he could step over in three paces. Bāli readily agreed. But to his surprise the Dwarf (Vishṇu) covered heaven and earth in two strides! However, due to Bāli's virtues he did not take the third step, and so left the infernal regions (Pātāla) to him.

With a mere boatman, the Lord Himself
Or just a man a boat who needed?
But in a flash then wisdom dawned
'Tis a part the Lord thus plays,
And she rejoiced that anon
The Lord's feet she would Bathe.

When Rāma had permitted Kewaṭ to wash his feet, *he went and* fetched water from the Gangā in a pot. He started washing the Lord's feet with great love and devotion. The gods sang his praises from heaven and rained flowers. 'There's none so blessed as this man', they said. Kewaṭ brought his whole family there. All of them drank the water which had laved the Lord's lotus-feet. Thus he not only redeemed himself and the members of his family, but also his ancestors above. Having done so he rowed them across the Gangā river.[220]

Getting down Kewaṭ bowed low
Rāma thought I haven't paid the hire
Sītā, knowning his desire,
Took off her gem-studded ring
Rāma said, 'take this as your wages.'
Clasping the lord's feet then Kewaṭ
Said, 'Lord what have I not got
This day ? All my griefs and faults
And all my poverty, have fled
By your lotus-feet thus blest.
For all my labours, only today
My true wages I have earned
Now I lack nothing; on return
Whate'er you give me I'll take
As a sacred gift, divine,

220. Apart from Rāma. Lakshmaṇa and Sītā. Nishāda was also with the trio. He was another low-caste devotee of Rāma.

From your hands, O Master mine.'
Much did Rāma prevail on him
To take as wages Sītā's ring
But Kewaṭ with firmness declined.
Seeing then that all persuasion
Failed to alter his resolve
On him conferred the gracious Lord
The priceless bounty of devotion.

[From *Ayodhyā-kāṇḍa*–99–102 Gītā Press Gorakpur edition].

RĀMA AND VĀLMĪKA

Rāma was brought by the Vālmika to his forest-abode. When the sage saw Rāma's splendour he was filled with peace and calm. Paying him due homage he brought him to his hermitage. He placed roots, fruits and herbs before Rāma, Sītā and Lakshmaṇa. After they had eaten and bathed, they sat before the sage who experienced great bliss by their presence. Rama joined his lovely lotus-like hand an spoke these pleasing words : 'O sage you are the knower of the three worlds. They are as clear to you as a plum placed in the palm of one's hand.' Having said This, he told the sage all the circumstances which had led to his exile.[221] and said 'O revered sage, it's my good fortune that I could keep my father's words, obey my mother, see my beloved brother, Bharata, as king of Ayodhyā and have the opportunity of paying homage to you. O supreme sage, by doing so today I have today reaped great merit. A king who brings grief on sages and ascetics is destroyed by his own evil deed. Honouring *brāhmins*, (i.e., the wise and the learned) is the source of all virtue, and a *brāhmin's* curse brings disaster to millions of one's generations. Tell me some place, O merciful one where I can put up my hermitage,

221. Rāma said that the sage knew everything. What was the need then to tell him all this in detail ? Vālmīka was destined to compose the (Sanskrit) Rāmāyana. So Rāma, who being God's incarnation of course, knew this. That was why he gave him the account in detail.

without causing any inconvenience to any such sage, and live with Sītā and Laksmaṇa for some time.' Hearing these gentle and unpretentious words of Rāma, Vālmīka said, 'O pride of the Ragu race, your gracious words are most befitting. You are the eternal protector of the Vedas.

O Rāma, in you the Vedas abide
You are their Lord, and Jānaki[222]
Is your *māyā* personified
Creator, Preserver, Destroyer, she.

Shesha, the thousand-headed Nāga
The Serpent-king who holds the earth
Of all creatures who's the lord,
He, as Laksmaṇa has taken birth.

As Saviour of the gods you come
To bring good, evil drive away,
The vexing demon-hordes to slay,
To end *adharma*, to usher *dharma*.

O Rāma, words cannot relate
Your glory, nor wisdom conceive;
Eternal, boundless, beyond speech
'Not this, not this' the Vedas e'er say.[223]

The world is but a puppet-show
You are the one that pulls the strings,
Shiva, Brahmā, Vishṇu you control
They know you not, then who can know?

222. i.e. Sītā, Janaka's daughter
223. That is to say the Vedas speak of you as the Unknowable

By your own will you are revealed
    Who knows you, you he becomes
As sandal-paste his heart you please
    Whom you choose as your favoured one.

Being-consciousness-bliss, Lord you are,
    Beyond change, by the worthy seen,
You are born, playing a king's part
Gods, saints and sages to redecm.

O Rāma, your form and deeds delude
    The fools, but the wise are pleased
Whate'er you say, that is the truth
    You act befittingly indeed![224]

Lord, you are asking me to say
    Where you may make your home and stay;
I ask you, tell me where's the spot
    O gracious Lord, where you are not?
Then, only then, Lord, can I tell
    Where the place is, for you to dwell!

Now listen, Rāma, I'll tell you where
    With Sītā and Lakshmaṇa you may live :
As rivers in the seas do pour
    Yet never can they flood the seas;
So are those, you who adore,
    Who never tire to hear your deeds :

224. The idea is that Rāma, who is Vishṇu himself, has descended on the earth as a man. So he plays a man's part, as indeed he should, just as an actor faithfully plays the part he is to play. And he plays it very well.

As *chātak* birds for the moon crave
Their eyes ever thirst for your sight,
O gracious Lord, in them abide,
Their pious hearts your dwelling make.

The waters of seas, lakes and streams
For whom are naught against a drop;
For whom e'en the three worlds seen
Are less than one glimpse of you, Lord;

With your glory and splendour slake
Who their thirst, as peck the swans
Pearls in the Mānsarovara lake :
With Sītā and Laksmaṇa, O Rāma,
Make their pure hearts your dwelling place.

Who ever smell the perfume sweet
Of your offering, who consecrate
To you first whate'er they eat,
And of that cloth their garments make
Your service blest which has received.
Who ever pay obeisance meek
To *brāmins*, preceptors and gods
Who worship e'er your lotus-feet
Whose refuge is none but you, Lord.
Dwell in the hearts of such as these.

Whose feet tire not in pilgrimage[224a]
To your sacred places; who chant

224a The idea is that such pilgrimage must be on foot. not by means of any conveyance, like the Canterbury pilgrims of Chaucer..

Your namc without fail every day,
And with their families, O Rāma,
Who worship you; in their hearts make
Your hermitage and these sojourn.

Who to ancestors offerings make[224b]
And in the fire oblations too;
Feast *brāhmins* and with open hand
Give charity : their gurus who
Revere even more than you
Serving them in every way;
And for all this seek, Lord Divine,
Love for your feet their sole reward,
With Sītā and Lakshmaṇa be enshrined
Within the temple of their hearts.

By pride and desire not enslaved
From arrogance and attachment free
With rage, greed, anguish not assailed
Nor by likes and dislikes swayed
Who are guileless, beyond deceit,
Nor by *māyā's* dark veil dismayed
O Rāma, live in hearts such as these.

Who cherish all, nor any hate,
Who in praise and blame are one
Whom grief grieves not, nor joy elates,
Who speak the truth, but yet hurt none
Whe seek support in you alone,
In their hearts, O Rāma, make you home.

224b Hindus offer food and water to their ancestors According to prescribed procedures as enjoined in the scriptures.

Who covet not another's wife
    Looking on her as on their mother,
Worse than poison in whose eyes
    Is wealth belonging to another.
Who're happy to see others rise
    And sorrowful to see them grieved;
Who love you as they love their life :
    In the heart of these be pleased
O gracious Lord Rāma, to abide.
    To whom you are master and friend,
Mother and father, teacher as well,
    Along with Sītā and Lakshmaṇa,
In the temple of their hearts, dwell.

Free from faults, who emulate
    The virtues of others, who protect
Brāhmins and cows and for their sake
    Who suffer : who by their conduct set
The norms of *dharma*, O Rāma, make
    Their lovely hearts your place of rest.
Who think that all their virtues stem
    From you, and all their faults are theirs,
Who on you in every way depend
    And for your loved ones great love bear :
Along with Jānakī, dwell in them.

Caste and creed, wealth, *dharma* and praise,
    Loved family, pleasure-giving home—
All these relinquishing, who stays
    In you, O Lord, and you alone :
Rāma, his heart is your dwelling-place.

For whom heaven, hell – liberation too;
    Are all one, for in every place
Bow-wielding Lord, he sees you:
    In thought, word, deed who is your slave;
His heart O Lord, your dwelling make.

Who never wishes aught to own
    Who is by nature drawn to you
And loves you for love's sake alone :
    His heart is your mansion true
Live there, it is for you fit home.

[From *Ayodhyā-kāṇḍa* : verses 124 to 131 (Gītā Press Edition)]

RĀMARĀJYA

[We have given Tulsidāsā's account of Kali-yuga, the present age when morals and character are at their lowest. This account of the Kali-age (*yuga* = age or period) has been given in the excerpt about this as in the *Bhāgavata Puraṇa* (q.v.) Now let us see what the *Rāmacharitamānasa* says about the rule of Rāma when he came back to Ayodhyā after slaying Rāvaṇa the demon-king and rescuing Sitā whom he had carried away by force. His rule, which fell in Tretā-yuga, is called Rāmarājya (*rājya* = rule, hence 'the rule of Rāma') reads much like the Utopia of Sir Thomas More. But while the Utopia was a figment of the imagination, Rāmarājya was real and existed in Ayodhyā when Rāma ruled. Will such a *rājya* ever come again ? Decidedly not. It will be the state of affairs of Kali-yuga, which we are experiencing now. Never a rule like Rāma's. The account is given by Kākbhushuṇḍi to Garuḍa].

The three worlds were thrilled to see
    Rāma enthroned; all sorrow fled;
By Rāma's grace, animosity
    Never raised its ugly head.

All people trod the path of *dharma*
    In all ways as the Vedas prescribe,
As was his duty so did one
    According to his stage of life.

Joy reigned supreme; no one knew grief
    Hearts were free from awe and fear,
Nor did one suffer from disease,
    All were healthy and of good cheer.
None was grieved by the three woes[225]
    Love only was the mutual bond
For what the Vedas said all men strove
    His own duty each man performed.

Four pillars were *dharma's* support–
    Largesse, mercy, pureness, truth–[226]
No one even dreamt of sin
    All the women, and the men
Were Rāma-devotees; all of them
Were worthy of achieving *moksha*

---

225. The three sorrows are 1. *daihika* (from *deha* or body) meaning the sorrows following from the body itself, like disease, hurts, wounds, fractures, loss of any of the senses etc. 2. *daivika* (from *daiva* i.e. gods) meaning sorrows given by the gods which are beyond our control like the death of loved ones, and 3. *bhautika* (from *bhūta* i.e. living creatures and that which is lifeless as for example a snake-bite or dog-bite.

226 The reference is to the four *yugas*–Krita, Tretā, Dvāpara and Kali. Righteousness (*dharma*) varied in these yugas. In the Krita-yuga *dharma* was four-footed i.e. firmly established Men effortlessly got fruits, there was no malice, pride, grief, deceit, hatred, cruelty, affliction, jealousy or envy. Everyone worked hard according to the duty he was meant to perform. In the subsequent *yugas dharma* progressively declined, becoming three-footed, then two and in Kaliyuga it hops along on just one foot! Thus righteousness declined a fourth in each *yuga.* And so in Kali-yuga (the present one it's only one-fourth.

Moksha means emancipation. The soul then unites with God and there is no more rebirth for it in the world of sorrows.

No one died an early death
    Nor with grief was ever vexed
None was diseased, all were handsome,
    No one was poor and anguished none;

And no one was badly off :
    There were no ignorant fools
Nor lacked goodness anyone,
    For virtue reigned where King Rāma ruled.

None was deceitful or vain
    And all persons were pure and pious;
All men and women in Rāma's reign
    Were skilful, clever and adroit.

Virtue was honoured, knowledge praised,
    Everyone was learned and wise;
And all were grateful when they
    Were for some kindness obliged.
No one was a fraud or knave
    And there was none was practised guile.

In Rāma's rule no one knows grief
    None is enslaved by works or time
Nor do the *guṇas* confuse his mind
    From all these bonds he is released.

Rāma rules in Ayodhyā, that land
Which is lapped by the seven seas.[227]
As a waist-ornament spans
A woman's waist—sole monarch he :
But for one from each body's down
Of whom the spheres of the universe spring
That power is of no account
Which is his as Ayodhyā's king.

To say that he wears a crown
Is as though to disparage him
For those who know him as he is
The Almighty, the Lord of lords,
O Garuḍa, their enraptured hearts
Are ever filled with endless bliss.

Enlightened saints of sense subdued
Say so and know this truth indeed,
Of the joy and splendour of Rāma's rule
Neither Sarasvatī nor Shesha can speak.

All are generous and benevolent
And men with one wife are content
The women in word, deed and thought
Have their husband's good at heart.

---

227. The seven, seas which are believed to surround the seven *dvīpas*, according to Hindu mythology are 1. Lavaṇa or salt water ? 2. Ikshu, that of sugarcane juice; 3. Surā, of wine : 4. Ghrita the sea of ghee; 5. Dadhi, the sea of curds; 6. Kshīra or the sea of milk; and 7. Jala or the sea of water.

Ḍanḍa is not punishment in Rāma's rule
For none errs; it's the hermit's staff,[228]
Nor are there rogues to be subdued
And how can one divide, when all
Are friends, and there is no strife?
It's only in the rise and fall
Of musical-notes that the difference lies!

There is no hate of any kind
Nor hostility, nor discord;
Victory means victory o'er the mind,
The spirit conquers, not the sword.

In all seasons on forest-trees
Fruits grow and the flower-buds sprout,
Lions and elephants amiably,
Abandoning enmity, roam about.
In Rāma's woods both birds and beasts
Have shed their hatred so that now
They ever live in loving peace.[229]

The chirping of the birds is sweet
And herds of beasts roam with delight,

---

228. According to the renowned Hindu administrator and policy-maker, Kauṭilya, there are four methods of administration—*sāma* (agreement), *dāma* (giving the enemy temptation in the form of gifts or money) *ḍanḍa* which means both punishment, and also a staff or stick (Kauṭilya, of course, means punishment—to which he gives primary importance) and *bheda*, i.e., creating division among the enemies. Tulsidāsa says that in Rāmarājya none of these is necessary, for all persons live amicably and do no wrong. There's a pun on the word '*ḍanḍa*'.

229. Cf., Bihārī : *kahlāne ekat basat, ahi mayūra mriga bāgha/jagat tapoban sau kiyau, dīragha dāgha nidhāga//* 'The serpent and the peacock, the gazelle and the lion, being troubled by the sizzling heat, have come together as though summer has turned their forced resting place into a sanctuary.' (*Satasaī*). But while in that case the truce is temporary and due to the heat, in *Rāmarājya* it's love which brings bird and beast together, not just the heat!

The gentle, cool and perfumed breeze
Keeps blowing, and the bumble-bees
On nectar-laden flowers alight
And with their precious burden flee
Humming softly as they fly.

Trees and creepers of themselves
Shed their nectar, and cows yield
Milk in plenty; and the fields
With golden grain are ever spread.
It seems the virtues of Krita-yuga
Have by Rāma grace, the Tretā blessed![230]

Knowing Rāma to be the World Soul
Mountains with mines are replete
The waters that in the rivers flow
Are satisfying, pure and sweet.

Within their bounds the oceans stay
And through their waves cast on the shore
Pearls for men to take away
And ponds have lotuses galore.

In every place all men are pleased,
The cooling moonbeams bathe the earth,
The sun gives heat that's just enough
To wrap the earth in pleasant warmth
And clouds rain where there is the need.

---

230. As we have said, of the four *yugas* (ages) the first, namely the Satyayuga or the Kritayuga tops in virtue and *dharma*. This is followed by the Tretāyuga, a close second. The poet says that it were as though in Rāma's rule (which was in the Tretāyuga), the virtues which rightly belong to the Satyayuga, have come to exist.

Lord Rāma performed millions of ashvamedha *yajñas* (sacrifices) and gave much charity to *brāhmins*. He is the respecter of the Vedas and the protector of righteousness. Beyond the reach of the *guṇas* (qualities), his heavenly glory is like that of Indra. Gentle soft-spoken Sītā, who is the personification of splendour, always agrees with everything he says. She knows that Rāma, who is always kind and merciful, is the Lord himself; and knowing this she devotedly worships his lotus-feet. Although there are many trained servants in the palace, both men and women, Sītā does the household chores herself. She always acts according to Shrī Rāma's behests and does everything which pleases him, for she is the knower of the natures of all persons. She looks after Kaushalyā and her other mothers-in-law and is never proud or arrogant in behaviour to them 'O Umā', says Shiva, 'Brahmā and the other gods revere Sītā. She is always full of bliss and has all good qualities. That same Sītā who is Lakshmī herself, and for even one favourable glance of whom the gods aspire, but who never even looks at them; worships the feet of her lord, Rāma with humble love.'

Rāma's brothers, obey him in all matters and have great love for him. They keep looking expectantly at his face, hoping he will ask them to do some service for him. Rāma, too loves all his brothers and instructs them in the art of polity. The people are happy and enjoy pleasures which even the gods obtain with difficulty. They keep praying to Brahmā to grant them continued devotion to Rāma's holy feet.

Two sons were born to Sītā, as the Vedas and the Purāṇas say. They were very lovely children, brave, gentle and virtuous. Rāma's brothers had two sons each, handsome, talented and amiable.

The Almighty Lord who is Unknowable by knowledge, words or the senses, who is Eternal and Unborn and beyond the reach of *māyā*, thought or the *guṇas*; has taken human birth for the good of all. After rising, he bathes in the Saryū river and then sits in the assembly of gentle folk and *brāhmins*. Although he is All-knowing, he listens attentively to Vashishṭha's readings from the Vedas and the Purāṇas.

He takes his meals with his brothers. All of Dashrath's wives are filled with rapture when they see him.

Bharata and Shatrughna go with Hanumān to some nearby grove and listen to the glorious deeds of Rāma which Hanumān narrates in his pleasing voice.[231] The two brothers rejoice when they hear of Rāma greatness and beseech Hanumān to tell of it again and again. The Purāṇas and the various deeds of Rāma are narrated in Ayodhyā's households. Men and women are delighted to hear of them and sing his praises. They are so engrossed in them that they have lost count of the days. Even thousands of Sheshas can't adequately narrate the people of happiness and prosperity of Ayodhyā' whose king is Rāma himself. Nārada, Sanaka and other sages come to Ayodhyā daily to pay their obeisance to Rāma. And when they see the splendour of that city they are so greatly charmed by it that they wish to stay on there, rather than wander about as hermits.

The attics are of gems and gold
With varicoloured jewelled floors,
Glorious ramparts circumscribe
The town, with towers that please the eyes.

The streets are paved with precious stones
Of various charming hues that steal
Even the settled minds of sages
The nine planets, it seems to me
Have, with a huge army, invaded
Indra's heaven, Amrāvatī![232]

231. Lakshmaṇa is not mentioned, for he accompanied Rāma and Sītā when they stayed for fourteen years in the forest. So he knows everything at first hand.

232. The nine planets are the sun, the moon, *mangal, buddha, guru shukra, shani, rāhū* and *ketu*. Their English equiv alents—Mercury Venus, Earth, Mars, Jupiter, Saturn, Uranus, Neptune and Pluto. The idea is that these planets have come and lent their grandeur to Ayodhyā. So that it surpasses haeaven's splendour.

The gleaming palaces are sky-high
    The glorious glints of their bright domes
Outshines the moon's and the sun's light,
    Myriad jewelled casements adorn
The palaces; and every home
    In Rāma's grand city is bright,
With lamps studded with precious stones.

The jewelled lamps make bright the homes
    The doorsills are of coral made
The pillars set with precious stones,
    The golden walls, with emeralds inlaid,
It seems as though Brahmā himself
    Has fashioned their fantastic shape.
Majestic spacious halls excel
    Each other : the courtyards are paved
With crystals; the golden doors set
    With diamonds that with splendour blaze.

In homes are picture-galleries
    With Rāma's paintings finely done
So captivating that they steal
    The hearts of hermits who see them.
There are lovely gardens and bowers
    With various charming flowers that please
And creepers in all seasons flower
    'Tis as though Spring is loath to leave!

Sweet is the hum of bumble-bees,
    Cool, gentle perfumed breezes blow,

Delightful the notes soft and low
Of tamed birds which the children please,
Their lovely bright plumages glow
When they flit forth from tree to tree.

Peacocks, pigeons, storks and geese
Strut gracefully on the rooftops,
When they their reflections see
In the jewelled roofs and walls
They think they're real, and dance with glee,
Pouring their joy in rapturous calls.

Parrots and starlings are taught
By children to say 'Raghupati', 'Rāma';
Splendid are the palace-doors
The lanes, the crossings and bazaars.

Beyond description are the market-places
Free of cost one gets there everything,
Of that place how can the wealth be narrated
Where Lakshmī's husband himself is the king![233]
Cloth-dealers, jewellers and other merchants
Seem as though they were verily Kuvera.[234]
Both young and old there are well-intentioned
Handsome, happy and content in every way.

---

233. Rāma being Vishṇu's incarnation. Shrī or Lakshmī is his wife. So Sītā is Lakshmī, and Lakshmī is believed to be the goddess of wealth.

234. Kuvera is one of the guardian deities of the world and the god of wealth. He is the regent of the north, and the keeper of gold, jewels, silver, pearls and all the treasures of the earth. That is why the merchants in the bazaar of Rāma's kingdom are likened to Kuvera.

Northward the Saryū river runs
Whose waters are deep, cool and clean
With bathing-ghats for everyone
Where no slime or slush is seen.[235]

Some way off there is a lovely place
Where horses and elephants slake their thirst.[236]
And charming ghats for women made
Where they fill their pitchers undisturbed.

The captivating Rajghāt is an eyeful
Here bathe the men of all four *varṇas*[237]
The temples along the Saryū are delightful
With a garden planted round each one.
Here and there live wise saints and sages
Whom worldly pleasures have ceased to enchant;
They have grown clusters of the *tulsī* plant[238]
Near their lovely peaceful hermitages.

Of the town's splendour words can't tell
So too of its outskirts splendid made

---

235. Ghat's are solid platforms built on river banks where people can bathe, dry themselves and change clothes.

236. Horses and elephants formed the royal stables for both of them were needed for warfare and on festive occasions. Hence they alone are mentioned. But the implication is that all such beasts come there in herds to drink water from the river.

237. The 'four *varṇas*' means the 'four classes (not castes). These have been divided by the *Gītā* according to their natures and occupations into *brāhmin, kshatriya, vaishya* and *shūdra.* It is significant that here the *shūdras* are not excluded. They bathe with the other classes.

238. The *tulsī* plant is considered by Hindus to be sacred. It is often worshipped by the women of the household.

With woods, groves, ponds and terraced wells.[239]
By a pilgrimage to this sacred land
The sins of all evil deeds are washed away.

There are matchless tanks and terraced wells
Whose lovely steps with gems inlaid
And sparkling waters, even amaze
Gods and sages when they dwell
Up on their beauty : in the tanks
Bloom lotuses of various hues
The notes of warbling birds enchant
And on the branches cuckoos coo
As though they're calling those who pass
To stop and this great grandeur view!
How can that kingdom be described
Which is ruled by Lakshmī's Lord himself,
In Ayodhyā the eight *siddhīs* reside[240]
Which bring prosperity and happiness.

Everywhere people sing Rāma's praises, and ask everyone to chant the name of Rāma who protects all those who take refuge in him, and who is the abode of splendour, gentleness, beauty and noble qualities. Chant the name of the lotus-eyed and dark-complexioned Lord, they say, who protects his devotees

---

239. A *bāvalī* is a tank or a large and wide well with steps on the inside surfaces. Those who wish to bathe or to take water from it descend to the surface by going down these steps. In some old cities e.g. Gonda, we still see thise *bāvalīs* though in a ruined condition.

240. *siddhis* are believed to be divine beings, very pure and holy who inhabit the region of the sky between the earth and the sun. They are identified with the eight accomplishments and miraculous powers which saints can acquire. They are, 1. Aṇimā, the power of becoming atomic, 2. Mahimā, the power of becoming very light, 3. Garimā, the power of becoming infinitely heavy, 4. Laghumā the power of becoming very small, 5. Prāpti, getting all desires, 6. Prākāmya fulfilling all wishes, 7. Īshisva, absolute supremacy, and 8. Vasitva, subduing all.

as carefully as the eyelids protect the eyes. Chant the name of the gentle Lord who bears the bow and a quiver of arrows and who lights the hearts of his devotees as the sun's rays open up the lotus-petals. Rāma is the destroyer of serpent-shaped Death. He removes affectation from the minds of those who desirelessly worship him. He is the destroyer of delusion. He delights the hearts of those who love him, and for those who are licentious, he is as fearful as a lion is to an elephant. Worship Rāma they say, who dispels doubt and anguish from the minds of men as the light of the sun removes the dense darkness of night; who destroyes the demons as a forest-fire burns down trees. Why don't you worship. Rāma who removes the woes of life and the fear of death? He is the destroyer of craving and desires as the flame of a lamp is the destroyer of the moths which fall on it. He is pure as the snows. He is the Lord eternal, Unborn and Indestructible. Worship Rāma who gives joy to the sages, who lightens the burden of his devotees and who is Tulsidāsa's merciful Lord. Thus do the people of Ayodhyā sing Rāma's praies. Shrī Rāma is ever kind and gracious to everyone.

[Utitarākāṇḍ. 19 (G) : 4 to 30]

Gītā Press Edition of the text]

THE GODLY AND THE GODLESS

[Shrī Krishṇa has given a vivid description of people who are of godly nature and those who are wicked. We have given this in the selections from the Bhagavadgītā q.v. – The Divine and the Demoniacal. Shrī Rāma also gives a similar account in the Rāmacharitamānasa which is reproduced in the passage which follows.]

The difference between the acts
Of the saints and the godless are such
As between the sandalwood, and axe
By whose sharp blade it is cut.

Even though cut, the sandalwood
    Gives its perfume to the blade;
So too the gentle, godly sage
    Pays back evil with the good.

But because of this the axe's blade
    Is in the fire heated red-hot
And firmly beaten into shape;
    While on the brows of the god
Resplendent shines sandalwood-paste.

The godly saints are not tempted
    By pleasures which the senses please,
They are virtuous, gentle and contented,
    To see others suffer makes them grieved;
And they're elated when they see
    Another happy; they are one
To all beings and from rancour free,
    For they are hostile to none.

Of minds detached, they have abjured
    The world ; by greed they're never swayed,
Nor by elation e'er disturbed
    And they have conquered fear and rage.
In their minds compassion resides,
    They are kind to the poor and needy,
In thought word and deed they strive
    With unaffected love to worship Me.

All beings these godly saints revere
 But seek no honour for their own selves,
O Bharata, they are to Me very dear[241]
 And in My Soul their spirit ever dwells.

These saints have forsaken all cravings. They are very near to Me, and chant My name With delight. They are the abode of peace, humility and happiness and have forsaken all worldly pleasures. They are calm, unostentatious and friendly to all, even to those who serve them. They are loving and devoted to *brāhmins* and are walk in the way of righteousness and virtue. O brother, know them to be saints in whom all these qualities are present. Their minds and senses are ever under their control. They are always disciplined and law-abiding, and never speak harshly to anyone. These godly sages to whom praise and disparagement are the same, and who love My lotus-feet are dear to me as My very soul.

Now of the wicked I'll speak
 Their friendship you should ever avoid
For it invariably brings grief
 As a wild unruly cow spoils
A gentle white one of good breed.

The wicked are of sorrowful minds
 Jealous of those who're in fair weather
And if they hear someone maligned
 They're glad as though they've found a treasure!

By desire, anger and greed swayed,
 Cruel crooked cunning, arrogant,
These vile men steeped in sin, always
 Without a cause envy all men;
And even their well-wishers they
 Are out to harm in every way.

---

241. Rāma is telling Hanumān, Bharata and others about the saints and the sinners. Therefore, 'O Bharata.'

In all things falsehood is their guide,
In eating drinking, give-and-take,[242]
Outside all smiles, but dark inside
As peacocks which eat deadly snakes.

To all persons they are malicious
Dispraise of others gives them pleasure,
These men evil-minded and vicious
Covet the wives and wealth of others.
These greedy men are demons indeed
And they imagine they'll never die!
Sex and food is all they seek
And if they hear one praised they sigh
As though by a burning fever seized!

The sorrows of others makes them elated
As though the world's monarch they've been made!
These selfish men in families sow hatred,
And they're filled with uncontrollable rage
When their greed and lust are not satiated.
They have no regard for their parents
Nor for *brāhmins* or their gurus;
Corrupt themselves, they are bent
Upon corrupting others too.
These deluded men are full of hate,
Neither the company of holy men
Nor the Lord's deeds, nor praise,
Ever attract them, or please them.

---

242. Although sometimes taken to be a cliche, the expression is used here as it conveys the meaning succinctly (see Fowler's *Dictionary of Modern English Usage*. Oxford 1965. p., 91 quotation of J.A. Spender and Clutton Brock).

Full of evil qualities
These foolish men of lustful thoughts
Despise the Vedas; by force they seize
The wealth of others; they hate all
But specially *brāhmins*; they keep
A fair exterior but at heart
Are full of vanity and deceit.

Such evil and depraved persons are not found in the Satya and the Tretā *yugas* (ages). A few of them may be encountered in the Dvāpara-yuga. In the Kali-age, however, they abound. There is no virtue greater then doing good to others, and O brother, there's no vileness greater than causing grief to others. Dear friend, this is what all the scriptures say. Wise men are aware of this truth. They who, being endowed with a human body, yet torment others, suffer greatly in this life and in the hereafter. A man commits innumerable sins for his own selfish interests, and thereby he suffers in afterlife. Brother, I am the giver of the fruits of good and evil deeds. And for evil-doers I am as fearful as Death. Therefore those men who are supremely wise know the world to be the vale of sorrows and chant My name in order to be delivered from it. These enlightened men, gods and hermits of unshakable faith worship Me. I have related to you the qualities of the godly and the godless persons. Those who can distinguish between them are freed of the rounds of births and deaths. Listen, dear friend, in truth all virtues and faults are born of delusion. There is no reality in them. The discriminating mind takes no notice of either of them. To see them as real is indeed lack of discrimination.[243]

[From *Uttara-kāṇḍa*, 36 : 3 to 41 Gītā Press edition of the text]

243. The sense is rather vague, but it could be interpreted thus : It is God who does everything. Human beings are only the agents. So it is a delusion to think that a man is doing what's right or what's wrong. As the divine will makes him do, so he does.

INDEX

Note : Information already given in the sub-headings is not repeated in the index.

INDEX TO 'A SOURCE BOOK OF HINDU PHILOSOPHY'

K.P. Bahadur